GREAT BRITAIN
AND THE ORIGINS OF
THE PACIFIC WAR

Dr Lowe is Senior Lecturer in History at the University of Manchester.

GREAT BRITAIN AND THE ORIGINS OF THE PACIFIC WAR

A Study of British Policy in
East Asia 1937–1941

BY
PETER LOWE
Senior Lecturer in History
at the University of Manchester

CLARENDON PRESS · OXFORD
1977

Oxford University Press, Walton Street, Oxford OX2 6DP

OXFORD LONDON GLASGOW NEW YORK
TORONTO MELBOURNE WELLINGTON CAPE TOWN
IBADAN NAIROBI DAR ES SALAAM LUSAKA ADDIS ABABA
KUALA LUMPUR SINGAPORE JAKARTA HONG KONG TOKYO
DELHI BOMBAY CALCUTTA MADRAS KARACHI

© *Oxford University Press 1977*

British Library Cataloguing in Publication Data

Lowe, Peter
  Great Britain and the Origins of the Pacific War..
  1. Great Britain — Foreign relations — East (Far East)
  2. East (Far East) — Foreign relations — Great Britain
  I. Title
  327.41'05   DS740.63

ISBN 0-19-822427-3

*Typesetting by Malvern Typesetting Services
Printed in Great Britain by
Billing & Sons Ltd, Guildford*

PREFACE

THIS study examines British policy towards the approach of the Pacific war between 1937 and 1941. From July 1937 onwards Great Britain was faced with the challenge of responding to the growth of Japanese expansion, at first in China and then with the escalating threat of Japanese aggression in south-east Asia and into the western Pacific. The crisis in East Asia coincided with the swift deterioration of the situation in Europe, exemplified in the development of Hitler's power, the coalescence of Germany and Italy, and the savagery of the Spanish civil war. British authority in East Asia had for many years rested on past prestige rather than current military might, and much of the interest of this study lies in witnessing the struggle to find the correct diplomatic means of defending a position that was no longer viable. It is surprising not that Britain encountered the rebuffs and humiliations that she did at the hands of Japan, as in the Tientsin crisis in 1939 and in the confrontation over the Burma road in 1940, but that she contrived to maintain her position as well as she did. That Britain managed moderately successfully is to be attributed to the reluctance of Japan to push matters too far prematurely and to the shrewd conduct of policy by a small number of British diplomats, above all by the underrated ambassador in Tokyo throughout this period, Sir Robert Craigie. Britain believed there was little justification for Japanese expansion, and she did not pursue the policy of positive appeasement in East Asia adopted by Neville Chamberlain in Europe between 1937 and 1939. Of British politicians and officials in Whitehall, R. A. Butler firmly advocated *rapprochement* with Japan in 1939–40, and ironically he subsequently became chairman of the committee responsible for tightening the economic screw in Anglo-Japanese relations in 1940–1. Sir George Sansom believed that it was of little assistance to draw distinctions between 'moderates' and 'extremists' in Japan, for most Japanese harboured the same ultimate objectives of

securing hegemony in East Asia: all that could be done was to
defend British interests as effectively as was possible while conducting a gradual retreat. Only the United States possessed the
resources to handle Japan and even the United States was
merely beginning serious rearmament in 1940–1. For China
Britain felt definite sympathy, allied with the belief that many
of China's problems were of her own making: in any case
Britain maintained that she could do little in tangible terms to
aid China because of the prior claims of her own armed forces
and because of the risk of excessively antagonizing Japan. The
decline in Britain's standing in the eyes of the Chinese was
accentuated by British concessions to Japan over Tientsin and
the Burma road. China looked to the United States to save her
from continued Japanese depredations; the hope was
eventually realized when the attack on Pearl Harbor occurred,
but American involvement came too late to rescue the ramshackle structure of Chiang Kai-shek's Kuomintang regime.

The most serious error made by British politicians,
diplomats, and defence planners was to miscalculate the
damage Japan could inflict if war came to the Pacific.
Objectively it was absurd to think of Japan taking on the might
of the United States and of overrunning British, American,
French, and Dutch colonial territories. In the long term Japan
could not expect to win unless Russia collapsed and the United
States agreed to a compromise peace with Germany and
Japan. In the short term, however, Japan could wreak great
havoc, as she proved in 1941–2. It is understandable that
Britain did not devote more resources to East Asia when she
was heavily committed in Europe and the Middle East; what is
still difficult to explain is the grave underestimation of
Japanese tenacity and vigour by the British and Americans.
This was most probably the outcome of feelings of racial
superiority and of ignorance of Japanese prowess; the latter
does not reflect creditably upon British and American
intelligence. Japan's inability to inflict a complete military
defeat on China contributed significantly to the fallacious
assessment of Japanese strength. Japan was eventually crushed,
but only after a particularly ferocious and savage struggle, in
the course of which Japan effectively demolished the moral
basis of European colonialism.

This study concentrates upon the immediate origins of the Pacific war. Origins of war can be traced back many years and the conflict in the Pacific is no exception to this generalization. However, the major impetus to the onset of the war sprang from the outbreak and escalation of the Undeclared War between Japan and China in 1937. The subject is, therefore, pursued from this date. More attention is paid to the period 1939-41, which is of great interest and has not been reassessed recently, as has the period from 1937 to 1939. There is a vast quantity of material in the British archives dealing with policy towards the crisis in East Asia, and it would have been possible to have produced a far longer work than the present one. However, there is much to be said for conciseness in concentrating the mind on the vital issues, which it is hoped has been achieved here.

ACKNOWLEDGEMENTS

IT is a pleasure for me to express my deep appreciation to those indivuduals and institutions who have assisted me during the preparation of this work. The bulk of the research was carried out at the Public Record Office, London, and I am most grateful for the help I received from the staff over a period of years. Transcripts/translations of Crown-copyright records in the Public Record Office, London, appear by permission of the Controller of H.M. Stationery Office. Quotations from the letters of Neville Chamberlain are reproduced by permission of the Librarian, Birmingham University. In addition, I wish to thank the staffs of the India Office Library, the John Rylands University Library of Manchester, and all other libraries in which I have worked. The following kindly allowed me to see, and cite from, material in their possession: the Keeper of the India Office Records for the Linlithgow papers; the Librarian of the John Rylands University Library of Manchester for the Auchinleck papers; Lady Brooke-Popham and the Trustees, Liddell Hart Centre for Military Archives, King's College, London, for the Brooke-Popham and Ismay papers; Lord Chatfield, Professor A. Temple Patterson, and the Librarian of Southampton University for the Chatfield papers, now deposited at the National Maritime Museum, Greenwich; Major A. J. McG. Percival for the Percival papers deposited at the Imperial War Museum. I wish to thank Leo Cooper Ltd. for permission to cite copyright material from B. Bond (ed.), *Chief of Staff: The Diaries of Lieutenant-General Sir Henry Pownall*, Vol. II (1974) and Stanford University Press for permission to cite passages from N. Ike (ed.), *Japan's Decision for War: Records of the 1941 Policy Conferences* (1967).

I have benefited greatly from the stimulus of scholars working in the field embraced in this study. I am particularly grateful to the following with whom I have either discussed aspects of the subject or raised questions that have been answered: Professor Asada Sadao, Professor David Dilks, Professor Akira Iriye, Dr. Ian Nish, and Mr. G. R. Storry. Many of the problems surveyed have been discussed with my former postgraduate students, Dr. Paul Haggie and Mr. Paul Wright, and I have gained from hearing their views. I would like to thank Colonel G. T. Wards for kindly discussing with me British policy towards Japan before the outbreak of war.

I am grateful to the following publishers for permission to reproduce maps: Weidenfeld and Nicolson Ltd. for Map I from H. McAleavy, *The Modern History of China* (1967), and Cassell & Co., Ltd. for Map II from S. Woodburn Kirby, *Singapore: The Chain of Disaster* (1971).

I would like to express my warm thanks to the staff of the Oxford University Press for their constructive advice and guidance.

I am once again indebted to Mrs. Margaret Gissop for so capably typing the work for me. In conclusion, I must state that I alone am responsible for any errors that remain.

Manchester PETER LOWE
October 1976

CONTENTS

LIST OF MAPS

ABBREVIATIONS

D.B.F.P.	*Documents on British Foreign Policy, 1919-1939*
D.G.F.P.	*Documents on German Foreign Policy, 1918-1945*
F.R.U.S.	*Foreign Relations of the United States*
Adm.	Admiralty records, Public Record Office, London
Air	Air Ministry records, Public Record Office, London
Cab.	Cabinet Office records, Public Record Office, London London
F.O.	Foreign Office records, Public Record Office, London
Prem.	Prime Minister's Office papers, Public Record Office, London
T.	Treasury papers, Public Record Office, London
H. C. Deb.	Parliamentary Debates: Official Report, House of Commons, fifth series
H. L. Deb.	Parliamentary Debates: Official Report, House of Lords, fifth series
E.H.R.	*English Historical Review*
I.A.	*International Affairs*
J.A.H.	*Journal of American History*
J.A.S.	*Journal of Asian Studies*
J.B.S.	*Journal of British Studies*
J.C.S.	*Journal of Commonwealth Studies*
J.I.C.H.	*Journal of Imperial and Commonwealth History*
J.M.H.	*Journal of Modern History*
M.A.S.	*Modern Asian Studies*
P.H.R.	*Pacific Historical Review*
Borg and Okamoto	*Pearl Harbor as History: American–Japanese Relations 1931–1941* edited by D. M. Borg and S. Okamoto
Ike	*Japan's Decision for War: Records of the 1941 Policy Conferences* edited by N. Ike
I.M.T.F.E.	International Military Tribunal for the Far East

Japanese names are given with surname first, followed by personal name.

INTRODUCTION

ON 15 February 1942 the supposedly indestructible fortress of
Singapore surrendered to the besieging forces of General
Yamashita. It was the greatest surrender in the history of the
British Empire and a shattering blow to the prestige and
authority of Great Britain. It was, however, an appropriate
admission of the bankruptcy of British policy in East Asia in
the twentieth century. The 'Singapore strategy' of developing
the island at the tip of the Malayan peninsula as a potential
naval base, axiomatic to the pursuance of a British campaign
against Japanese expansion, was a bogus policy that implicitly
recognized the chronic weakness of British power: only in a
dire emergency would Britain be able to dispatch a major fleet
to Singapore, and this was under the unwise assumption that
Britain would not be facing simultaneous grave crises in
Europe and the Mediterranean. The menace of Japan only
struck the policy-makers in the cabinet, Foreign Office, the
Treasury, the defence departments, and other relevant areas
in the early 1930s; the full reality, with all its consequences,
was not grasped until the massive defeats suffered in the first
few months of 1942. Yet the trend in the decline of British
might was not new in the 1930s and had been discernible for at
least a generation before.

Britain's political and economic role in East Asia had been
established during the nineteenth century when diplomats,
soldiers, sailors, merchants, bankers, and missionaries had
spearheaded the process of opening up China and Japan to
intercourse with the west. The United States, Russia, France,
and Germany were prominent, too, but Britain established
herself as the power with the greatest single interests in the
area. China was the magnet that attracted the British. The
myth of the China market exerted its seductive influence as it
continued to do until the second world war, if not, in certain
respects, to the present day—the belief that China offered a
huge potential market of a significance hard to exaggerate.
Britain, therefore, took the lead in compelling China to open
up her leading ports to trade and in erecting the system of

extraterritoriality as it functioned until brutally swept away by Japanese imperialism at the beginning of the Pacific war. Foreign nationals lived according to their own laws and led a privileged existence; the Chinese were not infrequently treated as manifest inferiors in their own country as the tentacles of informal imperialism grew. The high noon of the western presence in China occurred in the brief period between the suppression of the Boxer rising in 1900 and the outbreak of the first world war in 1914. The foreign powers competed vigorously to obtain railway concessions, and the freedom of the Chinese government was further restricted by the controls insisted upon as a condition of granting loans.[1] Ironically the same years saw the beginning of the emergence of modern Chinese nationalism, characterized by a new patriotism and a determination to reverse the process of occidental hegemony.[2] From 1919 the new spirit in China offered the most serious threat to the British presence until itself overtaken by Japanese nationalism after 1931.

Britain's assertiveness was the product of the self-confidence and dynamism created by the industrial revolution. While force was employed from time to time, as in the two Anglo-Chinese wars (1839–42 and 1856–60) and as symbolized by the ubiquitous gunboat, British influence rested ultimately on bluff. The Royal Navy existed to safeguard world-wide interests, to defend the British isles, and to keep open strategic sea lanes. When other countries began to build powerful navies, the task of maintaining an appreciable presence in waters adjacent to China became increasingly difficult. As for the British army, it was impossible to conceive of it playing more than an extremely limited role in the principal treaty ports, such as Shanghai and Tientsin; the army existed primarily to garrison India and to fight colonial skirmishes, and Britain could never become involved in large-scale military intervention in China. The constant theme of British policy from the middle of the nineteenth century to the middle of the twentieth century was the desire for stability and peace

[1] See P. Lowe, *Great Britain and Japan, 1911–15* (Macmillan, London, 1969), chs. 2–4.

[2] See M. C. Wright (ed.), *China in Revolution: the First Phase, 1900–1913* (Yale University Press, London, 1968).

in China so that trade could flourish with minimum handicaps.[3] Whenever another power challenged her position, Britain required assistance to repel the danger: this was illustrated by the conclusion of the Anglo-Japanese alliance in 1902 during the rise of Russia, by the request for Japanese aid against Germany in 1914, and by the need to secure American help against Japan in the late 1930s. By 1941 it was only possible to defeat the attempt to impose a 'new order' by a huge war extending from the borders of India to northern Australia.

Until the 1920s, relations between Great Britain and Japan had generally been close. From the dying years of the Tokugawa shogunate onwards, British nationals had contributed significantly to the modernization of Japan. Britain had advised Japan on the foundation of her navy. Extraterritoriality had been established in Japan, as in China, but it disappeared from Japan by the end of the nineteenth century. A more positive attitude was shown by Great Britain in terminating extraterritoriality than was shown by other countries. In 1902 the first Anglo-Japanese alliance was signed; it was subsequently revised and extended in 1905 and 1911. The alliance brought substantial benefits to each partner. For Britain it connoted the tangible support of an ally of growing strength, as the result of the Russo-Japanese war of 1904-5 testified: Japan would assist in defending Britain's stake in East Asia and the Royal Navy could be concentrated in home waters during the decisive confrontation with Germany in 1908-12. The alliance made an important contribution to British defence policy, the full extent of which became clear in 1914 when Japanese naval aid was needed to contain the German threat to communications with the Dominions of Australia and New Zealand and the threat to commerce. In addition, the alliance gave Britain some influence over the development of Japanese policy and prevented relations from becoming excessively strained. From Japan's viewpoint, the alliance was a most satisfying indication of the success of Japan's modernization programme: alliance

[3] See J. D. Gregory, *Great Britain and the Taipings* (Allen and Unwin, London, 1969), Lowe, *Great Britain and Japan*, and B. A. Lee, *Britain and the Sino-Japanese War, 1937-39* (Oxford University Press, London, 1973).

with the largest empire in the world only one generation after feudalism had been dismantled was no mean achievement. The alliance constituted a shield against outside intervention in the war with Russia and afterwards continued to be valuable as an insurance policy during a period of swift change in the Far East and, indeed, the world. Japan annexed Korea formally in 1910 and developed her economic and strategic interests in south Manchuria from 1905. In 1915 Japan delivered the twenty-one demands to China and compelled her to accept the majority of these.[4] The move was counter-productive in terms of the crisis that ensued, which assumed both an international and a domestic character.

There were ominous strains within the alliance, however, which pointed to the circumstances of its termination after the first world war. Japan wished to extend her economic interests in China, partly through competing with Britain's traditional dominance in the Yangtze valley. Japan intervened to some extent in the internal upheavals in China following the revolution of 1911-12. Friction between the allies resulted. Furthermore, there was little enthusiasm for the alliance in the British Dominions or in the United States. It was felt by the British government, after 1918, that the alliance could not be continued in its old form. At the same time it was highly desirable to retain an agreement that would avoid serious deterioration in co-operation. The outcome of the Washington conference of 1921-2, summoned on the initiative of the United States, was the replacement of the alliance by a new four-power agreement including the United States and France; this proved meaningless and was not regarded seriously by the signatories. The other two pillars of the Washington settlement, the five-power naval ratio treaty and the nine-power treaty concerning China, were of more concrete importance, at least in the short term. The disappearance of the Anglo-Japanese alliance removed a cornerstone of the international order in East Asia.[5] The manner of its termination rankled in Japan. Anglo-Japanese relations gradually cooled during the 1920s and 1930s, despite

---

[4] See Lowe, ch. 7.
[5] On the final years and the end of the alliance, see I. H. Nish, *Alliance in Decline* (Athlone Press, London, 1972), chs. 14-23.

periodic endeavours to reverse the trend. With the advent of the Sino-Japanese war in 1937, the clash became overt.

The more immediate threat to Britain's interests in China came from the militant nature of Chinese nationalism in the 1920s. Paradoxically, while centralized government disintegrated in China in the warlord era that followed the death of Yuan Shih-k'ai in 1916, nationalism became bellicose and dominant. This was manifested in the political, social, and cultural spheres. After 1923, Sun Yat-sen's Kuomintang and the Chinese communists demanded the restoration of unity and the overthrow of western imperialism. Great Britain was the chief target for Chinese animosity. Britain was regarded as the leading oppressor of the Chinese people, and demonstrations developed in the mid-1920s with a view to securing a surrender of extraterritorial privileges. The British commercial community in China was mainly unsympathetic to the new spirit in China and felt that the best response to 'bolshevik intrigues' was to reiterate British determination not to compromise; the image of the gunboat was still prevalent. The British government was at first inclined to favour a firm attitude while simultaneously adhering to the view that force could not be used. Anglo-Chinese relations became acrimonious in 1925-6 and prompted a change of policy: despite initial misgivings by the British minister to China, Sir Miles Lampson, the government embarked on a new, more progressive approach; Britain would be willing to negotiate for the gradual restoration of Chinese autonomy.[6] In 1930 China regained tariff autonomy and Wei-hai-wei was returned to Chinese suzerainty. Chiang Kai-shek rose to become the most powerful leader within the Kuomintang by 1927; the rupture with the communists made it more necessary than before for Chiang to rely on the foreign powers for support, so that the campaign against foreign imperialism became less vocal than formerly. The Kuomintang was a ramshackle regime comprising numerous corrupt vested interests and

[6] For an interesting portrait of Lampson, see H. Kane, 'Sir Miles Lampson at the Peking Legation, 1926-1933', unpublished University of London Ph.D. thesis (1975). See also E. Davies, 'Britain and the Far East, 1922-1931: A Study in Foreign and Defence Policy', unpublished University of Birmingham Ph.D. thesis (1973), pp. 204-360.

pressure groups; its diverse membership ranged from moderate radical intellectuals and treaty port bankers to die-hard reactionary landowners. The Kuomintang became far more conservative under Chiang's leadership, and in effect dropped the radical social reforms for which it had originally stood.[7] Nevertheless, Chiang was a genuine nationalist and detested western imperialism. There was no doubt that he desired the end of extraterritoriality, but the timing of this depended on Chiang's domestic struggle with the communists and on Japanese policy.

The Manchurian crisis of 1931-3 was the watershed when Japanese expansion began to replace Chinese nationalism as the greatest threat to British authority. It is necessary to distinguish between the dispute over Japan's actions in Manchuria between 1931 and 1933 and the separate but related crisis in Shanghai in 1932. For over twenty years British policy-makers had assumed that Manchuria was bound to fall into the Japanese sphere of interest; Japan was an expanding nation and had expended blood and treasure to secure the former Russian rights in south Manchuria, ceded to her in 1905. Manchuria as a province was in an anomalous situation and had not previously been ruled as an integral part of the Chinese empire. It was preferable for Japan to expand into Manchuria than into the Pacific, for the latter would mean confrontation with the United States and the British Dominions. This had been the attitude of Sir Edward Grey before 1914 and it was accepted by his successors. The advent of the League of Nations had modified international ethics, however. Manchuria was technically part of China, and action by the Japanese Kwantung army would justify a Chinese appeal to Geneva. Since Britain was one of the two most important members of the League, it would not be possible for her to condone Japanese aggression: Britain had to keep in mind the repercussions on the prestige of the League in Europe of a failure to support League principles in the Far

---

[7] For a valuable examination of the functioning of the Kuomintang, see Hung-mao Tien, *Government and Politics in Kuomintang China 1927-1937* (Stanford University Press, Stanford, Calif., 1972). See also, L. Eastman, *The Abortive Revolution: China under Nationalist Rule, 1927-1937* (Harvard University Press, Cambridge, Mass., 1974), and D. Lary, *Region and Nation: the Kwangsi Clique in Chinese Politics, 1925-1937* (Cambridge University Press, Cambridge, 1974).

East. Britain had sympathy for Japan's exasperation with
Chinese provocation in Manchuria, but could not endorse her
crude methods of expelling the regime of Chang Hsueh-liang
and of declaring Manchuria independent as the state of
Manchukuo. Sir John Simon tried to perform a diplomatic
balancing act in his criticisms of Japan and China for which he
was castigated at the time and subsequently. Simon's tendency
to vacillate and postpone decisions prevented him from being
a successful foreign secretary; however, given the weak state of
British defences and lack of interest in Manchuria, it is
difficult to see an alternative to his policy, unhappy as it was.[8]

Britain was far more worried by events in Shanghai between
January and May 1932. Conflict between Japanese and
Chinese forces had been precipitated by an incident staged by
the Japanese military attaché, and had led to bitter fighting in
the city where the bulk of British and other foreign
investments was concentrated. The dangers of a future war
between Britain and Japan struck the Foreign Office and
chiefs of staff forcibly. The incident occurred when Britain was
struggling to escape from the worst of economic depression
according to the conventional economic idea of the balanced
budget and limited government spending; the lowest defence
estimates of the interwar years were introduced by Neville
Chamberlain in 1932. The Shanghai crisis was settled in May
1932 because there was no wish in Japan to exacerbate matters
while the developments in Manchuria were proceeding. Japan
now loomed in the minds of defence planners as the most
serious menace after Germany. The United States had been
most prominent in censuring Japanese policy in Manchuria
through the fiercely moralistic pronouncements of the
secretary of state, Henry L. Stimson. The United States did
not belong to the League, however, and Stimson left office
with the defeated Hoover in March 1933. Japanese ire was
directed more at Britain, the outcome of the steady cooling in
Anglo-Japanese relations since 1922 and of resentment at
criticism emanating from Geneva for which Britain was held
responsible; the fact that the League inquiry into the
Manchurian dispute was headed by a British national, Lord

---

[8] For a thorough appraisal of the Manchurian crisis, see C. Thorne, *The Limits of
Foreign Policy* (Hamish Hamilton, London, 1972).

Lytton, appeared to reinforce British identification with the moral condemnation of Japan's behaviour.

After 1933 the British Treasury advocated a *rapprochement* with Japan and came for a time to dominate much of British policy in East Asia.[9] The Treasury was frightened of the financial consequences of a worsening of relations with Japan, and believed that the Americans would not translate moral indignation into resolute action. Neville Chamberlain was chancellor of the exchequer and was the strongest personality in the National governments of the period. Ramsay MacDonald and Stanley Baldwin were ageing leaders with the end of their political careers not far away; Chamberlain was dynamic and ambitious; he knew the premiership to be within his grasp and was determined to leave his mark on Treasury policies—and not only on Treasury policies. Chamberlain worked closely with the able but eccentric head of the home civil service, Sir Warren Fisher, who was vehemently critical of the United States. The Foreign Office supported the objective of improving relations with Japan but was less sanguine on the chances of securing it. The Treasury compelled the Foreign Office to accept the dispatch of Sir Frederick Leith-Ross, the chief economic adviser to the government, on a mission to the Far East designed to produce a settlement between Japan and China. The entire character of the mission was changed when Japan declined to co-operate with Leith-Ross and made it clear that she regarded his mission with grave suspicion. In the sardonic words of a Foreign Office official, Leith-Ross became 'this gallant hero of a lost cause' and devoted his energy to advising the Chinese government on the reorganization of the currency with the transition from a silver standard to a paper currency. The Leith-Ross mission, originally intended to improve Anglo-Japanese relations, finished by having the opposite effect.

British defence policy in East Asia in the mid-1930s rested upon the continued construction of the naval base at Singapore and on the hope that, if conflict with Japan

[9] British policy in East Asia from 1933 to 1937 has been surveyed in two thorough, complementary studies, Ann Trotter, *Britain and East Asia, 1933–1937* (Cambridge University Press, Cambridge, 1975) and S. L. Endicott, *Diplomacy and Enterprise: British China Policy 1933–37* (Manchester University Press, Manchester, 1975).

threatened, Britain could send a fleet to Singapore.[10] Chamberlain wished to restrict expenditure and preferred to expand the R.A.F. rather than the Royal Navy. He was vigorously opposed by the secretary to the cabinet, Sir Maurice Hankey, who stressed the real dangers inherent in the rise of Japan and the value of adequate naval strength. The cabinet decided that the navy should not be neglected but agreed with Chamberlain that any drastic increase in defence expenditure had to be averted. The hopes of improving Britain's ability to pursue a firm policy in East Asia were undermined by the Abyssinian crisis of 1935-6, which raised the acute danger of war with Italy. Until 1935 the chiefs of staff had discounted the contingency of a clash between Britain and Italy; now the full horror dawned that Britain could be involved in serious crises in three different theatres. The outbreak of the Spanish civil war in July 1936 accentuated the perils in the Mediterranean. British rearmament was slowly beginning, but was not to gather momentum until 1938-9. For a considerable period to come, Britain would have to meet the threat of aggression by diplomatic methods as skilful as could be contrived. In East Asia in the 1930s Britain lacked naval and air power of any strength: Britain simply could not afford to become involved in war with Japan. This weakness was partially but not fully recognized. British political leaders were extremely reticent when it came to spelling out the facts of life to the Dominions. The Dominions had advanced to greater independence in the interwar years but they still leaned heavily on Britain for their defences. British leaders thought of the Empire as a family that must be held together: assurances were repeatedly given at imperial conferences that Britain would protect the Dominions if necessary, and the promises were to be reiterated even in the war period of

---

[10] For a discussion of defence issues, see S. Roskill, *Hankey: Man of Secrets*, iii (Collins, London, 1974) and P. Haggie, 'The Royal Navy and the Far Eastern Problem, 1931-1941', unpublished Ph.D. thesis, Manchester University (1974). See also B. Bond (ed.), *Chief of Staff: The Diaries of Lieutenant-General Sir Henry Pownall*, i (Leo Cooper, London, 1972). For two important, thorough surveys of defence problems, including discussion of East Asia, see N. H. Gibbs, *History of the Second World War: Grand Strategy*, i (H.M.S.O., London, 1976) and S. Roskill,' *Naval Policy Between the Wars*, ii: *The Period of Reluctant Rearmament, 1930-1939* (Collins, London, 1976).

1940–1. The defect in British policy towards the Dominions was the failure to explain cogently how severely pressed Britain was and how, with the best will in the world, she could not satisfactorily defend her vast and far-flung possessions. Canada and South Africa were the most isolationist of the Dominions for a mixture of historical, geographical, and ethnic reasons; Australia and New Zealand were fervently loyal to the crown and mother country but were preoccupied with the problems of the Pacific rather than Europe. Britain was conscious of the natural anxieties of the southern Dominions but had to place her own interest first in the dilemma confronting her. The realization of how much Britain could actually accomplish in terms of assisting them dawned slowly, with sickening horror, on Australia and New Zealand in 1940–1.

Japan in the 1930s was moving rapidly into a climate of extreme nationalism.[11] In one sense this was consistent with the policy of building a tough, vigorous, self-reliant nation, confident of her role and purpose, which had been the intention of the Meiji leaders after 1868. Most Japanese accepted the justice of a more militant, abrasive foreign policy and believed that the problems of Japanese society, with a fast-expanding population and serious agrarian poverty, were not understood or viewed with sympathy in a hostile world. It was a decade in which the advance towards constitutional government, with growing power for the political parties, was sharply reversed. The political parties continued to operate, despite the overt antagonism displayed by the armed forces, and still obtained a substantial measure of support from the populace, as the elections of 1937 demonstrated. However, the governments after the assassination of Inukai Tsuyoshi, in 1932, were essentially bureaucratic administrations anxious to follow policies aimed at unifying the country and at eliminating the weakness and corruption associated with the political parties.[12] The most significant single feature was the position

---

[11] For assessments of Japan in the 1930s, see two admirable collections of essays, J. W. Morley (ed.), *Dilemmas of Growth in Prewar Japan* (Princeton University Press, Princeton, 1971) and the contributions on Japan in Borg and Okamoto.

[12] On the relationship between extremism and the armed forces, see T. R. H. Havens, *Farm and Nation in Modern Japan: Agrarian Nationalism, 1870–1940* (Princeton

of the armed forces. The army and navy had never been subordinated constitutionally to the governments of the day but were responsible directly to the emperor. The concept of a Showa restoration inspired many officers after the new emperor, Hirohito, succeeded to the throne in 1926: the restoration would connote purity of government and society and a foreign policy based on the realization of the just aim of true, if rugged, autonomy for Japan and East Asia. Controversy has surrounded the person of the emperor and the extent to which he should be personally identified with extremism. It was decided, in 1945-6, to exclude the emperor from the war crimes trial of former Japanese leaders; the decision was taken after it had been determined to retain the monarchy and to use the emperor to legitimize the American occupation of Japan. In such circumstances it would have been politically impossible to have put Hirohito on trial. It has been argued that Hirohito himself was an extreme nationalist responsible for masterminding Japanese expansion.[13] This radical interpretation has commanded little support among historians, but the precise way in which the emperor functioned politically is obscure and it is possible that he exercised relatively more influence than used to be thought. However, the available evidence suggests that Hirohito was a ruler of moderate inclinations and that he did not sympathize with extremism. The armed forces were dominated by a fanatical loyalty to the throne, which was integrally linked with Shintoism. The older cautious leadership of the armed forces, epitomized in Yamagata Aritomo, gradually declined as the older generals and admirals died or retired: the calibre of leadership in the armed forces declined in consequence. Factionalism developed, with younger officers determined to exert more influence over policy formulation. The army was more vociferous and openly ambitious, but it would be misleading to think in terms of a division between a bellicose army and a moderate navy: during the 1930s extremism developed

University Press, Princeton, 1974), pp. 133-321, R. J. Smethurst, *A Social Basis for Prewar Japanese Militarism: the Army and the Rural Community* (University of California Press, London, 1974), and J. B. Crowley, *Japan's Quest for Autonomy* (Princeton University Press, Princeton, 1966).

[13] See D. Bergamini, *Japan's Imperial Conspiracy* (Heinemann, London, 1971).

within the navy and there was a decisive break with the tradition of co-operating with Great Britain and the United States as symbolized by the Washington conference of 1921–2.[14] Factionalism characterized both services but was more severe in the army (where members of rival factions sometimes attacked each other physically), culminating in the Tokyo mutiny of February 1936. After the mutiny, discipline was reimposed to a considerable extent, but younger officers of middle rank were important in policy-making down to Pearl Harbor and beyond.

Japan's foreign policy from 1933 to 1937 was directed towards attaining a 'Monroe Doctrine' for East Asia, towards reiteration of Japan's right to lead the peoples of the region in future, and to persuading the western powers to acquiesce in this situation. The Amau doctrine of 1934, the Hirota points in 1935, and the principles of national policy approved in 1936 all pointed to this objective. There was no intention of embarking on a major war within the immediate future but there was wider recognition of the fact that war with Britain and the United States was ultimately probable. It was not expected that Japan would become embroiled in an interminable struggle in China, since Japanese leaders felt that Chiang Kai-shek would not be so foolish as to fight them when communism was the real enemy. They sadly failed to comprehend the tenacity of Chinese traditions and Chiang's new status as a national leader, itself ironically endorsed by the Chinese communists after the Sian mutiny in December 1936. Japan's involvement in China, gradually developing from 1931, led to the war of 1937–45 and to Pearl Harbor.

As for Great Britain, she had no wish for a clash with Japan. If possible, Britain desired the serious issues dividing the former allies to be removed, or papered over if removal were impracticable. Britain was not, however, prepared to do this at the price of making major concessions. Anthony Eden, foreign secretary from December 1935 to February 1938, was more interested in Europe and was personally critical of

---

[14] On attitudes within the navy, see Asada Sadao, 'The Japanese Navy and the United States', Borg and Okamoto, pp. 225-59, and S. E. Pelz, *Race to Pearl Harbor: the Failure of the Second London Naval Conference and the Onset of World War II* (Harvard University Press, Cambridge, Mass., 1974).

Japan. He welcomed the approaches in 1936 from Yoshida Shigeru, the Japanese ambassador in London, for a world-wide Anglo-Japanese agreement on political and economic objectives. Yoshida pushed the proposal on his own initiative and it did not have the full weight of Tokyo behind it.[15] The desultory Eden–Yoshida talks were to run into the sands in 1937 and were effectively buried by the Undeclared War. On the eve of the Sino-Japanese war, Britain to some extent recognized the grave weaknesses in defence which prevented her from acting with vigour. However, the full implications were not appreciated and it was hoped that it would be possible to defend British interests through diplomacy until the situation in Europe and the Mediterranean became less menacing.

[15] See Trotter, pp. 191–203.

I

THE OPENING OF THE UNDECLARED WAR IN CHINA

ON 7 July 1937 a minor skirmish between Japanese and Chinese troops took place near the Lukouchiao bridge, ten miles outside Peiping (Peking). The clash marked the first incident in the Undeclared War between Japan and China, which was only to terminate eight years later with Japan's surrender after the dropping of the atomic bombs on Hiroshima and Nagasaki. The origins of the initial clash lay in the penetration of north-east China by Japanese forces in the four years that followed the Tangku truce (May 1933). Resentment among Chinese soldiers and administrators grew, and conflict became increasingly probable. It is difficult to apportion exact responsibility for the Lukouchiao affair: it seems clear that the local Chinese troops were disinclined to submit meekly to Japanese truculence and similarly that Japanese troops were determined not to accept Chinese recalcitrance. It is fair to say that neither side was innocent but that the principal responsibility was undoubtedly Japan's, for her forces had embarked upon a policy of undermining Chinese authority on territory that was indisputably Chinese. Neither Japan nor China wished the original incident to escalate into a major war, and it was not until the serious fighting developed at Shanghai in August 1937 that the conflict assumed a grave character. It now appears certain that the Japanese prime minister, Prince Konoe Fumimaro, supported a more vigorous expansionist policy and co-operated with the field army in north-east China against the general staff in Tokyo; the general staff, notably General Tada Shun, felt that it was too dangerous to become involved in a serious struggle in China and maintained, prophetically, that it might prove difficult to extricate Japan from such involvement. Konoe and his supporters wished to seize the opportunity to compel China to make concessions. It was politically impossible for Chiang Kai-shek to comply, since he

MAP I. China

had encountered loud criticism in recent years for failing to respond more positively to Japanese encroachment since 1931. From the beginning of the war the differences between the two sides were too great to surmount and thereafter neither Japan nor China could lose face by offering appreciable concessions.[1]

In Great Britain the gravity of developments in China took some time to register fully. The government was headed by a new prime minister, Neville Chamberlain, and was pre-occupied with European issues embracing the German threat to central Europe, the repercussions of the Abyssinian crisis, and the nature of the Spanish civil war. The foreign secretary, Anthony Eden, had not, in any case, exhibited much interest in the Far East. The new ambassador in Tokyo, Sir Robert Craigie, had not yet arrived to take up his appointment and the British embassy was in the temporary charge of James Dodds. In one of his first reports, on 12 July, Dodds stated that the military attaché had been assured by the general staff and the ministry of war that every effort was being made to prevent the crisis from spreading.[2] Dodds was distinctly sympathetic to Japan but was nevertheless uneasy at the way in which events were shaping; later on 12 July he proposed to Eden that he should, 'in certain eventualities', inform the Japanese foreign minister that, while Great Britain desired an understanding with Japan, any attempt at repeating in north-east China the policy so recently pursued in Manchuko would prevent further improvement in their mutual relations.[3] Eden agreed that Dodds should so act if necessary.[4] The foreign secretary himself decided to convey concern to the Japanese ambassador; he spoke to Yoshida the same day, incorporating a veiled warning on the future of Anglo-Japanese relations. On 13 July Eden saw the Chinese ambassador, Quo Tai-chi, and listened to a sombre assessment of the future as seen by the Kuomintang government. China feared the launching of a general offensive and desired the mediation of disinterested

[1] For a discussion of the first phase of the Undeclared War, see J. B. Crowley, *Japan's Quest for Autonomy*, pp. 301–78. See also J. W. Morley (ed.), *Dilemmas of Growth in Prewar Japan*, pp. 342–54, and Borg and Okamoto pp. 35–8, 66–9, 116–18.
[2] Dodds to Eden, 12 July 1937, F4019/9/10, F.O.371/20949.
[3] Dodds to Eden, 12 July 1937, F4035/9/10, F.O.371/20949.
[4] Eden to Dodds, 12 July 1937, F4071/9/10, F.O.371/20949.

governments. Eden replied that, 'There was I felt some danger that both parties would take up a rigid position in part on account of prestige, when we might find ourselves involved in tragic consequences which neither desired.'[5] Britain wanted a swift and amicable resolution of the crisis. Quo defined China's position as flexible to some extent, but warned that his country could not accept an enhanced Japanese military presence in northern China. Sir Ronald Lindsay, the British ambassador in Washington, visited the State Department and learned that Cordell Hull had seen the Chinese and Japanese ambassadors and emphasized the need for a peaceful solution to problems. The United States believed that it would be salutary for Britain to tender the same advice but representations should be parallel rather than joint; the vociferous nature of isolationism precluded the United States from acting too overtly with Britain.[6] Dodds, who was on close terms with the American ambassador, Joseph C. Grew, informed Eden on 14 July that he and Grew were agreed that Japan was not behaving in too bellicose a manner and that it was preferable not to make representations that were too pointed.[7] In the Foreign Office Eden and Sir Alexander Cadogan, the deputy under-secretary, expressed more anxiety than the officials of the Far Eastern department. Cadogan, whose suspicions of Japan had been fostered during his term as ambassador to China from 1933 to 1936, minuted on 14 July:

. . . in spite of reassuring messages from Tokyo, I can't say I like the look of things. The Japanese assurances remind me forcibly of six years ago, and I wouldn't like to put too much faith in them *yet*. They can mass troops behind the Wall, whence they can move them comparatively quickly to the scene of action. I hope my pessimism will prove unfounded.[8]

Cadogan's doubts were well founded, for the situation gradually worsened over the following days, with reports of Japanese bombing raids being received on 18 July. On 20 July Eden saw Robert Bingham, the American ambassador, and

---

[5] Eden to Knatchbull-Hugessen, 13 July 1937, F4085/9/10, F.O.371/20950.

[6] Lindsay to Eden, 14 July 1937, F4087/9/10, F.O.371/20950.

[7] Dodds to Eden, 14 July 1937, F4108/9/10, F.O.371/20950.

[8] Minute by Cadogan, 15 July 1937, on Cowan (Peiping) to Eden, 14 July 1937, F4130/9/10, F.O.371/20950.

discussed matters with him. Eden explained that Britain was reluctant to act alone and that action taken in conjunction with the United States was desirable. Bingham was sympathetic, and thought it should be easier to secure American co-operation in view of the apprehension of Japan in the western states of the country. At the same time he could not see what action could be taken that would lead to a significant improvement; neither Britain nor the United States could contemplate war with Japan. The next day Bingham called to see Eden. The ambassador put forward, as entirely his personal idea, a proposal that Britain and the United States should implement a joint embargo on Japanese trade, affecting both imports and exports. Eden inquired whether the neutrality legislation in the United States would permit such action. Before considering Bingham's suggestion further, he felt that it would be wise to see what moves the United States was prepared to take immediately.[9] Eden believed the two countries should combine in a joint approach to Japan; he urged the suspension of troop movements and put forward proposals for solving the existing crisis. Lindsay reported on 21 July that joint action seemed unattainable in the light of the attitudes prevailing within the State Department.[10] Eden in turn reported to the cabinet that he was maintaining contact with the United States but that he had no encouraging information to convey.[11]

There was some dissension within the Foreign Office over Anglo-American intervention. When Sir Hughe Knatchbull-Hugessen reported that China wished Britain and the United States to act as guarantors of a settlement, N. B. Ronald minuted: 'I cannot help thinking that the less we and the U.S. allow ourselves to be involved, the better for all concerned and the sooner the trouble will be ended.'[12] C. W. Orde and Sir Lancelot Oliphant agreed, Orde referring to the Chinese as 'such inveterate wrigglers and self-deceivers'.[13] Presumably it was thought that China would settle for the best terms she

[9] Eden to Lindsay (secret and personal), 21 July 1937, ibid.
[10] Lindsay to Eden, 21 July 1937, F4317/9/10, F.O. 371/20950.
[11] Cabinet meeting, 21 July 1937, 31(37)3, Cab. 23/89.
[12] Minute by Ronald, 28 July 1937, on Knatchbull-Hugessen to Eden, 26 July 1937, F4562/9/10, F.O.371/20951.
[13] Ibid., minutes by Orde and Oliphant, 29 July 1937.

could secure if Britain and the United States declined to assist her: such an outlook was curiously naïve and ignored the pressures experienced by Chiang Kai-shek, which effectively ruled out acceptance of Japanese terms. The Foreign Office view of the Japanese prime minister conformed to the widely held contemporary opinion of Konoe as a well-meaning but vacillating figure. When news was received that Konoe might be considering resignation, Ronald was alarmed. He minuted that Konoe resembled the late British prime minister, Lord Rosebery, in his reactions and that the departure of such a 'reasonable mouthpiece' would be most disturbing.[14] On 30 July the American ambassador called to see Sir Robert Vansittart, the permanent under-secretary. He said that his government wished to know what action would be deemed advisable by the British government, and the United States wondered whether a withdrawal of all military personnel from Peiping might not offer a possible solution. Bingham added that parallel action had failed and the only hope lay in joint action.[15] Eden regarded the American response as encouraging, commenting, 'We must lose no opportunity of cooperating with U.S. Govt.'[16] A memorandum was prepared in reply, stating that the two governments could offer their good offices in providing neutral territory for the plenipotentiaries to meet and that they could aim to minimize mutual suspicions. It was important to prevent the reinforcement of troops from proceeding further.

Shanghai became the focus of attention in August 1937. The situation in some respects was analogous to that of 1932, when bitter fighting had broken out between Japanese and Chinese forces.[17] The Chinese felt a greater compulsion to defend Shanghai, for it was geographically a considerable distance from the principal sphere of Japanese infiltration in northern China and a resolute Chinese policy in Shanghai was

---

[14] Minute by Ronald, 2 Aug. 1937, on Dodds to Eden, 31 July 1937, F4732/9/10, F.O.371/20951. For the views of a historian who inclines towards the contemporary impression of Konoe, see G. R. Storry, 'Konoye Fumimaro: the last of the Fujiwara', in G. F. Hudson (ed.), *St. Antony's Papers*, No. 7: *Far Eastern Affairs*, No. 2 (London, 1960), pp. 9-33.
[15] Minute by Vansittart, 30 July 1937, F4890/9/10, F.O.371/20952.
[16] Minute by Eden, 30 July 1937, ibid.
[17] For an analysis of the events in 1932 see C. Thorne, *The Limits of Foreign Policy*, pp. 202-72.

bound to influence the foreign powers, in view of the volume of foreign investment and commerce concentrated there. Shanghai was the metropolis of East Asia, and there were major British interests at stake. The atmosphere in Shanghai rapidly worsened between 9 and 12 August, culminating in the outbreak of savage fighting. An emergency meeting was convened in the Foreign Office on 13 August attended by representatives of the Foreign Office, the Admiralty, and the War Office. There were 50,000 foreigners in Shanghai, including 9,000 British residents, and evacuation would be an extremely formidable operation. General Sir Robert Haining, the director of military operations at the War Office, referred to the vulnerable position of the small number of British troops stationed in Shanghai. As regards the navy, few ships were in Shanghai but the commander-in-chief, China station, Admiral Sir Charles Little, was advancing to Shanghai. The first sea lord, Chatfield, wrote to Little on 6 August, 'It is very unfortunate that this China-Japanese [clash] has broken out at this time because we were all hoping here that we were going to make real friends with the Japanese once more and it has always been the China situation that has stood in the way, so I do hope that war will not come after all, but at present it looks very like it . . .'[18] Appeals were made by Britain and the United States to both sides, but the fighting continued. The full gravity of the Sino-Japanese war became inescapably clear.[19] On 12 August N. B. Ronald set down his reflections on the course of events. He saw little prospect of Britain being able to influence matters significantly. The extent to which British interests suffered would depend on the duration of the war, although they would inevitably be affected whether China decided to resist wholeheartedly or to acquiesce. He believed, on balance, that it might be best for Japan and China to fight it out, as a more stable situation might ensue. The fundamental problem was the inefficient and corrupt state of Chinese society. Defeat might lead to a radical restructuring of China which would assist her subsequent development. Otherwise:

[18] Letter from Chatfield to Little, 6 Aug. 1937, Chatfield papers.
[19] For a fuller discussion of developments in Shanghai and the British response, see B. A. Lee, *Britain and the Sino-Japanese War 1937–1939*, pp. 35–8.

they may never be brought to recognise that sham soldiers and sham politics gave no practical utility . . . Until the Chinese are brought to face the fact that their whole political system is riddled with shams by seeing it reduced to ruins, they are likely to go on in the bad old way.

Paradoxical as it may seem, it may therefore be in their ultimate interest that they should move towards the crushing defeat which probably awaits them at the hands of the Japanese.[20]

Japan would most likely emerge economically weakened from the struggle. Orde minuted substantial agreement with Ronald's analysis, and drew the conclusion that Britain could not pursue a more positive policy than the one she was already following.[21] Orde and Ronald were influenced by the realization of British defence weakness, the sluggishness of China, and the brutal tenacity of Japan. Orde commented on 22 August that since Britain was in no position to fight should the need arise, she should follow a policy calculated to avert embroilment with Japan.[22] The best course would be to reduce criticisms of Japan to the minimum at the League of Nations and recognize that a state of war existed, if necessary insisting on the latter contrary to Japan's formal opinion.

The adoption of this policy was made more difficult by developments in late August. Knatchbull-Hugessen's car was machine-gunned from the air on 26 August as the ambassador was travelling to Shanghai; he was seriously wounded.[23] His car was decorated with a large Union Jack but, far from warning off the Japanese aviators, the flag in practice made it simpler for them to hit the car. The prime minister was incensed at this grave incident, as was Eden. A vehement protest was made to the Japanese government with a demand for an apology and promise of condign punishment for those responsible. Eden was prepared to order the newly appointed

[20] Minute by Ronald, 12 Aug. 1937, F5393/9/10, F.O.371/20953.

[21] Minute by Orde, 12 Aug. 1937, ibid.

[22] Minute by Orde, 22 Aug. 1937, F5720/9/10, F.O.371/20954.

[23] For Knatchbull-Hugessen's account, see his memoirs, *Diplomat in Peace and War* (John Murray, London, 1949), pp. 120-4. Neville Chamberlain wrote to his sister Hilda: 'Now this stupid and outrageous attack has occurred upon our ambassador and it is to be hoped that the Japs. will accept without demur the very reasonable and moderate demands we are making upon them.' Letter from Neville Chamberlain to Hilda, 29 Aug. 1937, Neville Chamberlain papers, NC18/1/10/8, Birmingham University Library.

ambassador, Sir Robert Craigie, to leave Tokyo, unless Japan complied. Craigie, meanwhile, persuaded the Japanese government to make a fuller statement of regret than was contained in the interim reply, and this was reluctantly accepted in London. Apart from the attack on Knatchbull-Hugessen, Britain was antagonized by Japan's policy of intercepting British ships in the course of the application of a boycott of the Chinese coast.[24] It was decided, at a meeting of ministers held on 2 September, to approve the policy advocated by the Foreign Office of submitting to interception, subject to a reservation of rights for damages incurred. The cabinet endorsed this decision on 8 September.[25]

The earlier indications from Bingham that the United States might be prepared to co-operate more meaningfully were not borne out in August and September. Cordell Hull felt it would be inviting trouble from Congress if the United States switched from parallel to joint action; he was much influenced by Stanley Hornbeck, the chief specialist on the Far East in the State Department.[26] The counsellor of the British embassy in Washington, Victor Mallet, sent a private letter to Orde on 31 August discussing a candid conversation with Hornbeck. He had found Hornbeck in a somewhat irritable mood. 'No doubt this can largely be attributed to the fact that he had been spending about an hour and a half with the Secretary of State; apparently these conferences take up at least an hour a day and about seven of the principal figures in the State Department meet in the Secretary's room and talk over the day's China telegrams in his presence, which must be a rather trying way of doing business.'[27] Hornbeck spoke bluntly but off the record; he did not like joint action because parallel action was politically preferable and he thought it was often wiser to ignore Japanese actions than to complain too frequently. Hornbeck said that he would consult Hull over the British anxiety regarding the Japanese shipping measures. He asked what would be done if Japan merely treated protests with in-

[24] Lee, pp. 40-1.
[25] Lee, pp. 41-2.
[26] For an interesting assessment of the State Department under Hull, which is essentially an appraisal of Hornbeck, see J. C. Thomson, Jr., 'The Role of the Department of State' in Borg and Okamoto, pp. 81-106.
[27] Letter from Mallet to Orde, 31 Aug. 1937, F6303/9/10, F.O.371/20955.

difference. Mallet observed: 'American public opinion is so strongly non-interventionist that the State Department are terrified of being dragged out of their depth or even of wetting the tips of their toes. They don't like joint action for several reasons, one of which I think is that they are afraid of criticism here that they are being dragged along by us.' It would be erroneous, despite these discouraging signs, to conclude that the United States did not favour exchanges with Britain; it was, remarked Mallet, a matter of method more than anything else. The vigour of American public opinion was the obstacle. Mallet was sympathetic to the political dilemma confronting Roosevelt and Hull. He reiterated in a further letter to Orde a week later, 'I believe the State Department to be going just as far as public opinion will allow them and they are certainly not in favour of a scuttle and run policy in the Far East.'[28] Mallet's analysis was confirmed by an interview with Hull on 7 September, in which the secretary of state and the assistant secretary, Sumner Welles, emphasized that they were in no way embarrassed at communications from London relating to East Asia. 'Mr. Hull, while not entirely ruling out joint action if its utility could be proved, said he decidedly preferred parallel action as more expeditious and less liable to involve him in criticism here, but once again asked me to tell you that he was *not* embarrassed.'[29]

The American position was perhaps mildly encouraging but no more than that. The Foreign Office became steadily more gloomy as September proceeded. Craigie, having first accustomed himself to the political climate of Tokyo, sent a telegram to Eden on 25 September accurately warning that the coming weeks would be crucial in the development of the Undeclared War and that Japan's terms would become more onerous the longer the war lasted. Craigie advocated a British attempt at mediation; there were risks in adopting such a policy but even greater risks in not adopting it.[30] The reply was largely drafted by Cadogan with some amendments by Eden. The foreign secretary largely concurred in Craigie's appraisal, but added:

[28] Letter from Mallet to Orde, 7 Sept. 1937, F6496/9/10, F.O.371/20955.
[29] Mallet to Eden, 7 Sept. 1937, F6284/9/10, F.O.371/20955.
[30] Craigie to Eden, 25 Sept. 1937, F6972/9/10, F.O.371/20956.

I only wonder whether it would be possible to get in touch with the forces that in fact direct Japanese policy. It is conceivable that statesmen in Tokyo may have moderate and long-sighted views, but have they any influence on events, and with the passage of time are they more likely to regain ascendancy?

However that may be, H.M.G. would always be ready to further any effort towards restoration of peace, and for that purpose their good offices would always be available . . .[31]

In late September British animosity towards Japan was accentuated by indiscriminate bombing and by increasing use of the international settlement in Shanghai by the Japanese as a base for operations. Simultaneously the League of Nations was continuing its deliberations, protests from sections of British public opinion were growing in press and parliament, and the Foreign Office had to reassess matters. Orde received a letter from Dodds in late September; Dodds held that Britain must reassert her interest in East Asia, and one argument was that Britain was a greater Asiatic power than Japan. Orde drafted his reply, revealing how he had become far more critical of Japan himself compared with the position he had taken a month earlier:

We are fully in agreement with your views on how to behave with the Japanese. It is unquestionably a fact that one can talk very bluntly to them as long as one is not rude . . . Anyway it is becoming increasingly clear that this is the only method of obtaining the desired effect. In the past the western powers, ourselves included, have treated them gently and with marked forbearance, and it is perhaps not astonishing that as a result they have come to believe that a policy of swagger and bluster can sweep all before it. By all means let us now try methods of firmness and standing up for our rights on every possible occasion. It is, of course, exhausting and exasperating to have to keep on hammering away at people who are blinded by an overweening national vanity; but when we know, as we do, how large an element of bluff there really is in the pretensions when one looks behind the surface we are, I think, justified in assuming that the dangers attending such a process are for the most part largely imaginary and it is well worthwhile to keep on hammering away in spite of the tedium and strain involved. Of course, there is a point at which they may go off their heads, and sanctions may be that point.

Your point that we are a much greater Asiatic power than Japan is

---

[31] Eden to Craigie, 27 Sept. 1937, ibid.

excellent. This they must be made to realise and accept. They are fond of talking of 'the realities of the case', but let us also be realistic and keep this facet well in the forefront of our mind in framing our attitude towards their claims to Asiatic supremacy.

When they have a case and have learned to state it properly and reasonably, we will, I do not doubt, be prepared to listen to them with respect and magnanimity: but meanwhile we shall have to let them see we are not to be intimidated and we must endeavour, with or without their gratitude, to open their eyes as often as possible. In this I agree with you that if no one else will do so, it is all the more necessary that we should, in our own interests as well as those of the world in general.

The poor things would like to 'enlighten' us, 'correct' and 'rectify' our attitude but they are hard put to it. We are getting shoals of letters and telegrams from people full of indignation at the bombings.[32]

Both Dodds and Orde favoured a tougher approach; nevertheless their emphasis on Britain's importance as an Asiatic power, while undeniably true in terms of territorial possessions and political and economic interests, conveniently ignored the fact that Britain lacked the resources to act like a major power.

The League of Nations, no longer the body it had been before the Manchurian and Abyssinian crises had undermined it, had to grapple with the new far eastern conflict as best it could. It was not clear what positive action could be taken until aid came from an unexpected quarter. President Roosevelt, on 5 October 1937, made the most important address on foreign issues that he had so far delivered since entering the White House. Controversy continues to surround the speech, the precise meaning of which was veiled in calculated ambiguity and obscurity.[33] The basic theme was clear: the president's determination to awaken the uncomprehending American masses to the unpleasant features and inherent dangers of the world scene. Isolationism, inward-looking nationalism, or pacifism were each foolish paths to follow and could afford no ultimate guarantee of American

[32] Letter from Orde to Dodds, 1 Oct. 1937, F7287/9/10, F.O.371/20956.
[33] For a discussion of Roosevelt's speech, see D. M. Borg, *The United States and the Far Eastern Crisis of 1933–1938* (Harvard University Press, Cambridge, Mass., 1964), pp. 369–98.

survival in a hostile world. The contention begins thereafter. What did Roosevelt have in mind in referring to the need for law-abiding nations to co-operate and possibly mount a 'quarantine' of the aggressor states? The most likely answer is that he had nothing specific in mind, although subsequent developments, which will be discussed below, suggest that he may have been toying with the idea of an economic blockade of Japan, reinforced by appropriate naval measures. Immediately after delivering the speech, Roosevelt retreated into vague generalizations when questioned as to its meaning. Hull was appalled at Roosevelt's initiative in inserting the quarantine reference without consultation, and maintained in his memoirs, rather dubiously, that the speech so offended the isolationists as to set back the cause of achieving a more positive foreign policy by six months.[34] From the vantage point of Geneva, Roosevelt's speech was highly apposite. The president could hardly reject an invitation for American representation at a conference of the countries that had signed the nine-power treaty in 1922, with the addition of the Soviet Union, Norway, and Denmark. The invitation was duly transmitted and accepted by Roosevelt; as Hull was reluctant to attend, it was decided to send the ubiquitous Norman Davis.[35]

The British cabinet discussed the implications of Roosevelt's speech on 6 October. Neville Chamberlain was preoccupied with the domestic repercussions, and stated that the speech would be utilized by the Labour and Liberal parties for their own purposes. 'It would be important for the Government not to be manoeuvred into a position in which it could be said that the United States had offered to cooperate in economic sanctions if the United Kingdom would join them and that we were standing in the way of such action.' Chamberlain felt that in his next public speech he would have to welcome the president's remarks, with particular reference to the sanctity of treaties. Hore-Belisha, the secretary of state for war, emphasized his alarm at the course of the war in China. Chamberlain concurred and held that Britain must not

[34] C. Hull, *The Memoirs of Cordell Hull*, 2 vols. (Macmillan, N.Y., 1948) i, 544-5.
[35] For American reactions to the Brussels Conference, see Hull, *Memoirs*, i, 550-6, Borg, pp. 399-401, N. H. Hooker (ed.), *The Moffat Papers: Selections from the Diplomatic Journals of Jay Pierrepont Moffat* (Harvard University Press, Cambridge, Mass., 1956), pp. 156-87.

become involved militarily in China. 'He could not imagine anything more suicidal than to pick a quarrel with Japan at the present moment when the European situation had become so serious. If this country were to become involved in the Far East the temptation to the Dictator States to take action whether in Eastern Europe or in Spain, might be irresistible.'[36] The prime minister continued, citing a recent article from the *Manchester Guardian* in support, that it might be wise to ask the United States outright whether she contemplated economic sanctions and if she would be prepared for war in fulfilment of applying sanctions. The first sea lord, Chatfield, was perturbed lest Roosevelt's remarks encouraged his political masters to cast discretion aside:

I am concerned about the Far Eastern situation and where we may find ourselves dragged by the sentimentalists. I am afraid that Roosevelt's speech will do us more harm than good. It encourages the anti-Japanese enthusiasts — and yet you may be quite sure that if it ever comes to any trouble in the Far East the Americans will stand aside. We have got quite enough troubles on our hands in Europe to make it most undesirable to send the Fleet out to the Far East. Sanctions are just as likely to mean sending the Fleet out to the Far East as the sanctions against Italy meant sending the Fleet out to the Mediterranean. I have, however, warned the Foreign Office of the danger, and I hope that wise counsels will prevail . . .[37]

Chamberlain reflected at length on Roosevelt's speech and its repercussions in a letter to his sister Hilda:

I read Roosevelt's speech with mixed feelings. What did it really mean? It sounded very fierce but when one examined it carefully it was contradictory in parts and very vague in 'essentials'. What does he mean by 'putting them in "quarantine" '? And seeing that patients suffering from epidemic diseases do not usually go about fully armed is there not a difference here and something lacking in his analogy. Of course our opposition have interpreted it as I knew they would, as meaning that U.S.A. would put economic sanctions on Japan if we would do the same and they are preparing the way for an accusation that we as usual are standing in the way and preventing the courageous and altruistic Americans from saving the Chinks from aerial bombs. But the conversations of our man in

---

[36] Cabinet meeting, 6 Oct. 1937, 36(37)5, Cab.23/89.
[37] Letter from Chatfield to Backhouse, 8 Oct. 1937, Chatfield papers.

Washington draw a very different picture and speak of the American Gvt's 'fear of encouraging boycott' and their anxiety to know what *we* would propose to do! This confirms my first impression that the President's pronouncement was intended to sound out the ground and see how far his public opinion was prepared to go but that he himself had thought nothing out and in any case had no present intention of doing anything that wasn't perfectly safe.

Now in the present state of European affairs with the two dictators in a thoroughly nasty temper we simply cannot afford to quarrel with Japan and I very much fear therefore that after a lot of ballyhoo the Americans will somehow fade out and leave us to carry all the blame and the odium. It is not a pleasant prospect, but I am setting my mind now to see how we can avoid it and I think some straight speaking to U.S.A. (in private) before they go any further will be necessary . . . However there is just one point on the other side—the psychological effect of this sudden abandonment of America's attitude of complete detachment. If the totalitarians get the idea that they can't entirely count on her remaining outside while they eat up the democracies it may give them some pause and for that reason I have thought it wise to give the appearance of believering that R. meant much more than in fact he did. But you will have seen that I was extremely cautious and committed myself to absolutely nothing at all.[38]

At a later cabinet meeting, Chamberlain and Eden pessimistically surveyed the course of the war; the prime minister feared that China might soon collapse, in which case Chiang Kai-shek would end up in the same plight as the unfortunate emperor of Abyssinia. Chamberlain thought that conciliation must be the keynote at the forthcoming conference.[39] Eden regarded it as most improbable that Japan would attend, and entirely agreed with Chamberlain in ruling out economic sanctions, unless the United States and other signatories of the nine-power treaty were willing to enforce them. The cabinet decided that the British attitude should be fully explained to the United States and that it was essential to tread warily in formulating policy.

On 18 October Eden sent Mallet a lucid analysis of British policy for the consideration of the Roosevelt administration. It was almost certain that Japan would refuse to attend the

[38] Letter from Neville Chamberlain to Hilda, 9 Oct. 1937, Neville Chamberlain papers, NC18/1/1023, Birmingham University Library.
[39] Cabinet meeting, 13 Oct. 1937, 37(37)5, Cab.23/89.

Brussels conference: the powers would have to determine their course of action without Japanese co-operation. There appeared to be three alternatives: to postpone action in the hope that matters would improve, to censure Japan morally but without proceeding further, or to approve a positive response comprising direct assistance to China or the application of economic pressure against Japan. The first two alternatives would amount to acquiescence in Japanese aggression, while the third would alienate Japan to no purpose. The significance of the latter should be more carefully considered, however.[40] Material assistance to China would have to be conveyed by sea and would involve the danger of a direct clash with the Japanese navy. Economic action against Japan could prove effective if strictly enforced through agreement among the powers. There was a definite risk of war resulting, however, and Britain believed that no country could afford to impose sanctions without undertakings of support from other powers. The issues were left open for discussion when Norman Davis arrived in Europe.

The Belgian government reluctantly agreed to act as host to the conference, which accordingly met in Brussels on 3 November 1937. It gathered in inauspicious circumstances, with Japan conspicuous by her absence and by her animosity towards the conference and with little agreement among the powers on the action that could be taken. As is often the case, the cynical argument for the conference was that at least it created the impression of activity. There was much discussion at Brussels, but unhappily it led nowhere. Craigie urged from Tokyo that the conference should refrain from attributing responsibility for the conflict in China and that ample room should be left for conciliation; in his opinion, the most satisfactory solution would be to appoint a small committee to keep in touch and offer mediation if it seemed appropriate.[41] Great Britain was represented by Anthony Eden and by Malcolm MacDonald, the secretary of state for the Dominions. The principal members of the American delegation were Norman Davis and Stanley Hornbeck. Davis was well-intentioned but garrulous and not infrequently unreliable

---

[40] Eden to Mallet, 18 Oct. 1937, F8013/6799/10, F.O.371/21015.
[41] Craigie to Eden, 30 Oct. 1937, F8783/6799/10, F.O.371/21016.

in his explanations of American policy; Hornbeck was much tougher but always conscious of American public opinion, and he tended to underestimate Japan. Lengthy consultations took place between the British and American delegations outside the formality of the conference chamber.[42] Eden and MacDonald talked to Davis just before the opening and re-iterated the British desire for a close working relationship with the United States. Hornbeck told Sir Robert Clive, the British ambassador in Brussels who had formerly served in Tokyo, that Britain was too cautious and that Japan did not constitute a serious threat to Britain or the United States.[43] Davis discussed Roosevelt's views in a private conversation with Eden:

Mr. Davies [*sic*] . . . made it plain that the President is deeply concerned at world outlook and sincerely anxious to cooperate in an attempt to stop the rot. Mr. Davies explained that the President had put it to him that the conference would either succeed or, having failed, would confront the world with a futile situation in which further action by the United States could not be excluded. All liberty depends in the President's view upon the course of the conference and state of American public opinion at the end of it. Mr. Davies also intimated that the President was deeply perturbed at the prospects in the Far East. He thought that Great Britain might be compelled to withdraw from her position there and that as a consequence United States might some day have to deal, may be alone, with a greatly strengthened Japanese Power across the Pacific Ocean. It was this formidable prospect that was making the President wish, if he could, to do something to check the tendency now.[44]

Eden deduced that the American delegates regarded the conference as important in educating their own public but that the United States had no resolute policy in mind.

The conference meandered along in the hope that Japan could be persuaded to behave constructively towards it. The hope gradually faded, as it was realized that Japan regarded it with contempt. The British delegates listened with diminishing patience to the windy rhetoric of Norman Davis

[42] For Eden's views of the conference, see Lord Avon, *The Eden Memoirs: Facing the Dictators* (Cassell, London, 1962), pp. 536-40. See also J. Harvey (ed.), *The Diplomatic Diaries of Oliver Harvey, 1937-1940* (Collins, London, 1970), pp. 54-8.
[43] Clive to Eden, 2 Nov. 1937, F9046/6799/10, F.O.371/21016.
[44] Clive to Foreign Office, 3 Nov. 1937, F9072/6789/10, F.O.371/21016.

and adhered to the cabinet's policy of not accepting commitments that would place Britain in an exposed position. Eden informed the cabinet on 17 November that any impression that Britain was lingering behind the United States had been eradicated. He alluded to the difficulty of producing a statement that would be tolerated by Japan. The cabinet decided that the existing policy of caution and restraint must be continued. It was optimistically held that there was scant evidence that Japan wished to remain in occupation of Chinese territory; more significantly, it was again recalled that Britain's military position in the Far East was weak. Even if the United States should advocate a firm policy, which was unlikely, Britain should discourage the pursuit of such an approach. It was felt that the best way out of a dismal predicament was for Britain and the United States to be nominated to a mediatory committee; if the conference rejected this course, it might be followed independently.[45] MacDonald sought to implement this policy at Brussels. Assisted by Lord Cranborne, the parliamentary undersecretary at the Foreign Office, and by Cadogan, he pressed Davis and Hornbeck to accept a mild concluding statement with a joint offer of good offices from Britain and the United States. Davis vigorously opposed the suggestion. He castigated any decision to adjourn the conference as premature and deprecated the contemplated offer of good offices. MacDonald then forcefully pointed to the absurdity of indulging in strident criticism of Japan while simultaneously being unable to meet Japan with force if necessary. Davis at last concurred. The Brussels conference simply confirmed the interest of the powers in the crisis and repudiated the Japanese argument that the dispute involved only Japan and China and should be settled between them. It was emphasized, when the conference adjourned on 24 November, that the aim should be to obtain a settlement compatible with the nine-power treaty of 1922. The conference was a manifest failure. The idea of holding it was a mistake; it succeeded only in conveying accurately enough the feeling of helplessness dominating the nations represented at it.

On 24 November the cabinet decided that thought should

[45] Cabinet conclusions, 17 Nov. 1937, 42(37)4, Cab.23/90A.

be given to the possible dispatch of a naval expedition to the Far East. Cadogan saw Chatfield on 26 November and Chatfield indicated the complexity of the operation. There would be no point in sending a small fleet in case the Japanese defeated it before conjunction with the American fleet was effected. The British force would have to be strong enough to cope on its own with the Japanese fleet and this would necessitate mobilization. Chatfield preferred a tentative sounding-out of the United States rather than the advancement of a concrete proposal. A telegram was drafted in suitable terms and sent to Lindsay in Washington on 26 November.[46] The United States was asked to consider whether the time had not come for a powerful naval display in East Asia. Britain was willing to enter staff conversations to this end. When Lindsay spoke to Hull on 29 November, the secretary of state underlined the need to maintain secrecy in any naval exchanges so as to obviate trouble with the isolationists in Congress. Lindsay was pessimistic as to the likelihood of the administration assenting to naval exchanges.[47] It is unlikely that Roosevelt would have encouraged naval exchanges had it not been for a deterioration in relations with Japan in December 1937.

In November-December 1937 Japan pursued a successful offensive which forced the retreat of the Kuomintang armies; the Chinese capital, Nanking, symbol of the supposed rebirth of China, was captured in early December amidst scenes of rape and pillage that discredited the Japanese army. Shortly afterwards two grave incidents occurred on the Yangtze when the British gunboat, H.M.S. *Ladybird*, was attacked and the American ship, the *Panay*, was sunk. The incidents arose from the extremism of the Japanese field armies and from the contempt for the effete west openly expressed by military personnel. The incidents seriously embarrassed the Japanese government, and the foreign minister, Hirota, hurried round to the American embassy to apologize.[48] An apology was also sent to the British government. The cabinet reviewed the crisis at length on 15 December. Eden explained that the United

[46] Eden to Lindsay, 26 Nov. 1937, with minute by Cadogan, 26 Nov. 1937, F10024/9/10, F.O.371/20959.

[47] Lindsay to Eden, 29 Nov. 1937, F10254/9/10, F.O.371/20960.

[48] See J. C. Grew, *Ten Years in Japan* (Simon and Schuster, N.Y., 1944), p. 235.

States had sent a note of protest to Tokyo without waiting for Britain's opinion, as Eden had suggested. Eden stated that he was urging on the United States the importance of resolute action to impress Japan. After discussing matters with Chamberlain and Duff Cooper, he had drawn up a further telegram proposing that the two countries should each send battle fleets to the Far East. The prime minister commented that it was essential to emphasize that Britain would only act if the United States moved. Duff Cooper doubted the wisdom of sending the telegram because the United States would merely be irritated. The secretary of state for India, the Marquess of Zetland, supported a show of naval force in eastern waters. It was decided that Eden should consult Lindsay before formally approaching the United States.[49] The worsening situation jolted Roosevelt into deciding to send a naval officer to London to hold urgent and highly confidential talks with the Admiralty. Roosevelt had been contemplating the possible implementation of a naval blockade of Japan for some time; it was now fitting that there should be an exchange of views with London on naval problems.[50]

Roosevelt and Hull met Lindsay on 17 December.[51] Roosevelt proposed that there should be a comprehensive exchange of information between the Admiralty and the American navy on a basis similar to that of the exchanges in 1915-17, when Roosevelt had been assistant secretary of the navy. The president spoke of a possible blockade and quarantine of Japan with the objective of cutting Japan off from access to raw materials; it might take eighteen months to have full effect and Roosevelt did not envisage a blockade leading to war. He hoped that Britain could send cruisers, destroyers, and submarines to the Far East. He indicated that he was considering the imminent dispatch of an American officer to conduct conversations in London. The Foreign Office received the news with a mixture of satisfaction and scepticism. Ronald commented:

[49] Cabinet conclusions, 15 Dec. 1937, 47(37)3, Cab.23/90A.
[50] For reassessments of Roosevelt's thinking, see J. McV. Haight Jr, 'Franklin D. Roosevelt and a Naval Quarantine of Japan', *P.H.R.* xl (May 1971), 203-26, and L. Pratt, 'The Anglo-American Naval Conversations on the Far East of January 1938', *I.A.* xlvii (Oct. 1971), 745-63.
[51] Lindsay to Eden, 17 Dec. 1937, F11201/9/10, F.O.371/20961.

The plan sketched out by the President may be a fantastic chimera as it stands but it has the supreme merit of being his, the President of the U.S.A.'s, own creation. With care and patience on our part it should not be impossible to preserve the lion's head while yet transforming the goat's body into something more congruous. I submit therefore that our first reaction must be to applaud the creator of the plan and to express readiness to consider with Captain Ingersoll how it could, if need arose, be translated into practice.

The plan as it stands is no doubt impractical as well as fraught with every kind of danger, but it should not be impossible to lead the Americans away from the silliness and still leave them the idea that what results is their very own.[52]

Eden and Cadogan believed that it was essential to strike while the United States was in a positive mood.[53] Eden advocated preparatory measures within the two navies, perhaps involving the dispatch of ships to Singapore. On 24 December Lindsay reported that an American cruiser squadron would leave in about ten days' time for visits to Sydney and Singapore.[54] In the cabinet there was general support for holding naval talks.

Captain Royal E. Ingersoll of the United States navy was dispatched from Washington immediately to conduct exchanges in London. Ingersoll met a number of top personnel in the Admiralty and, in addition, saw Eden and senior Foreign Office officials. According to Ingersoll's own account, a copy of which is to be found in the Admiralty archives, he met Eden and Cadogan on 2 January 1938; Herschel Johnson, counsellor at the American embassy, was also present. Ingersoll stated that, on the president's instructions, Admiral Leahy had sent him to London, 'to obtain information on which to place and base decisions, if necessary, as to future action'.[55] Ingersoll clearly regarded his mission as concerned primarily with long-term exploratory exchanges; the foreign secretary, however, was more occupied with the near future. 'I got the impression that Mr. Eden was more interested right now in immediate gestures to impress the Japanese than he was in long-term future planning.'[56] Ingersoll met Chatfield on the

[52] Minute by Ronald, 19 Dec. 1937, ibid.

[53] Minute by Cadogan, 19 Dec. 1937, ibid.

[54] Lindsay to Eden, 24 Dec. 1937, F11473/9/10, F.O.371/20961.

[55] Records of conversations with Captain Ingersoll (1937-8), report by Ingersoll, Adm.1/9822.

[56] Ibid.

following day. Chatfield referred to political pressure to send inadequate forces to the Far East, which he had resisted. The first sea lord observed that the Admiralty had been preparing a force for some time and that it should be feasible for it to be ready to depart on 15 January if required. Mobilization would be necessary to ensure adequate reserves to cope with the danger of a European crisis; the eastern Mediterranean would be held by occupying Egypt, but Malta and Cyprus would most likely have to be abandoned. Chatfield commented that political and naval decisions must be kept in step, as should Anglo-American co-operation.[57] Ingersoll then explained the position of the United States. The navy could not be mobilized unless a national emergency was proclaimed. The first American action would probably be to adopt a position of readiness covering the west coast and Hawaiian islands, but an advance of the entire fleet beyond this position was not desirable. Chatfield expressed concern over the defence of British trade routes in the Atlantic. With regard to the base at Singapore, two docks were ready but the repair of large ships could not be undertaken and the base would not be completed for about eighteen months. Ingersoll was informed that the British force would comprise nine battleships, one battle-cruiser, two aircraft carriers, fifteen cruisers, fifty-four destroyers, and ten submarines. It was important to arrange for common codes, signals, and procedures with the American fleet as soon as possible. On 4 January the question of implementing a blockade or quarantine was debated. No firm understanding was reached, but Ingersoll believed that the British were prepared to cover the line from Singapore via the southern Philippines as far east as the New Hebrides and the United States could cover the area to the eastward via Fiji, Samoa, Hawaii, and the United States. Britain was interested in using Manila as a base, but it was not thought likely that the Japanese would endeavour to capture the Philippines while they were occupied in China. Ingersoll reported that the British believed that a demonstration by the two fleets in the Pacific would be required in order to remind Japan of Anglo-American interest in the fate of China and so obtain more acceptable peace terms for China at the end of the Sino-

[57] Ibid.

Japanese war. Britain did not expect to receive much assistance from France, other perhaps than the use of French ports in Indo-China. If joint action was to be taken, then the British and American fleets should reach Singapore and Hawaii at about the same date. In a further discussion on 5 January the Admiralty indicated that, if a blockade was established, the Royal Navy would stop all Japanese traffic crossing a line extending approximately from Singapore through the Netherlands East Indies, New Guinea, New Hebrides, and around to the east of Australia and New Zealand. It was held that the United States should be able to control the entire Pacific coast. The number of capital ships to be sent by the British was eight, and not nine as previously believed, with eight battleships and a battlecruiser.

At the end of his visit, on 13 January, Ingersoll once more met Chatfield. Chatfield spoke warmly of the value of Ingersoll's mission.[58] He felt that as much progress had been made as was feasible. He continued to discuss the action that could be taken by the signatories of the 1936 naval treaty to compel Japan to supply information on whether she was building vessels whose characteristics exceeded those of the treaty. If Japan was exceeding the limitations or declined to give satisfactory information, then the escape clause should be utilized to exceed the existing limits for cruisers, both tonnage and guns. Japan should be left in no doubt as to the consequences of her actions in rapidly expanding her navy. In the agreed record of the conversations, signed by Ingersoll and Tom Phillips, it was noted that the state of readiness of the U.S. fleet was: submarines and aircraft on the Pacific coast (100 per cent); an advance force, consisting of two squadrons of heavy cruisers and two squadrons of destroyers with one aircraft carrier; in addition, capital ships, cruisers, destroyers, and auxiliaries on the Pacific coast other than advance forces, 85 per cent complement. On the Atlantic coast, the Americans would station three battleships, the *Wyoming*, and one squadron of destroyers used as a training force with about 50 per cent complement. The U.S. navy would send the advance force to Honolulu first, together with fifteen submarines; these would join seventy-five patrol planes and about twenty sub-

[58] Ibid.

marines at Honolulu. There would be six submarines and thirty-six aircraft in the Panama Canal zone. All available capital ships would probably be sent to Honolulu. It should be possible for nine or ten capital ships to sail ten to fifteen days after the declaration of national emergency. A gradual advance across the Pacific was then contemplated, using Japanese mandated islands, with the base being ultimately established at Truk or some other position in the same general area.[59]

Ingersoll's mission was important as one of the first tangible signs of the extent of Roosevelt's alarm at the deteriorating world situation and of his determination to begin taking action to combat it. The significance was qualified, however, by the strictly confidential nature of the exchanges, and the president's initiative was not helped when news of Ingersoll's activities was leaked to Congress by hostile elements in the Navy department. As a result of the leak, Roosevelt was discouraged from pursuing the idea of naval co-operation further until the Hampton mission in June 1939. The Ingersoll mission had no practical effect on British policy in the Far East: it did not lead to joint co-operation against Japanese expansion.[60] The central dilemma of British defence remained unchanged. Roosevelt indicated to Lindsay in early January 1938 that he was willing to send three American cruisers to Singapore, to announce that the ships in the American Pacific Fleet were to have their hulls scraped, and to advance Pacific manoeuvres to February if Britain announced definite plans to send a fleet to the Far East within a few days. It was clear that the onus would fall principally upon Britain and that there was no guarantee that the United States would act resolutely. Eden supported action on the basis of the American response, but he was away from London on holiday and not in the best position to influence decision-making. In addition, his relations with Chamberlain were worsening and led to his resignation in February 1938. Chamberlain was opposed to mobilizing the British fleet owing to events in Europe, and it was decided not to act.[61]

[59] Ibid.

[60] For Cadogan's views, see D. Dilks (ed.), *The Diaries of Sir Alexander Cadogan, 1938-1945* (Cassell, London, 1971), pp. 33-4.

[61] For further discussion of this aspect, see Pratt, *I.A.* (1971), 757.

At the beginning of 1938 the Foreign Office reluctantly recognized that the Sino-Japanese war was more serious and was unquestionably going to last longer than had been expected a few months earlier. The two principal specialists in the Far Eastern department, Sir John Pratt and Sir John Brenan, submitted memoranda in early January 1938 reviewing the terms of a possible future peace settlement. Brenan observed that it was certainly in Britain's interest to preserve the integrity of China in so far as this could be achieved. Since the Japanese controlled north China, little could be done to defend this area. British aims had to be seen in a world context:

It is essential . . . if we are to disarm the antagonism of our political opponents in Europe and to have the support of world opinion and especially American opinion, that our aims should be recognised as unselfish and fair to all. If anything, we must err on the side of altruism and indeed we can well do so, because all we desire, apart from the safety of Hong Kong, is the maintenance of the general principle embodied in the nine-power treaty, an open door and no discrimination against our trade with China.[62]

Brenan suggested recognition by Japan of the sovereignty and independence of China and withdrawal of Japanese forces to the south of the Great Wall; Chinese acceptance of Manchukuo's retention of the international customs administration on existing lines with tariff amendments in Japan's favour; the reorganization of the Shanghai area under one administration; a possible termination of extra-territoriality at the end of the war. Brenan concluded that a settlement on these lines would include abandonment 'of some of the political pretensions no longer justified by our military strength in that part of the world', but the opportunities for British trade with Japan and China would be enhanced.

Pratt urged that if Britain proposed peace terms, she should send a naval force strong enough to defend vital British interests. Britain desired peaceful conditions for trade and equality of commercial opportunity, objectives common to other nations in the Far East. British interests were particularly threatened in Shanghai, where Japanese action

---

[62] Memorandum by Brenan, 6 Jan. 1938, F335/16/10, F.O.371/22053.

'was undermining the international settlement and the maritime customs. What Britain wanted was evacuation of islands
off the southern coast of China; abandonment of attacks on
southern China, notably Canton; complete withdrawal of
Japanese forces from the international settlement; and
assurances on the maritime customs. Of these, Pratt felt that
Japan would be most reluctant to leave the international
settlement unless compelled to do so. Concessions from all
sides would be required to produce a fair agreement. The
most sensible solution might well be to end extraterritoriality.
The international settlement could be absorbed within one
municipal authority for the whole of Shanghai; an answer to
the problem of the maritime customs would have to be found.
In north China, Japan and China could be left to reach an
agreement.[63]

C. W. Orde indicated approval of the memoranda and of
Pratt's suggestions on Shanghai: however, he believed that
north China must be included. Cadogan commented that the
method of approach need not be discussed at this stage. He
was interested in terms that could be imposed if Britain were
able to dictate, an improbable contingency. Cadogan was encouraged by the recent improvement in Anglo-American
relations. Eden concurred, although he was not to hold office
for much longer.[64] The memoranda were subsequently
merged and sent by Cadogan to Stanley Hornbeck for his
personal information.[65]

In February 1938 a debate proceeded as to whether it was
desirable for the war to continue. Sir Robert Craigie trenchantly maintained that continuation of the struggle would
create further problems, and was not inclined to favour such a
development:

As I have more than once ventured to urge, British interests
(strategic as well as economic) stand to suffer most from a prolongation of this struggle and I see great risk in accepting the com-
placent theory that on balance we stand to gain from the progressive
(though slow) economic weakening of Japan. My conclusions are that
it would be most unwise from our *own* point of view to take any step

[63] Memorandum by Pratt, 5 Jan. 1938, ibid.
[64] Minutes, 17-28 Jan. 1938, ibid.
[65] Cadogan to Hornbeck, 14 Feb. 1938, ibid.

calculated to encourage Chiang Kai-shek to prolong resistance (notwithstanding his obvious personal advantage in doing so) and that we should watch carefully for any sign that nationalist Government might be prepared to make peace on terms which leave China temporarily weakened, it is true, but still capable of ultimate resuscitation .. .[66]

W. J. Davies minuted agreement with Craigie, but J. Thyne-Henderson thought it would be fallacious to assume that the war would develop further in Japan's favour; in economic terms, Japan's position was bound to worsen. Orde predictably concurred, as did Cadogan, who believed that extension of the war would not result in harsher peace terms for China but rather the reverse. Eden evidently harboured some doubts. While remarking, 'I hesitate to enter the controversy among experts', he pointed out that Japan was doing reasonably well out of north China economically and could manage.[67] The foreign secretary contemplated China's predicament unenthusiastically. Whatever happened, it was clear that there would be numerous difficulties for Britain to navigate with the best diplomatic skill she could muster. In any event, it made little difference whether the extension of the war was in her favour: Britain could not intervene to bring the conflict to an end. German good offices and mediation had been employed from September 1937 to January 1938 to little avail.[68] The two sides were too far apart in their respective attitudes, and Japan's price for a settlement had risen appreciably after her successes in the offensive late in 1937.

The principal issues down to the summer of 1938 sprang from the growing Japanese pressure on the foreign concessions and the possibility of providing economic aid for the Chinese government. Logically enough, Japan wished to gain as much control as she could over the concessions and the international settlement at Shanghai in order to further her policy of pressurizing China and gradually eliminating western interests. The customs revenues quickly became the centre of controversy in 1937-8. The customs administration still operated as it had done for nearly eighty years, under the

[66] Craigie to Eden, 9 Feb. 1938, F1679/84/10, F.O.371/22107.
[67] Minutes, 10-12 Feb. 1938, ibid.
[68] For Germany's attitude in this period, see *D.G.F.P.*, D, i, 780-825.

direction of a British national, currently Sir Frederick Maze. Japan worked to gain control of the revenues, the pressure becoming especially intense at Shanghai and Tientsin. Britain's chief aim was to defend the functioning of the customs administration and to ensure that foreign loans were properly met. Negotiations were conducted in Tokyo from February 1938. Britain had hoped to persuade Japan to agree to the revenues being put in a neutral bank, but when the Japanese proved obdurate, Britain gave way. In the agreement reached in April and announced on 3 May 1938, customs revenues from the ports under Japanese control were to be placed in the Yokohama Specie Bank, which would allow foreign obligations to be met.[69] China bitterly resented the agreement: it was correctly interpreted in Hankow as connoting the sacrifice of China's rights to protect British trade. The Chinese were oblivious of the argument that the agreement at least prevented Japan from taking more extreme action. The United States regarded it critically, as a retreat from the policy of upholding the nine-power treaty. As Bradford Lee has observed, the customs agreement 'represented the first notable instance of British appeasement of Japan during the Sino-Japanese conflict'.[70] It was not to be followed by another major act of appeasement until the Tientsin crisis in the summer of 1939.

The continuation of the war and the approach of the first anniversary of its outbreak led within Whitehall to a deeper consideration of the possibility of extending British economic assistance to China. Britain had pledged moral support for China at Geneva, but had not reinforced this with more tangible encouragement. Between May and August the new foreign secretary, Lord Halifax, took the lead in endeavouring to convince the Treasury of the importance of helping China. In a letter to the chancellor of the exchequer, Sir John Simon, on 9 May, Halifax talked of China's resilience in resisting Japan and of the willingness of France, Germany, and Russia to send arms to China. He continued:

China is fighting the battle of all the law-abiding States and she is incidentally fighting our own battle in the Far East, for if Japan wins,

[69] Lee, p. 119.
[70] Ibid.

our interests there are certainly doomed to extinction. The Japanese Army and other high authorities have left us in no possible doubt about that. Our immense vested interests in North China and Shanghai will be the first to go and the Japanese Army and Navy set no limits to their appetites on the Continent and in the South Seas. It seems to me that if China can only fight Japan to a stalemate, we and the Americans will then be able to intervene with effective results and safeguard our position for another generation.

Moreover we are committed by a Resolution of the League of Nations to give every assistance we can to China. Every consideration, therefore, of honour and self-interest impels us towards doing what we can to keep China alive. We are embarking on an expenditure of two milliards of pounds in preparation for war. Here for an infinitesimal fraction of that sum, we may be able, at no risk to ourselves, to preserve our vital interests in the Far East.[71]

Halifax hoped that Simon would respond positively. Sir Archibald Clark Kerr, the new ambassador in China, warmly advocated economic aid to China, while Craigie was hostile because of the repercussions in Tokyo. Brenan held that, while Craigie was right in forecasting renewed pressure on British interests, it was necessary to support the suggested loan, as it 'would be good policy from a wider imperial point of view'.[72] R. G. Howe reiterated support for the extension of credits to China through the Exports Credits Guarantee Department, based on the security of antimony and silver. The Treasury predictably showed no enthusiasm in supporting a loan. Halifax brought the matter before the cabinet on 6 July 1938. The Foreign Office contemplated a loan of £20 million, supporting the proposal with arguments arising from the need to defend direct British interests and prestige in China, and indeed Asia generally. Simon put forward an alternative memorandum, reminding his colleagues of the perils of intervening in the Sino-Japanese war. The ensuing discussion appeared to reveal an equal division of opinion in the cabinet, but the prime minister was dubious of the wisdom of providing the loan and emphasized the dangers of a clash with Japan and the difficulty of securing American co-operation. The discussion was adjourned to 13 July. By that time Halifax and

[71] Letter from Halifax to Simon, 9 May 1938, F4582/84/10, F.O.371/22108.
[72] Minute by Brenan, 11 May 1938, on Craigie to Halifax, 6 May 1938, F4865/84/10, F.O.371/22108.

Malcolm MacDonald had spoken to Joseph Kennedy, the American ambassador, and to Stanley Bruce, the Australian high commissioner: Kennedy had not been encouraging but Bruce had stated that his government would support a loan. Neville Chamberlain opposed a loan, owing to the gravity of the European situation, including the attitude of Italy; he commented on Mussolini's 'curious and somewhat inexplicable frame of mind'.[73] The prime minister referred with approval to Kennedy's observation that the British Empire had more than enough to contend with already. Halifax recognized the strength of the opposition, and agreed to explain tactfully to the Chinese government why it would not be possible to proceed with the loan. Despite adverse comments from Zetland, who warned of the consequences for British prestige, the cabinet formally decided that no loan should be advanced.[74] Chamberlain's influence was decisive, and the situation in Europe was worsening with the build-up to the climax of the Czechoslovak crisis. The issue of British economic aid for China was postponed for subsequent consideration in 1938-9.

Thus in July 1938 the first year of Great Britain's response to the Sino-Japanese war closed. The war had already lasted longer than had been thought probable in July-August 1937, and there was no likelihood of it ending in July 1938. British policy had vacillated to some extent but had, in the main, leaned increasingly towards sympathy for China. However, the fundamental principle guiding British policy was understandably that of safeguarding British interests in China, and it was, therefore, essential not to antagonize Japan unduly. Vigorous protests had to be made where necessary, as for instance following the attacks on Knatchbull-Hugessen and on H.M.S. *Ladybird*. At the same time, account had to be taken of Japan's actions, hence the customs agreement of May 1938. Chiang Kai-shek received sympathy but little solid economic or technical assistance. It was, however, recognized that the Kuomintang regime was failing to rally support significantly.

---

[73] Cabinet conclusions, 6 July 1938, 31(38)6, Cab.23/94. For the views of the Treasury, see Leith-Ross papers, T188/205, 208. See also memoranda by Halifax and Simon, 1 July 1938, C.P.152 and 157(38), Cab.24/277.
[74] Cabinet conclusions, 13 July 1938, 32(38)8, Cab.23/94. Cadogan believed that the European crisis was too dangerous to permit a loan to China, see Dilks, p. 86.

A. L. Scott commented on 18 March 1938 that, while there was respect in China for Chiang Kai-shek as a military leader of the resistance to Japan,

> the influence of the Communists is bound to increase as that of the Kuomintang becomes less, and attention has frequently been called to the moribund state of the Kuomintang party. While the intelligentsia and youth in China may recently have rallied to Chiang Kai-shek as a military leader their sympathies for Communism are probably none the less strong. Certainly the Communists for their part are confident that when the war is over they will gain the supremacy, in which case we may expect the establishment of a regime similar to that now existing in Mexico . . .[75]

Relations with the United States had grown somewhat more cordial, but it was improbable that the parallel approach would be replaced by a joint one within the near future. British policy-makers placed their hopes on the growing strains imposed by the war upon the Japanese economy having salutary repercussions on Japanese policy. How far these hopes were justified was not clear as the second year of the Undeclared War began.

[75] Minute by Scott, 18 Mar. 1938, F2944/53/10, F.O.371/22082.

II

THE ADVENT OF THE NEW ORDER

IN the summer of 1938 there appeared to be some possibility of securing an improvement in Anglo-Japanese relations. Japan did not seem to be making progress in the war. The British air attaché in China commented adversely on the competence of the Japanese air force. It could not be deemed comparable to the air force of 'a First Class Power' because the performance of the aircraft was inferior; there was poor coordination between the services; tactics were bad and there was insufficient attention paid to military targets; air bases were insecure; the wrong type of bomb was used; the Japanese underestimated their enemy.[1] Here were the seeds of the British complacency and arrogance that were to reap a bitter harvest in 1941-2. The magnitude of the challenge confronting Japan in coercing or defeating China was immense. It was dangerous to infer from the inability to secure complete victory that Japan's forces were incompetent. The faith in China's ability to resist was bolstered by a cautiously optimistic assessment from Sir Archibald Clark Kerr:

It is futile to attempt to prophesy but my own impression formed after consulting every source within reach is that in spite of all its weaknesses and handicaps Central Government — or rather the dictatorship which has to all intents and purposes replaced it — is full of life, vigour and determination, and that even on the worst hypothesis its complete destruction is beyond the power of the Japanese armed forces. I consider that even if Hankow falls in the immediate future it will be a long time before the slow process of disintegration which the military experts foresee will become as marked as to enable

[1] Report by air attaché, British embassy, Shanghai, to H.M. embassy, 10 May 1938, F6467/1/10, F.O.371/22039. In a fuller subsequent report the attaché, Wing-Commander H.S. Kerby, stated that it was difficult to assess Japanese strength accurately *vis-à-vis* major powers because Japanese planes had encountered little opposition in China. However, aircraft performance and quality of technical equipment were inferior to those of first-class powers; it was doubtful whether Japan had enough reserves of pilots or aircraft in existing conditions. See report by Kerby, 20 Dec. 1938, Air 2/3558.

the Japanese to slacken their effort. I am convinced that no one in Hankow is yet prepared to consider peace on any terms likely to be acceptable to Japanese and I fear that future holds no prospect of anything in a continuation of arid struggle.[2]

In late May 1938 General Ugaki Kazushige assumed office as foreign minister, replacing Hirota Koki. Ugaki's appointment reflected Konoe's desire to achieve a settlement in China if possible.[3] Ugaki was relatively liberal by the standards of the Japanese army; he had actually presided over a reduction in the size of the army while war minister in 1924. He had been regarded as a possible prime minister in January 1937 but his appointment had been blocked by the army.[4] Ugaki believed firmly in Japan's mission, but appreciated that a more subtle approach was required where the foreign powers were concerned. He was, therefore, willing to exchange views with Sir Robert Craigie on ways of improving relations between Britain and Japan. Craigie had long wished to seize any opportunity to ameliorate the situation. He realized that concessions would inevitably have to be made to Japan at China's expense but hoped that, by shrewd diplomacy, he could restrict the concessions to the minimum. This aim fitted in with inquiries from China in early August 1938 as to the likelihood of Great Britain, the United States, and France being willing to mediate if Hankow were captured.[5] On 16 August Craigie reported that Japan definitely desired peace and that she might accept 'good offices from the right quarter'. He held that the best chance of success would lie with an Anglo-German combination, since Germany enjoyed better relations with Japan than either the United States or France; he recognized that much would depend on whether the United States would be prepared to participate.[6] Meanwhile Craigie had pressed, on 26 July, for the satisfactory resolution of a number of thorny problems in his somewhat desultory conversations with Ugaki. These comprised the position in the

[2] Clark Kerr to Halifax, 20 July 1938, F7853/2/10, F.O.371/22044.
[3] B. A. Lee, *Britain and the Sino-Japanese War, 1937-39*, p. 140.
[4] See J. B. Crowley, *Japan's Quest for Autonomy: National Security and Foreign Policy 1930-1938*, p. 130.
[5] *D.B.F.P.* 3, viii, 2 and 4-5, Clark Kerr to Halifax, 4 Aug. 1938 and Halifax to Clark Kerr, 4 Aug. 1938.
[6] *D.B.F.P.* 3, viii, 22, Craigie to Halifax, 16 Aug. 1938.

northern district of Shanghai; the navigation of the Yangtze; the termination of restrictions on British-owned or controlled firms; facilities for the inspection of railways which were not involved in major military operations; and the removal of measures inhibiting the work of the Whangpoo River Conservancy.[7] Ugaki expressed the hope that outstanding differences could be settled to mutual satisfaction but stressed that the navigation of the Yangtze presented considerable difficulties; the Japanese government doubted whether it would be feasible for foreign ships and nationals to visit Wuhu and Nanking. Ugaki was less forthcoming when Craigie met him again on 18 August. Ugaki welcomed the British decision not to proceed with a loan to China, but criticized the tone of parliamentary statements in London and referred to a rumour that Clark Kerr was advising Chiang Kai-shek on the choice of a new temporary capital when Hankow should have fallen.[8] Craigie was clearly disappointed at the negative response:

I detected a great change in General Ugaki's attitude though he remained personally friendly and courteous . . . Rumour has it that the Cabinet had been strongly pressed to discontinue conversations altogether and the decision to mark time is the obvious compromise . . . I am afraid moment is approaching when we must conclude that method of friendly negotiations here has failed and that such other methods of pressure as are available must be tried but no final decision should be taken on this point until I have had my interview at the end of the month, but it would be as well that forms of pressure open to us should meanwhile be examined.[9]

The Foreign Office viewed the position pessimistically. Sir John Brenan thought Japan would aim to monopolize trade with China and would ignore the earlier bland assurances of respect for foreign rights. 'The Japanese are prosecuting the war with great ruthlessness and our main safeguard against even worse treatment is not so much considerations of past friendship as the fear of the consequences. There is no sign yet that the military rulers of Japan are prepared to abate their demands or consider peace terms acceptable to ourselves and our only hope and policy is still to play for a stalemate and the

[7] *D.B.F.P.* 3, viii, 5–6, footnote.
[8] *D.B.F.P.* 3, viii, 27–8, Craigie to Halifax, 18 Aug. 1938.
[9] *D.B.F.P.* 3, viii, 29, Craigie to Halifax, 18 Aug. 1938.

further exhaustion of the aggressor Power.'[10]

When Craigie saw Ugaki again on 20 August, however, the foreign minister adopted a more positive attitude and emphasized that he favoured cordial co-operation between Britain and Japan in the future, and invited Craigie's opinion as to the chances of such co-operation developing. Craigie welcomed Ugaki's sentiments but observed that much depended on the interpretation of the word 'co-operation'.[11] The Foreign Office deprecated the concept of co-operation, which was regarded as the thin end of the wedge for compelling Britain to accept Japanese policy. Brenan irately commented:

If we wish to know what is meant by cooperation we must look at the Japanese complaints of the ways in which we have not cooperated. We have sold arms to China and have kept open the Hongkong channel for the supply of munitions. We have criticised Japan in Parliament and the press, and have given moral and material support to the Chinese Government. The British authorities in China have adopted an unfriendly attitude and are always making protests; and on occasion they have done things to impede the Japanese operations.

The bargain therefore is that if we will cease our moral and material support of Chiang Kai-shek's administration and recognise Japan's new position on the mainland, if we will abandon the League of Nations attitude and condone the Japanese aggression by helping to finance the development of the occupied areas on Japanese lines, then the Japanese will see what they can do to remove some of our more immediate complaints. Our reward will be, possibly, the payment of the railway loans and debts, permission to resume some of our commercial activities in the restricted districts at Shanghai, to continue our shipping trade in a modified form, and fewer insults and pinpricks. We are to make the very great concession of a reversal of our whole attitude towards the Far Eastern conflict in return for minor and problematical advantages of a temporary kind . . .

The present moment is not suitable for making concessions to them and we shall 'miss no opportunity' by marking time until the situation in the Far East and Europe changes for the better.[12]

[10] Minute by Brenan, 18 Aug. 1938, on Craigie to Halifax, 14 July 1938, F.O.371/22051.

[11] *D.B.F.P.* 3, viii, 34–5, Craigie to Halifax, 20 Aug. 1938.

[12] Minute by Brenan, 30 Aug. 1938, on Craigie to Halifax, 27 Aug. 1938, F9256/12/10, F.O.371/22051.

Craigie wavered between a feeling that Ugaki might yet be able to secure significant concessions and a sense of growing disillusionment. His interview with the foreign minister on 9 September strengthened the latter reaction. Ugaki reiterated the fundamental importance of Japan's mission in China, and called for abandonment of British support for Chiang Kai-shek. He then discussed the specific points raised by Craigie in late July. He offered little in the way of reassurance except on the Whangpoo conservancy, which he believed was about to be settled. Craigie replied that he was extremely disappointed: the Japanese government had shown no sympathy or even understanding of British complaints.[13]

The Craigie–Ugaki talks were overtaken in the middle and latter part of September by the climax of the Czechoslovak crisis in Europe and by a political crisis in Tokyo concerning Ugaki himself. Japan's reaction to events in Europe was to voice strong support for Germany's demands coupled with condemnation of the Czech approach, which was obscurely attributed to the machinations of the Comintern. There appeared to be some danger of Japan joining Germany if war resulted in Europe but, in retrospect, it is most likely that Japan would have preserved a benevolent neutrality to Germany. On 22 September Craigie again visited Ugaki. The foreign minister spoke at length of Britain's unfair support for Chiang Kai-shek: 'The short cut out of our difficulties would be for Great Britain to assume towards the Japanese authorities in China an attitude similar to that which she had adopted *vis-à-vis* the Franco Government in Spain.'[14] Ugaki dealt with the specific causes for British complaint repeatedly pursued by Craigie; it was obvious that improvements could only be attained if Britain agreed to co-operate on terms decided by the Japanese. Craigie expected to see Ugaki again, but this hope was frustrated by the foreign minister's resignation on 29 September. Ugaki resigned in protest against the scheme to establish the China Affairs Board, a method of facilitating greater control over the formulation of foreign policy for the more extreme nationalists. The Craigie–Ugaki talks stood little chance of success, for Ugaki could not retreat

[13] *D.B.F.P.* 3, viii, 75–6, Craigie to Halifax, 9 Sept. 1938.
[14] *D.B.F.P.* 3, viii, 97–8, Craigie to Halifax, 22 Sept. 1938.

on the basic aims of Japanese policy, even had he wished to do so, and the British government had no intention of compromising upon essentials. Ugaki's resignation marks a watershed in that it was the end of hopes that some advance could be made in the direction of improving Anglo-Japanese relations, no matter how thin the hopes had been. Relations steadily deteriorated from September 1938 until the conclusion of the Nazi–Soviet pact of non-aggression in August 1939.

On 12 October 1938 the Japanese army launched new offensives against the Wuhan complex in the heart of the wealthy Yangtze valley and in southern China, directed at Canton. The operations brought the Japanese closer to important centres of British trade and investment. There is no evidence that British policy in Europe, culminating in the Munich settlement, affected the timing of the military campaign but there can be little doubt that it fostered the image of British weakness: Japanese contempt for Britain was certainly more overt than before. The offensives were overwhelmingly successful. Canton was taken on 21 October, and Hankow, the temporary Kuomintang capital, fell shortly afterwards. Elation and supreme self-confidence characterized the Japanese response. Several major policy statements were issued in November and December 1938, enunciating the essence of the 'New Order' in East Asia. The principal features consisted of an explanation of Japan's divine purposes in fulfilling the new order; repudiation of the Kuomintang regime; and an underlying theme that Asia belonged to the Asians. The first important statement was issued on 3 November for publication the next day.[15] The Foreign Office took a gloomy view of the prospects and determined to make it abundantly clear that Britain would not acquiesce in the establishment of the new order. The parliamentary under-secretary, R. A. Butler, stated in the House of Commons on 10 November that British policy was governed by the Washington treaty settlement and, therefore, was the same as American policy as reiterated by Cordell Hull on 4 November.[16] Craigie spoke to the new foreign minister, Arita Hachiro, on 17 November. Arita

[15] For the key passages of the statement see below, Appendix, pp. 70–1.
[16] *D.B.F.P.* 3, viii, 212–13, Halifax to Craigie, 10 Nov. 1938.

defended Japan's concept of the new order, referring in particular to the growth of powerful economic blocs in the world, such as those associated with the British Empire, the United States and Latin America, and Russia. He alluded to the need for Japan to defend her sphere of interest; Arita hoped the powers would greet the advent of the new order with appropriate understanding and promised to study Britain's earlier complaints over the activities of the Japanese military.[17] Craigie warned Arita of the dangers of pursuing economic blocs to extremes and denied that the 'open door' and equality of opportunity were applied in China alone. Clark Kerr denounced the new order and trenchantly argued that Britain should continue to oppose Japanese designs and assist China. The Foreign Office generally concurred but simultaneously contemplated indicating to Japan, 'at a carefully selected opportunity', that the existing international treaties could be modified by negotiation. Craigie was instructed to confer with his American colleague, Grew, and, if they both agreed, to intimate to the Japanese that Britain and the United States would consider proposals for modifying treaties. There was a feeling that it would perhaps be unwise for a totally negative response to be advanced. However, it was imperative to carry the United States along with Britain if such a view were to be communicated to Japan.

On 22 December another major policy pronouncement was made by Prince Konoe, as an extension of a radio broadcast he had made on 4 November. Konoe bluntly expounded the purpose of the new order and Japanese antagonism to the Kuomintang. A sop was thrown in for foreign powers by way of consoling them, to the effect that Japan did not intend to erect an economic monopoly in China:

The Japanese Government are resolved . . . to carry on military operations for the complete extermination of the anti-Japanese Kuomintang Government, and at the same time to proceed with the work of establishing a new order in East Asia together with those far-sighted Chinese who share in our ideals and aspirations. A spirit of renaissance is now sweeping over all parts of China and enthusiasm for reconstruction is mounting ever higher . . .
Japan, China and Manchukuo will be united by the common aim of

---

[17] *D.B.F.P.* 3, viii, 234–5, Craigie to Halifax, 17 Nov. 1938.

establishing a new order in East Asia and of realising a relationship of neighbouring amity, common defence against communism, and economic cooperation. For that purpose it is necessary first of all that China should cast aside all narrow and prejudiced views belonging to the past and do away with the folly of anti-Japanism and resentment regarding Manchukuo. In other words, Japan frankly desires China to enter of her own will into complete diplomatic relations with Manchukuo.

The existence of Comintern influence in East Asia cannot be tolerated. Japan, therefore, considers it an essential condition of the adjustment of Sino-Japanese relations that there should be concluded an anti-Comintern agreement between the two countries in consonance with the spirit of the Anti-Comintern Agreement between Japan, Germany and Italy, and in order to ensure the full accomplishment of her purpose, Japan demands, in view of the actual circumstances prevailing in China, that Japanese troops be stationed as an anti-Communist measure at specified points during the time the said agreement is in force, and also that the Inner Mongolia region be designated as a special anti-Communist area.

As regards economic relations between the two countries, Japan does not intend to exercise economic monopoly in China, nor does she intend to demand of China to limit the interests of those third Powers who grasp the meaning of the new East Asia and are willing to act accordingly . . .

If the true object of Japan in conducting the present vast military campaign be fully understood, it will be plain that what she seeks is neither territory nor indemnity for the costs of military operations . . . Japan not only respects the sovereignty of China, but she is prepared to give positive consideration to the questions of the abolition of extraterritoriality and the rendition of Concessions and Settlements — matters which are necessary to the full independence of China.[18]

The Foreign Office was already moving towards the conclusion that a formal note should possibly be addressed to Tokyo, refuting the basis of the new order while indicating a willingness to surrender extraterritoriality. Sir John Brenan and Sir George Mounsey held that Britain should give aid to China. Cadogan, never noted for his sympathy to Japan, minuted:

In this age of broken faith — and Treaties — there has been nothing so blatant as Japan's aggression in China. It would go sorely against the

[18] *D.B.F.P.* 3, viii, 343–4, statement by Konoe, 22 Dec. 1938.

grain to compound with it in any circumstances. But we have America to consider and we should lose the last shreds of respect and sympathy that we may enjoy in that country if we did so.

Unfortunately, with our other commitments and anxieties, there is little we can do actively. We must leave the Chinese to fight their battle—or ours for us—and give them such assistance as we can. It is an unpleasant and rather humiliating role, but I am sure it is right. We should get nothing, in the end, by making up to the Japanese. If they win all their points they will still throw us over—and out.[19]

Halifax commented that 'we should be prepared to take our part in the revision of Treaties, that may be held to require reconciliation, but that we could not accept unilateral modification of them.'[20] When Konoe's statement was examined in the Foreign Office, M. E. Dening observed that it was significant for what was left unsaid. The ultimate aim was to control strategic points throughout China in pursuit of Pan-Asian ideas. Brenan concurred, remarking that the statement had a deceptive air of moderation. He did not envisage Konoe's sentiments appealing to China, 'Nevertheless, Mr. Wang Ching-wei and the peace party may feel that these terms offer a basis of negotiations.'[21] The closing remark was accurate enough, for Wang Ching-wei broke with Chiang Kai-shek shortly afterwards and began to tread the lonely and invidious path of collaboration, which was to lead him to the formation of the Nanking regime in 1940.

The formal note, which had been in preparation since November, was sent to Craigie on 5 January 1939. Halifax hoped that the United States and France would decide to submit notes in similar terms. Reference was made at the start to the spate of new order pronouncements in November and December. Britain wished to emphasize that she would not recognize changes in the *status quo* in China accomplished by force. However, it was accepted that treaties were not eternal and that there must be room for amendment. Such amendment must be the product of negotiation and must be arrived at by mutual consent. If Japan had any constructive proposals to offer, Britain would be prepared to consider them. The

---

[19] Minutes by Howe, Mounsey, and Cadogan, 14–23 Dec. 1938, with memorandum by Brenan, 29 Nov. 1938, F/3096/84/10, F.O.371/22110.
[20] Minute by Halifax, 25 Dec. 1938, ibid.
[21] Minutes by Dening and Brenan, 29–30 Dec. 1938, F13735/84/10, F.O.371/22111.

note concluded by welcoming 'a more precise and detailed exposition of the Japanese conditions for terminating the hostilities and of the Japanese policy towards China'.[22] Thus the onus was placed on Japan to bring forward any modifications she wished to suggest. Britain did not do so because she did not herself wish to promote any changes and, more significant, neither did the United States. It was believed that Japan did not have a case, yet it would be tactically unwise to reveal this too openly. Japan was, therefore, being given the opportunity to put forward her views if she chose to do so. The hardening of Japanese policy in 1937-8 and the expansion of the territory under her control in China greatly accentuated the dilemma of the future evolution of policy—should it lie in economic retaliation or in economic aid to China?

The feasibility of applying economic retaliation against Japan had been debated since the investigation by the advisory committee on trade questions in time of war, in the autumn of 1937. It was appreciated that it would be extremely difficult to enforce rigorous economic sanctions, owing to the problem of obtaining the necessary co-operation from the various countries concerned and because of the danger of economic action provoking a violent response from Japan. However, the Foreign Office could not ignore the loud complaints from British firms and nationals at the damage inflicted by Japanese forces. A China liaison committee, comprising representatives from the Federation of British Industries, the China Association, and the London, Bradford, and Manchester chambers of commerce, had been formed to press for reasonable compensation. Japan's policy was that claims for damages resulting from the Japanese army's occupation of property would be considered but that Japan would not admit liability for claims resulting from bombing, shelling, and other similar actions. The Foreign Office disliked Japan's attitude and Sir John Brenan suggested, in March 1938, that a press campaign against Japanese outrages should be encouraged.[23] When Clark Kerr inquired as to the advice that should be given to British firms, when they asked if it were wise to accept

[22] *D.B.F.P.* 3, viii, 371-3, Halifax to Craigie, 5 Jan. 1939.
[23] Minute by Brenan, 28 Mar. 1938, F3209/62/10, F.O.371/22087.

collaboration with the Japanese or with puppet regimes, Brenan concluded that while each case must be regarded on its merits, the Foreign Office could not dissuade firms from making whatever arrangements were essential to preserve their trade.[24] British embassy and consular officials must exercise proper care not to condone violations of the nine-power treaty and of arrangements affecting the administrative integrity of the Chinese government. Consultations took place with other government departments. Sir Frederick Leith-Ross, chief economic adviser to the government, pointed out that most methods of retaliation were double-edged and care was necessary in appraising their possible use.[25] Restrictions on Japanese textile credits could be imposed and would assist Lancashire textile interests, which had been to the fore in expressing criticism of Japanese competition. However, complications could ensue with native populations in the colonies. On balance, Leith-Ross favoured tightening textile quotas and hindering Japanese firms operating in British territories. When other departments were approached, the Colonial Office indicated measures that could be taken in the colonies against Japan, such as discriminatory duties on imports, and stressed that denunciation of the Anglo-Japanese commercial treaty of 1911 would be required.[26] The Dominions Office was doubtful as to reactions in the Dominions; and regarded it as unlikely that the Dominions would wish to co-operate.[27] The Board of Trade was sceptical about economic pressure and warned that economic sanctions could lead to war; the Treasury reacted in similar vein and thought the Foreign Office's suggestion of establishing a new interdepartmental committee under Sir Hughe Knatchbull-Hugessen to handle the subject to be inappropriate.[28] The interdepartmental committee met on 12 July and concluded once again that there were formidable difficulties involved in applying reprisals. The Foreign Office was more inclined to contemplate reprisals than any other department of government, since it inevitably

[24] Minute by Brenan, 11 June 1938, on Clark Kerr to Halifax, 30 May 1938, F5880/62/10, F.O.371/22089.
[25] Letter from Leith-Ross to Howe, 30 June 1938, F7043/62/10, F.O.371/22090.
[26] Colonial Office to Foreign Office, 8 July 1938, F7316/62/10, F.O.371/22091.
[27] Dominions Office to Foreign Office, 5 July 1938, F7201/62/10, F.O.371/22090.
[28] Board of Trade to Foreign Office, 8 July 1938, F7316/62/10, F.O.371/22091.

bore the brunt of the complaints made by British nationals and firms. When J. S. Dodds, the M.P. for Oldham, wrote to the Foreign Office on 12 August 1938 protesting at Japanese action against Chinese cotton mills in which British capital was invested, J. Thyne-Henderson minuted:

The position is, of course, that we know all about it, that we have made the 'necessary representations' and that they have been ignored. We are apparently precluded from using force or reprisals, the only arguments which will be listened to, owing to the uncertainty of the European situation and importunity is our only weapon. It is already blunted by too much use but we shall continue to use it.

It would be a good thing if M.P.s realised the full hopelessness of the position.[29]

Renewed exchanges with other departments took place in the autumn of 1938. The Foreign Office drew a clear distinction between limited measures, directed either at Japanese trade or at the activities of Japanese nationals in British territories, and sanctions proper: it should be possible to demonstrate British disapproval of Japanese actions without allowing the British counter-measures to reach the point of inviting hostile Japanese moves. However, the reactions were, as before, singularly lacking in enthusiasm. The most positive reply came from the India Office, which had not answered earlier inquiries made in the summer; no statement had been obtained from the Indian government but it was believed that India would co-operate if satisfied that the measures would be effective and that the United States would support Britain's policy. It was significantly added, however, that in 1936–7 India took 9·5 per cent of Japan's total exports, including 15 per cent of Japanese exports of cotton goods.[30] There were, in fact, doubts as to the Indian position. The Dominions Office stated that the Dominions had a favourable trade balance with Japan and would be loath to co-operate.[31] After further exploration, it appeared to the Foreign Office that three courses of action could be pursued, only one of which counted as direct retaliation—export credits, currency assistance to

[29] Minute by Thyne-Henderson, 28 Aug. 1938, F3945/62/10, F.O.371/22093.
[30] India Office to Foreign Office, 30 Nov. 1938, F12715/62/10, F.O.371/22098.
[31] C. W. Dixon (Dominions Office) to Ronald, 15 Sept. 1938, F9873/62/10, F.O.371/22095.

China, or the denunciation of the Anglo-Japanese trade treaty of 1911. G. F. Fitzmaurice, one of the legal authorities in the Foreign Office, dissented from the views of the Treasury and Board of Trade:

I should have thought that the matter was by no means merely an economical or financial one, at any rate not in the narrow sense in which it is regarded by the Board of Trade and Treasury. Surely the real issue is whether the Empire can afford to see the British commercial position in the Far East destroyed with the inevitable repercussions not only of a financial and economic but of a political character. If the answer is that the Empire cannot afford this, then it follows that action to prevent it cannot be ruled out merely on the ground that it will temporarily cause loss to British trade elsewhere. This is to my mind the main consideration which definitely outweighs any arguments of a purely economic character. It is strongly reinforced by the great importance of keeping on the right side of the Americans and not giving them a handle for arguing that they were prepared to do something but that we refused to cooperate.[32]

On 3 November the United States had approached Britain to inquire about action that should be taken if Japan did not give satisfaction to the representations to be made over the navigation of the Yangtze. Craigie urged that Britain must prepare retaliatory measures. It was manifest from the outcome of the extensive consultations with other departments that it would be extremely difficult to apply economic measures effectively. The Sino-Japanese war had exacerbated the problems confronting Japan, and would shorten the period in which an embargo on Japanese trade would bite. It would still be awkward to secure adequate co-operation between the powers. Denunciation of the Anglo-Japanese commercial treaty of 1911 could not produce immediate results owing to the notice of termination that had to be given: notice of termination itself would be a serious step, however. In a note summarizing these views and sent to Washington on 23 January 1939, the views of the Roosevelt administration were requested. The final tone was one of sombre warning, not calculated to inspire the United States to resolute action:

A policy of retaliation cannot be embarked upon without a clear realisation as to what it will lead to if pursued to the end — and the

[32] Minute by Fitzmaurice, 30 Dec. 1938, F13603/62/10, F.O.371/22100.

objections to embarking on such a policy and then being forced to retract are self-evident. Whatever may be the initial step in a policy of retaliation, the real problem is the political dilemma that non-retaliation may involve the failure to protect the Treaty rights and legitimate interests of British and American nationals against discrimination and the danger of eventual elimination by Japanese aggression, while retaliation involves the danger of counter-measures and of war.

His Majesty's Government have hitherto been disposed to think that, in the present state of Europe, the right policy for the present is not to embark on retaliation . . .[33]

In the United States the predominant feeling in the State Department was against retaliation for the present, largely because of the political problems involved in Congress. Grew and his colleagues in the American embassy in Tokyo were opposed to sanctions.[34] The Foreign Office still hankered after retaliation, but continued to encounter opposition from other departments.

The reverse side of the coin and one that was, in some respects, more attractive was economic aid to China. Chiang Kai-shek had appealed for assistance repeatedly but had met with a discouraging response. The Foreign Office supported economic aid but had been blocked by the resistance of the Treasury in July 1938; Chiang was being compelled, by force of circumstances, to rely more heavily on the Soviet Union for succour. German aid diminished sharply when Hitler ordered the withdrawal of the military mission headed by Falkenhausen in May 1938. The thought of China slipping into the Russian orbit was offensive, and inspired feelings of guilt at the inadequacy of British help. A. L. Scott commented on 7 October 1938: 'We have been disgracefully slow in coming to China's assistance. Short of a personal visit by Sir A. Clark Kerr to Chiang Kai-shek I can see no way of arresting the slide towards complete dependence on the U.S.S.R.'[35] R. G. Howe concurred: 'I sympathise with Mr. Greenway [consul at Hankow]. I feel the same as he does when

[33] *D.B.F.P.* 3, viii, 411–14, Halifax to Mallet, 23 Jan. 1939.
[34] See *F.R.U.S. 1938*, iii, 400–2 and 406–9, for the views of Grew and the State Department.
[35] Minute by Scott, 7 Oct. 1938, on Greenway to Halifax, 3 Oct. 1938, F10540/10, F.O.371/22062.

the Chinese Ambassador asks me, as he does frequently, what we are doing to implement our pledges of assistance to China . . .'[36] The Chinese ambassador, Quo Tai-chi, visited Halifax on 17 October and conveyed the strong desire of the generalissimo that Britain should follow a more resolute policy. The ambassador referred to the recent American moves in discouraging the export of aeroplanes to and the provision of credit for Japan. He thought that the United States was considering further steps, and hoped that Britain would take analogous action. Halifax promised to review the position.[37] On 6 November Clark Kerr had a long interview with Chiang. It was a melancholy occasion, coming, as it did, shortly after the capture of Hankow and the fall of Canton. Chiang admitted to being shaken by the latter development, which he regarded as a serious blow to Britain as well as China. Chiang professed astonishment at the British failure to react more vigorously to the Japanese incursions:

For sixteen months now China had been fighting single-handed, to save herself it was true, but also to save our interests. She had looked and was still looking to us for help. If we gave it we should find that her memory was long and that we should be amply recompensed. If we withheld it disillusionment would drive her into a bitterness that would be lasting and vindictive. He and his Government would not be able to ignore this . . .

The undertakings we had entered into at Geneva justified him in asking what was our policy in the Far East. Were we going back from China or were we going to truckle with Japan in hope of saving something from the wreck? We should dismiss that hope, for if Japan won Asia we would save nothing at all . . .

His present appeals for our help are the last he would make. If Great Britain turns her back upon her principles and upon China he would never bring up the questions again. He would never again concern himself with our policy in the Far East or consult us about China's future policy or anything else . . .[38]

Chiang added that he was prepared, if necessary, to declare war formally on Japan, since he believed there was nothing to be lost by such a decision. When Halifax saw the Chinese

---

[36] Minute by Howe, 10 Oct. 1938, ibid.
[37] *D.B.F.P.* 3, viii, 145–7, Halifax to Clark Kerr, 17 Oct. 1938.
[38] *D.B.F.P.* 3, viii, 216–18, Clark Kerr to Halifax, 11 Nov. 1938.

ambassador on 18 November, he assured him that he British section of the Burma road was nearing completion and the Foreign Office had asked the Export Credit Guarantee Department to regard support for China in connection with the purchase of lorries for the road as a matter of urgency.[39] The Foreign Office decided that a renewed attempt must be made to obtain cabinet approval for a loan to bolster the Chinese currency: the battle with the Treasury would be fought once more. Halifax and Simon submitted memoranda to the cabinet on 30 November. The foreign secretary advocated a loan of £3 million to the Chinese currency stabilization fund. The chancellor of the exchequer commented on the risks involved: a change of policy would lead to growing intervention in China. In the cabinet debate Halifax outlined the gravity of China's position and her need for assistance: he did not believe that a loan on the lines proposed would provoke conflict with Japan. The first lord of the Admiralty, Lord Stanhope, expressed alarm at the menace of Japanese retaliation. Neville Chamberlain vacillated, explaining that he had initially felt that the proposal should be accepted but that the risks now struck him as too great. Simon sceptically remarked that any money lent would simply be a façade and would be diverted into China's war chest. Lord Zetland, the secretary of state for India, supported the loan. The cabinet determined that the United States should be consulted, as should Sir Robert Craigie, before a final decision was reached.[40] Halifax told the cabinet on 7 December that the British military attaché in Tokyo, General Piggott, considered a loan to be undesirable because of the repercussions on Japanese policy. The cabinet concluded that the attitude of the United States was crucially important.[41] A week later the prime minister informed his colleagues that he had spoken to Joseph Kennedy, the American ambassador, and had urged support for action to be taken in the Far East.[42] In mid-December the Export and Import Bank of America authorized credits of 25 million dollars for financing exports to China.

[39] *D.B.F.P.* 3, viii, 244–5, Halifax to Clark Kerr, 19 Nov. 1938.
[40] Cabinet conclusions, 30 Nov. 1938, 57(38), 9, Cab. 23/96.
[41] Cabinet conclusions, 7 Dec. 1938, 58(38)1, Cab. 23/96. For views within the Treasury, see Leith-Ross papers, T188/224, 237.
[42] Cabinet conclusions, 14 Dec. 1938, 59(38)1, Cab.23/96.

When the news reached the cabinet, support for British action increased; Zetland emphasized that the India Office wanted help to be extended to China, as did the Indian general staff. The cabinet empowered Chamberlain, Halifax, and Simon to reach a decision on guaranteeing a contribution of £3 million to the Chinese currency stabilization fund on certain conditions, provided the United States took parallel action.[43] A telegram was sent to Washington on 6 January 1939 explaining that legislation would soon be introduced to permit Britain to support the Chinese currency, assuming the United States would act similarly. It was recognized that the Roosevelt administration had already rendered valuable assistance to China in the form of silver purchases and the recent 25 million dollars' credit. The British government was considering guaranteeing the Hong Kong and Shanghai Bank against loss, but the United States must decide on the most appropriate method of proceeding. 'The essential points in the view of His Majesty's Government are that it should be made clear that action is being taken by both Governments to maintain our respective interests in China which would be seriously threatened by a collapse of the Chinese currency and that the proposed assistance and encouragement should be given to China at a very early date.'[44]

When the United States replied, it was made clear that action similar but not identical to the British action would be taken. Halifax told the cabinet that the American response was encouraging but vague.[45] Craigie felt that Britain could weather the storm that would ensue in Japan without excessive difficulty. More consideration was given to the subject in the latter part of January and February 1939. The occupation of the island of Hainan by Japanese forces in February stimulated the feeling that no more time should be lost and that Britain should conclude an agreement as soon as practicable.[46] On 22 February Simon produced a memorandum for his colleagues setting out a scheme for maintaining the stability of the Chinese dollar and the establishment of an exchange sta-

[43] Cabinet conclusions, 21 Dec. 1938, 60(38)2, Cab.23/96.
[44] *D.B.F.P.* 3, viii, 373–4, Halifax to Mallet, 6 Jan. 1939.
[45] Cabinet conclusions, 18 Jan. 1939, 1(39)3, Cab.23/97.
[46] Cabinet conclusions, 15 Feb. 1939, 7(39)4,5, Cab.23/97.

bilization fund; Simon now held that a sum of £10 million would be necessary, a larger amount than had previously been considered, and the fund would be managed by a committee in the form of a banking operation. The arrangements were swiftly completed and the announcement of the loan was made by Simon in the House of Commons on 8 March. Simon stressed that the stability of the Chinese dollar was 'a matter of great importance to this country in view of our financial and economic relations with China'. The fund of £10 million would be provided equally by the two official Chinese banks and by two British banks, the Hong Kong and Shanghai Bank and the Chartered Bank. The British contribution would be guaranteed by the Treasury.[47] The cabinet, viewing the issue in the international context, were concerned that the official announcement should come at the same time as the formal recognition of General Franco's government in Spain, so as to balance the consideration of accepting a situation detested by the proponents of liberal democracy by action calculated to please the same circles.

Britain, therefore, moved to assist China in the manner that was deemed most satisfactory, given the need to reconcile constructive support for China with a sensible determination not to antagonize Japan unduly. It had been a long-drawn-out and contentious subject but the Treasury had at last accepted the validity of the case put forward by the Foreign Office. The amounts of money involved were small when placed in perspective, but they did underline British sympathy for China more positively. Chiang Kai-shek courteously expressed appreciation for the crumbs of comfort which would, he hoped, 'mature to the ultimate mutual benefit of British and Chinese Governments and peoples'.[48]

The remaining aspect in British policy towards the deteriorating Far Eastern situation hinged on defence problems, with particular reference to naval strength. The Foreign Office had long felt that a naval force should be sent to Singapore to boost British prestige and demonstrate that diplomacy could be reinforced by realistic measures when the situation warranted. In November and December 1938 Sir

---

[47] *D.B.F.P.* 3, viii, 505–6, Halifax to Craigie, 9 Mar. 1939.
[48] *D.B.F.P.* 3, viii, 477–8, Greenway to Clark Kerr, 28 Feb. 1939.

Josiah Crosby, the British minister in Bangkok, and Sir Robert Craigie both argued that the Admiralty should be approached to reconsider the proposal. In his dispatch of 14 December, Craigie indicated the salutary effect on Japan of witnessing a British squadron. 'Since my appointment to this post it has always been my hope that the situation in Europe would, before long, permit of the despatch to Singapore of a squadron of capital ships or battle cruisers of sufficient strength to readjust the position from the political, if not from the naval point of view . . .'[49] Craigie argued that naval action would reap dividends in Anglo-American relations, in that the United States undeniably harboured the suspicion that Britain was endeavouring to involve her in the defence of imperial interests which Britain could not protect herself. Craigie was far more knowledgeable on naval matters than most diplomats, since he had specialized in handling naval disarmament questions before moving to the Tokyo embassy. He had tried to combat in advance the Admiralty reaction by expounding the opinion that a small squadron of three or four capital ships would be adequate. Craigie believed that the Japanese would be deterred from attacking a British force based on Singapore by the realization that the United States might send a powerful battle fleet to Honolulu. He urged that action be taken urgently, 'because I feel that events here may be moving rapidly towards a crisis in the Far East and because the evolution of American opinion may soon render possible the adoption of a more resolute British policy . . .'[50]

The Foreign Office heartily approved of the sentiments of Craigie and Crosby. A memorandum advocating a change in policy was drawn up by G. F. Fitzmaurice and sent to the Admiralty. It began by stating the British possessions in the Far East would have to be defended against aggression and that Britain would have to fight Japan, if compelled to do so, at the same time that she fought Germany even if the Mediterranean had to be abandoned temporarily. The existing official policy of concentrating on home waters while hoping to be able to send a fleet eastwards if a crisis developed was no

[49] *D.B.F.P.* 3, viii, 320–2, Craigie to Halifax, 14 Dec. 1938 (received 16 Jan. 1939). Crosby had reported in similar vein in a dispatch dated 7 Nov. 1938.
[50] *D.B.F.P.* 3, viii, 320–2, Craigie to Halifax, 14 Dec. 1938.

longer suitable. It should be possible to decentralize and to build up a far eastern force that could operate independently. Fitzmaurice accurately identified the weakness in the official policy by pointing out that if Britain had to send a force capable of meeting the Japanese fleet on equal terms, this would effectively eliminate the feasibility of sending one at all, given the threat from Germany in Europe. 'The situation in which we could, in theory, send a Fleet to the Far East in case of need but might not, in practice, be willing or able to do so at the critical moment, is really one of the most dangerous possible, since it encourages a policy of adventure both on the part of Japan and of her associates, and creates for us a very serious strategic and diplomatic weakness.'[51] Fitzmaurice considered the question of numbers to be irrelevant to stationing a capital ship fleet at Singapore in time of peace. He went on to argue for stationing five to seven capital ships at Singapore; a minimum of four and a maximum of seven could then be retained for Europe, which should suffice on the assumption that France would cope with Italy. Looking to the future, Fitzmaurice maintained that it would be wise to send the five oldest capital ships, which would be scheduled for scrapping in 1942-4, to the Far East instead. He continued:

To put it at its lowest, it would seem that these five ships would be better than nothing at Singapore. If the alternative is to scrap them altogether, would it not be better to keep them and put them in the Far East for what effect they can produce? At least we would be no worse off than we are at present when we have no capital ships there and we may be considerably better off, for not only would these ships produce at least some appreciable deterrent effect, but they would also give valuable practice to the Singapore base in the care and maintenance of capital ships and form a nucleus for the defensive operations of our entire Far Eastern forces.[52]

In the covering letter to the Admiralty, the Foreign Office stated that the naval issue should be considered 'from the broadest aspect of vital imperial needs' so as to devise a policy capable of defending British interests in East Asia. The

---

[51] *D.B.F.P.* 3, viii, appendix I, 545, memorandum by Fitzmaurice, 27 Jan. 1939. See also P. Haggie, 'The Royal Navy and the Far Eastern Problem, 1931-1941', pp. 277-99.

[52] *D.B.F.P.* 3, viii, appendix I, 545.

problem was acute given the proclamation of the Japanese new order:

The problem would appear to be one of preventing Japan from creating a vast closed area from which she would be able to draw nearly all the raw materials which are essential to her and thereby attaining such strength as might enable her subsequently to absorb into that area other territories producing two at least of the other raw materials of really vital importance to her, oil in the Netherlands East Indies and of high-grade iron ore in Malaya. The power thus acquired by Japan would enable her to present, either in combination with Germany and Italy or even alone, a permanent and formidable threat to British interests throughout the Eastern Hemisphere.[53]

Attention was drawn to the more positive attitude recently displayed by the United States. The Foreign Office also refuted the commonly held view that Japan might act in a 'volcanic' manner and suddenly attack British territories. Japan was a calculating nation and it was unlikely that she would take extreme action unless convinced that the time was right to do so.

The Admiralty replied on 29 March.[54] It was emphasized that in war it was imperative to provide sufficient cover of the main fleets for the activities of the detached forces behind them. Such cover must be adequate to engage an enemy fleet at a particular moment. Under no circumstances could the British navy simultaneously engage the German, Italian, and Japanese navies: it was highly improbable that Britain would ever possess a navy strong enough to face all three powers at once. In addition, a considerable part of the fleet had to be stationed at home for practical training reasons, apart from political aspects. The Admiralty held that it was impossible to station capital ships in East Asia at present or in the near future: with luck it should be possible to station one capital ship in the area by 1942. The situation was rendered more awkward currently with three ships undergoing reconstruction and it would not improve before 1940 or 1941, when the new battleships were completed. The Admiralty believed that the existing policy would have to be continued of stationing one

[53] Ibid., appendix I, 542-3, letter from Foreign Office to Admiralty, 13 Feb. 1939.
[54] Ibid., appendix I, 549-50, letter from Admiralty to Foreign Office, 29 Mar. 1939.

major fleet at home with the other in the Mediterranean. If a grave crisis occurred in the Far East, the Admiralty would consider sending a fleet to the east. The letter ended on a somewhat ironic note with the Admiralty explaining the dependence of foreign policy upon defence resources:

The Admiralty welcome this opportunity of emphasising the close relation that exists between naval strength and foreign policy. Unless the Navy is maintained at a strength sufficient to secure our position in those parts of the world which are vital to the existence of the Empire, it is impracticable to carry out our chosen policy as and when we wish. But while, in theory, naval strength must be based upon foreign policy, in practice there is a limit, governed by money, men and material, and determined by the Government of the day, beyond which our armaments cannot be advanced; and when this is reached the tables are turned and foreign policy must depend upon naval strength, unless risk of war, and even of unsuccessful war, is to be incurred . . .[55]

The correspondence between the Foreign Office and the Admiralty was overshadowed by a reappraisal in the committee of imperial defence of the commitment to send a fleet to the Far East in certain circumstances. The reassessment took place in the first few months of 1939. The chiefs of staff produced a new European appreciation in February 1939 and this was discussed at a meeting of the committee of imperial defence (C.I.D.) held on 24 February 1939.[56] Air Chief Marshal Sir Cyril Newall introduced the appreciation; it included a statement that the size of the fleet that could be dispatched to Singapore would depend upon the extent of British commitments and on the state of conflict in Europe. Lord Stanhope, the first lord of the Admiralty, expressed concern at the possibility of the Mediterranean being denuded of capital ships in the event of the fleet being sent to Singapore. He thought that one or two capital ships could constitute a deterrent to Japanese action, especially if the American fleet moved to Honolulu: Japan would be reluctant to send a large fleet as far south as Singapore because of the danger of being cut off if the United States intervened.

[55] Ibid.
[56] Minutes of the 348th meeting of the committee of imperial defence, 24 Feb. 1939, Cab.2/8.

Chamberlain reminded the committee of past promises made
to the Dominions, particularly at the imperial conference held
in 1937. Lord Chatfield made a lengthy speech favouring the
dispatch of a fleet to the Far East. Chatfield felt that the
morale of the Dominions must not be undermined and some
risks were unavoidable in time of war: he pointed out that, on
a staff appreciation, Britain would have lost at Trafalgar since
the British were the weaker side.[57] He disputed Stanhope's
view that the Mediterranean was now more important than
the Far East. It was decided to refer the whole issue to the
strategical appreciation sub-committee comprising Chatfield
as chairman with Stanhope, Sir John Anderson, Leslie Hore-
Belisha, Sir Kingsley Wood, W. S. Morrison, and the chiefs of
staff. The deliberations of the sub-committee clearly revealed
the swing towards placing greater emphasis on the importance
of the Mediterranean. The explanation of the change in
thinking is to be found in growing anxiety concerning the
policies of Germany and Italy and awareness of the extent of
British commitments in the Mediterranean and Middle East.
Guarantees were extended to Greece, Romania, and Turkey
in March–April 1939 following Hitler's decision to occupy the
rump of Czechoslovakia in March 1939. In addition, Britain
was already committed to defend Egypt and Iraq. Britain's
naval problems were exacerbated by the fact that only ten out
of fifteen capital ships were available for immediate deployment. In a memorandum for the strategical appreciation sub-
committee, the deputy chief of the naval staff, Vice-Admiral
Sir Andrew Cunningham, concluded that: '. . . there are so
many variable factors which cannot at present be assessed that
it is not possible to state definitely how soon after Japanese
intervention a Fleet could be despatched to the Far East.
Neither is it possible to enumerate precisely the size of the
Fleet that we could afford to send.'[58] The sub-committee
accepted Cunningham's analysis and endorsed the conclusion
reached, pointing out the importance of defeating Italy and of
honouring Britain's commitments to other countries in the
eastern Mediterranean and the Middle East.

The C.I.D. considered matters further on 2 May. Chatfield

[57] Ibid.
[58] Cited by N. H. Gibbs, *Grand Strategy*, i (H.M.S.O., London. 1976), 425.

described the position concerning capital ships: the numbers currently available made matters extremely difficult. Stanhope stressed the consequences of the new commitments in the eastern Mediterranean. The Dominions secretary, Sir Thomas Inskip, referred to the scaling-down of British undertakings to Australia and New Zealand. Chamberlain remarked that the most important aspect was the fate of Great Britain upon which the fate of the Dominions hinged. Halifax thought that Japan was too preoccupied in China to pose an additional threat in the Pacific and failed to recognize that Japanese activities in China could lead to a grave crisis, as was to be demonstrated in June–July 1939. The C.I.D. decided to accept Vice-Admiral Cunningham's report that, with so many variable factors involved, it was impossible to state definitely how soon after Japanese intervention a fleet could be dispatched to the Far East.[59] Nor was it possible to indicate the size of the fleet that could be sent. It was decided that the change in policy should be communicated to the United States.

The most delicate feature concerned relations with Australia. Doubts had been voiced in Australia for at least a decade as to whether Britain would actually send a fleet to the Pacific when the need arose.[60] British spokesmen had repeatedly sought to allay the apprehensions with ritualistic promises of support if Japan became extremely aggressive. Through an unfortunate oversight, the minutes of the C.I.D. meeting of 24 February had been supplied to the Australian high commission. Ismay, the secretary of the C.I.D., had to extricate himself from the ensuing confrontation with Stanley Bruce, the high commissioner. Ismay told Bruce, in March

[59] Minutes of the 355th meeting of the C.I.D., 2 May 1939, Cab.2/8.

[60] For a valuable discussion of Australian attitudes towards British naval policy in the Pacific, see I. Hamill, 'The Strategic Illusion: the Singapore Strategy and the Defence of Australia and New Zealand, 1919-1942', unpublished Leeds University Ph.D. thesis (1975), especially chs. 7, 10, and 11. For earlier defence papers dealing with the Dominions, see 'Australian Co-operation in Imperial Defence', note by the joint planning sub-committee, 31 Mar. 1938, C.O.S.703(J.P.), Cab.53/37; 'New Zealand Co-operation in Imperial Defence', note by the joint planning sub-committee, 31 Mar. 1938, C.O.S.704(J.P.), Cab.53/37; 'Singapore: Reinforcement from India', note by the joint planning sub-committee, 9 Dec. 1938, C.O.S.805(J.P.), Cab.53/42; 'Malaya–Period Before Relief', draft report of the joint planning sub-committee, 27 Feb. 1939, C.O.S.848(J.P.), Cab.53/45.

1939, that the matter was simply being discussed and that there was no need for undue anxiety. Bruce informed his government of the direction in which British policy was moving. In reply to Australian approaches, Neville Chamberlain stated, on 20 March 1939, that Britain was not reneging.[61] Now on 2 May it was candidly recognized that 'there had been a considerable scaling down of our undertaking to the Dominions to send a fleet to the Far East in all circumstances' and that there had been 'a reversal of the basis of calculation previously used for determining the scale of reserves necessary for Singapore'.[62]

As a result of the new appreciation of Britain's European commitments, the question of the time to be allowed for the relief of Singapore came under review in 1939. The joint planning sub-committee recommended on 27 February 1939 that the period allowed for the arrival of the fleet from Europe should be raised from seventy days to ninety days. Careful calculation was needed; Japan could interrupt sea communications and it would be wise not to count on being able to send supplies to Singapore in an emergency after the outbreak of war and before the fleet arrived in the Far East. If Japan embarked upon war at the same time that Germany and Italy attacked Britain, it would be possible for Britain's enemies to enjoy a period of vigorous naval activity before the reserve fleet was mobilized or fully worked up. It was recommended that the new proposed period before relief of ninety days should be based on thirty days for concentration and preparation; forty-five days' passage via the Cape of Good Hope; fifteen days for contingencies such as fuelling delays and bad weather. The recommendation was eventually accepted by the C.I.D. on 6 July.[63]

The simple truth was that Britain was dangerously overextended in her world-wide commitments and was only beginning serious rearmament in 1938–9. British policy towards Japanese expansion in China and the advent of the new order was, to a large extent, unavoidably lacking in

[61] See appendices to the minutes of the 362nd meeting of the C.I.D., 26 June 1939, Cab.2/9.
[62] Cited Gibbs, *Grand Strategy*, i. 425.
[63] Minutes of the 364th meeting of the C.I.D., 6 July 1939, Cab.2/9.

cohesion and tenacity. Economic retaliation was too dangerous to embark upon, despite the inclination of the Foreign Office towards it. Economic aid for China was easier to implement, once the Treasury had been coaxed into co-operation. However, the reality had to be faced that there was little Britain could do beyond improving means of communic-ation with China, as in the completion of the Burma road, and assisting the Chinese currency. The Tientsin crisis, which was about to erupt in the spring of 1939, was to demonstrate beyond any doubt how tenuous Britain's true position was.

APPENDIX

Key passages from the first 'New Order' statement, issued on 3 November 1938 (*D.B.F.P.* 3, viii, 177-8, footnote).

By the august virtue of His Majesty, our naval and military forces have captured Canton, the three Wuhan cities Hankow, Hanyang and Wuchang, and all the vital areas of China have thus fallen into our hands. The Kuomintang Government exist no longer except as a mere local regime. However, as long as they persist in their anti-Japanese and pro-Communist policy, our country will not lay down arms until that regime is crushed.

What Japan seeks is the establishment of a new order which will ensure permanent stability in East Asia.

This new order has for its foundations a tripartite relationship of mutual aid and coordination between Japan, Manchukuo and China, in the political, economic, cultural and other fields. Its object is to secure international justice, to perfect joint defence against Communism, to create a new culture, and to realize close economic cohesion throughout East Asia. This, indeed, is the way to contribute towards the stabilisation of East Asia and the progress of the world.

What Japan desires of China is that that country should share in the task of creating this new order in East Asia. She confidently expects the Chinese people fully to comprehend her true intentions and to respond to the call of Japan for their cooperation. Even the participation of the Kuomintang Government would not be rejected if, repudiating the policy which has guided them in the past and re-moulding their personnel to translate their rebirth into fact, they were to come forward to join in the establishment of the new order.

Japan is confident that other Powers will for their part correctly appreciate her aims and policy, and adapt their attitude to the new conditions prevailing in East Asia . . .

III

THE TIENTSIN CRISIS

THE Sino-Japanese war had given rise to a number of serious incidents in Anglo-Japanese relations involving the danger of a rapid deterioration possibly culminating in war: the shooting at Knatchbull-Hugessen and the attacks on British and American vessels were the most obvious examples. The most alarming crisis of all developed in June and July 1939 and brought the two countries to the verge of conflict. It revolved round the British concession at Tientsin, in the north-east of China. The area had been infiltrated by the Japanese from the middle of the 1930s and had been swiftly captured by the Japanese army in the early stages of the war. The foreign concessions became symbolic obstacles preventing the complete triumph of Japanese militarism. In practical terms, Tientsin was important to China because the foreign concessions helped to strengthen *fapi*, the Chinese currency, which the Japanese were seeking to undermine and replace with the federal reserve bank currency, issued by the Japanese-backed puppet regime. There were, in addition, appreciable quantities of silver owned by the Chinese government deposited in banks in the British and French concessions in Tientsin. Lastly, the freedom afforded by the existence of the concessions assisted Chinese guerrillas in their sporadic campaign of violence against those Chinese who chose to collaborate. Each of these aspects aroused the ire of the local Japanese military authorities and, to a lesser extent, of the government in Tokyo. Restrictive measures against the British concession were instituted by the Japanese in 1938-9, including the erection of a barrier around the concession and passport checks. Great Britain clearly sympathized strongly with the Chinese and made her sympathy too overt. The Foreign Office was worried by the situation at the beginning of 1939, and realized that the activities of Chinese agents would have to be curbed. Sir John Brenan minuted on 16 January: '. . . Chiang Kai-shek has been warned informally that if Chinese

Government agents carry on anti-Japanese activities in the concession we may have to hand them over to the local authorities. It is a question of political expediency and we had better not be drawn into a discussion of its legal aspect.'[1] However, the atmosphere in Tientsin slowly worsened. On 22 March Sir Robert Craigie warned that he was concerned at the trend of events and suggested that his military attaché, General Piggott, might visit Tientsin to consult the Japanese commander, General Homma, who was an old friend of his. While A. L. Scott was predictably unenthusiastic at this idea, Brenan dissented:

Like Sir R. Craigie, I am uncomfortable about the way the Tientsin situation is developing. Our people on the spot are putting up a brave front and I do not think that we should discourage them from doing so, within limits, but I fear that they are supported by the belief that in the last resort His Majesty's Government will in some way come to their assistance with the might of the Empire. In present European conditions such a hope is less likely than ever to be fulfilled, and it is desirable to secure a local *détente* if it can be done without too great a sacrifice of principles.[2]

The Foreign Office wished to secure a settlement yet could not see how this could be attained. It was impossible to make major concessions to Japan involving the rights of British citizens, for this would provoke renewed cries of appeasement in the face of aggression; it was equally impossible to sacrifice Chinese interests and antagonize Chungking and Washington in the process. The problems at Tientsin were to be further complicated by the contrasting attitudes adopted by the British ambassador to China, Sir Archibald Clark Kerr, and the British consul in Tientsin, E. G. Jamieson. Clark Kerr was passionately devoted to the Chinese cause and sometimes allowed his zeal to outrun his discretion; when the crisis broke in May-June, Clark Kerr constantly reiterated that no concessions should be made to Japan and that Britain must remember the impact of her actions on the Chinese war effort. Jamieson, on the other hand, was exposed directly to the menacing behaviour of the Japanese and believed that con-

[1] Minute by Brenan, 16 Jan. 1939, on Craigie to Halifax, 12 Jan. 1939, F384/1/10, F.O.371/23395.
[2] Minutes by Scott and Brenan, 23-4 Mar. 1939, F2867/1/10. F.O.371/23396.

cessions had to be made to avoid occupation of the concession. Unfortunately Jamieson became frightened at the perils of the predicament and failed to report with sufficient clarity to London. The Foreign Office experienced difficulty in following the tortuous course of events, and Jamieson's erratic telegrams led the government to pursue a tougher policy than would otherwise have been the case. It was only with the astute negotiating skill of Craigie in July-August 1939 that a strategic withdrawal from direct confrontation was accomplished. It must be remembered that the Tientsin crisis occurred during a period of mounting tension in Europe and while Britain and France were negotiating with the Soviet Union for a possible alliance. The cabinet and defence chiefs were forced to contemplate the nightmare that had dominated the middle and later 1930s—the danger that Britain would be involved in simultaneous wars with Germany, Italy, and Japan.

While matters had steadily deteriorated in 1938-9, the immediate impetus was provided by the assassination on 10 April of Cheng Lien-shih, manager of the Federal Reserve Bank and recently appointed superintendent of customs; Cheng was murdered in a theatre in the British concession.[3] The enraged Japanese demanded that the British authorities change their policy and suppress anti-Japanese movements. Jamieson felt that the Japanese demand for the expulsion of Chinese against whom there was evidence of plotting was reasonable.[4] The Foreign Office concurred but wished to ensure that expulsion could be implemented 'humanely' so that the persons concerned did not inevitably fall into Japanese hands; they would instead be given the Englishman's conception of a sporting chance of averting the singularly unpleasant fate in store for them if arrested by the Japanese. The formula laid down was that 'persons against whom there is convincing evidence of crimes of violence against the Japanese or their puppets such as complicity in assassination or its attempt should be handed over to the *de facto* Chinese authorities and that other political offenders whose activities become a serious nuisance should be compelled to leave'.[5]

[3] *D.B.F.P.* 3, ix, 1, Jamieson to Clark Kerr, 10 Apr. 1939.
[4] *D.B.F.P.* 3, ix, 19-20, Jamieson to Clark Kerr, 21 Apr. 1939.
[5] *D.B.F.P.* 3, ix, 29, Halifax to Broadmead, 28 Apr. 1939.

Clark Kerr consulted Chiang Kai-shek, and reported that he and the generalissimo had agreed that internment followed by swift transfer to Hong Kong offered the most satisfactory solution for those not guilty of acts of violence. Chiang was predictably opposed to severe punishment for those guilty of lesser crimes which amounted simply to 'excessive patriotism'.[6] Halifax rejected this proposal because the colonial government in Hong Kong had enough difficulties to contend with already; he believed that, for existing cases, the most serious should be expelled and the less serious released with a warning, while *future* cases should either be expelled or handed over to the *de facto* authorities depending on the nature of the crime.[7] The British government had, therefore, decided to follow a tougher policy in future. Meanwhile the British and Japanese authorities in Tientsin had consulted each other in the hunt for Cheng's murderers and, acting on information received from the Japanese, the British arrested four men on suspicion of involvement in the crime. Two of the men confessed responsibility to the Japanese, but the men subsequently alleged that they had been tortured while in Japanese hands. Jamieson reported that the British police believed that the men had been water-tortured. However, the consul-general held that the men unquestionably belonged to a terrorist gang and he considered that they should be handed over for trial. He warned that the Japanese reaction would be militant unless the men were handed over.[8] What Jamieson foolishly did not state was that he had given an assurance that the men would be handed over; this highly significant aspect did not emerge until some six weeks later, by which time the crisis had assumed an extremely grave character.

Clark Kerr conceded that the Chinese were to blame to some extent for jeopardizing the neutrality of Tientsin. He could not, however, subscribe to Jamieson's view that the four men should be surrendered:

This imposes upon me a decision from which I confess I flinch. The problem reduces itself to a repugnant simplicity to sacrifice the four or perhaps even more scapegoats in the hope that by this sacrifice

[6] *D.B.F.P.* 3, ix, 33–4, Clark Kerr to Halifax, 1 May 1939.
[7] *D.B.F.P.* 3, ix, 55–6, Halifax to Clark Kerr, 8 May 1939.
[8] *D.B.F.P.* 3, ix, 66–7, Jamieson to Halifax, 13 May 1939.

Japanese may be persuaded to hold their hand for a time at any rate and give Concession a breathing space. But it offers little hope of freedom from more and equally repugnant sacrifices in the early future. I mean demands from Japanese for surrender of this person or that on evidence as convincing to them and as unconvincing to us as in present case . . .

The truth is that we should be handing over these four men to be killed and that is a thing with [*sic*] which I for myself cannot at present reconcile with my conscience and I would beg to be excused from the duty of giving the Consul-General the authority for which he asks . . .[9]

Craigie sided firmly with Jamieson; only the prompt handing-over of the four men could avert a grave crisis in Tientsin. The Foreign Office uneasily reflected on the alternative courses of action. R. G. Howe helplessly and appropriately observed, 'I do not see how the Foreign Office can be expected to give a decision to hand these men over to the Japanese authorities since we do not know whether their offence is such as to bring them within our ruling that terrorist cases should be handed over and until they are tried in some way or some kind of court of enquiry has been able to establish their complicity or otherwise, we are in no position to form any judgement on the matter.'[10] Howe considered that the only answer was to keep them in Tientsin and assure the Japanese that they were being held incommunicado. With future cases Jamieson should be authorized to hand over suspects where he was satisfied that the culprits were involved in terrorist activities. At the end of May the Foreign Office decided that two of the four men should be surrendered and the Japanese informed accordingly; since there was no evidence against the other two men they should be interned and subsequently expelled from the concession unless evidence was produced against them.[11] Jamieson continued to press for permission to hand over the four men.[12] Meanwhile the Japanese military authorities at Tientsin were growing more exasperated at the British reluctance to fulfil the assurances given by Jamieson. On 31 May

[9] *D.B.F.P.* 3, ix, 83, Clark Kerr to Halifax, 19 May 1939.
[10] Minute by Howe, 22 May 1939, on Clark Kerr to Halifax, 19 May 1939, F4808/1/10, F.O.371/23397.
[11] *D.B.F.P.* 3, ix, 117–19, Halifax to Clark Kerr, 30 May 1939.
[12] *D.B.F.P.* 3, ix, 121, Jamieson to Halifax, 1 June 1939.

General Homma demanded a reply within eight days indicating whether or not Britain would surrender the men. The Japanese then began to prepare their measures for the blockade of the concession.

The blockade started on 14 June. It was very rigorous, including restrictions on food supplies and thorough searches of British nationals entering and leaving, ostensibly to ensure that they were not carrying the outlawed *fapi*. In reality the searches were intended to humiliate the British inhabitants of Tientsin and the British government, to demonstrate the helplessness of Britain's position, and secure compliance with Japanese demands. On a number of occasions men were stripped naked in public during the searches; there was at least one instance of a woman being stripped. Naturally the press in Britain reported the incidents fully and a mood of profound indignation developed. *The Times* deplored the blockade and warned that counter-measures would have to be taken; it was pointed out, with less cause for comfort than was implied, that close contact was being maintained with the United States and France.[13] On 24 June a veiled warning of resort to force was uttered. 'But if the language of diplomacy is not understood by the Japanese Government then other methods more intelligible to them will have to be employed.'[14] *The Economist* was fiercely hostile to Japanese policy in China and declared that there could be no question of Britain acquiescing in Japanese domination of China:

This is a demand that Japan cannot seriously expect us to comply with; and, even if we did stoop to becoming Japan's accomplice in international crime and the coercion of Japanese menaces there is no probability that this would save our material interests in the Far East. If the Japanese have their way at Tientsin, it is already clear that they will promptly apply the same methods in all the other foreign concessions and settlements in China, including the French concession and the International Settlement at Shanghai. It is this that lends the Tientsin problem its particular importance. On the spot, we can do little. But the Japanese are not the only people who can impose embargoes, and the cooler heads at Tokyo have reason to be alarmed at the news that reprisals are being planned in London . . .[15]

---

[13] *The Times*, leading articles, 15, 19, 21 June 1939.
[14] Ibid., 24 June 1939.
[15] *The Economist*, 17 June 1939.

It was realized that Britain could do little to halt Japan's advance in China and that 'Japan could immediately seize all or nearly all British, French and American continental and insular possessions and holdings in Eastern Asia and the Western Pacific between Singapore and Hawaii'.[16] It was viewed as the culmination of the weak policy pursued by the National government since 1931. In the House of Commons numerous anxious questions were asked and the former foreign secretary, Anthony Eden, inquired whether Craigie had stressed that the government could not acquiesce in the blockade and that supplies to Tientsin would be maintained.[17]

The dispute had rapidly escalated from being the concern of the Foreign Office on a departmental basis to being a first-class crisis requiring urgent consideration by the cabinet and defence chiefs. Neville Chamberlain disliked Japan, disapproved of her war with China, and was not disposed to consider Japanese grievances with the sympathy he displayed towards the policy of Germany down to March 1939. However, Chamberlain had to give meticulous attention in his calculations to the state of British defences, and it was appreciated that these dictated a policy of conciliation. On 14 June Halifax summarized the situation for his cabinet colleagues in broadly optimistic terms. He thought that Japan might accept American mediation. With regard to the intended blockade measures announced by the Japanese, Halifax commented that the proposals amounted to a 'damp squib' in the opinion of his advisers:

The view of his Foreign Office advisers (including Mr. Howe, who had recently served in China) was that the Japanese would soon find that the arrangements which they proposed to carry out would give them considerable trouble, more particularly as there were several hundred United States citizens in the Concession. It was felt that the Japanese action in this matter was in conformity with the methods which they were likely to adopt of making some attempt to 'save face'. Generally, his advisers thought that after a time a way out of the difficulty might be found.[18]

[16] Ibid., 24 June 1939.
[17] See H. C. Deb, 348, 1508–10, 1794–8, 2199–222, for questions asked on 15, 19, and 24 June 1939. For Eden's intervention, see col. 2201.
[18] Cabinet conclusions, 14 June 1939, 32(39)2, Cab.23/99.

If this forecast proved erroneous, Halifax held that possible recourse to economic retaliation would have to be contemplated. The Foreign Office felt that it would be relatively
easy to adopt certain measures, principally requiring consular
certificates for exports from north China, which would embarrass the Japanese but have little effect on British interests. On
the whole his impression was that it was unlikely that there
would be catastrophic developments in Tientsin.[19] The
president of the Board of Trade agreed to investigate
retaliatory measures. Chamberlain expressed concern:

We had acted in this matter in flat contradiction to the advice given
by our Consul-General at Tientsin. The Prime Minister quoted from
Telegram No. 193 from Tientsin, in which Mr. Jamieson had
reported that in the case of the four men we were definitely on un-
sound ground; not only were the men members of a terrorist gang,
but they had confessed to complicity in murder and we were not in a
position to prove these confessions were obtained by torture.

The Prime Minister noted that it was now proposed to consider
economic sanctions. This weapon had not been very successful in the
past . . .[20]

Halifax's optimism was not justified by the deterioration in
Tientsin within the next few days. The indignities inflicted on
British nationals and the irate reaction in Britain compelled
the cabinet to assess the situation in depth.

Chamberlain wrote to his sister Hilda on 17 June:

Once more I ask myself whether any Prime Minister ever had to
contend with such a series of critical events as I have. The behaviour
of the Japs has been increasingly insolent and aggressive for a long
time, and the Tientsin incident is only the culmination of successive
acts of provocation. The worst of it is that I believe we were in the
wrong about the four men. We have acted in flat contradiction to the
advice of the man on the spot and although it is true that our ambassador's advice was not to give them up he has not been in China long
and as far as I know never in Tientsin. On this occasion the F.O. did
not consult me and though I was very uncomfortable about the way
things were going I can't always be interfering in their job so I left it
alone. I did tell the Cabinet my doubts but the F.O. were still confident that it would be all right and that the blockade would turn out

[19] Ibid.
[20] Ibid.

to be only a 'damp squib'. Of course now they sing a very different tune and in a way the new demands are a relief to them as they put us on a better wicket. But how it will turn out I don't know. If the Americans would come in with us of course it would be all over directly. But I am sure they won't. The F.O. have been talking vaguely about retaliation but they cannot deny that retaliation is only another name for sanctions and Abyssinia has shown us that sanctions are no good unless you are prepared to use force . . .[21]

The cabinet committee on foreign policy met on 19 June to consider memoranda submitted by the Foreign Office, the Board of Trade, and the chiefs of staff. The last report was examined first. In introducing the discussion, Chamberlain reverted to his anxiety over the repercussions of applying economic sanctions. 'If economic sanctions were ineffective they amounted to nothing more than pinpricks. If, on the other hand, they were effective, then the country against whom they were applied might be stung to retaliate. In effect, the kernel of the position as he saw it was that, before deciding to apply sanctions, one must be prepared if necessary to use force.'[22] The report of the chiefs of staff was examined somewhat critically by Chatfield, minister for co-ordination of defence and former first sea lord. The chiefs of staff were opposed to any policy that might connote retaliatory action. Chatfield admitted that the chiefs of staff had tended to emphasize the problems of Britain's predicament rather than to determine what would be done if a major crisis developed. The chiefs of staff warned that it would be impossible to send more than two capital ships to reinforce the China squadron without withdrawing from the Mediterranean. Chatfield stated his disagreement with the view that a fleet including only two capital ships would be sent if necessary. He maintained that a larger fleet should be sent, sufficiently strong to engage the Japanese fleet. On the world strategic situation, Chatfield reviewed the change in priorities that had occurred within the previous two or three years. Formerly it had been foreseen that Britain might be at war with Germany and Japan simultaneously and it had been expected that Italy would be

[21] Letter from Neville Chamberlain to Hilda, 17 June 1939, Neville Chamberlain papers, NC18/1/1103.
[22] Cabinet committee on foreign policy, 19 June 1939, F.P. (36), 52nd meeting, enclosed in F6110/1/10, F.O.371/23400.

kept out of a conflict. The Mediterranean would then be abandoned. In recent months the dilemma had been re-assessed. The priority was now to avoid war with Japan, since the first principle of strategy was to eliminate the weakest foe first. The crisis at Tientsin had occurred at an unfortunate time. There was no point in dispatching a battle fleet unless it was accompanied by other vessels. Chatfield thought some parts of the report should be considered further, as, for example, that dealing with the state of readiness of the Japanese fleet. He suggested sending three capital ships to Suez to strengthen the ships already there. Despite his criticisms, Chatfield closed his remarks by stating his con-currence with the conclusion of the chiefs of staff that 'it was most undesirable that we should become involved in the Far East'.[23]

Halifax then outlined the diplomatic developments with particular reference to consultations with the United States; he had been assured by Joseph Kennedy that he would telephone President Roosevelt for his reactions. Halifax next referred to Craigie's proposal that he should informally sound out the Japanese foreign minister on the prospects for a settlement in-corporating the withdrawal of the blockade measures; that Britain would be willing to discuss the outstanding problems at Tientsin provided that British authority in the concession was maintained intact and that actions contrary to observance of neutrality be curbed; and that negotiations be started in Tokyo for a general settlement involving local British and Japanese representatives from Tientsin. Halifax doubted if Craigie could reach an acceptable settlement on this basis; it was, however, essential to weigh the dangers of not reaching a settlement. Provided Britain would receive American dip-lomatic support, it might be wise to proceed as Craigie en-visaged. The foreign secretary fully agreed with the chiefs of staff that conflict with Japan should, if possible, be averted.

---

[23] Ibid. The committee of imperial defence had discussed the repercussions of the guarantees given to Greece, Romania, and Turkey on 2 May 1939. Stanhope referred to the consequences of the greater involvement in eastern Europe bordering the Mediterranean, and it was decided to endorse the conclusions reached by the deputy chief of the naval staff that it was impossible to state how soon after Japanese inter-vention a fleet could be dispatched to the Far East or how strong a fleet could be sent. See C.I.D. (355), 2 May 1939, Cab.2/8.

Chamberlain said that he could foresee grave perils in the crisis. 'He himself would have thought that our best course would have been to endeavour to reach some settlement with the Japanese on the most favourable terms obtainable, though, no doubt in so doing we should open ourselves to considerable humiliation and criticism.'[24] Later in the debate he modified his approach, observing that it was not inevitable that negotiations in Tokyo would culminate in 'a very humiliating surrender'. The attitude and role of the United States was regarded as one of the key aspects: assured of American support, Britain could advance with some confidence, but American policy so far had not been particularly encouraging. In reply to a detailed inquiry on naval strength, Chatfield stated that it should eventually be feasible for Britain to send seven capital ships to the Far East but all seven could not be sent before mid-September owing to the prior claims of the Mediterranean. The cabinet committee agreed to consider the subject again at a later meeting. It was clear from the wide-ranging review that the argument in favour of negotiating with Japan was cogent: the weakness of British defences rendered it imperative to reach a diplomatic solution. Simultaneously it would be necessary to avoid making concessions that were too extreme and which would antagonize public opinion.

On the same day Halifax summoned Shigemitsu, the Japanese ambassador, to see him. In forceful terms he stated the shock and anger of the government at the extreme measures taken against the British concession. 'I told the Ambassador that, whatever justification might exist for the blockade in the mind of the Japanese authorities, behaviour such as that reported was unworthy of any civilised people, and I was certain that he would be just as shocked by it as I was myself. The Ambassador seemed to assent to this and said that he would at once make representations on the subject to Tokyo.'[25] Halifax then urged that food supplies should be allowed to enter the concession again for humanitarian

---

[24] Ibid. See also J. Harvey (ed.), *The Diplomatic Diaries of Oliver Harvey, 1937-1940*, p. 298, where Oliver Harvey records the impact made by the report from the chiefs of staff.

[25] *D.B.F.P.* 3, ix, 205-6, Halifax to Craigie, 19 June 1939.

reasons. He followed by emphasizing the dangers of fostering further escalation and appealed for restraint to avert a dangerous 'head-on collision'. Halifax told Shigemitsu that there was no wish in Britain to permit the use of Tientsin for activities hostile to Japan. The interview ended in a more friendly spirit. Clearly the advice of Craigie and the defence chiefs was governing Halifax's policy. The more responsible leaders of the Japanese government shared the wish to reduce the growing acrimony, but naturally on their own terms. Craigie reported on 20 June that he had received a personal message from Baron Hiranuma, the prime minister, to the effect that he was watching developments closely and that he supported the holding of a conference in Tokyo dealing only with issues peculiar to the concession.[26] Craigie was using his military attaché, General Piggott, as an intermediary in negotiations with a certain 'M' representing Hiranuma. The Foreign Office frequently criticized Craigie for relying too heavily on Piggott, renowned for his pronounced Japanese sympathies. This is an excellent example of Craigie skilfully using Piggott, who had many contacts in the Japanese government and army, to defuse the dangers inherent in Tientsin. In a private letter to Cadogan, the permanent under-secretary, Craigie discussed the importance of Hiranuma's approach. The prime minister was willing to curb the army's desire to dictate policy decisions relating to China, and had taken a more resolute line than Arita, the foreign minister.[27] Craigie's confidence in Hiranuma's moderation was exaggerated, for the prime minister had consistently supported the proposed alliance with Germany, blocked by the reservations of the navy. However, it was apparently the case that Hiranuma did not wish a major confrontation with Britain at this time.

The cabinet foreign policy committee met again on 20 June. Chatfield stated that the chiefs of staff would give further consideration to the measures that might have to be taken if the crisis worsened. If the cabinet decided that a fleet had to be sent, seven capital ships would be dispatched. The fleet would have to be mobilized on 1 July so as to bring into commission

[26] *D.B.F.P.* 3, ix, 209, Craigie to Halifax, 20 June 1939.
[27] Letter from Craigie to Cadogan, 30 June 1939 (received 28 July 1939), F8061/1/10, F.O.371/23403.

reserve ships to replace the cruisers and destroyers going to the
Far East. Chatfield stressed that the fleet could only prevent
Britain from suffering a major disaster: it could not directly
restrain Japanese actions in China. It was essential to keep in
mind the political repercussions in Europe of diverting a large
proportion of naval resources to East Asia. Chatfield made it
clear that the Admiralty expected the cabinet to shoulder the
political responsibility if the fleet went to Singapore:

He [Chatfield] wished to make it clear that he understood that the
Admiralty would not advocate sending to the Far East a Fleet of
seven capital ships. It would be for the Cabinet to decide whether the
circumstances made it necessary to risk sending a Fleet to the Far
East, or whether we should make the naval position quite safe at
home and in the Mediterranean.[28]

Chamberlain emphasized the need to reach a solution by
negotiation and Halifax spoke of the relevance of the United
States. Inskip, the Dominions secretary, warned of the reactions in Australia and New Zealand when the decisions
reached were learned. Chatfield expressed the personal
opinion that the Americans would be more likely to act
positively if Britain sent a substantial fleet; he wondered
whether it might be concentrated at Alexandria, so that it
could be deployed either in the Mediterranean or the Far
East.[29] The discussion underlined the crucial role of
diplomacy in escaping from the dilemma.

The cabinet considered matters further on 21 June. Halifax
explained that little could be decided until Craigie indicated
the formal Japanese reply to his approach. He drew the
cabinet's attention to a recent telegram from Jamieson, which
revealed that the consul-general had seemingly given the
Japanese to understand that the four men accused of assas-
sinating Cheng would be handed over. Sir John Simon referred
to the economic problems of the crisis, with special reference
to the Japanese aim of securing the wider acceptance of
federal reserve board currency. Halifax commented that the
currency was not a matter that could be settled in Anglo-
Japanese talks, nor could it be pursued at Tientsin. Chamber-

---

[28] Cabinet foreign policy committee, 20 June 1939, F.P.(36)53, Cab.27/625.
[29] Ibid.

lain once more commented on the perils implicit in economic sanctions; such measures could only be implemented if there was an assurance of American support. In the existing situation this was not the case. It had to be remembered too that sanctions should be effective but that, if they were fully effective, Japan might retaliate and strategic implications could not be ignored. 'It seemed clear that our right course was to endeavour to reach a settlement with the Japanese, rather than to embark on measures of retaliation which might involve us in sending out a Battle Fleet to the Far East at a later date.'[30] In addition, if retaliation were pursued, the advice of the chiefs of staff to the effect that the China Fleet be withdrawn from the northern Chinese ports to a safer place would have to be followed. Chamberlain said that, in case matters worsened at Tientsin, he had requested Chatfield to produce a paper on action to be taken in such a contingency. The prime minister described the situation as most serious in a letter to his sister Ida, and castigated the Foreign Office for mishandling the earlier stages of the crisis:

It looks now as if we might get negotiations started pretty soon at Tokyo in which case the blockade should at once begin to abate. The trouble is that the Govt. have hardly any control over the army and have to deny the truth of the accounts of the brutal behaviour of their soldiers although they know well enough they are accurate. But a few more 'incidents' like those which have already occurred would make negotiations impossible and the situation would then be pretty serious. It is maddening to have to hold our hands in face of such humiliations but we cannot ignore the terrible risks of putting such temptations in Hitler's way. If we can get out of this mess into which our Foreign Office has so rashly landed us we shall have a further brief respite but no one would care to prophesy what may happen in August and September.[31]

Craigie continued to employ all his diplomatic gifts both to reiterate British disgust at the odious measures enforced at the Tientsin barrier and to explain his government's wish for an amicable settlement. It was important to keep in mind American reactions if a decision were reached to compromise

[30] Cabinet conclusions, 21 June 1939, 33(39)3, Cab.23/100.
[31] Letter from Neville Chamberlain to Ida, 25 June 1939, Neville Chamberlain papers, NC18/1/1104.

with Japan. The cabinet decided to propose that negotiations should begin to discuss local issues at Tientsin, provided that the humiliating searches at the barrier ceased. Craigie would be entrusted with the negotiations and Halifax confirmed his confidence in the ambassador's judgement. Craigie favoured a dual, flexible approach. He urged that legislation be introduced permitting the adoption of economic reprisals against Japan if necessary. He sought to persuade the Japanese to modify their actions against Tientsin; at the same time he desired as much freedom as he could for compromising on the controversial aspects of Tientsin without going too far. The government agreed with Craigie, but had to exercise care that compromise did not lead to the harsh accusation of yet more inept appeasement.[32] Warren Swire, a prominent figure in the China trade and in the China Association, wrote to Howe expressing his fear that Britain 'will be led up the garden path at Tokyo to an undesirable compromise which will react disastrously on this country all over the East . . .'[33] Brenan mordantly commented on Swire's warning, 'Unless we are prepared to retaliate, or compromise, we shall be not so much led as kicked down the garden path and over the garden wall.' The danger was undoubtedly more acute than was appreciated by British opinion and it could be expected that a settlement would lean more towards the Japanese interpretation of justice than the British. Nevertheless Halifax pressed Oliver Stanley, the president of the Board of Trade, to prepare for action against Japanese goods. Stanley replied that he was sympathetic and believed that the test should be discrimination against British trade or subjects contrary to treaty rights; with regard to the form he favoured an embargo on importation into Britain of Japanese goods, which would be relatively simple to apply. Stanley added that Japan would certainly retaliate, most probably against British shipping.[34]

[32] *D.B.F.P.* 3, ix, 225-6, Halifax to Craigie, 25 June 1939. Chamberlain wrote to his sister Hilda: 'The Tientsin incident shows some prospects of relief now that Craigie has very skilfully managed to get the venue removed to Tokyo. Discussions haven't yet begun so that I don't know what are the extent of the Japanese claims but the Minister of Foreign Affairs has promised to confine them to the vital issue'. 2 July 1939, Neville Chamberlain papers, NC18/1/1105.

[33] Letter from Swire to Howe, 6 July 1939, with minutes, F7009/6547/10, F.O.371/23527.

[34] Letter from Stanley to Halifax, 14 July 1939, F7330/44/10, F.O.371/23439.

The three services' attachés to the British embassy in Tokyo opposed embarking on retaliatory action; in their opinion such a move could lead to war.[35] Retaliation was examined again by the advisory committee on trade questions (A.T.B.) on 20 July, which concluded that while there was certain action that Britain could take, co-operation with the United States would be extremely desirable in rendering action·effective. The same conclusions emerged, therefore, as from previous studies. By the time the cabinet examined the report, on 2 August, a temporary agreement had been reached with Japan, but the outlook was still grave and the cabinet decided to send copies to the Dominions and India with a summary to be sent to the American and French governments.

Before Craigie could begin the talks in Tokyo, he had to handle pressure from Hiranuma to include the whole field of British policy towards China in the scope of the discussion. Hiranuma's intermediary visited Craigie and stated that the prime minister personally appreciated the desirability of restricting the talks to local issues but 'he [Hiranuma] had been greatly impressed by public insistence upon a change in our policy towards Chiang Kai-shek forming an essential part of the forthcoming discussions'.[36] Craigie replied that 'quite apart from the fact that we had reached a prior understanding to confine conversations to local issues, demand that British foreign policy should be changed at the dictation of a foreign Power was obviously unacceptable.'[37] Craigie stressed that the wisest procedure was to dispose of the problems arising from Tientsin and hoped that this would lead to more harmony generally. The intermediary was disappointed at the reply, and blamed Clark Kerr for much of the acrimony·in Anglo-Japanese relations; Craigie loyally defended his colleague from the onslaught.[38] Equally, Craigie was anxious to remove any doubts in London as to the consequences of adopting a tough stand with Japan. He entirely agreed with his service attachés that such an attitude should be eschewed unless Britain could reinforce a policy of economic retaliation with force if

[35] War Office to Foreign Office, 17 July 1939, enclosing military attaché, Tokyo, to War Office, 15 July 1939, F7388/44/10, F.O.371/23439.
[36] *D.B.F.P.* 3, ix, 261, Craigie to Halifax, 12 July 1939.
[37] Ibid.
[38] *D.B.F.P.* 3, ix, 276–7, Craigie to Halifax, 15 July 1939.

required. The Foreign Office received Craigie's warnings critically. Dening commented on an earlier telegram from Craigie, referring to the inflamed state of Japanese opinion, that there was no public opinion in Japan and that it was accordingly impossible to accept his allusion to the Hiranuma government being forced into a more militant posture:

There is no public opinion in Japan and it is only too obvious that the Japanese public has been instructed to demonstrate. It has done so with the prompt obedience one expects of the Japanese people and in the process the usual native hysteria has manifested itself. I decline to believe that the Japanese Govt. is at all impressed, or that the demonstrations would not cease instantly if orders were given from the same source which instigated them.

But there is no doubt that the demonstrations have served the purpose which inspired them, since they have given rise to this telegram. I feel H.M. Ambassador might have been better advised by members of his staff who have a considerable experience of the Japanese and their tactics. However disagreeable these demonstrations may be for people on the spot, one must hope that they will not lose their sense of proportion.[39]

Nigel Ronald observed that part of Craigie's telegram appeared to have been drafted by General Piggott, the military attaché. 'Tokyo Embassy have intimated to us privately that they know we can distinguish "Piggotries" from serious reports and they evidently rely on us to prevent the former from receiving too wide publicity or reaching the eyes of those who have neither the experience nor the time to sift the grain from the chaff . . .'[40]

The prime minister's view of Craigie was very different. He wrote to his sister Hilda on 15 July:

The only thing that gives me any confidence is Craigie's attitude. He always seems to preserve his calm and never to get rattled. I fancy he must have established particularly good relations with Arita and that may save us. But the anti-Japanese bias of the F.O. has in the past

[39] Minute by Dening, 19 July 1939, on Craigie to Halifax, 10 July 1939, F7163/6457/10, F.O.371/23527.
[40] Minute by Ronald, 19 July 1939, ibid. The Far Eastern department of the Foreign Office was critical of Craigie, regarding him as weak and too much of an appeaser, see D. Dilks (ed.), *The Diaries of Sir Alexander Cadogan, 1938-1945*, p. 194. The accusation was unjust.

never given him a chance. If he gets us through this mess I shall insist
on his having an honour to mark our gratitude.[41]

Craigie's immediate objective was to secure an agreed statement terminating the extreme bitterness in Anglo-Japanese
relations and, he hoped, opening the door to a full settlement
of the issues involved in Tientsin.[42] He discussed the problem
with Arita Hachiro a week before signing an agreement on 22
July. Arita had made it clear, when they met on 15 July, that
Japan desired a statement in which Britain would accept the
special war conditions prevailing in China and that Japanese
forces had to cope with the conflict as they thought best. In
effect, Japan wanted Britain to give her *carte blanche* in
China. The British wish was to reduce this recognition to the
minimum compatible with compromise. The impact of any
statement on the United States had to be borne in mind.
Both the United States and France were closely involved in the
currency and silver questions and their interests had to be safe-
guarded, apart from the more vital political motives in the
case of the United States. The Japanese were reluctant to push
Britain too far: it was important for Japan to secure a partial
diplomatic victory and boast of it afterwards. The terms of the
statement read as follows:

His Majesty's Government in the United Kingdom fully recognise
actual situation in China where hostilities on a large scale are in
progress and note that, as long as that state of affairs continues to
exist, the Japanese forces in China have special requirements for the
purpose of safeguarding their own security and maintaining public
order in regions under their control, and that they have to suppress
or remove any such acts or causes as will obstruct them or benefit
their enemy. His Majesty's Government have no intention of
countenancing any act or measures prejudicial to attainment of the
above-mentioned objects by Japanese forces and they will take this
opportunity to confirm their policy in this respect by making it plain
to British authorities and British nationals in China that they should
refrain from such acts and measures.[43]

Neville Chamberlain warmly welcomed news of the agree-

---

[41] Letter from Neville Chamberlain to Hilda, 15 July 1939, Neville Chamberlain
papers, NC18/1/1107.
[42] *D.B.F.P.* 3, ix, 278–80, Craigie to Halifax, 15 July 1939.
[43] *D.B.F.P.* 3, ix, 313, Craigie to Halifax, 23 July 1939.

ment and praised Craigie's talents as a negotiator: 'Craigie has, with great skill, got an agreement with the Japs about the preliminary formula and if only a little restraint can be exercised on our side the inflammation should gradually subside.'[44]

Britain had moved a considerable distance towards accepting the legitimacy of the Japanese military operations in China. It was undeniably a departure in verbal terms from the previous British policy of neutrality benevolently weighted towards China. However, the stress is on the verbal element. In practice, Britain still leaned towards China and aided her financially. Chiang Kai-shek, as anticipated, was hostile and regarded the agreement as a regrettable retreat by the British. The United States deprecated it, but the Tientsin crisis had the effect of at last galvanizing the United States to a measure of retaliation for the humiliations heaped on westerners in Japanese-occupied regions of China. Roosevelt and Hull comprehended the dilemma facing Britain but nevertheless maintained that she should have stood up to Japanese pressure. As Britain had not done so, the United States must make a move to convey disapproval. The United States gave notice to Japan of her intentions of terminating the American-Japanese commercial treaty of 1911 at the end of the statutory period of six months' notice. The American action was taken abruptly without consultation with Britain, and entirely in keeping with Roosevelt's somewhat cavalier methods of conducting policy. The president's attitude was admirably conveyed in the tone of a casual conversation between Roosevelt, Mallet, the counsellor of the British embassy, and the Maharajah of Tripura, who was visiting Washington, which took place at the White House on 31 July:

The President after a conversation on quite other subjects volunteered the following entirely unsolicited statement regarding Japan. He had not contemplated any immediate abrogation of Commercial Treaty but at noon on July 26 he had learned that the Foreign Relations Committee of the Senate had decided to shelve both Pittman and Vandenberg resolutions for this session. He sent for Secretary of State at 1.0.p.m. and they decided that they must act immediately 'in order that the dictators should not imagine that they could get away with it'. Accordingly note to Japanese Government

---

[44] Letter from Neville Chamberlain to Ida, 23 July 1939, NC18/1/1108.

was drafted and delivered that very afternoon. President said that he hoped we should not think he had been trying to go behind our back but that there had been no time to inform us.

Mr. Mallet said that he imagined President's action to be very helpful to His Majesty's Government in the United Kingdom and President replied that he thought so too and hoped so as something had to be done to warn the dictators.[45]

At the beginning of August Sir George Sansom drafted a lengthy, reflective memorandum on the broader implications of the Tientsin crisis. Sansom possessed profound knowledge of Japanese culture and society through his life's work in the diplomatic service together with his research as a historian. Unfortunately his relations with Craigie had not been happy, perhaps because of incompatibility of temperament and because of a certain pomposity in Craigie's manner. Craigie was basically more sanguine as to the chances of averting further deterioration in Anglo-Japanese relations. Sansom felt that the divergent interests of the two powers made a conflict virtually inevitable. He thought it unlikely that the talks over Tientsin could produce a settlement without surrendering fundamental principles:

Sir Robert Craigie, in assessing the strength of the forces in Japan which we have to meet, distinguishes between an extremist party, which he hopes may be conciliated, and a moderate party which he hopes may be encouraged, by the settlement of outstanding issues without sacrifice of principle. He agrees that the Japanese Government are at present unable to control the extremists adequately, but he thinks that if we adopt a suitable policy this may enable them to gain control. He believes that we have useful friends in Japan whom we shall lose if we do not help them by deferring to the extremists. But it is open to serious doubt (which the memory of past experience does nothing to remove) whether in present conditions we have any really useful friends in Japan. All Japanese want a 'new order' in Asia, and a 'new order' involves the ultimate displacement of Great

---

[45] *D.B.F.P.* 3, ix, 370–1, Lindsay to Halifax, 31 July 1939. Chamberlain wrote to his sister Hilda that the talks in Tokyo were progressing 'and should be helped by Roosevelt's action [which] would have been still more helpful if it had come earlier. The attitude of the military in China itself, especially at Tientsin, Peking and Shanghai remains intolerably provocative and offensive. But we must exercise what patience we can and hope that it will gradually get better. After all the worst outrages the stripping, searching and slapping may now come to an end.' 30 July 1939, Neville Chamberlain papers, NC18/1/1109.

Britain in the Far East. The difference between the extremists and the moderates is not one of destination, but of the road by which that destination is to be reached and the speed at which it is to be travelled.[46]

The last sentence was particularly apposite and there can be no doubt that it was an accurate statement. Sansom conceded that there were some liberals, bankers, and industrialists who were frightened of the growing consolidation of a military-inspired totalitarianism. These elements could assist the purposes of British policy in certain circumstances but this result could only be attained by pursuing a tough approach to Japan's easy victories, for the extremists would not aid the moderates. In Sansom's opinion, it was preferable to compel the Japanese to employ coercion and thus leave Britain's moral position intact. It would be feasible, although admittedly difficult, to adopt an attitude of non-resistance to Japan in China. If carefully planned and frankly explained to the British public, it could create appreciable difficulty for the Japanese involving (as it would) the withdrawal of British nationals and services. The alternative to evacuation was the implementation of economic reprisals. There were risks in this policy, too, but Sansom regarded them as acceptable if they were applied after the intensification of measures against British interests. He believed that most Japanese leaders were cautious and calculating and that, in existing conditions, it was improbable that Japan would wish to go to war; it was, however, always possible that the two countries would drift into war. Sansom concluded that there could be a *rapprochement* with Japan only if Great Britain and the United States made major concessions in the direction of accepting the new order. He suggested that Britain should propose such concessions in return for the Japanese refraining from pressing Britain further in Tientsin.

Is there any good reason why we should not attempt to penetrate the home front in Japan by announcing openly that we are prepared, in the proper conditions, to surrender a great deal of what we have hitherto held in China? We have said something of the sort in general terms from time to time and no harm could come from publicly

[46] *D.B.F.P.* 3, ix, appendix I, 528, 'Memorandum on British policy in the Far East' by Sansom, 3 Aug. 1939.

repeating our statements in more precise terms, saying for instance that we are ready to carry out our announced programme of rendition of extraterritorial privileges etc., and to give Japan all reasonable assistance in securing a large share of the economic benefit to be drawn from trade and industry in China. Perhaps we might even go further and promise reconsideration of colonial quotas. In any case, if we can substitute for what Sir R. Craigie calls our 'unmeasured and sustained condemnation' of Japan a method of address which at least admits that Japan has some legitimate aspirations and grievances, even the extremists might be put in a better frame of mind. There is no doubt that our and the Americans' preaching has infuriated the Japanese in recent years.

Even if the extremists prefer not to trust our offer, it puts them in a difficult position and is a more hopeful method than any other of widening the breach between them and the moderates. The moderates can be helped only if they have something to propose which the extremists cannot by their methods produce.[47]

Sansom's views were generally cogent but ended less convincingly, for he did not face up to the logical implications of his concluding remarks: if the Japanese new order was accepted, it could only be at the expense of China. This was to remain the principal obstacle to *détente* down to Pearl Harbor. Even if the western powers had decided to make the concessions, they would have had to convince their own public opinion. In the aftermath of Munich and the reaction against appeasement, it would not have been an easy task.

The Tientsin crisis caused great concern in Australia and led to an exchange of telegrams between London and Canberra, followed by meetings between leading ministers and Dominion representatives. On 26 June Neville Chamberlain informed the committee of imperial defence that he had received a telegram from Robert Menzies, the Australian prime minister, requesting an assurance that, if war broke out with Japan, Britain would send a fleet to Singapore to defend Australia. The Dominions secretary, Sir Thomas Inskip, suggested that he might see Stanley Bruce, the Australian high commissioner, and Walter Nash of New Zealand to discuss the impact of recent developments on naval strategy. Chamberlain agreed and suggested that he, too, should see Bruce and Nash. A meeting took place in the prime minister's room at

[47] Ibid. 531–2.

the House of Commons on 28 June. Chamberlain, Inskip, and Chatfield were present with the two high commissioners. At the beginning of the meeting Chamberlain read out the telegram he was sending to Menzies; this mostly consisted of a repetition of the salient passages from Chamberlain's telegram of 20 March 1939 to Menzies's predecessor, J. A .Lyons.[48] The prime minister went on to observe that the danger in which Britain found herself differed from that which had been foreseen in that it now appeared possible that Britain would become involved in war with Japan first, and that Germany and Italy would subsequently join in. Previously the reverse situation had been anticipated. Britain's growing commitments in Europe made matters far more difficult. If a British fleet was to be sent to Singapore, it was vital that it should be strong enough to accept battle if necessary. Britain was determined to resolve the Tientsin issues peacefully and there now seemed a better opportunity of achieving this objective. It was, however, possible that the Japanese might force war on Britain, but Chamberlain did not consider this probable in view of Japan's commitments in China. Japan had to keep the attitude of the United States in mind.[49]

Bruce said he would explain how he personally thought Australia would react. In his opinion, the Foreign Office had mishandled matters and should not have adopted the line which it had followed. He was sure that his government would applaud efforts to reach a diplomatic solution. If it became necessary to retaliate against Japan, Australia would favour assisting China, and even the imposition of sanctions, if Britain felt this was the best course. Bruce stated that as far back as 1938 he had doubted whether Britain would send a fleet to Singapore if conflict with Germany, Italy, and Japan occurred simultaneously;[50] he had been given firm assurances on the subject by the Admiralty, however. Chatfield commented that the situation had changed, in that Japan had

[48] In the telegram of 20 March Chamberlain had confirmed the promise of British support but had added that 'the size of that fleet would necessarily be dependent on (a) the moment when Japan entered the war, and (b) what losses, if any, our opponents or ourselves had previously sustained' in the event of war with Germany, Italy, and Japan. See appendix II to C.I.D. minutes, 26 June 1939, Cab.2/9.

[49] Minutes of meeting held on 28 June 1939, appendix III to C.I.D. minutes, 26 June 1939, Cab.2/9.

[50] Ibid.

become far more of a menace than envisaged in 1938.

A second meeting was held at the Dominions Office on 11 July, attended by Inskip, Chatfield, Stanhope, Pound, the chief of the naval staff, and Bruce. Bruce pressed for information on the size of the fleet to be sent to the Far East. He stressed the concern felt in Australia and stated dramatically that Chamberlain's telegram of 20 March had come 'as a bombshell' to his government.[51] Chatfield once more explained how developments in Europe had compelled a fundamental change in thinking. Bruce demanded a clear answer as to what Britain would do if war with Japan began: was a fleet going to be sent or not? Had a secret decision been reached?[52] Inskip replied that no decision had been taken and no plan formulated, owing to the current uncertainties. Chatfield described the consequences of a withdrawal from the eastern Mediterranean: the French would be deeply alarmed and might concentrate their resources in the Mediterranean at the expense of the Atlantic. Chatfield favoured basing the fleet on Alexandria so that it could be deployed in the Mediterranean or Far East as desired. Chatfield added that at the last C.I.D. meeting, held on 6 July, it had been agreed to extend the period before relief for Singapore to ninety days. The meeting closed with Bruce still confessing his confusion as to the outcome in the event of grave trouble developing in East Asia rather than Europe.[53] The exchange did not promote Australian confidence in British policy.

As a result of important staff talks held between Britain and France in the spring of 1939, an Anglo-French conference was held at Singapore from 22 to 27 June 1939. The French had understandably attached more significance to the Mediterranean and maintained that the defeat of Italy should take priority over reinforcement of the Far East.[54] The contribution to be made by the Singapore base towards any action against Japan was accepted by France. The Singapore conference was preoccupied with plans for the defence of the base and the report stressed that the army, air force, and navy each

[51] Meeting held on 11 July 1939, appendix IV to C.I.D. minutes, 26 June 1939, Cab.2/9.
[52] Ibid.
[53] Ibid.
[54] Gibbs, *Grand Strategy*, i, 429.

required strengthening,[55] the provision of additional air strength being deemed 'of paramount importance'.[56] The C.I.D. decided, in July 1939, that two squadrons should be sent to Singapore. The minutes recorded the statement of the secretary of state for air: 'Sir Kingsley Wood said that the Air Staff had weighed up the conflicting claims of Great Britain and the Far East, and had come to the conclusion that these two squadrons should go. The aircraft could fly out at once and the remaining personnel and stores would go by sea, taking about five weeks to reach Singapore.'[57] At last some slight appreciation of the role of air power in far eastern defence was shown, albeit inadequately. The air officer commanding, Far East, Air Vice-Marshal J. T. Babington, repeatedly and cogently advanced the arguments for giving more weight to air defence in a series of letters and memoranda to the Air Ministry between 1938 and 1940. He castigated the stereotyped thinking of the army and navy; the older services did not fully understand the relevance of air power. 'There is so much bow-and-arrow tradition, so much wishful thinking by the older services, and so much vague reliance on economic factors to be removed before anything can be clearly appreciated.'[58]

Meanwhile, highly secret Anglo-American exchanges on naval issues were taking place in June 1939. The confidential discussions were an extension of the talks held in London during the visit of Captain Ingersoll in January 1938. The initiative was taken by the Admiralty, who expressed the wish that a British naval officer visit the United States to review the current world situation as it affected the two powers. The Admiralty would have preferred the talks to be held in London, as previously, and hoped that they could be conducted on the American side by a new naval attaché; the post had been vacant since the departure of the previous incumbent. It is clear that the Admiralty hoped in this way to exercise effective control over the conversations and to achieve

[55] Ibid. 429-30.
[56] Ibid. 430.
[57] Minutes of 367th meeting of the C.I.D., 21 July 1939, Cab.2/9.
[58] Letter from Babington to Peirse, 28 July 1939, with memorandum, Air 19/2130. Note also letter from Babington to Peirse, 28 Oct. 1938, ibid.

the desirable objective of securing a new American naval attaché. Roosevelt did not wish to appoint another attaché at this stage, because of his bid to amend the neutrality laws with the concomitant need to handle Congress with particular care. More important than the question of the attaché was Roosevelt's determination to prevent any leakage of information about the discussions, as had happened after Ingersoll's visit. The Admiralty had to bow to the president's wish, for the importance of complying with American preferences took precedence. At first Sumner Welles suggested that Britain send a naval officer in disguise, who would take over from the British naval attaché in Washington, the latter returning to London; the replacement would reside in a city other than Washington. This curiously complex proposal was disliked in London, particularly because of the danger of the disguise being penetrated: if this occurred, the resulting furore would be embarrassing in the extreme.[59] Eventually a compromise was approved whereby Commander T. C. Hampton was to be sent to the United States, sailing under the name of 'Mr. Hampton' and landing first in Canada. Hampton's visit was regarded as highly confidential, to such an extent that only two senior officers in the American Navy Department knew of his presence; it was even emphasized to Hampton that news of his visit should not be communicated to the director of intelligence in the American navy. The Americans aware of the visit were Roosevelt, Hull, Welles, Admiral Leahy, chief of the naval staff, and Admiral Ghormley, director of plans. Hampton, in company with Captain L. C. A. Curzon-Howe, the British naval attaché, saw Leahy and Ghormley twice, on 12 and 14 June 1939. Hampton explained the strategic rethinking within the Admiralty provoked by the serious deterioration of relations with Germany and Italy. The situation was more dangerous than at the time of the Ingersoll mission, and it was more difficult for Britain to contemplate the dispatch of a fleet to the Far East. Leahy explained that if a European war broke out, Roosevelt would send the fleet to Hawaii as a warning to Japan. He was reluctant to enter into a

---

[59] For the Admiralty view, see papers relating to Commander T. C. Hampton's visit, Adm.116/3922. I am grateful to Dr. P. Haggie for drawing this reference to my attention.

detailed analysis of policy in the event of the United States becoming involved in a war as an ally of Great Britain, and Hampton wisely refrained from pressing him. Leahy indicated that it would be the function of American forces to guard the Pacific while the allied fleets protected European waters, the Atlantic, and the Mediterranean. The American fleet would proceed to Singapore with sufficient strength to engage and defeat the Japanese fleet if encountered: in Leahy's opinion, at least ten capital ships would be required in the Far East. He was adamantly opposed to sending an inferior force to confront the Japanese, coinciding in this respect with the outlook of the Admiralty in London. The Americans had no detailed plans for the voyage to Singapore but Leahy thought it might take up to sixty days to organize the operation. Leahy was unhappy with the official period of relief of ninety days and held that it should be raised to 120 days, a conclusion already reached in London. Hampton conveyed the British view that it would be most satisfactory for the British naval forces in the Far East to be under the strategical direction of the American commander-in-chief, but the final decision would have to be taken subsequently. American policy towards the Philippines resembled British policy towards Hong Kong in foreseeing that delaying action was the best to be hoped for.

Hampton concluded that while the talks had not achieved outstanding results he was certain that Leahy had welcomed his visit and had deemed it to be helpful. It was essential to appreciate that Roosevelt was far more advanced in his approach to foreign affairs than most American citizens; that Leahy was fervently Anglophile and that he was shortly to be succeeded as chief of staff by a man of similar outlook in Admiral Stark; and that a leakage of information would have serious consequences. It was manifest that the American navy had no detailed plans for co-operation with the British fleet in war; however, what was revealed by Leahy confirmed the information given to Hampton by Rear-Admiral T. S. V. Phillips, the deputy chief of the naval staff, before his departure. The Hampton talks emphasized Roosevelt's desire to maintain and improve contacts with Britain in the defence sphere so long as the contacts were kept strictly confidential. The drawback was the president's unwillingness to advance too quickly lest such action stimulate opposition in the isolationist lobby. The effects of the Tientsin crisis resulted, as has been seen, in Roosevelt's decision to give notice of termination of the American-Japanese trade treaty. By the end of July 1939 the likelihood of the United States pursuing a firmer policy seemed less remote than at the end of Hampton's visit a month before.

Discussions on the issues involved in Tientsin were resumed in late July. It became clear that Japan wished to compel Britain to compromise over the Chinese silver deposits in British and French banks in the concession and over the circulation of Chinese currency. Heartened by the more resolute attitude discernible in Washington, and in the knowledge that these matters directly involved the United States and France, Britain declined to compromise further. Preparations were made for the possible denunciation of the Anglo-Japanese commerical treaty of 1911 and for the evacuation of British nationals from north China. Japan's attitude was unyielding and further progress could not be achieved. The talks were officially adjourned on 20 August, to be continued in changed circumstances after the outbreak of the war in Europe.

As the menace of war temporarily receded in East Asia in August 1939, so the war clouds in Europe became more threatening. The desultory talks between Great Britain, France, and the Soviet Union dragged on until overtaken by the dramatic announcement of the Nazi–Soviet pact on 22 August. From Stalin's viewpoint, there were compelling reasons why he should make the agreement despite the ideological gulf between the signatories and the ensuing shock to marxists throughout the world. The economic transformation of Russia, the effects of the huge purges and the serious conflict between Russia and Japan on the borders of Mongolia and Manchukuo were powerful arguments for reaching an accommodation with Germany. For Hitler it was an essential short-term measure to secure the swift liquidation of Poland. The major advantage of the Nazi–Soviet pact in the far eastern context was that it shocked Japan at least as deeply as Britain and France. The Hiranuma government was identified with warm support of the Anti-Comintern pact and of close relations with Germany. Japan had not been consulted or informed of the trend of German policy; Hiranuma and his cabinet were disgraced and resigned promptly, assuming responsibility for the reverse in foreign policy. Japanese politics were thrown into turmoil and even some sections of the army voiced dissatisfaction. A retired general, Abe Nobuyuki, took office as prime minister in a caretaker capacity. A perceptibly warmer tone entered Anglo-Japanese relations, induced by the common experience of having been jilted by actual or potential partners rather than by any fundamental incentive for *rapprochement*. Halifax met Shigemitsu on 28 August. 'I informed the Ambassador that I have been much entertained by a report which our Ambassador in Berlin had brought home with him to the effect that Herr Hitler had been furious at the action of the Japanese in protesting against the new German-Soviet Pact. The Ambassador laughed, and said there was a strong feeling against the pact in his country. This new fact must have considerable bearing on the attitude of the new Japanese Government, and the Ambassador agreed that the double-crossing of Japan by Germany and of ourselves by Russia must cause both the Japanese and British Governments to reconsider the positions in which they found themselves and to consider a possible improvement in their mutual relations.'[60] The next day A. H. F. Edwardes, formerly acting head of the Chinese Maritime Customs Inspectorate and now adviser to the Japanese government on 'world affairs', called to see R. A. Butler at the Foreign Office and stressed that the Nazi-Soviet pact was encouraging Japan to reconsider relations with Britain. Edwardes suggested that the deadlock at Tientsin could be surmounted through neutralizing the silver by sealing it and by avoiding any reference to *fapi*; he assured Butler that there was no intention of preventing the circulation of *fapi*.[61] Butler expressed interest, but it was obvious that little could be achieved until the Abe government was securely installed. It was necessary to resolve the vexed topic of the four Chinese in British custody in connection with the assassination of Cheng Lien-shih. Craigie had consistently pointed out that progress could not be made until the men had been handed over. The Foreign Office informed Clark Kerr on

[60] *D.B.F.P.* 3, ix, 507-8, Halifax to Craigie, 28 Aug. 1939.
[61] *D.B.F.P.* 3, ix, 511, Halifax to Craigie, 29 Aug. 1939.

4 September that 'for reasons of State', the men should be handed over immediately.[62] Even so, while a real attempt was being made to compromise with Japan over Tientsin, it was not until the following summer that an agreement was signed.

The descent into war in Europe was rapid in late August, culminating in the German attack on Poland on 1 September. Two days later Britain and France declared war. The Abe government determined to concentrate exclusively on the affairs of East Asia, in particular on achieving a diplomatic victory in the war with China. There was naturally much interest in the events in Europe but an equal determination to keep out. Craigie was handed an *aide-mémoire* on 5 September stating Japan's position:

Now that a war has broken out in Europe, Japanese Government intend not to be involved therein but to concentrate their efforts on the settlement of the China affair. In this connexion Japanese Government, to whom attitude and conduct of the Powers towards China incident is a matter of deep concern, desires to request that the British Government appreciating said intention . . . will refrain from taking any such measures as may prejudice Japan's position in regard to the China affair.

Furthermore, with regard to those regions of China which are under the control of the Japanese forces, it is apprehended that presence therein of troops and warships of countries taking part in the European War may give rise to untrue reports of incidents and create a situation not in keeping with Japan's intended policy of non-involvement. Japanese Government, therefore, consider it necessary to offer friendly advice to belligerent Powers concerned that they should voluntarily withdraw their troops and warships from regions referred to above. It may be added, upon the withdrawal of such troops and ships, Japanese authorities are prepared to do their utmost for protection of the lives and property of nationals of belligerent Powers.[63]

Japan wanted a free hand in China, and the statement contained the not too subtle hint that Britain must moderate and preferably cease encouragement to Chiang Kai-shek. It would be feasible for Britain and Japan to continue in a state sus-

---

[62] *D.B.F.P.* 3, ix, 524, Halifax to Clark Kerr, 4 Sept. 1939. The decision to hand over the four men had been reached a month earlier but had been delayed by legal action.
[63] *D.B.F.P.* 3, ix, 526, *aide-mémoire* communicated to Craigie, 5 Sept. 1939.

pended between the acrimony of the Tientsin crisis at its climax and reconciliation for a limited time, but not indefinitely. Ultimately a choice would have to be made between friendship with China and a worsening of relations with Japan, or a *détente* with Japan attained at the price of surrendering China to Japanese domination.

The dispute over Tientsin demonstrated the fragility of peace in the Far East. Politicians and service chiefs appreciated how stark was the state of British defences and how patent was Britain's inability to fight Japan. It was the gravest crisis so far encountered in Anglo-Japanese relations in the twentieth century. The situation foreseen by Sir John Pratt and Sir Robert Vansittart in 1932, at the beginning of the Shanghai crisis, had arrived with a vengeance: Britain was having to swallow increasing humiliation inflicted by Japan while the United States observed from the sidelines. Tientsin showed clearly that the United States and only the United States could confront Japan decisively. The United States was beginning to flex her muscles but a positive, forthright policy could not be expected for some time ahead.

IV

THE REPERCUSSIONS OF THE EUROPEAN WAR

THE advent of war in Europe produced a situation in East Asia substantially different from that which had been expected for several years beforehand. Relations between Great Britain and Japan were better than they had been since the beginning of the Sino-Japanese war. The shock of the Nazi–Soviet pact created a mixture of anger and indignation in Tokyo precluding a policy of co-operation with Germany, which endured until the outstanding successes enjoyed by Hitler in the spring and summer of 1940. For both Britain and Japan the brief period of 1939–40 marked an interlude of relative tranquillity in their relations, before the deterioration resumed its course to culminate in the events of December 1941. In London and Tokyo a desire manifested itself to examine afresh the growing rift and to see if a *rapprochement* could be arrived at. For Britain the urgency of the defence predicament greatly strengthened the argument for reaching an agreement; in Japan the political scene was one of turmoil and the government of General Abe Nobuyuki needed time to take stock and reappraise matters. Time was to show that the importance of maintaining and improving relations with the United States and of keeping China in the struggle would not permit Britain to advance far along this path. Equally, the ambitions of expansionists in Japan prevented any significant modification of Japan's terms.

The immediate issue in September 1939 arose from the Japanese wish for the withdrawal of foreign garrisons from China and the desirability of securing a permanent solution to the crisis at Tientsin. It was essential to discuss policy frankly with the United States, in continuation of the prewar policy of encouraging more positive initiatives from Washington; in addition, Britain's dependence on the United States for support in the European war made close co-operation axiomatic. Shortly before the British declaration of war, the British ambassador in Washington, Lord Lothian, reported that Dr. Hornbeck was warning against any British surrender over Tientsin.[1] Ashley Clarke minuted that a settlement of the Tientsin dispute was the first step towards an over-all peace settlement in East Asia; France and the United States should be involved but major concessions should not be made to Japan. As regards a wider settlement:

How we are to proceed . . . will depend on the extent to which Americans are disposed either to resist and give us concrete assistance in resisting with them or on the other hand to take upon themselves the responsibility of an initiative towards a peace settlement. I would submit that the moment has now come to place these two alternatives squarely before them.[2]

During September considerable debate occurred within and between the Foreign Office, the chiefs of staff, and the cabinet over the wisdom of intervening more vigorously to promote a settlement between Japan and China. Halifax saw Quo Tai-chi, the Chinese ambassador, on 8 September and asked him if it was likely that an approach might be made by Japan to Chiang Kai-shek to end the conflict; Quo replied in the negative. Halifax then requested the ambassador's opinion of Wang Ching-wei. Quo stated that Wang was 'an undoubted patriot' who had allowed himself to be outmanoeuvred and exploited. He warned Halifax against a change of policy aimed at encouraging Wang:

He had, however, been instructed by Chiang Kai-shek to inform me that if His Majesty's Government gave up supporting Chiang and came to terms with the Japanese, this would play straight into the hands of Mr. Wang's movement . . .
I told the Ambassador that, as has been repeatedly said, His Majesty's Government were not in the habit of changing their policy overnight. That policy might not have been entirely satisfactory to the generalissimo, but at all events he knew where we stood and we had no surprises in store for him.[3]

Three days later Halifax met Shigemitsu, the Japanese ambassador; it is interesting to note that the foreign secretary had been briefed beforehand by A. H. F. Edwardes, special adviser

[1] Lothian to Halifax, 1 Sept. 1939, F9938/8457/10, F.O.371/23533.
[2] Minute by Clarke, 12 Sept. 1939, ibid.
[3] Halifax to Clark Kerr, 8 Sept. 1939, F9935/87/10, F.O.371/23459.

to the Japanese embassy.[4] Halifax expressed the government's appreciation of Shigemitsu's contribution towards the release of Colonel Spears, the military attaché in China who had been incarcerated for a lengthy period. He continued to state that Britain had no political aims in China. Shigemitsu replied that the Japanese wanted to establish order in China; he believed that Wang Ching-wei would formally establish a new government within the next month or so and that this would become the future administration of China. He urged Britain not to rely too heavily on the United States, adding that in any reshaping of East Asia Japan was opposed to consultations with several powers simultaneously. Halifax said there could be no drastic change in British policy and that the Chungking government would be recognized in the future, as in the past, as the official government of China. Shigemitsu commented that all Japan wished was a more realistic alignment in British policy.[5] M. E. Dening minuted that Japan was clearly going to establish Wang Ching-wei as a puppet and stupidly compel Chiang, as a consequence, to lean to a greater extent on Russia and Germany for support.[6]

Debate in high political circles in London concerned the terms of a conceivable settlement. One of the principal advocates of a policy of appeasement, incorporating appreciable concessions to Japan, was the parliamentary under-secretary at the Foreign Office, R. A. Butler. Owing to the increasing pressure of business in the Foreign Office, Butler began to specialize in far eastern issues for the remainder of his term of office, until he was transferred to the Board of Education in 1941. Butler favoured an agreement with Japan with some enthusiasm, and was one of the few in the Foreign Office to show no regret at the partial surrender to Japan over Tientsin. In the debate over the response to Japan's demand for the withdrawal of garrisons at Tientsin, Butler, with the concurrence of Sir John Brenan, supported withdrawal in contrast to the views of Craigie, Cadogan, Clarke, and Howe. Butler observed: 'I can see positive advantages in withdrawal in our time and my mind envisages the possibility with calm and without

---

[4] Note by R. A. Butler, 11 Sept. 1939, F10074/87/10, F.O.371/23459.
[5] Halifax to Craigie, 11 Sept. 1939, F10074/87/19, F.O.371/23459.
[6] Minute by Dening, 13 Sept. 1939, ibid.

shame. I do not wish my minutes to look too like those of the Chevalier Bayard—sans peur et sans reproche.'[7] He formulated his views at length in a minute for Halifax on 22 September. He began by stressing that it was important to improve relations with Russia or Japan; for the moment, he intended to concentrate on relations with Japan. Butler 'stated that he had talked to Hugh Dalton, the Labour party's chief spokesman on foreign affairs; to W. N. Ewer, diplomatic correspondent of the *Daily Herald*; to Sir John Wardlaw-Milne, the influential Conservative back-bencher; and to Stanley Bruce, the ubiquitous Australian high commissioner. Dalton envisaged the withdrawal of all British troops from China and would liquidate all concessions, retaining only Hong Kong. Ewer did not go so far but favoured withdrawal from north China. Wardlaw-Milne and numerous other Conservative M.P.s were less explicit but advocated positive steps to improve Anglo-Japanese relations. Bruce was less forthcoming, contemplating withdrawal only under duress. Looking at the broader perspective, Butler felt that the development of Russian policy was extremely significant:

Russia and Japan are bound to remain enemies, and with our position in India and the East it would pay us to make a return to the Anglo-Japanese alliance possible. It does not appear that there are the makings of a war between America and Japan; the American interests in the Far East are insufficient to justify a major war. I do not believe it will in the end pay us to keep Japan at arm's length and distrust everything she does for the sake of American opinion. I have never been happy since the Japanese Treaty was allowed to lapse. I believe it is still possible to obtain American interest on our side in fighting dictators in the West, while improving relations with Japan.

I am fortified in wishing to draw nearer to the Japanese by the continued lack of fighting skill, and indeed fighting at all, shown by the Chinese. We have from time to time submitted to taunts that we are about to break faith, that we are not fulfilling our obligations, in fact that we are dishonest in our policy. Meanwhile the Chinese have done little to encourage us. The fall of Canton [in October 1938] without any organised resistance destroyed my confidence in the Chinese as a military force.[8]

---

[7] Minute by Butler, 23 Sept. 1939, F10193/87/10, F.O.371/23459.

[8] Minute by Butler, 22 Sept. 1939, F10/10/176/23, F.O.371/23556.

He continued that the establishment of Wang Ching-wei's regime heralded the danger of civil war breaking out between Wang's supporters and opponents, although he was prepared to accept the expert view that Wang was not a 'winner'. Butler believed that British policy was not sufficiently realistic and that a settlement of the Tientsin question should be reached, including the withdrawal of British garrisons. He rejected the prevalent Foreign Office attitude, expressed particularly by Cadogan, that any agreement with Japan would encourage her to demand more. 'I feel this is the wrong method of approach. I believe there is in the Japanese a desire to improve their relations with us. I believe that they are a nation who keep their word when given.'[9] After agreement had been attained on Tientsin, Butler advocated barter agreements whereby Britain supplied raw materials to Japan in exchange for war material. Finally he urged that closer contact be established with Chiang Kai-shek, who was living 'in great isolation', and that Britain should strive to achieve 'a negotiated peace between China and Japan'.[10] Sir Robert Vansittart expressed full concurrence.[11] The consensus among officials in the Far Eastern department was that it was unwise to try to move too quickly. Dening wrote: 'This Department, I trust, shares the view that our concessions in China should ultimately be liquidated in any final settlement of the Far Eastern situation, and indeed that view has been held for many years. But it is not a decision which can be made rashly or which can be put into effect at a moment's notice.'[12] Brenan thought that Britain had to face the fact that eventually her political interests in north China would face extinction and her commercial interests would be severely reduced. Undoubtedly a readjustment in policy to accept the change would be necessary 'in a way that will achieve the much desired *détente* with Japan without unduly alienating Chinese or American goodwill.'[13] This could not be satisfactorily accomplished either by hastening to reach quick agreement

---

[9] Ibid.
[10] Ibid.
[11] Minute by Vansittart, 29 Sept. 1939, ibid.
[12] Minute by Dening, 22 Sept. 1939, F.10356/87/10, F.O.371/23461.
[13] Minute by Brenan, 25 Sept. 1939, ibid.

with Japan at all costs or by retreating only when confronted by force. Brenan outlined a 'middle solution' under which the garrison would be withdrawn from Tientsin without any commitments, and the obstructive attitude to the Japanese economic schemes in north China abandoned in return for a firm Japanese offer to protect British nationals. He did not expect to meet the Japanese in central China, notably at Shanghai, since the United States attached special significance to preserving the foreign position there.

A further impetus to intervention to promote a general settlement in China came on 24 September when Craigie sent an urgent telegram to London reporting that he had pursued an informal approach, from a source apparently in touch with the Japanese prime minister, to ascertain what opportunities existed for British mediation between Japan and China. Craigie explained that he had not originally intended examining the proposal before the Tientsin dispute had been resolved, but he had reflected on the Nomonhan truce, marking the end of the bitter fighting on the border between Manchukuo and Mongolia that had lasted since May 1939, and believed that the contingency of rapidly improving relations between Japan and Russia rendered delay most undesirable. He had, therefore, sent the military attaché to see General Koiso; Koiso had discussed the approach with Abe and the minister of war, General Hata, and the Japanese attitude was cautiously favourable. Japan drew two matters to the attention of the British government: a wish that sympathy should be shown towards the Wang Ching-wei regime and the resumption of the Tientsin conference at an early date. Craigie wished to act promptly in continuation of the exchanges by conveying willingness to provide facilities at Hong Kong for Sino-Japanese negotiations, and suggested that Clark Kerr be instructed to see Chiang Kai-shek.

Halifax decided to bring the subject before the war cabinet immediately. A full discussion took place on 25 September. Objections to the proposed course of action were voiced on the grounds that no impression that Britain was anxious to reach a settlement at China's expense should be communicated, and that it was arguable whether an end to the Sino-Japanese war was in Britain's interest as it might encourage Japanese expansion south. It was also held that Chiang Kai-shek personified the new spirit of China and Japan could ultimately be defeated by the force of Chinese nationalism. The cabinet requested the chiefs of staff to assess China's ability to continue fighting and to indicate whether or not it was sensible to encourage negotiations.[14] The following day the chief of the air staff presented the conclusions of the chiefs of staff. In their view, there was no reason to expect the collapse of Chinese military resistance; it was essential for Britain to avoid military involvement in East Asia while the neutrality of Italy was not assured; and from the narrowly military assessment, it was preferable that the Sino-Japanese war should go on. In the ensuing debate in cabinet, the approaching formation of Wang Ching-wei's regime was regarded as possibly presaging civil war in China and it was felt that a solution of the conflict in China could lead to a Japanese attack on the Netherlands East Indies. Other members of the cabinet alluded to the danger of the Soviet Union playing a mediatory role, which would be most undesirable. It was decided that Clark Kerr should see Chiang Kai-shek and inform him of the Japanese position but that it should be emphasized to Chiang that Britain had no wish to undermine his resistance.[15] On 9 October Halifax told the cabinet that as doubt had now arisen as to the reliability of Craigie's intermediary, he believed it was best for Clark Kerr not to raise the matter with Chiang on his visit to Chungking.[16] There the intense consideration of British mediation lapsed.

However, the Foreign Office, the Treasury, and the Board of Trade proceeded to examine relations to see if limited improvements in the economic sphere were possible. R. A. Butler supported such a development and a leading part in the reappraisal was played by Sir George Sansom. Sansom had now retired from the Tokyo embassy and was temporarily assisting the Foreign Office in London. The major difficulties in seeking a trade agreement lay in the exigencies of the wartime crisis, with the inevitable pressure to reduce purchases to

[14] War cabinet conclusions, 25 Sept. 1939, 26(39)7, Cab.65/1.
[15] War cabinet conclusions, 26 Sept. 1939, 28(39)7, Cab.65/1.
[16] War cabinet conclusions, 9 Oct. 1939, 42(39)7, Cab.65/1.

essentials and eschew over-committing sterling.[17] Shudo, commercial counsellor of the Japanese embassy, suggested that Britain and Japan should enter into an informal 'gentlemen's agreement' concerning the balance of payments. The suggestion was prompted by the implementation of import controls by Britain resulting in a fall in Japanese exports to Britain. Shudo stated that Japan would be willing to supply considerable quantities of foodstuffs, raw materials, and other commodities in return for whatever could be supplied in the field of machinery, metals, and chemicals. Japan wanted to obtain supplies of raw materials from the Commonwealth, especially raw wool from the Australian and New Zealand clip. Sansom saw Shigemitsu on 9 October to discuss the general prospects of using trade to improve relations. He told the ambassador that while the British government ardently desired to improve relations, Shudo's proposals could only be met with difficulty or at the expense of other neutrals: he felt that the first priority was to alleviate tension between Britain and Japan in China. Shigemitsu said British interests in China were suffering owing to the refusal to recognize realities there and it would be otiose to expect improvement until Britain made a gesture herself: it would be unwise to link the political situation in China and Anglo-Japanese economic relations too directly.[18] Butler minuted that he supported a barter agreement that would have indirect results on the British position in China.[19] After discussions with the Board of Trade, the Foreign Office concluded that three kinds of agreement were theoretically possible — a multilateral agreement extending to the Dominions and India to assure supplies to Japan, a normal war trade agreement or a restricted and informal commercial agreement dealing with Great Britain alone. The first two alternatives were undesirable, since in the former case protracted exchanges with the Dominions would be unavoidable and a normal war agreement would be inappropriate as there was no question of Japan's securing

---

[17] Board of Trade to Foreign Office, 11 Oct. 1939, F10970/1054/23, F.O.371/23568. For the standard account of British trade policy, see W. N. Medlicott, *The Economic Blockade*, 2 vols. (H.M.S.O., London, 1952-9).

[18] Minute by Sansom, 9 Oct. 1939, F10898/1054/23, F.O.371/23568.

[19] Minute by Butler, 12 Oct. 1939, ibid.

commodities which could subsequently be sent to Germany. If the third alternative were applied special inducements would have to be included because the volume of trade would otherwise be too small. Such inducements might comprise additional authorization by the Treasury and Ministry of Supply of sterling available for expenditure in Japan, no increase in import licences to private traders to give Japan part of commodities in Britain's possession, such as wool from Australia, and the modification of export regulations in favour of Japan. The benefits to be derived from such an agreement would be concrete, such as the release of frozen yen balances in Japan, a small increase in exports, and the possible prevention of shipments of soya beans to Germany through Siberia. The disadvantages would be that the political gains would be intangible and not apparent for some time. More seriously, it could be objected that the repercussions of such an agreement in the United States would be regrettable at a time when the United States was preparing for the termination of the commercial treaty.[20] An interdepartmental meeting was held on 24 November to discuss the preparation of a cabinet memorandum; the Treasury and the Ministry of Supply vehemently opposed any agreement to purchase specific quantities of Japanese goods and any assistance to Japan to obtain raw materials in the British Empire. The reason was that purchases would increase Japan's sterling balances; a British undertaking to buy stipulated amounts would force prices to rise prematurely and it was too early in the war to estimate with accuracy what future requirements would be. Sansom concluded, after a careful appraisal of the circumstances, that it would not be advisable to pursue this matter further. If it was thought necessary to send a communication to Tokyo, Sansom believed that it could be pointed out that Britain was not treating Japan as stringently as she herself was being treated and that nearly £2 million of balances were frozen in

---

[20] Foreign Office memorandum, 8 Nov. 1939, enclosed with Board of Trade to Foreign Office, 13 Nov. 1939, F11899/1054/23, F.O.371/23568. Among the commodities which Japan obtained from the Commonwealth the following were prominent: iron ore (Malaya and Australia), pig iron (India), manganese ore (India and Malaya), zinc (Canada and Australia), tin (Malaya), lead, nickel, and aluminium (Canada), raw cotton (India), wool (Australia), jute (India), rubber (Straits Settlements and Malaya), F11960/1054/23, F.O.371/23568.

Japan under exchange control.[21] Butler expressed regret that
no more progress could be made but thanked Sansom 'for ex-
ploring the question from every angle'.[22] Later in December
Sansom minuted that Craigie should be informed that Britain
could definitely not make an agreement with Japan; meanwhile, it was hoped to take appreciable quantities of Japanese
products if no difficulties were encountered with prices,
tonnage, and other factors. It was possible that talks currently
being held by the Bank of England and Japanese financial
authorities would lead to a limited payments agreement
embracing British purchases from Japan and the sale to Japan
of goods from the Commonwealth.[23] Butler commented that
he would welcome a payments agreement, adding: 'I understand from Viscount Kano that these talks were going well.
Remember that I am just as nervous of being left at the post by
the U.S.A. as of galloping nimbly round the course with her.
In the latter context, we may well go lame, particularly if the
recent frost returns.'[24] Yet again, therefore, an avenue for
improving relations was explored and rejected. The attitude of
the Treasury was decisive but, in addition, apprehension concerning the effects on the United States were important.
Butler was willing to discount such fears to a greater extent
than others in the Foreign Office and cabinet but his views did
not convince Halifax. Butler, as was often the case, tended to
exaggerate the concrete benefit to be derived from offering
concessions to Japan. British policy was tied closely to the
United States by the over-all demands of the war.

As the new year of 1940 opened, the endless debate was
resumed as to the best means of helping the 'moderates' to
resist the 'extremists' in Japan. The American State Department was sceptical of the advantages supposedly stemming
from supporting the moderates: it was first necessary to discover how influential the moderates were and what they could
produce, if anything, and the United States doubted whether
Japanese frustrations in China would lead to expansion south.

[21] Minute by Sansom, 27 Nov. 1939, F12160/1054/23, F.O.371/23568.
[22] Minutes by Sansom and Butler, 2 and 4 Dec. 1939, F12464/1054/23, F.O.
371/23568.
[23] Minute by Sansom, 21 Dec. 1939, F13010/10/15204/23, F.O.371/23568.
[24] Minute by Butler, 8 Jan. 1940, ibid.

A summary of the American assessment was sent to Craigie, who dispatched his own comments on 1 January 1940.[25] Craigie maintained that it was extremely superficial to ignore the difference between moderates and extremists; the moderates wanted gradual economic progress through achieving control of major raw materials and the expansion of overseas markets, whereas the extremists aspired to world domination. The moderates were, he felt, now more powerful in Tokyo because of current disillusionment with Germany and Italy. Craigie feared that if the United States applied serious economic measures against Japan, it could lead to an extremist government taking office with a possible re-orientation in policy towards the Soviet Union and a re-appraisal of policy over the European war as a consequence. He rejected the view that the settlement of minor disputes simply encouraged Japan to insist more strongly on the larger issues as revealing ignorance of Japanese psychology. There was much uncertainty in the Japanese political scene and rising popular dissatisfaction with inflation; the Abe government relied for its survival on successes in foreign policy and was working for better relations with Great Britain and the United States.[26] Craigie clearly thought that a more sympathetic approach to this aspiration should be shown in London and Washington. In the Foreign Office minutes dissent was expressed. Dening observed that the weakness of the moderates was that they took advantage of the actions of the extremists, claiming simultaneously that they were powerless. With regard to American economic action against Japan, Dening wrote: 'I think we are of opinion here that an embargo by America would frustrate Japan's aims in a comparatively short space of time, though not immediately. That would not necessarily deter Japan from proceeding to an act of desperation but it is important to note that an act of desperation would *not* solve Japan's problems.'[27] He agreed that there was a danger of a more extreme administration assuming office in Tokyo, although it did not inevitably follow that the con-

---

[25] Craigie to Halifax, 1 Jan. 1940 (received 12 Jan. 1940), F297/1193/61, F.O.371/24708.
[26] Ibid.
[27] Minute by Dening, 12 Jan. 1940, ibid.

sequences would be disastrous. Sansom, who had frequently clashed with Craigie in the past, observed succinctly:

The views with which Sir R. Craigie disagrees may be mistaken, but they are not superficial. It is my firm conviction, after many years of study and observation, that there is no really *effective* moderate opinion in Japan; and that the only way in which such opinion may become effective is through the defeat of extremists by outside forces—a defeat which the moderates cannot compass by their own determination and efforts.[28]

R. A. Butler preferred, to some extent, to accept Craigie's opinions:

We are in danger of counting on the Americans and then being let down. But I agree that an act of desperation would not solve Jap problems . . . I think we must be very careful to consider with the respect which they deserve our ambassador's views. He has had a very difficult time. He may overrate the importance of the Japanese moderates and in this connection I have studied Sir G. Sansom's views.[29]

In all essentials, Sansom's judgement was correct. There were few Japanese, and these were uninfluential, who were fundamentally opposed to the more bellicose policy pursued since 1931. There was a wide measure of consensus in Japan that the country's problems were not appreciated or understood in the west and that Japan was entirely justified in implementing a policy of expansion throughout East Asia. As has been observed, there was a unique character to Japanese nationalism between 1931 and 1945 and near unanimity within Japanese society in support of it.[30] The new government of Admiral Yonai Mitsumasa, with Arita Hachiro at the *Gaimusho*, was anxious to secure improved relations with Great Britain and the United States but on condition that these powers were willing to meet Japan by making considerable concessions to her in return; inevitably such concessions would prominently involve the position of China.

[28] Minute by Sansom, 15 Jan. 1940, ibid. For Sansom's disagreements with Craigie, see K. Sansom, *Sir George Sansom: A Memoir* (Diplomatic Press, Tallahassee, Fla., 1972), pp. 96, 97, 99, 115–17.
[29] Minute by Butler, 1 Feb. 1940, ibid. See also *I.M.T.F.E.*, Record, Exhibit 1015, pp. 9672–3.
[30] See J. W. Morley (ed.), *Dilemmas of Growth in Prewar Japan*, pp. 489–510.

A triangular exchange of views developed in January and February 1940 between Craigie, Clark Kerr, and the Foreign Office. Craigie explained that the tougher American policy was mistimed and should have come a year earlier, when it would have stood a greater chance of achieving a satisfactory response from Japan in the face of economic pressure; this was indeed the policy advocated by Craigie at the time.[31] With the war in Europe, the situation was radically different. There seemed to be two courses of action for Britain to follow, either to persevere with the existing policy of encouraging the United States in a firm attitude or of offering compensation to Japan in areas outside China, which would not conflict with American policy. The latter would involve recognition of Japan's basic problems of lack of raw materials and rapid growth of population. Clark Kerr fundamentally disagreed in a broadside from Chungking. For years, he remarked, Britain had been unable to translate her expressions of verbal sympathy at Geneva into tangible forms; further, she had been compelled to submit to humiliating and abusive Japanese actions. It would be absurd to dissuade the United States from its new policy:

The new order in East Asia has been something which we have told ourselves that we can in no circumstances accept because it promises early destruction of all that we value in the Far East, and after that still greater dangers. About the meaning of the new order there can now be no doubt despite the occasional friendly assurances which Sir R. Craigie is obliged to put in the balance against the outbursts of the Tokyo press and assertions of the Japanese Generals. We now know it is the purpose of the Americans to use the power they possess to frustrate the new order and it is clear their Government has popular opinion behind it. It is obviously in our interests to see this frustration takes place . . .[32]

Equally it would be foolish to risk antagonizing the United States by making concessions to Japan. The Americans understood that Britain could do little to assist in the Far East but it was vital that 'we . . . at least mark time until the day comes when we shall be able to catch them up'. In his rejoinder

[31] Craigie to Halifax, 1 Jan. 1940 (received 12 Jan. 1940). F.297/193/61, F.O. 371/24708.

[32] Clark Kerr to Halifax, 4 Feb. 1940, F870/193/61, F.O.371/24708.

Craigie stated that there was justification for cautious optimism, for the Japanese nation was becoming increasingly conscious of the application of the law of diminishing returns in China; he believed that the imminent establishment of Wang Ching-wei's government demonstrated a wish to retire from China as soon as this could be accomplished in keeping with saving face. The extension of aid to Chiang Kai-shek by foreign powers was at once seized on by Japanese militarists as an insult to the nation. To Craigie's mind, it was preferable to leave China to continue the struggle as at present, which would undoubtedly culminate in Japan's withdrawal from south and central China; he admitted that it would be far more difficult to force Japan out of northern China. To intervene with limited aid for Chiang Kai-shek would anger the Japanese without being sufficient to defeat them. In the world context, Britain and Japan had much in common in their mutual hostility to the Soviet Union. It might suit Japan in the future to make peace with Chiang on terms acceptable to the generalissimo in order to join 'a strong combination of the Powers bent on settling accounts with the U.S.S.R. once and for all'.[33] A tough American attitude was valuable so long as the United States did not embark on drastic economic measures; the threat was more significant than the actual imposition of sanctions. Craigie's two telegrams of 1 January were sent to the prime minister for his consideration. Chamberlain commented that Craigie's proposal of meeting Japan's grievances on raw materials and overseas markets should be examined 'though the prospect is not attractive at first sight'.[34]

In the main the Foreign Office sided with Clark Kerr rather than Craigie. In a memorandum for the prime minister, Dening pointed out that, within the previous half-century, Japan had acquired Formosa, Korea, the southern half of Sakhalin, the Marshall and Caroline islands, and Manchuria and could not convincingly claim that she lacked territory. However, she did lack some raw materials and adequate overseas markets for her manufactures. If Britain were not at war,

[33] Craigie to Halifax, 26 Feb. 1940, F1429/193/61, F.O.371/24708.
[34] Syers (prime minister's office) to Mallet, 15 Jan. 1940, F420/193/61, F.O.371/24708.

it would be appropriate to consider concessions to Japan including the abolition of colonial quotas and access to raw materials, assuming the Dominions and India assented. In war conditions, the sole means of advance lay in the exploratory conversations proceeding between the Bank of England and the Bank of Japan to reach a payments agreement relating to wool and other commodities. If the cabinet, the Dominions, and India concurred, it would in addition be feasible to inform Japan that, at the end of the war and as part of a peace settlement, a reorganization of the world economy incorporating a new deal for Japan might take place. Dening agreed this would not satisfy Japan but he felt that all Britain could do was to impress upon Japan that victory in Europe offered the hope of a solution to Japan's economic problems.[35] Sansom reviewed matters in a lengthy minute written on 6 February.[36] It was prompted not only by the controversy surrounding Craigie's opinions but by a letter from Henry L. Stimson, the former American secretary of state and vociferous advocate of resistance to Japanese aggression, and by an article by Walter Lippman. Sansom deemed it wise to reflect on the evolution of American far eastern policy and the form it would assume in the future. The aim of American policy was to halt Japanese expansion and to ensure the vindication of the moral principles to which Cordell Hull attached so much importance. If, therefore, the United States expected Japan to make peace with China in accordance with the terms of the nine-power treaty, the question had to be posed as to how Japan would react to full-scale American economic sanctions designed to achieve this objective. Japan could react in one of three ways: submit to the pressure and make peace in accordance with the *status quo* of 1937 or even 1931; declare war on the United States or take the risk of war; or decline to submit and simply continue with her existing policy. Sansom believed Japan would never surrender except if defeated in war. Neither did he think Japan would go to war so long as the Japanese believed they could pursue their policy in China without recourse to such action. Therefore, he held that Japan would continue the war in China with such changes as were

---

[35] Memorandum by Dening, no date, enclosed in Mallet to Syers, 25 Jan. 1940, ibid.
[36] Minute by Sansom, 6 Feb. 1940, F924/193/61, F.O. 371/24708.

rendered necessary by American economic measures. These changes could include reaching agreement with the Soviet Union so that the appreciable volume of Russian aid to China would be stopped, and accepting a reduction in living standards and harsher conditions. Sansom felt that preparations must be made for economic sanctions leading to war:

Should the argument set forth above be sound, we are bound to conclude that, if the object of United States policy is not only to stop further Japanese aggression in China but to repair the damage already done to China, and if the United States Government is determined to achieve that object, she must inevitably go to war with Japan. I am not here endeavouring to state as a general proposition that economic sanctions cannot be effective without war or the determination to go to war, but merely stating that, in circumstances now foreseeable, the United States cannot hope to compel Japan to surrender her gains in China by the mere imposition of economic pressure.[37]

On the other hand, it was possible that the United States would apply partial, rather than comprehensive, economic sanctions. This would not compel the Japanese to retreat and the United States would be in a dilemma. Ultimately the United States would have to decide whether or not to go to war. Britain had to determine her policy in the light of this analysis: should she keep in step with the Americans, what were the dangers of a Japanese move south, and would the Japanese adopt a policy more favourably disposed to Russia? Sansom urged that the whole subject be taken up in Washington; in particular, Britain needed to know if the United States had assessed the respective problems of being too stringent or too soft. Meanwhile, he agreed with Dening that the best means of advancing British interests lay in co-operating closely with the United States. Brenan and Howe minuted agreement, Brenan noting that the State Department had indicated that the United States was prepared to maintain a policy of limited pressure and moral disapprobation for twenty years.[38] In late February Lothian spoke to Cordell Hull and Stanley Hornbeck; they believed that Japan's economic position was

[37] Ibid.
[38] Minutes by Brenan and Howe, 15 Feb. and 4 Mar. 1940, ibid.

deteriorating and that Chinese morale was high. A further American loan to China was under consideration but it was uncertain if action would be taken on the resolution for an embargo of Japan, moved by Senator Pittman, until the attitude of Congress became known. Lothian expressed satisfaction with Anglo-American co-operation whereby the navies of the two powers defended each other's interests in the Atlantic and the Pacific. Hornbeck inquired if Britain still feared that American policy could lead to a Japanese attack on British and Dutch possessions in the Far East, to which Lothian skilfully replied that he did not think Britain was worried at the present American approach but that she was apprehensive about developments that could promote Japanese aggression while there was no British fleet at Singapore.[39] Lothian felt that the Americans regarded Japanese expansion in the near future to be improbable. On the whole, the Foreign Office inclined to agree with the American estimate; however, Dening believed that the worsening economic climate in Japan could result in an internal explosion. Optimistically he thought this could lead to a reversion to 'Shidehara policy' although he recognized that the opposite might also occur.[40] He added that he doubted whether the Australian government, 'whose strange fear of Japanese aggression it seems just hopeless to allay', would be satisfied with the American assessment. Cadogan commented that he would not object to an explosion so long as it did not assume the form of southward expansion. Butler succinctly remarked: 'Let's have another metaphor. On the whole I prefer the therapeutic to the lancing method of dealing with boils.'[41] Whatever the consequences, Britain was tied to American policy.

One episode of Anglo-Japanese conflict promoted by the European war arose in January 1940, when a Japanese liner, the *Asama Maru*, was stopped by a British destroyer in order to take off some German passengers. German ratings in the United States were known to be planning to return to Germany via Japan and it was important to prevent the addition of recruits to the German navy. It was, however, a

---

[39] Lothian to Halifax, 24 Feb. 1940, F1398/193/61, F.O.371/24708.
[40] Minute by Dening, 27 Feb. 1940, ibid.
[41] Minutes by Cadogan and Butler, 28 Feb. 1940, ibid.

delicate operation to halt a Japanese vessel and remove passengers; maximum discretion would be necessary in the conduct of the enterprise. The original aim was to stop the *Asama Maru* some one hundred miles from the Japanese coast. The ship was late and not at the estimated location so that the interception occurred thirty-five miles from Yokohama. A vigorous Japanese protest ensued. Halifax was disturbed at the danger of a deterioration in relations with Japan and suggested the possibility of an agreement whereby the Japanese would undertake not to permit German nationals capable of.joining the armed forces from travelling on their ships. The Japanese foreign minister, Arita, initially demanded the return of the twenty-one Germans removed, but a compromise was eventually reached whereby Britain returned nine of the Germans and both sides felt that it should be feasible to avoid future difficulties. The swift resolution of the dispute was attributable yet again to the diplomatic skill of Sir Robert Craigie in negotiating with the *Gaimusho* and to the fact that the Yonai government did not desire a serious crisis to develop at this juncture in view of the uncertainties of the European situation. Craigie was correct in implicitly criticizing the government and, in particular, the Admiralty, for implementing a policy of questionable sagacity given the broader issues involved.[42]

In the constant reflection and reconsideration of British policy and the wish to secure a better relationship with Japan if possible, the emergence of the Wang Ching-wei regime in 1939-40 is of considerable interest. Wang Ching-wei had long been one of the most prominent and attractive figures in the Kuomintang, with impeccable revolutionary credentials extending back to his role in the plotting against the Ch'ing dynasty before 1911. A close friend of Sun Yat-sen, he had originally been identified with the left wing of the Kuomintang and its co-operation with the Chinese communists. After disillusionment with the communists in 1927, Wang had veered back towards the centre of the party. He was unhappy with his position, principally owing to the rivalry and ani-

---

[42] For a brief discussion of naval aspects, see P. Haggie, 'The Royal Navy and the Far Eastern Problem, 1931-1941', pp. 359-62. See also, E. L. Woodward, *British Foreign Policy in the Second World War*, ii (H.M.S.O., London, 1971), pp. 89-90.

mosity between Chiang Kai-shek and himself. In the later 1930s Wang moved away from the Kuomintang, his independence having been accentuated by an unsuccessful attempt to assassinate him. While he was no slavish admirer of the Japanese, Wang believed it was counter-productive to pursue a hostile line towards Japan. Since China was too weak to resist Japan on her own, Wang wished to come to terms with Japan on conditions that would, he hoped, permit a substantial measure of autonomy. This was not as surprising or unpatriotic as it might appear, for there had always been a tradition of friendship with Japan beginning with the co-operation between Sun Yat-sen and the Japanese nationalist adventurers at the beginning of the twentieth century.[43] Japan was a source of inspiration to Asian nationalist movements in the outstanding success of her modernization, even if the success had some disturbing concomitants. As John Hunter Boyle has pointed out, Wang's motives comprised a mixture of genuine concern for his country and of personal ambition.[44] At any rate, by the summer of 1939 Wang had established amicable contacts with the authorities in Tokyo, and rumours proliferated about his intention to set up a new reorganized Kuomintang regime in Nanking. Clark Kerr, the ambassador in China, and the Foreign Office viewed the prospect with concern but, in addition, with fascination. There was, in the autumn of 1939, more willingness to envisage some degree of acceptance of Wang Ching-wei than might have been expected. Wang at first offered, or seemed to offer, the prospect of escape from the stalemate in China and of easing Britain's heavy burdens which was most desirable given the war in Europe. The early hopes were soon to be disappointed.

In early October 1939 Clark Kerr reported that Wang might soon establish a government in Nanking. If so, it would have the warm support of Japan, might be recognized by Italy

---

[43] For the most recent study of Wang, see J. H. Boyle, *China and Japan at War 1937-1945: the Politics of Collaboration* (Stanford University Press, Stanford, 1972); see also G. E. Bunker, *The Peace Conspiracy: Wang Ching-wei and the China War, 1937-41* (Harvard University Press, London, 1972) and H. L. Boorman, 'Wang Ching-wei: China's Romantic Radical', *Political Science Quarterly*, lxxix (1964), 504-25. See M. B. Jansen, *The Japanese and Sun Yatsen* (Harvard University Press, Cambridge, Mass., 1954) for an illuminating discussion of this aspect.

[44] Boyle, pp. 336-63.

and even perhaps France, which was flirting with Wang. Clark
Kerr assumed that Britain and the United States would continue to recognize the Chungking government. However:

I feel . . . that while we are bound to maintain a formal attitude of
non-recognition, we can do a good deal to mitigate its effects if we
are allowed a wide discretion in regard to our informal relations with
the new Government and its satellites.

I consider that we should try to prepare the ground now by making
(and encouraging consuls to make) as many friendly personal contacts as possible with people like Chu Min Yi who are likely to be in a
position to pull strings in Nanking. We should explain to them that
the question of recognition does not arise at present and cannot in
any case arise unless and until the new regime has shown that it is not
a puppet of Japan but is a genuine Chinese Government accepted as
the Government of China by consensus of Chinese public opinion;
but that if they are genuinely actuated by patriotic motives they have
nothing to gain and everything to lose by allowing or encouraging the
Japanese to destroy all foreign interests but their own in occupied
China, and that we look to them to put the brake on their friends and
avoid forcing us into a position of hostility.[45]

He added that Britain should emphasize that she had not
wanted to intervene in China's internal affairs and that her
actions had been governed by her commitments to the League
of Nations, but that, if a Chinese government commanding
the confidence of the Chinese people stated that it did not
want assistance, then the position would be different. Clark
Kerr thought that the United States had already gone further
than Britain in communicating with Japanese puppets: the
American consul-general had met the mayor of Shanghai and
an American representative had visited Wang Ching-wei.[46]
The officials of the Far Eastern department expressed some
agreement with Clark Kerr but warned that it would be rash to
proceed too rapidly. A. L. Scott believed that it would be premature 'for us to get down off the fence on which we have sat
for so long and we must at all times consider American reactions with a view to their support in the war against
Germany, but to act as suggested would seem a reasonable

---

[45] Clark Kerr to Halifax, 5 Oct. 1939, F10814/4/10, F.O.371/23407.
[46] Clark Kerr to Halifax, 5 Oct. 1939, ibid.

policy of re-insurance.'[47] Sir John Brenan, the leading authority on China in the department, held that the situation could develop into a civil war between the communists and anti-communists, .with Russia and Japan supporting the two sides respectively. 'In that case we should certainly not want to take sides, or at all events not the side against Japan. Our policy of support for the Chungking government would have to be modified in order to meet the new situation.'[48] Brenan endorsed Clark Kerr's assessment, but feared the consuls in China might be encouraged to go too far in their anxiety to meet local officials.

At the beginning of November 1939 Craigie expected Wang's regime formally to be proclaimed at any time; the warning came too soon, for the regime was not set up until March 1940 and not fully until November 1940. Craigie stated that Wang was proving tough in his negotiations with the Japanese, which was encouraging. He advised that Britain's approach should be one of 'reserve and caution'.[49] Brenan approved the advice. A month later Craigie went further and an argument ensued with the Foreign Office, who felt the ambassador was advocating an unacceptable measure of appeasement. Craigie said he had spoken to an important Japanese official, who had intimated that after an agreement on Tientsin had been reached, Britain and Japan should advance to more complex issues, the first of which would involve the new regime in China. The new government would be primarily occupied with central China but would be involved, too, in north China; the chief distinction between the two regions would be the establishment of a special area to act as a *cordon sanitaire* against Russia. The aim of the negotiations between Wang and Japan was to ensure that the regime would be strong enough to warrant official Japanese recognition. The principal policy of Wang's government would be opposition to communism, which should attract opinion in Chungking. Japanese troops would remain until Wang was securely established. When this stage was arrived at, efforts would be made to improve trade and it was hoped that Britain

---

[47] Minute by Scott, 9 Oct. 1939, ibid.
[48] Minute by Brenan, 10 Oct. 1939, ibid.
[49] Craigie to Halifax, 3 Nov. 1939, F11542/4/10, F.O.371/23407.

would assist in currency stabilization; there would not be a new currency but separate banking arrangements for the occupied part of central China would be necessary to facilitate trade.[50] The Far Eastern department showed alarm at the report. Scott observed that Japan's true intentions were revealed — 'we are in fact expected to be Japan's stalking horse in China'.[51] Brenan wrote that it entirely confirmed the views of the Foreign Office. Japan intended to use a settlement of the Tientsin crisis as an alleged change of policy by Great Britain connoting acquiescence in the new order. The price to be paid would be acceptance of Japan's 'virtual annexation' of north China and Inner Mongolia plus recognition of a puppet regime which would only be allowed the freedom deemed adequate by the Japanese army:

If it were really necessary to placate Japan now, at all costs, in view of our European difficulties, that is how we could do it — for a while — but the cost would include the alienation of American opinion and the abandonment of our existing interests in China. Moreover, how long would the appeasement last? There is no reason to suppose that if we now help the Japanese to establish themselves in China they will be deterred from using their increased strength in the future to continue their expansion at our expense; especially if we show signs of weakness in the European war and have in the meantime forfeited our claim to American support by our change of policy.

It seems to me that our response to overtures of this sort should be one of polite scepticism; we should, of course, not go out of our way to provoke Japanese hostility; but Japan is in a mess and we should leave her to get out of it, if she can, without our help. Let us see how much genuine Chinese support her new regime in China can command before we take an attitude towards it. And above all let us see how Japan is going to satisfy the United States Government in the forthcoming struggle about the commercial treaty, without allowing a wedge to be driven between ourselves and the Americans, which of course is one of the more important objectives of the present Japanese scheme.[52]

Dening criticized Craigie for having listened uncritically to the exposition of future Japanese policy. He urged that the ambas-

[50] Craigie to Halifax, 8 Dec. 1939, F12503/4/10, F.O.371/23407.
[51] Minute by Scott, 9 Dec. 1939, ibid.
[52] Minute by Brenan, 11 Dec. 1939, ibid.

sador be instructed to exercise care, 'Otherwise on the parallel of the present negotiations about Tientsin, we may find that he has committed us to discussing the future of the regenerated China.'[53] Ashley Clarke dismissed the Japanese approach as 'all very old stuff', consisting of a rehash of Konoe's peace proposal of December 1938 and of Hirota's three points of 1935. He was disturbed at the fact that Craigie seemed to believe that they offered the basis for agreement.[54]

A telegram incorporating the substance of these minutes was sent to Tokyo on 14 December. The telegram ended somewhat abruptly, 'I feel sure that these considerations are very much present to Your Excellency's mind and that in any further conversations of this kind, you will bear in mind that an improvement in Anglo-Japanese relations along these lines would appear very difficult of reconciliation with the professed policy of His Majesty's Government.'[55] In his reply, Craigie termed the rebuke 'a little hard': Britain was not being asked to recognize a puppet regime. It could not be expected that the Japanese could tolerate a fully independent regime from the start, but it should be possible for the regime to obtain more autonomy as it evolved. In a lengthy minute, Dening stated that there was unfortunately a marked divergence of views between the Foreign Office and the Tokyo embassy as to whether it would be feasible to reach an agreement with Japan without sacrificing principles. In Dening's opinion, any negotiation with Japan involving trade would violate article two of the nine-power treaty. Furthermore, it was most unlikely that Japan would ever allow any regime a genuine measure of independence. He ended on a more considerate note by commenting that Craigie faced arduous problems and that another exchange of views with him was desirable.[56] The subject was not urgent since the formation of Wang's regime had again been postponed. The right policy, as Craigie had suggested himself, was to insist amicably on Britain's rights and trust that Japan would eventually be persuaded to accept their validity, just as the effects of geography and economics

[53] Minute by Dening, 11 Dec. 1939, ibid.
[54] Minute by Clarke, 11 Dec. 1939, ibid.
[55] Halifax to Craigie, 14 Dec. 1939, ibid.
[56] Minute by Dening, 21 Dec. 1939, ibid.

were eroding Japan's military fortitude. Sansom and Brenan concurred; Butler and Cadogan minuted that the matter could be left there for the present.[57]

In the middle of January 1940 Craigie spoke to the vice-minister of foreign affairs, who indicated that it would take some time for Wang's new administration to establish itself. Craigie's exchange with the Foreign Office apparently led him to talk more robustly, for he said there was only one way of securing peace in China and that was to come to terms with Chiang Kai-shek. The vice-minister replied that this was impossible because of Chiang's insistence on the complete withdrawal of Japanese forces and of Chiang's refusal to break with the communists. Brenan aptly observed that the Japanese were putting the 'cart before the horse' because Chiang could only break with the communists after he had made an acceptable peace. The Chungking government was clearly un-easy about the coming formation of Wang's regime, for Quo Tai-chi asked Butler what would be done to discourage Wang. Butler could offer little solace, simply referring to Britain's present problems in Europe. Feeling in the Far Eastern department had become more critical both of Wang and of Japan early in 1940. The protracted talks between the two sides underlined all the difficulties inherent in the situation. Butler was alone in enigmatically discerning some grounds for optimism: 'I yet think it possible that Wang will form a bridge. There are several circumstances including the particularity of his own character which are intriguing.'[58] In March Japan in-formed Britain that Wang's regime would shortly be in-augurated.[59] Shigemitsu, the Japanese ambassador, told Butler that a conference was taking place in Nanking attended by representatives of the various Japanese-sponsored regimes in China and Mongolia to decide formally on the choice of the capital city of the new government; he said that it would be Nanking. Shigemitsu hoped Britain would regard the develop-ment benevolently:

The Ambassador said that he need not ask me whether we should acknowledge the new government, but trusted that British policy in

[57] Minutes by Sansom and Brenan, 21 Dec. 1939, ibid.
[58] Minute by Butler, 1 Feb. 1940, F772/27/10, F.O.371/24659.
[59] Minute by Butler, 4 Mar. 1940, F1116/27/10, F.O.371/24659.

the Far East would develop along such lines as would lead to an ultimate peace settlement. In his view this could best be reached by setting up Wang Ching-wei's Government. He hoped that contact would thereafter be established by that Government with Chungking and that thereby, with time, a settlement would be effected.[60]

Butler replied that British policy on recognition of the Chinese government was clear and firmly based; Great Britain naturally desired a fair solution to the struggle in China and would follow developments with much interest. Shigemitsu warned that it would only be a matter of time before Japan went to war with Russia. Brenan reviewed matters with the aim of determining policy towards Wang's regime:[61] Wang's previous career did not suggest he was a traitor and the answer was that Wang was endeavouring to secure genuine autonomy; however, the Japanese would not grant it. Wang's policy would doubtless be based on ending extraterritoriality and privilege and seeking to gain as much as he could from Japan. Both Chinese and foreign interests would be compelled to give Wang partial *de facto* recognition, but there could be no likelihood of translating this into *de jure* recognition. Essentially British policy was to wait and see what success Wang enjoyed. It would be too dangerous to greet Wang's regime with any enthusiasm since it would encourage the Japanese to become more truculent, sacrifice friendship with Chungking, and alienate the United States. In reality Wang was to enjoy virtually no success whatever. The Japanese army had no intention of giving him real autonomy and Wang had committed himself too far to Japan to be able to retreat without abject humiliation. Against his wishes he became a Japanese puppet and died in 1944, a sad and broken figure.

The chief item of unfinished business in Anglo-Japanese relations in 1939–40 concerned the situation at Tientsin. While the most delicate phase had been averted through the temporary agreement negotiated by Craigie in July 1939, the atmosphere in Tientsin remained difficult and rumbles of further trouble were periodically heard. The problems, as before, involved the silver deposits belonging to the Chinese

---

[60] Minute by Butler, 21 Mar. 1940, F2073/27/10, F.O.371/24660. See also *I.M.T.F.E.*, Record, Exhibit 1016, pp. 9675-7.
[61] Minute by Brenan, 26 Mar. 1940, F2247/27/10, F.O.371/24660.

government, the circulation of the federal reserve currency in place of *fapi*, and the continued presence of the British garrison. The familiar ingredients of the far eastern dilemma were implicit. Britain ideally wanted to settle the dispute but had to bear in mind the attitudes of the United States and China, especially the former. The United States was strongly of the opinion that no concessions should be made to Japan and that Britain should stand firm, accepting the consequences; Japan sought to put pressure on Britain to accept her case in order to drive a wedge between Britain and the United States. British policy-makers unhappily attempted to make the best of the dilemma and repetitive debates continued between London, Tokyo, and Tientsin in 1939–40. At last agreement with Japan was reached in June 1940, to be overshadowed and dominated by Hitler's victories in Europe. On 1 September Hornbeck told Lord Lothian bluntly that the United States would deprecate any compromise with Japan over Tientsin.[62] The American attitude was subsequently instrumental in the decision not to withdraw the British garrison, although the Foreign Office and the War Office would have preferred to do so. Craigie pursued informal discussions with the *Gaimusho* to see if agreement was within reach. On 15 September he supported the proposal of Jamieson, the consul-general in Tientsin, that the silver deposits should be used to alleviate the suffering caused by the severe floods in Tientsin.[63] Brenan disliked the idea because the Chinese would not agree to it; they would rightly interpret it as further surrender to brute force, as had been the surrender of the four Chinese prisoners in August.[64] Butler indignantly dissented:

I cannot accept the above minute which says that we 'surrendered once more to the Japanese demands' over the four Chinese. We acted on evidence and I have no sense of surrender or shame whatever. My only doubt is whether the evidence could not have been with us before and whether there should ever be any shadow of doubt that our Concessions were used for concealing or harbouring suspects.[65]

[62] Lothian to Halifax, 1 Sept. 1939, F9938/8457/10, F.O.371/23533.
[63] Craigie to Halifax, 15 Sept. 1939, F10216/6457/10, F.O.371/23533.
[64] Minute by Brenan, 18 Sept. 1939, ibid.
[65] Minute by Butler, 20 Sept. 1939, ibid.

Butler disagreed with the American-inspired view that it was best for the Japanese to seize the silver by force; such 'self-immolation' would not necessarily be sensible. Except for a brief period in October, when he veered in the other direction, in deference to the United States, Craigie strongly supported persevering with discussions in Tokyo. It was in his view essential to wider improvement of relations with Japan. He reported on 18 September that Japan was unlikely to assent to the retention of silver in the bank of communications or its transference to a neutral bank; he saw the alternatives as using the silver for flood relief or transferring it to the Yokohama Specie Bank.[66] The drawback to the latter suggestion was that the Yokohama Specie Bank could hardly be considered neutral. Halifax told Craigie that great care was required to preserve American goodwill. The government wished, as regards silver, to have it sealed in the bank of communications or sealed in a neutral bank; as a last resort, the Yokohama Specie Bank would be acceptable but only in this context. If used in connection with flood relief, silver would probably have to be sold and funds provided for an organization such as the Red Cross; alternatively some form of Anglo-Japanese co-operation in flood relief could be envisaged. Craigie was instructed to approach the *Gaimusho* to see if talks could be re-opened.[67] When he saw Admiral Nomura, the foreign minister, Craigie was informed that the Japanese government was reluctant to resume negotiations unless there was a guarantee of success; Craigie replied that talks could not be pursued on such a basis.[68] Nomura's unenthusiastic response was attributable to the weakness of the Abe government and the pressure it faced from militant quarters, in both the *Gaimusho* and the army.[69] In the middle of October, Craigie had an interesting discussion with his American colleague, Joseph C. Grew. Grew told Craigie that American public opinion was turning against Japan and that if Japanese policy

[66] Craigie to Halifax, 18 Sept. 1939, F10278/6457/10, F.O.371/23533.
[67] Halifax to Craigie, 23 Sept. 1939, ibid.
[68] Craigie to Halifax, 1 Oct. 1939, F10600/6457/10, F.O.371/23533.
[69] A struggle for power was being waged within the *Gaimusho* between the extreme nationalists and those who were less bellicose. In addition, Nomura was not a career diplomat; as his later career as ambassador in Washington showed, he was an amiable, well-meaning man but lacking in assertiveness.

were not modified, an embargo of crucial Japanese imports would ensue. Craigie advised that, in these circumstances, it was vital not to risk offending the United States and he recommended that no further initiative be taken to reopen the Tientsin talks. Halifax brought Craigie's request to the attention of the war cabinet and successfully persuaded his colleagues to defer any action to withdraw the British garrison.[70] At the same time the consul-general at Tientsin warned that more demonstrations against the British were taking place and that the outlook was bad.[71] Halifax spoke to Shigemitsu on 20 October; the ambassador said that progress could only be made if the British attitude towards silver changed so as to recognize that it belonged to the north China regime.[72] He regarded currency as less difficult: it was a matter of local administration. Shigemitsu proposed that the contentious issues be resolved singly instead of reconvening the Tientsin conference. Halifax observed that a compromise was required and the ambassador's arguments would be considered. Craigie duly consulted Kato of the *Gaimusho* once more, and believed that progress was being achieved on the silver issue.[73] Brenan investigated the nature of silver stocks in a memorandum, and concluded that ownership was not as crystal clear as had been believed in London. The branches of the Currency Reserve Board were in fact semi-independent in north China; nevertheless the Chinese government's case was still convincing.

After further tedious exchanges with the *Gaimusho*, Craigie suggested that a settlement on silver should be proposed comprising sealing in a neutral bank and the use of the sum of £100,000 for flood relief.[74] The Far Eastern department considered the idea to be sanguine but worthy of support; Craigie was authorized to proceed accordingly but it was emphasized that the blockade of Tientsin, which had recommenced, must be lifted. Grew saw Craigie at the end of November and told him that if a settlement arising from sealing in a neutral bank

[70] War cabinet, 17 Oct. 1939, 50(39)6, with telegram from Craigie to Halifax, 16 Oct. 1939, F11083/1/10, F.O.371/23405.
[71] Jamieson to Halifax, 17 Oct. 1939, F11057/1/10, F.O.371/23405.
[72] Halifax to Craigie, 20 Oct. 1939, F11185/6457/10, F.O.371/23534.
[73] Craigie to Halifax, 25 Oct. 1939, F11302/6457/10, F.O.371/23534.
[74] Craigie to Halifax, with minutes, 25 Nov. 1939, F12132/6457/10, F.O.371/23534.

could be concluded, this should be done.[75] Craigie was anxious to conclude matters and envisaged a British retreat on the other major issue of *fapi* and federal reserve currency, but the Foreign Office opposed this suggestion: Britain had compromised on silver and it was Japan's turn to compromise on currency.[76] Clark Kerr consulted the Chinese government on the modified British line over silver and encountered predictably hostile reactions. China deplored any compromise because the silver was the legal possession of China.[77] A firm reply was sent to Chungking, defending the informal talks held in Tokyo: 'The solution we have proposed is the best we can obtain to safeguard Chinese interests and although we do not expect the Chinese Government to welcome it, we do not think it should be beyond them to accord it their tacit acquiescence and to inform their representatives in Tientsin accordingly.'[78]

The stage had been reached for proceeding more swiftly if Japan would agree. Britain suggested that four separate agreements should be signed dealing respectively with police matters, silver, currency, and British desiderata, which should constitute enclosures to semi-official letters to be exchanged simultaneously between the *Gaimusho* and the British embassy. The Japanese government was willing for the talks to develop; a more settled political atmosphere prevailed in Tokyo with the assumption of office by the Yonai government with the experienced Arita Hachiro as foreign minister. It was unrealistic to expect rapid agreement: a period of bargaining and mutual concession was inevitable. Craigie handled the discussions with tactical astuteness; he was revealed at his best in the protracted resolution of the problems at Tientsin and the Foreign Office appreciated his patience and persistence. After advances had been made on silver and currency, Halifax emphasized that guarantees must be secured to prevent the recurrence of the odious blockade and searches which had caused so much acrimony in the past:

[75] Craigie to Halifax, 28 Nov. 1939, F12207/6457/19, F.O.371/23534.
[76] Craigie to Halifax, 9 Dec. 1939, with minutes, F12524/6457/10, F.O.371/23535.
[77] Clark Kerr to Halifax, 13 Dec. 1939, F12663/6457/10, F.O.371/23535.
[78] Halifax to Clark Kerr, 17 Dec. 1939, ibid.

Now that we appear to be approaching a settlement of the silver, currency and police problems, we must not lose sight of our own desiderata in connexion with the withdrawal of the blockade and the suppression of anti-British activities in the occupied areas.

I consider it essential that after the agreement has come into force, we should have assurance that the Japanese army will not again resort to forcible measures for blockading the concession, and I shall be glad if you will endeavour to secure the insertion in our formula about the withdrawal of the blockade of a clause to the effect that, in the event of any differences of opinion as to the application of the terms of the agreement, the Japanese authorities at Tientsin will not reimpose the blockade or any similar restrictive measures . . .[79]

China was understandably extremely suspicious of developments in Tokyo, but did eventually assent to the allocation of £100,000 for flood and drought relief. Japan agreed to the remainder of the silver being sealed in the bank of communications; Britain compromised by accepting the circulation of federal reserve currency in return for the Japanese dropping their demand for the prohibition of the circulation of *fapi*. Arrangements for policing the concession were envisaged analogous to those in force in the international settlements at Shanghai and Amoy. Japan was willing to terminate the blockade at Tientsin. In reply to the repeated expression of Chinese doubts on various aspects of the contemplated settlement, Clark Kerr was informed that Chinese interests had been protected as far as possible and that the settlement was compatible with the basic principles of the nine-power treaty and of British policy.[80] Chinese objections centred on the length of time the silver would be sealed, to the method of administration for the £100,000, and to the circulation of federal reserve currency. Butler assured the Chinese ambassador that the suspicions were unjustified and, in an attempt to sweeten the pill, said that Britain hoped to give more aid to China under the export credits agreement.[81] The China Association protested at news of the talks and castigated British policy as 'most dangerous', involving the risk of antagonizing both China and the United States. The Foreign Office rejected the criticism; Brenan commented that

[79] Halifax to Craigie, 1 Apr. 1940, F432/5/10, F.O.371/24649.
[80] Halifax to Clark Kerr, 17 Apr. 1940, F2597/5/10, F.O.371/24651.
[81] Minute by Butler, 20 Apr. 1940, F2860/5/10, F.O.371/24651.

the protest represented the views of E. M. Gull, secretary of the association, 'with perhaps a few aggressive amendments by Mr. Warren Swire'.[82] Chiang Kai-shek took an increasing personal interest in the subject and Clark Kerr described his mood as very 'mulish'; Chiang seemed to think that the change of governments in Britain and the Netherlands denoted a change of policy, and wanted Churchill to investigate.[83] The prime minister did indeed request a short memorandum from the Foreign Office. In the face of the spirited Chinese protest, the Far Eastern department showed some concern over signing the agreement, since the Chinese had withdrawn approval of the sale of part of the silver for relief purposes. Dening and Brenan, while criticizing the Chinese for obduracy, held that it would be unwise to proceed without their consent. B. E. F. Gage thought the Chinese should be dissuaded from continuing to oppose signature of the agreement and if the attempt failed, the assistance of the United States should be invoked.[84]

Halifax and his senior advisers believed the agreement must be concluded. The situation in Europe was worsening daily, with France visibly crumbling against the German offensive. Neither Churchill nor Halifax was disposed to allow the Chinese objections to prevent settlement. A strongly worded telegram was sent to Clark Kerr:

While I understand the Chinese point of view, the fact remains that the Tientsin agreement as at present constituted involves no sacrifice of principle. The National Government of China have at no time had physical possession of the silver at Tientsin and they were unable to obtain it even before the outbreak of the present hostilities. In reaching agreement with the Japanese we are taking the far-reaching step of constituting ourselves guardians of the silver. We have no desire whatever to assume this role and it is solely for the benefit of the Chinese Government and to safeguard what they regard as their property that we are doing so. If they wreck the present negotiations by their intransigence, we shall be divested of our responsibility in the matter, and they will have only themselves to blame if the silver is seized.

---

[82] China Association to Foreign Office, 23 Apr. 1940, with minutes, F2931/5/10, F.O.371/24651.
[83] Clark Kerr to Halifax, 17 May 1940, F3288/5/10, F.O.371/24652.
[84] Minutes by Dening, Brenan, and Gage, 4 June 1940, F2957/5/10, F.O.371/24651.

The constant suspicion shown by the Chinese Government that we are about to do a deal with Japan at the expense of China shows little understanding and contributes nothing to their cause or ours. We are engaged upon the gigantic task of defeating Germany. Our success is the greatest service we can render to China, and for her to seek to embroil us with Japan merely helps our enemies . . .[85]

The settlement was duly completed and signed in Tokyo on 12 June by Craigie and Tani, the vice-minister of foreign affairs. Britain agreed to co-operate with the Japanese authorities in the enforcement of law and order in Tientsin. The silver coin and bullion were to be jointly sealed in the bank of communications until subsequent decisions were taken, with the exception of the sum of £100,000 to be employed for relief purposes: the fund was to be administered by experts appointed by the British and Japanese consuls-general in Tientsin. The British Municipal Council agreed not to hinder the use of federal reserve bank currency within the municipal area. The settlement was a compromise from which Japan gained considerably. At the same time, Japan did not gain all she had originally wanted; she had failed to obtain sole possession of the silver and had not secured a ban on the circulation of *fapi*. Given the essential weakness of the British position, it was a triumph for Craigie's patient negotiating skill. Had it not been for the catastrophic developments in Europe, and their prompt repercussions in the Far East, the agreement might have been followed by a greater cordiality in Anglo-Japanese relations. In the event, it was succeeded by a period of grave tension and crisis.

Therefore, British policy in East Asia in 1939–40 functioned in even more of a vacuum than had been the case before the outbreak of war in Europe. The priority, as previously, was to promote close co-operation with the United States but this aim acquired far more urgency because of the European conflict. The second priority was to improve relations with Japan, but only in so far as it was compatible with the first principle. The third priority was to encourage the Chinese in their struggle with Japan; it was essential that large numbers of Japanese troops should be occupied in China to preclude their use else-where. The policy might be summarized as endeavouring to

---

[85] Halifax to Clark Kerr, 5 June 1940, F2871/5/10, F.O.371/24651.

reconcile the manifestly irreconcilable, rendered more difficult by Britain's virtual nakedness in defence. The anxieties and alarms of the prewar period were much accentuated. The solace was the distant prospect of American diplomatic and possibly military embroilment with Japan. The prospect was still a distant one but less so than formerly.

V

THE BURMA ROAD CRISIS

THE spring and summer of 1940 saw a rapid deterioration in the situation in East Asia caused primarily by events in Europe, which had the effect of revealing the position of Great Britain, France, and the Netherlands as even weaker than before and, consequently, of stimulating Japanese expansion. Apart from the initial savage onslaught on Poland by Germany and the Soviet Union in September 1939, the war in Europe had been largely static and uneventful until April 1940 when Hitler dramatically launched his lightning campaigns in Scandinavia. Denmark, Norway, Holland, and Belgium were defeated in swift succession. In France allied resistance disintegrated in the course of May and early June; France, now under the leadership of the aged Pétain, sued for peace on 17 June. Italy had entered the war on 10 June. A month before the Third Republic was effectively brought to an end, the old order fell in England with Neville Chamberlain's resignation as prime minister (9 May). Ironically the immediate cause of Chamberlain's fall was the disastrous campaign in Norway for which his successor as prime minister, Winston Churchill, was largely responsible. Chamberlain was discredited by a long succession of failures; his resignation was overdue. Churchill radiated vigour, dynamism, and self-confidence; it was his hour, just as it had been Lloyd George's hour in 1916.[1] As in other aspects of his world policy, Churchill left his mark on the development of British strategy in the Far East. However, most of Churchill's time was necessarily occupied by events in Europe and the Middle East with the addition of Anglo-American relations, in which Churchill continued his personal correspondence with President Roosevelt.[2] To summarize

[1] Although Churchill came to represent unyielding resistance to Nazi Germany, even he recognized the possibility of a negotiated settlement with Hitler in late May 1940: see D. Dilks, 'Allied Leadership in the Second World War: Churchill', *Survey* 1/2 (94/95) (Winter-Spring 1975), p. 21.
[2] A considerable proportion of the correspondence may be found in F. L.

Churchill's far eastern policy briefly, it may be said that he wished to avert conflict with Japan for as long as he could but that he underestimated the resolution and tenacity of Japan, with consequences that became depressingly evident after the outbreak of the Pacific War in December 1941. The United States firmly supported Great Britain morally, and the Roosevelt administration acted to translate the sympathy into tangible terms in securing the repeal of the requirement that goods purchased by Britain could be carried only in English ships (October 1939). American public opinion did not wish to proceed too far and risk direct involvement in the war; as Duff Cooper remarked after a visit to the United States, most Americans wanted Britain to win but without American lives being sacrificed.[3] The attitude of Roosevelt was enigmatic, as was frequently the case. Most probably the president shared the feelings of most Americans at this time.[4] The most pressing problem from Roosevelt's viewpoint in 1940 was the campaign to secure re-election to the presidency in the summer and autumn of 1940. Roosevelt declined to make his position clear before the Democratic party's nominating convention in July 1940. The gravity of the external crisis and the absence of any obvious successor within his party made it certain that Roosevelt would again be the candidate. The Republican party's convention had witnessed a major reversal for the party establishment in the surprise nomination of Wendell Willkie; Willkie's nomination was both reassuring and alarming to Roosevelt: reassuring because Willkie was an internationalist in foreign affairs, more progressive than any of his rivals, but alarming because Willkie was a popular, charismatic personality who perhaps stood some chance of defeating the president.[5] Roosevelt's far eastern policy would be dictated by

---

Loewenheim, H. D. Langley, and M. Jonas (eds.), *Roosevelt and Churchill: Their Secret Wartime Correspondence* (Barrie and Jenkins, London, 1975).

[3] See N. Nicolson (ed.), *Harold Nicolson: Diaries and Letters*, ii: *1939–1945* (Collins, London, 1967), p. 72.

[4] This theme is pursued in R. Divine, *Roosevelt and World War II* (Johns Hopkins, Baltimore, 1969).

[5] The American ambassador in London, Joseph Kennedy, told Lord Halifax on 17 July that he thought it not unlikely that Willkie would defeat Roosevelt. Kennedy was, however, disenchanted with Roosevelt and was becoming extremely isolationist himself so that his opinion may have been prejudiced. See Foreign Office to Lothian, 17 July 1940, F3590/43/10, F.O.371/24667.

the demands of the campaign. The policy was in part formulated by Cordell Hull, who still supported a cautious, moralizing policy, if somewhat more decisive than previously. In Japan the impact of the events in Europe was profound. Doubts about the reliability of Germany persisted, not least concerning the long-term aims of German policy, but the doubts were submerged in the tide of huge German successes and the necessity to rearrange Japanese policy accordingly. The Yonai government, as will be seen, sought to switch from a policy that had been in the main conciliatory to one of belligerence in an attempt to save itself and outmanoeuvre the more extreme nationalist and military elements. Yonai was disliked in military circles and his government fell in mid-July, to be succeeded by the second administration headed by Prince Konoe Fumimaro with the egregious Matsuoka Yosuke as foreign minister. This government represented the widespread desire in Japan for a bellicose policy of expansion epitomized in the emphasis on the new order.

Before the culmination of Germany's brilliant onslaught had been reached, Japan had expressed interest in the fate of European colonial possessions in East Asia with particular reference to the Netherlands East Indies. The chain of innumerable islands stretching from Malaya to northern Australia was of crucial economic and strategic significance to Japan. It was essential that Japan should extend her influence and obtain some control over vital raw materials, especially oil; the East Indies would furthermore be an integral area for Japanese southern defence should war begin in the Pacific. Japan was determined to prevent British or American intervention in the East Indies in the event of the Netherlands being conquered by Germany or, for that matter, German intervention, although the latter was clearly remote. A statement confirming the Japanese interest in the East Indies was issued by Arita, the foreign minister, in April 1940. It encountered a firm statement of disapproval from the United States.[6] The overt Japanese interest accentuated growing alarm and uneasiness in the southern Dominions, notably in Australia. A sense of isolation, and of not being adequately understood in London, was exacerbated by the acrid political atmosphere in

---

[6] For the statements by Arita and Hull, see *F.R.U.S. 1931-41*, ii, 281-4.

Australia where the Labour opposition bitterly opposed the Menzies government.[7] The Australian dimension was significant, since it reflected the growing division between London and Canberra over policy towards Japan and because the Australian desire to avoid the contingency of war in the Pacific influenced British policy to a limited extent during the crisis over the Burma road.

The confrontation between Great Britain and Japan over the Burma road in June-July 1940 was extremely important, since it demonstrated the nature of Japanese ire with Britain for helping to sustain Chinese resistance and the paucity of British defences to combat a Japanese attack. While it was followed by a major defence review and a reorganization of the British defence structure, the lessons were unfortunately not applied as thoroughly as they should have been. The contribution of the Burma road to the Chinese campaign against Japan lay both in the sphere of morale and in the realm of practical aid. From the beginning of the Sino-Japanese war in 1937, there had been three principal routes for conveying arms and other supplies to China. These were the railway from French Indo-China to Yunnan; the long overland road from Soviet Central Asia to western China; and the Burma road. The role of the Burma road increased in importance as the Japanese control of the China coast was extended and as the French administration in Indo-China was frightened into reducing and eventually terminating the transport of goods by rail. The Burma road ran for some 770 miles, through extremely rugged terrain, from Lashio in northern Burma to Kunming (Yunnanfu), the capital of Yunnan province. Goods for China were usually transported by sea to Rangoon and from there to Lashio by rail. The road was not in a satisfactory condition owing to a combination of the mountainous countryside, severe wet weather, and reluctance of the authorities, particularly in Burma, to spend adequate money on developing and maintaining it. The government of Burma held that there was no long-term commercial incentive to improve communications with China; in addition, there had

---

[7] See P. Hasluck, *The Government and the People* (Australian War Memorial, Canberra, 1952), pp. 211-63. For a discussion of the role of Australia in the approach of the Pacific war, see P. Wright, 'Great Britain, Australia and the Pacific Crisis, 1939–41', unpublished M.A. thesis, Manchester University (1974).

been difficulties with China over the undefined border between Burma and Yunnan. Nevertheless the Burma road was assuming growing significance for China. According to figures supplied by the Burma Office in June 1940, during the six months from December 1939 to May 1940 the total value of arms and ammunition imported into Rangoon for re-export to China was 262·83 lakhs of rupees (£2,022,000); of these 100·32 lakhs (£771,000) or about 38 per cent were of United States origin while 97·09 lakhs (£747,000) or about 37 per cent were of Russian origin. The comparable figures for April to October 1939 were 401 lakhs (£3,085,000) of which 15 lakhs (£108,000) were of United States origin and 76·5 lakhs (£588,000) were of Russian origin. Before September 1939 most arms came from Germany, Czechoslovakia (under German control from October 1938), France, and Belgium. The dismal contribution of Great Britain was underlined by the statistic that, out of a total of £7,028,362 worth of munitions imported into Rangoon for outward transit to China between 26 March 1939 and 31 March 1940, only about £239,000 or 3·4 per cent originated in the British Empire.[8]

The crisis began in the middle of June 1940 when the British military attaché in Tokyo was summoned to see the director of military affairs in the War Ministry, and told that Britain must close the Burma road and the Hong Kong frontier if war with Japan was to be averted.[9] This semi-official approach was soon followed by a formal request to Craigie by Tani, the vice-minister at the *Gaimusho*, that 'the British Government will urgently give effect to measures necessary to put a stop to transportation via Burma not only of arms and ammunition, but also of transport supplies, such as fuel, fuel oil especially gasoline, trucks and railway materials.'[10] Tani said that it was 'a friendly communication', which he agreed was not based on international law. Craigie at once consulted his staff on the advice to be tendered to London. Everything depended on the policy of the United States, but Craigie assumed that nothing more than vague sympathy would be forthcoming from Washington.[11] In his sober assessment, Craigie stated that he

[8] Statistics supplied by Burma Office to Foreign Office, 29 June 1940, F3529/43/10, F.O.371/24666.
[9] For the text see *F.R.U.S.* 1940 iv, 26-7.
[10] Craigie to Foreign Office, 24 June 1940, F3479/43/10, F.O.371/24666.
[11] Ibid.

did not believe refusal would be followed by a Japanese attack on British possessions. However, Japan would undoubtedly begin to take action, perhaps in the form of a blockade of Hong Kong or a bombing offensive against the Burma road. Relations between Britain and Japan would then decline rapidly and extremist elements in Tokyo, wishing to form an alliance with the European Axis, would be greatly encouraged. In the light of the grave situation in Europe, with Anglo-French relations worsening after the appearance of the Vichy regime, Craigie counselled that it was no time to take needless risks in the Far East. China would be affronted and there would be American criticism, but these aspects had to be subordinated to the prior aim of averting conflict with Japan. 'I therefore have no doubt in my own mind that we should agree to this Japanese request and do so promptly i.e., before some incident occurs which renders acceptance yet more difficult.'[12] He believed that submission to Japan's demands should be accompanied by a serious effort to resolve outstanding problems and secure a broad settlement in East Asia. The Foreign Office was not happy with Craigie's appraisal, holding that he had underestimated the effects on China and, more important, on the United States.[13] It was not simply a matter of what action the United States might or might not take, but of general American support for the British cause. The whole matter transcended departmental limitations and needed consideration by the chiefs of staff and by the war cabinet.

The chiefs of staff had for many years rightly stressed the extreme inadequacy of British defences and the importance of avoiding entanglements elsewhere. The Japanese approach led them to reiterate the familiar theme once again, for the European situation was desperate. Britain faced the danger of war with Vichy France over the issue of the French fleet and the prospect of an imminent German invasion of the British Isles. The chiefs of staff committee met on 1 July. An *aide-mémoire* had been prepared by the joint planning subcommittee, itself commenting on views expressed by the Foreign Office. General Sir John Dill suggested that the correct course was to discuss with Japan the possibility of an

---

[12] Craigie to Foreign Office, 25 June 1940, ibid.
[13] Foreign Office to Clark Kerr, 27 June 1940, ibid.

over-all settlement in the Far East on the widest terms. Such a settlement might include withdrawal of the British garrison from Shanghai and even demilitarization of Hong Kong. The Foreign Office envisaged limited concessions falling short of the closure of the Burma road but, in Dill's opinion, this involved the risk of war and was therefore unwise. His colleagues agreed and decided to forward their conclusions to the war cabinet.[14] In cabinet Halifax urged that Japan's demands be rejected; at the same time, in view of the Australian fears of antagonizing Japan, an offer to restrict the volume of traffic on the road should be made.[15] The colonial secretary, Lord Lloyd, warned that closure would provoke a strong reaction among the Chinese in Hong Kong. Some members of the cabinet supported the idea of a broad settlement but others referred to the obvious difficulty of achieving terms that would be acceptable to Japan and China. Leopold Amery, the secretary of state for India, adamantly opposed closure.[16] The Dominions secretary, Lord Caldecote, defended Australian apprehension and Neville Chamberlain stated that the aim was to avoid the risk of war. Churchill and Attlee supported Halifax. The provisional decision was made to meet the demand for withdrawal of the garrison at Shanghai, provided that the Italian garrison was similarly withdrawn, for the garrison had long been a hostage to fortune; the demand for closure of the Burma road would be politely declined on the grounds that the road did not carry large quantities of war materials.[17]

A disturbing report was received from Craigie late on 1 July that he had obtained information pointing to pro-German elements among the younger army officers having virtually got

---

[14] Chiefs of staff committee, 1 July 1940, C.O.S.202(40)3, Cab.79/5.

[15] War cabinet conclusions, 1 July 1940, 189(40), Cab.65/8.

[16] Ibid. In a private letter to the Viceroy of India, Lord Linlithgow, Amery wrote 'With regard to the Burma-China road I have taken a strong line at the Cabinet against any yielding to Japan because I am convinced that it will only lead to fresh demands and that just because we are in a difficult position the only thing for us is to show a brave face to the world and refuse to be intimidated. After all, Japan is not in so comfortable a position in China or *vis-à-vis* Russia or America as to be willing to risk a war with us . . .' Letter from Amery to Linlithgow, 4 July 1940, Linlithgow Collection, MSS. Eur. F125/9, India Office Library, London.

[17] Dominions Office to the governments of Canada and South Africa, enclosing exchange of telegrams with the Australian government, 2 July 1940, F3544/43/10, F.O.371/24666.

out of control. He was now alarmed to hear of the war cabinet's decision. He stated in an urgent telegram that it would not satisfy the Japanese and that to offer a form of restriction of traffic would give rise to the problem of inspection and would mean releasing confidential figures on the use of the road.[18] He eloquently called for reconsideration of the decision. Craigie felt that excessive emphasis had been placed on refraining from offending Chiang Kai-shek, and the political consequences for British prestige in India and Burma would be still worse if Japan embarked on a campaign to enforce her demands. He considered that the Burma road crisis offered a dangerous opportunity for Germany to urge Japan into attacking British possessions. He concluded:

I feel that I am entitled to enquire whether in fact His Majesty's Government are prepared to risk drifting into a state of war with Japan on this issue? Evidently you rate the chances of this lower than I do and my staff. Admittedly this is a matter on which none can forecast with absolute certainty; but even if there is only 50 per cent chance—and I put the risk higher than this—are we justified in taking it? Or for that matter taking even a 10 per cent risk? This is of course for His Majesty's Government to decide but I should be failing in my duty if I did not state in emphatic terms that the risk is considerable; that we shall be playing straight into the German hands, and that in the final analysis we shall be serving less our own vital interests than the interests of Chiang-Kai-shek [*sic*] and his Government.

It is most repugnant to me to have to urge compliance with this Japanese request but I do so in a hope and belief that when we have defeated Germany we and the United States of America will be able to teach Japan a lesson which she will never forget. To precipitate the crisis unnecessarily . . . will in my opinion mean jeopardising the prospect of that ultimate reestablishment of a strong British position in the Far East on which I pin all my hopes . . .[19]

The same view was taken by the chiefs of staff when they met on 4 July. 'The committee considered that the War Cabinet should be left in no doubt as to the apprehension which the Chiefs of Staff felt regarding the military necessity of avoiding any steps which might lead to war with Japan for

---

[18] Craigie to Foreign Office, 1 July 1940, F3479/43/10, F.O.371/24666; Craigie to Foreign Office, 4 July 1940, F3544/43/10, F.O.371/24666.
[19] Ibid.

the reasons which they had discussed . . . particularly in the light of the possibility that we might find ourselves in a state of hostilities with France.'[20] The arguments against pursuing the Foreign Office policy of partial concessions were gathering added force. A full debate proceeded in the war cabinet with the foreign secretary's dogged adherence to his line of refusing to close the road commanding diminishing support, especially when the prime minister switched sides. In cabinet on 5 July Halifax reiterated his views and said he did not believe that Japan would launch a major offensive; he admitted, however, that an attack might be made on Hong Kong. He thought the Japanese were indulging in bluff and that it should be called. In the discussion much attention was paid to Craigie's warnings and it was felt that rationing of traffic on the road would be impracticable. China relied on the commodities carried, for example oil, lorries, and materials for an aircraft factory in China, although the goods were not carried in large quantities. The effect on public opinion was assessed, since it was believed that hostility to any surrender to Japan was important. The Dominions secretary, Lord Caldecote, stated that while Australia had approved the proposed action of the Foreign Office, her reactions might have been different had she been aware of the state of Anglo-French relations. To Churchill the essential point was that, if Britain resisted, the burden would fall entirely on her shoulders instead of falling where it rightly belonged — on the United States. The Americans should be asked what they would do in the event of Japanese aggression, for instance against the Netherlands East Indies. 'In the present state of affairs he did not think that we ought to incur Japanese hostility for reasons mainly of prestige.'[21] Chamberlain unsurprisingly concurred. The debate turned to examining the consequences should Japan go to war: her fleet could cause great difficulties through chaos in trade and the menace to the southern Dominions. The cabinet concluded that it would be foolish to take risks that might lead to war. If Britain had to yield, attention should be given to the advice from Roosevelt that it was preferable to submit to *force majeure* rather than make an agreement of appeasing

---

[20] Chiefs of staff committee, 4 July 1940, 208(40)3, Cab.79/5.
[21] War cabinet conclusions, 5 July 1940, 194(40)1, Cab.65/8.

character, as France had done. Halifax repeated his dissent but was asked to draft telegrams to Washington and Tokyo explaining that it might be necessary to give way to Japan.[22]

Lord Lothian saw Cordell Hull on 5 July and informed him of Craigie's growing alarm at the contingency of a Japanese attack. Hull recognized the problem, but asked if Britain could continue negotiations in Tokyo 'rather than formally undertake to close a road of commercial importance to India, Burma, China and the outside world at the dictation of Japan'.[23] Hull thought the British action against the French fleet at Oran would have a salutary impact on Tokyo. The United States was, according to Lothian, still willing to discuss the possibility of a general far eastern settlement. The ambassador thought the European powers should give Japan access to oil and rubber in return for generous concessions to Chiang Kai-shek and an agreement to keep the Pacific neutral in the European struggle. Lothian optimistically ended that such an agreement would solve the issue of the Burma road.[24] Dening minuted that the Americans were obviously against British submission over the Burma road. He added that Lothian's comments on an overall settlement were unrealistic, for he underestimated the numerous complications. 'Not only that, but he seems to assume too readily that the Japanese would be willing to play, whereas present indications are to the contrary.'[25] Craigie reported urgently that the assistant military attaché, Colonel Wards, had seen Major Sugita at the War Ministry and had been told bluntly that British refusal to close the road would definitely lead to war.[26] Dening criticized Craigie irately and unfairly for gullibly swallowing Japanese bluff:

What does cause surprise, and not a little sadness, is that Sir R. Craigie who has so frequently been subjected to these threats and blandishments in the past, should always be impressed by them. Experience apparently does not teach and we shall no doubt have to endure one of those dreary moral defeats which do so much to damage an already tarnished reputation in the Far East. We are told

---

[22] Ibid.
[23] Lothian to Foreign Office, 5 July 1940, F3544/43/10, F.O.371/24666.
[24] Ibid.
[25] Minute by Dening, 7 July 1940, ibid.
[26] Craigie to Foreign Office, 4 July 1940, ibid.

that we must consider our strategy and not our prestige. But what
has maintained our strategy in the Far East for many years past if not
prestige? Certainly not force, neither its presence nor the threat of
it.[27]

The last sentence was unquestionably accurate but it was unjust to censure Craigie for reporting significant information to
London, which was part of his work. Therefore, on the one
hand, advice came to resist Japan for as long as possible and,
on the other hand, a serious warning of the perils of following
such a course. The Dominions' high commissioners urged that
the road be closed and an effort made to reach a general
settlement. The most vocal of the high commissioners was
Stanley Bruce of Australia, which was understandable given
the intense concern and political tension within the country.
Bruce suggested Britain should tell Japan clearly that she
would allow readier access to raw materials and trade and
would give financial assistance—it was not clear where this
would come from—in return for the restoration of peace in
China. Massey and Waterson, representing Canada and South
Africa, supported Bruce. Jordan of New Zealand was absent
from the meeting.[28]

The official British reply in accordance with the war
cabinet's decision was sent to Craigie on 6 July. In his covering
instructions to Craigie, Halifax stated that the cabinet had
considered various relevant aspects, including relations with
the United States, China, and the Soviet Union. While Britain
did not desire war with Japan, neither did she wish to comply
with the demands if Japan was bluffing. Halifax asked Craigie
to negotiate as best he could and, unlike Dening, praised the
ambassador's diplomatic skill. 'Your difficulties are fully
realised, but I feel satisfied that no one can handle them better
than yourself and I leave you full discretion as to how you can
best play a very awkward hand.'[29] For the present, Halifax
preferred not to discuss withdrawal of garrisons from China,
but Craigie could give assurances on the need to avoid embarrassing incidents if pressed. Craigie was instructed to point out
that Britain's response was friendly and that there was no

[27] Minute by Dening, 7 July 1940, ibid.
[28] Caldecote to Halifax, 6 July 1940, ibid.
[29] Foreign Office to Craigie, 6 July 1940, ibid.

desire for a confrontation.[30] Halifax continued:

You may say, if you see fit, that our reluctance to comply with the Japanese request does not mean that we are not willing to meet the Japanese on questions which in our view are far more vital to their welfare. It must have been apparent to the Japanese Government that, during the course of recent discussions between His Majesty's Government and the Japanese Government on economic questions, there has been evident on the part of His Majesty's Government a desire to understand Japan's economic needs and to make, as far as possible, provisions for them. His Majesty's Government are both willing and anxious to assure to Japan supplies of raw materials which Japan needs and which the British Empire can supply and they would urge that the pace of negotiations already in progress should be accelerated in order that our trade relations may be placed on a more satisfactory footing.[31]

In the accompanying text of the official reply to Japan, it was stated that no arms had passed over the frontier of Hong Kong since January 1939 and Japanese requirements had, therefore, already been met. With regard to the Burma road, it was admitted that arms reached China by this route. However, the quantities were limited and could not be considered to constitute a prominent source of material support. Britain could see no justification for halting supplies of fuel, fuel oil, petrol, trucks, and railway materials. Such trade was entirely legitimate and contributed to the economies of India and Burma. The bulk of the goods concerned came from third powers, and British action to stop supplies would be unneutral and discriminatory against China. It was tartly pointed out that, 'In strict neutrality a request to cut off the materials in question from China should involve a similar stoppage of supplies to Japan, but this of course is in no way the intention of His Majesty's Government.'[32] A comparison was drawn with the recent British request to Japan to prevent certain goods being sent to Germany; the reaction of Japan, while she agreed under stipulated conditions to arrange not to re-export goods purchased from the British Empire, had been a refusal to give assurances on other Japanese imports. The statement ended:

[30] Ibid.
[31] Ibid.
[32] Ibid.

For all these reasons it will be evident to the Japanese Government that, were they to press their request, they would place His Majesty's Government in a position of great embarrassment. This could not but cause a serious crisis in Anglo-Japanese relations, and His Majesty's Government are unwilling to believe that this is in fact the desire of the Japanese Government. His Majesty's Government fully appreciate the anxiety of the Japanese Government to bring to an end the hostilities which His Majesty's Government have themselves from the outset deplored. But the closing of the Burma Road could at best furnish only a partial solution of the problem which the Japanese Government have set themselves. His Majesty's Government venture to express the view that only by a just and equitable peace acceptable to both parties will the present unfortunate dispute be terminated and thus pave the way to a general and constructive settlement which will bring lasting peace and prosperity to the Far East. His Majesty's Government for their part are ready and willing to afford their cooperation and to enter upon discussions to achieve this end.[33]

The Yonai government refused to accept the reply. Yonai and Arita were encountering growing pressure from the vociferous militarists; Britain's plight in Europe was so grave that they were confident she would give way, the only cause for caution arising from possible harsh reactions in the United States. When the British war cabinet met on 10 July, Halifax referred to a suggestion from Craigie that a solution might be found in agreeing to closure of the Burma road for three months on the understanding that special efforts to reach a general peace settlement would be made during that period.[34] Thus a fig leaf would help to cover the act of surrender. Australian apprehension was once again borne in mind and the predominant feeling was that Craigie's proposal was cogent. As Halifax wished to give the matter further thought, it was deferred until the next meeting. Lothian at this moment

[33] Ibid.
[34] Amery wrote to Linlithgow on 9 July that there was strong feeling against submitting to Japan. 'But a good deal of information has come through to show that they really are prepared to make war over this issue and if that were the result it would knock the bottom out of the whole of our schemes for combining the defence of the Empire in those parts, for I suppose it would mean Japanese cruisers and submarines interfering with all reinforcements of the Middle East by the Cape, as well as with communications between Australia and India and the Middle East. We have put in a temporising reply, but you must not be too greatly shocked if in the end we have to give way.' Letter from Amery to Linlithgow, 9 July 1940, Linlithgow Collection, MSS. Eur. F125/9, India Office Library, London.

reported a change in the American attitude; the situation in the Atlantic was giving rise to such alarm, with the likelihood that the American fleet might be moved to the Atlantic, that if Britain felt she had to compromise with Japan, Lothian thought it would be understood and condoned in the United States.[35] The problem of alienating the Americans seemed to have diminished and Halifax lost no time, after consultations with his officials, in accepting Craigie's solution. The cabinet endorsed the view that agreement should be reached with Japan at once.[36] Neville Chamberlain fully supported the decision, writing to his sister Hilda:

In the meantime we have made a concession to the Japs which I hope and believe has extricated us from a dangerous crisis. Some think the Japs were bluffing but if they were mistaken—and we have to duel not with the Foreign Office but with truculent and ignorant Army officers who think we are going to be beaten by the Germans—we have not got the forces to fight Japs, Germans and Italians at once. I would hardly say that the Americans, while anxious to see us take a 'bold' line have made it clear that they are not prepared to use force to help us. So I was relieved and gratified to find that Winston, with the responsibilities of a P.M. on his shoulders, was firmly against the bold line.[37]

Lothian was instructed to explain the decision fully to the State Department and express the hope that the United States would sympathize with Britain's invidious position; it was stated at the end of the telegram that Britain was anxious to achieve a general settlement in the Far East.[38] Halifax added that if the United States could leak a report indicating concern at interruptions to American supplies reaching China, and hinting that supplies to Japan might be halted, this would be of much assistance. The latter might well have contributed to Hull's public statement on the closure and to Roosevelt's decision to begin restricting trade with Japan, notably in high-quality gasoline and scrap metal.[39] Craigie was told to secure agreement if he could on the basis of the Burma road being

---

[35] Lothian to Foreign Office, 10 July 1940, F3568/43/10, F.O.371/24667.
[36] War cabinet conclusions, 11 July 1940, 200(40)13, Cab.65/8.
[37] Letter from Neville Chamberlain to Hilda, 14 July 1940, Neville Chamberlain papers, NC18/1/1165.
[38] Foreign Office to Lothian, 11 July 1940, F3568/43/10, F.O.371/24667.
[39] See H. Feis, *The Road to Pearl Harbor* (Princeton University Press, Princeton, 1950), pp. 88–100. For Hull's public statement, see *F.R.U.S.* 1931–41 ii, 101.

kept open but carrying the same quantities as in the corresponding period in 1939; if this was impossible, he was authorized to accept closure for three months:

You should conclude by making it clear that His Majesty's Government are making this very considerable concession to Japanese opinion in the face of great opposition, but that they do so in the confident hope that it will lead to a genuine improvement in Anglo-Japanese relations. Their position will become very difficult if, nevertheless, there is to be a continuance of hostility on the part of the Japanese public and press . . . You have given us to understand that once this difficult corner in Anglo-Japanese relations is turned there will be an end to threats and demands. It is for the Japanese Government to ensure that this forecast is correct.[40]

Craigie met Arita and, after lengthy exchanges, it was agreed on 17 July that the Burma road would be closed for three months as from 18 July to the transport of the following goods — arms, ammunition, petrol, trucks, and railway material. Closure was conditional on a special effort being made during the following three months to secure peace; at the end of this period, Britain was free to decide whether or not to extend the closure. The governments of Burma and Hong Kong would notify Japan of steps being taken to prevent arms shipments.

The reaction of the United·States was one of private sympathy but official regret that Britain had submitted. Lothian spoke firmly to Hull, saying that Japan had been encouraged by the fall of France and by statements emanating from Senator Walsh, an isolationist Democrat from Massachusetts, and by President Roosevelt's press secretary, Stephen Early; in remarks presumably intended to mollify the isolationists, Early had reflected that there might be justification for a Monroe doctrine in Asia. In view of American inability to assist and of strong pressure from Australia to avert the threat of war with Japan, Britain had compromised. 'Mr. Hull said he was sorry we had had to take this decision but did not demur to its being inevitable in view of inability of United States to give us armed support.'[41] Joseph

---

[40] Foreign Office to Craigie, 11 July 1940, F3568/43/10, F.O.371/24667.
[41] Lothian to Foreign Office, 12 July 1940, F3597/43/10, F.O.371/24667.

Kennedy, embittered and discontented, castigated his own government when he visited Halifax on 17 July. He understood Britain's dilemma 'and took this part of our conversation as a text for reproaches against his own Government for the extent to which they preached morality to the world without being prepared to give it practical support'.[42] The criticism was merited, if ironical, coming from this source. However, the exigencies of the election campaign now about to commence in earnest required Roosevelt to use his shrewd political judgement to maximum success. The president had to strike a balance between sympathy for the British cause and reassurance that the United States was not going to be involved in war. Neville Chamberlain, mortally ill, reflected bitterly on American inaction in a letter to his sister Ida:

. . . I confess that when I read Cordell Hull's comments on our decision to close the Burmah [*sic*] Road for 3 months my blood boiled, and the Press comments in U.S.A. since have done nothing to cool me down.

Before replying to the Japs we pointed out to the U.S.A. Govt. we could not afford to take on Japan in addition to Germany and Italy alone, but that if they would be prepared to stand by us we would take the risk. Their answer was that they understood our difficulties but we *must not count on any material help from them*. I don't complain of that, but when, without saying a word about this correspondence, they take up a superior attitude and reproach us for being too submissive to the Japs my feelings are almost too much for me.[43]

China's reaction was predictably bitter. The Chinese ambassador, Quo Tai-chi, made repeated visits to the Foreign Office to emphasize to Halifax and R. A. Butler the importance of maintaining the transport of supplies to his country in the heroic fight against Japanese aggression. On 12 July Halifax spoke of British concern for China and stressed that the Burma road was not regarded as a minor matter. 'But

[42] Foreign Office to Lothian, 17 July 1940, F3590/43/10, F.O.371/24667.
[43] Letter from Neville Chamberlain to Ida, 20 July 1940, Neville Chamberlain papers, NC18/1/1166. Chamberlain showed courage in facing the collapse of all his hopes and the loss of the premiership in 1939–40. He worked honourably and closely with Winston Churchill in the final phase of his life; Churchill reciprocated Chamberlain's feelings. Chamberlain suffered from inoperable cancer; he resigned from the war cabinet in October 1940 and died the following month.

at present the British people were fighting for their lives and an attack might at any moment be made on Britain itself. General Chiang Kai-shek, I was sure, would not fail to appreciate the British point of view, which was that we could not in present circumstances afford to add to the number of our enemies if we could avoid it.'[44] Given the gravity of the war in Europe, it was impossible to expect Britain to take unnecessary risks with Japan. Britain appreciated how repulsive the agreement would be to Chinese opinion, but Halifax hoped it would be a temporary closure in the course of which a serious attempt could be made to end the Sino-Japanese war:

Dr. Quo thought it unlikely that this would be possible. The attitude of the Chinese Government towards Japanese aggression was the same as that stated by the Prime Minister to be that of His Majesty's Government towards Hitler; and there was no thought of negotiations with Japan whose Government had been since 1931 dominated by the military clique. He feared that any peace reached now would inevitably be at China's expense. If any such intimation of our purpose were given at the same time as concessions were made to Japan over the Burma Road, it might be construed, Dr. Quo feared, as an attempt to bring pressure to bear on China. To this I replied that His Majesty's Government had always stressed the necessity for a just and equitable settlement which obviously implied Chinese assent. Dr. Quo urged that the termination of hostilities in China would not be in the interests of His Majesty's Government, and that a settlement there would increase the threat by Japan to the British position in the Far East generally.[45]

The closing observation was the most convincing from Britain's viewpoint, and had been strongly held by the chiefs of staff until the reversal of their thinking when the Burma road crisis broke. Four days later Quo called again to say that China would reluctantly accept closure on condition the road was reopened from October onwards and that facilities were granted in Burma for outward transmission into China of goods that had accumulated already in Burma. However, Chiang Kai-shek deeply resented the action taken, interpreting it as a stab in the back; British prestige declined in Chungking and was not to recover significantly. While, in

---

[44] Foreign Office to Clark Kerr, 12 July 1940, ibid.
[45] Ibid.

retrospect, it seems clear that Japan was bluffing in threatening war over the Burma road, the war cabinet had acted wisely in determining not to call the bluff. Craigie's telegrams arguably erred on the pessimistic side but, in his grasp of the essentials, he was surely correct. Again Craigie handled the actual negotiations very ably, just as he had done over Tientsin in June-July 1939 and once more in 1940. Japan had recognized that the closure might be temporary and that an attempt must be made to secure peace in East Asia. Bearing in mind that Britain was so weak in defence terms, it was a not inconsiderable achievement to gain these concessions from Japan.

The closure of the Burma road was followed by detailed consideration within the Foreign Office and other interested departments of the numerous aspects to a peace settlement between Japan and China, which would also embrace the other powers concerned in the Pacific region. In some preliminary reflections on 10 July, Sir John Brenan wrote that a broad settlement was advocated by the British ambassadors in Tokyo and Washington, by the chiefs of staff, and by the Australian government. It would mean consulting the United States, the Netherlands, France, and China. The American position was that no discussions would be initiated by the United States but that the Americans were willing to examine proposals. Fundamental to any peace between Japan and China would be a guarantee of the integrity and independence of the latter. In order to persuade Japan to make a magnanimous settlement, the other powers would have to offer inducements. These would have to satisfy Japan's economic requirements, principally in supplying raw materials and financial assistance. Japan would be expected to recognize the integrity of the various colonial territories in East Asia and the Pacific and to agree to remain neutral for the duration of the European war. The next problem lay in opening the discussions. Craigie and Clark Kerr could try to persuade the Japanese and Chinese governments to appoint plenipotentiaries to meet to arrange a truce. Japan would have to modify the Konoe statement and clarify some of its opaque features; Britain would make a generous contribution in the form of financial aid to both countries and a guaranteed supply of raw materials to Japan; when the European war ended, extraterritoriality in China would terminate. Since Craigie deemed it best for the initial approach to come from Japan, Brenan recommended that Craigie be given full discretion to sound out Japan. The head of the Far Eastern department, J. C. Sterndale Bennett, did not believe Brenan's minute went far enough: a fuller review was needed.[46] A lengthy debate followed between R. A. Butler and the permanent officials. Butler produced a long minute, once again deploying his not unfamiliar arguments in favour of a *rapprochement* between Britain and Japan:

The 'complete defeat' of Japan can only be brought about by the enlistment in the war of a first class nation. We should be unwise to undertake the task and I doubt whether the Russians or Americans will.

Therefore I think that we should work for as good a settlement in the Far East as we can manage. We and the Americans have economic weapons against Japan. Under cover of these we should attempt to secure a modification of the Konoye terms. I should like to see, as soon as possible any draft proposals for utilising the 3 months that the Dept. can produce.[47]

Butler continued that China should be handled carefully, with no attempt to force her into peace talks. In the Japanese context, the danger was that Japanese irritation at her unending struggle with China could lead to attacks on the Chinese from the rear through invasions of northern Indo-China or Thailand. It was essential to use the coming three months to promote a settlement:

To be successful we must be much more active with the American Govt. than hitherto. We cannot have them sniping at us in public while privately telling us that they understand our motives.

I should like to take this line with them:- 'Your and our interests are very similar. In the Far East let us try, under cover of our economic weapons, to secure a fair settlement, and to revise our position in China (extraterritoriality etc.). If we look like failing then can we count on your aid, when the Japs. start pouncing on other people's property? Joint British and American action will help influence China'.

---

[46] Minute by Sterndale Bennett, 11 July 1940, ibid.
[47] Minute by Butler, 23 July 1940, F3633/193/61, F.O.371/24708.

It may be said that the weakness of the above policy is that Japan will have her hands free for adventure elsewhere. If we are going to succeed in the settlement policy we must show courage and determination and not fall between two stools as we have done in our European policy since the war. There seem to me to be two alternative developments in the Far East. Either we carry our settlement policy to its logical conclusion and produce a joint U.S.A., Japan, British Treaty securing order in the Far East and Chinese independence; or we let Japan run into the U.S.A. and ourselves by continuing her policy of *taking* what she wants and more.[48]

Neither alternative, he noted, would obviate the fact that Japan was the most powerful nation in East Asia. The first course would place British policy on a realistic footing again, connoting a coalescence between the Lansdowne tradition (the Anglo-Japanese alliance) and the Balfour tradition (the Washington conference). The second course would terminate in war of truly world dimensions, for the United States would be involved against Japan and the Soviet Union might choose to enter too. He ended:

With this comforting reflection at the back of our minds I do not see why we should not set out hopefully and actively to secure alternative number one. It is to be remembered that the preliminaries to securing this objective are by no means complicated, but rather made more simple by any decision on the part of the U.S.A. to impose restrictions on the passage of war materials to Japan. Moreover such an action would make the Chinese less suspicious of our attempts to secure an honourable ending to one of the great wars with which the world is cursed.

If in company with America we can achieve a happy result we shall have our hands freer for our European commitments. Though, through alternative one, the U.S.A. may paradoxically be less likely to join in the war against Germany, yet practically they will be more likely to embrace alternative one if they realise that, through its success, they may save themselves fighting in East and West, or at any rate confine their action in the west to their navy which will have been freed from the East. They will also be freer to send us the munitions which we need.

The place of the U.S.S.R. in alternative one is problematical and it will be under alternative two, and whatever we do, we would have to prevent Chiang falling under Soviet influence and be as polite and frank to the Soviet as we can.

[48] Ibid.

We may in the end have to carry on our 'middle' policy but the above is an attempt to reach out for something more definite.[49]

Butler's minute was a full and frank exposition of his views. The defect with his analysis, as Sterndale Bennett commented, was that it oversimplified matters. Butler tended to think that Britain could achieve a peace settlement on her own initiative, which was erroneous. A successful policy needed force behind it and the fact was that Britain had no force:

Broadly speaking, we have to go slow and avoid further trouble in the Far East for the next three or four months until (a) the German threat to this country is exploded and (b) the United States Presidential election is over. During this period we can only sound the Japanese and Chinese Governments to see how far they are respectively prepared to go to meet each other, and meanwhile clear our own minds as to the type of peace which would be fair and as the contribution which we can make. We can of course keep in close touch with the United States in all this.[50]

Sterndale Bennett closed with renewed emphasis on the vital importance of strengthening British defences in the Far East. Without it Britain would continue, in Butler's phrase, to fall between two stools. Sir Alexander Cadogan issued a salutary note of warning:

Let us for our own education, discuss what we think might be a just settlement . . . But let us not, so long as the military situation remains as it is, imagine that we are going to have much influence in imposing it and we shan't get the Americans to help. We lived on bluff from 1920-1939, but it was eventually called. Until we have made ourselves strong enough to maintain the position that we then agreed to hold, we shall have to play for time, which is neither dignified nor comfortable.[51]

After further discussion, Sterndale Bennett completed the draft of a memorandum explaining the views of the Foreign Office in detail, for circulation to other government departments. The first aim in any settlement should be to end the Sino-Japanese war. Japan's military commitments and the resulting economic strain undoubtedly acted as a factor restraining Japanese expansion. For this reason, extremists in

---

[49] Ibid.
[50] Minute by Sterndale Bennett, 25 July 1940, ibid.
[51] Minute by Cadogan, 27 July 1940, ibid.

Japan desired an early end to the conflict so that the Japanese sphere of interest could be extended to include south-east Asia. British support for China, limited though it was, plus the damage to British economic interests arising from the war, formed an ever-present cause of friction. There was always anxiety, and the danger that Japan might join the European Axis was a real one. Therefore, it was probably desirable to bring the Sino-Japanese struggle to an end if this could be attained on reasonable terms. Special inducements would be necessary to bring Japan to the negotiating table; these inducements would be of a political, economic, and, most likely, financial character. Sterndale Bennett then pursued the subject under two sub-headings, peace between Japan and China and the broader settlement that would, it was hoped, ensue. Japanese peace terms, according to the Konoe statement of December 1938, and the later rumoured treaty between Japan and Wang Ching-wei (December 1939) would include the recognition of Manchukuo; acceptance by China of the new order; a mutual agreement to oppose communism; autonomy for Inner Mongolia under Japanese protection; economic privileges for Japan in north China and the Yangtze; a new status for Shanghai; the appointment of Japanese political advisers in Inner Mongolia and north China; tariff changes; cessation of anti-Japanese propaganda; the presence of Japanese garrisons on Hainan island and at Amoy; phased withdrawal of troops over a period of years; ultimate agreement to the abolition of extraterritoriality. Chinese peace terms were thought to be vague but would involve the full restoration of Chinese sovereignty, probably including Manchuria. Withdrawal of Japanese forces would be an essential prerequisite. It was manifest, therefore, that extreme difficulty would be experienced in reconciling the adversaries. The power or powers acting in a mediatory capacity would have to coax and cajole the two countries until each gradually compromised. It would be particularly important to offer Japan economic inducements and the aid of the United States would have to be invoked.[52]

---

[52] Memorandum, 'General Settlement with Japan', 8 Aug. 1940, enclosed in Foreign Office to Treasury, Board of Trade, Ministry of Economic Warfare, Colonial Office, Dominions Office, India Office, Burma Office, Petroleum Department, 10 Aug. 1940, F3633/193/61, F.O. 371/24708.

As regards a broad settlement of outstanding issues, Japan's demands would most likely include recognition of Japan's special position in East Asia; acceptance of the new order; recognition of racial equality and acceptance of Japanese immigration into the Dominions and the United States; withdrawal of foreign troops from China; credits, for exploitation of China and for financing essential imports; free trade with the Netherlands East Indies, Indo-China, and other regions bordering the Pacific; abolition of colonial quotas and of the Ottawa tariff structure; assurance of access to vital raw materials, notably oil, rubber, iron ore, nickel, manganese, cotton, and wool; and increased trade with the British Commonwealth. Sterndale Bennett believed there were serious problems with a number of these items, especially racial equality in the United States and the Dominions. China's desiderata would spring from her economic and political revival after the war and would principally comprise a guarantee of territorial integrity; revision of the 'unequal treaties'; a consolidated and stable currency; and loans for rehabilitation. From the British viewpoint, it would be easier to meet Chinese requirements than Japanese, which was hardly surprising. In return for concessions by the powers, Japan would be expected to undertake formally to remain neutral in the European war; to respect the territorial posessions of the powers; and to give comprehensive assurances concerning the re-export of goods to enemy powers. China would be expected to respect foreign rights and to permit equal opportunities for participation in economic restoration and development. This would have to be reconciled with the Japanese demand for privileged status in north China. Sterndale Bennett concluded that no further progress could be realized until all the interested departments had considered the subject — 'It will be necessary in particular to survey Far Eastern and Pacific resources with a view to determining where our own essential interests lie and the direction in which concessions can be made with the minimum detriment to their interests.'[53] In his covering letter to other departments, he briefly recapitulated the background and stressed that the situation had deteriorated following the formation of the new Konoe

[53] Ibid.

government, which was more bellicose than its predecessor: a number of British nationals had been arrested and maltreated resulting in 'an atmosphere of tension in which it is clearly impossible to discuss the question of a Far Eastern settlement'.[54] Nevertheless, it would be valuable to have the considered opinions of other departments on record for use if a future opportunity of raising the matter presented itself.

Over the next six weeks replies gradually arrived. The Treasury stated that little could be accomplished in the financial sphere. Japan and China each had a favourable balance of payments with the sterling area. Therefore, sterling credits or loans would hardly attract them unless they could convert the sterling into other currencies; such a course of action would not be acceptable to the Treasury. With regard to the Chinese currency, Britain could not promise to support it indefinitely.[55] The Ministry of Economic Warfare expressed considerable scepticism about the whole subject, because it felt it was undesirable for the Sino-Japanese war to be terminated. Any attempt to mediate might be interpreted as weakness by Japan. It was imperative not to modify the economic blockade of areas dominated by Germany and Italy; equally the United States must not be offended.[56] The Dominions Office also wondered whether Britain should try to end the war in China.[57] The India Office declined to comment until the interdepartmental meeting was held.[58] The most entertaining reply came from the Colonial Office which, after outlining the difficulties inherent in making concessions to Japan, remarked that any peace conference should be utilized to obtain an extension of the lease of the New Territories in the crown colony of Hong Kong or, indeed, the permanent acquisition of the area.[59] The officials of the Far Eastern department agreed there was much force in the fundamental objection made to ending the Sino-Japanese war; the objection gathered cogency during August and September when the

---

[54] Sterndale Bennett to Treasury and other departments, 10 Aug. 1940, ibid.
[55] Treasury to Foreign Office, 25 Sept. 1940, F4417/193/61, F.O.371/24709.
[56] Ministry of Economic Warfare to Foreign Office, 2 Sept. 1940, F4108/193/61, F.O.371/24709.
[57] Dominions Office to Foreign Office, 27 Aug. 1940, F3859/193/61, F.O.371/24709.
[58] India Office to Foreign Office, 26 Aug. 1940, ibid.
[59] Colonial Office to Foreign Office, 17 Aug. 1940, ibid.

Konoe government put pressure on the Vichy administration in Indo-China to grant Japan bases in the northern half of the colony, and then aligned Japan overtly with Germany and Italy in the tripartite pact. The exercise of examining the divisive problems had been beneficial, if only in starkly demonstrating the numerous different aspects dividing Japan from China and the other powers and the improbability of bridging these to mutual satisfaction or acceptance.

Thus the hopes of improving Anglo-Japanese relations during the three-month closure of the Burma road petered out. The other major reassessment stimulated by the crisis concerned the state of British defences in East Asia. A new appraisal was urgently necessary, for the last substantial report by the chiefs of staff had been written for the imperial conference in 1937 before the outbreak of the war in China. The European situation had completely overshadowed the Far East before July 1940, just as it continued to do afterwards. However, the menace of Japan had to be recognized as more immediate than before, even if differences persisted in high quarters over the precise nature of the threat; Churchill, in particular, tended to dismiss the threat as a distraction from the 'real wars' in Europe and the Middle East. The strident alarm emanating from Australia reinforced the pressure to examine the poverty of far eastern defences once more. The full report by the chiefs of staff was submitted to the war cabinet on 31 July 1940.[60] The report merits careful analysis, since the issue of defence assumes greater significance and controversy from this time onwards. In the introductory memorandum Newall, Pound, and Dill, the chiefs of staff, stated that the report had been compiled on the assumption that the military predicament in other theatres would not improve noticeably, necessitating the retention of a fleet in the eastern Mediterranean; the policy of the United States would be unchanged; that Britain would resist if attacked by Japan; that whether Britain would assist the Netherlands East Indies, if attacked, would have to be determined by the British government at that time, although the chiefs of staff had anticipated that Britain would do so for the purposes of drafting

---

[60] 'The situation in the Far East in the event of Japanese intervention against us', report by chiefs of staff committee, 31 July 1940, C.O.S.(40)592, also W.P.(40)302, Cab.66/10.

the report. If Britain were to co-operate effectively with the Netherlands East Indies, joint staff talks would be needed; such talks could not be held at this juncture, however, since Britain could not provide any significant military aid.

The report opened by recalling the basic thinking underlining the previous review in 1937. It had then been assumed that any threat to British interests would be seaborne, and that a fleet of ample strength could be dispatched within three months to protect the Dominions and India and to defend communications in the Indian Ocean. The Japanese advance into the coastal areas of China, the development of communications in Thailand, the weakness of the French regime in Indo-China, the wider scope of aircraft, had all increased the Japanese threat to such an extent that Malaya was menaced by land and air as well as sea. The war in Europe, including the unexpected collapse of France, meant it was at present impossible to send a fleet to the Far East. The report proceeded to subdivide the issues under the heading of general considerations: the defence problem; strategy in the absence of a fleet; and defence requirements in the absence of a fleet. Japan's aim was to exclude occidental influence from the Far East and secure control of vital raw materials. The existence of British possessions would be incompatible with this aim, and attacks could eventually be expected on Hong Kong and Malaya. The factor deterring Japan from too rapid an advance was fear of American reactions. Since Britain was so heavily committed in Europe, a collision with Japan must be avoided. The original copy of the report sent to the Foreign Office contained the sentence, 'A general settlement including economic concessions to Japan, should be concluded as soon as possible.' This was subsequently amended to read, 'A general settlement, including economic concessions to Japan, is desirable. But the prospects are not at present favourable.'[61] Ideally a British fleet should be sent to Singapore but this was impossible for the foreseeable future; the aim must accordingly be to contain Japanese expansion as far as possible, retaining a foothold from which a counter-attack would be launched. The courses open to Japan consisted of a direct attack on British possessions; penetration of Indo-China

---

[61] Copy of report in F3765/193/61, F.O.371/24708.

or Thailand; an attack on the Netherlands East Indies; or seizure of the Philippines. The chiefs of staff thought it most likely that the Japanese would advance gradually, moving at first into Indo-China or Thailand and then into the Netherlands East Indies before attacking Singapore. Japanese penetration of Thailand would be extremely dangerous to Malaya but would have to be tolerated in view of the lack of defence resources. The Netherlands East Indies would be a vital region, and Japanese control of the East Indies would jeopardize the entire British position. It was desirable that Britain and the Netherlands should agree on mutual co-operation. The British garrisons in north China were strategic-ally so vulnerable that they should be withdrawn; Hong Kong could not be held for long but should resist as best it could. The essence of Britain's plight was summarized in the following succinct but plaintive paragraph: 'In the absence of a Fleet our policy should be to rely primarily on air power. The air forces required to implement that policy, however, cannot be provided for some time to come. Until they can be made available we shall require substantial additional land forces in Malaya, which cannot in present circumstances be found from British or Indian resources.'[62] Because of the Japanese expansion, a serious attempt must be made to defend the whole of Malaya without relying so heavily on the fortress of Singapore itself.

The report was a mixture of the accurate and the mis-leading. British weakness was manifestly revealed but the emphasis on reaching a settlement with Japan was excessive and unrealistic; in addition, Singapore was still overvalued as a powerful base and the Japanese were underestimated, especially in the air.[63] It was estimated that to afford adequate security for British possessions and trade routes centring on Malaya, an air strength of 336 aircraft was required, approximately four times the existing air strength. No doubt in order to forestall the outburst from Downing Street, the chiefs of staff explained that this large increase was rendered necessary by the appreciable improvement in Japan's power and the decline in Britain's position: the absence of a battle

---

[62] Ibid.
[63] Ibid., paragraphs 67 and 69.

fleet was the cardinal feature. Army strength would similarly have to be improved: to defend the Malayan peninsula at least six brigades with ancillary troops would be needed. It was impossible to provide the equivalent of three divisions and attached troops recommended by the G.O.C.[64] The sole immediate source of reinforcement would come from the provision of a division by Australia.[65] Current British naval strength consisted of 1 eight-inch cruiser, 2 modern six-inch cruisers, 4 old six-inch cruisers, 6 armed merchant cruisers, 5 old destroyers, 3 A/S escorts, and 8 M.T.B.s—'These are entirely inadequate for a war in the Far East.'[66] The report was to constitute the official guide to defence policy, but it remained curiously ambivalent in its effects. The prime minister did not accept important sections of the report, particularly the proposed increase in forces necessary to hold the whole of Malaya. This reflected his single-minded concentration on Europe and the Middle East and failure to appreciate the Japanese threat. There was no disagreement over the fact and extent of weakness but over the proximity and probability of that weakness being successfully exploited by Japan. The defence chiefs exaggerated the might of Singapore, and Churchill did so even more.

One of the crucial questions raised involved Britain's attitude to the Netherlands East Indies. Should Britain promise to help the East Indies or not? The subject arose in late July 1940, when the chiefs of staff considered the first draft, by the joint planning sub-committee, of the Far East appreciation. The chief of the naval staff and first sea lord, Admiral Sir Dudley Pound, objected to a guarantee being given on the grounds that the navy was so stretched already that it could not possibly implement the promise; it would be necessary to accept Japanese occupation of the East Indies, unpleasant and difficult though this would be. The chief of the imperial general staff and the chief of the air staff dissented and the matter was referred to the war cabinet.[67] The cabinet

---

[64] Ibid., paragraph 79.
[65] Ibid., paragraph 81.
[66] Ibid., paragraph 84.
[67] See chiefs of staff 23, 26, and 27 July 1940, C.O.S.230(40)2, 234(40)3, and 236(40)3, Cab.79/5. As with other defence problems, the role of the Netherlands East Indies had been discussed before the start of the European war in 1939 with the same

began to consider it on 29 July. Halifax reiterated doubt as to the likelihood of a Japanese declaration of war. Pound said it would be foolish for strategy to be determined by sentiment. The Netherlands government in exile was co-operating with Britain in Europe to restore the mother country. The position in the Far East was entirely different: Europe must come first and a Japanese landing in the East Indies could not be prevented. Britain's sole aim should be to hold the base at Singapore until a fleet could be dispatched. Halifax said frankly that Britain's authority would be gravely diminished if the Japanese conquered the East Indies: Australia and New Zealand would be directly threatened. He thought the Japanese always moved carefully and with calculation, and the fact was that their interests were best served by remaining at peace. Churchill agreed:

THE PRIME MINISTER said that, to his mind, the central fact of the situation, if Japan obtained the mastery of the Netherlands East Indies, was that she would be able to prepare strong positions facing Singapore, including a base for her fleet. If we did not fight, she would be able to prepare these positions in peace, and to use them against us at the moment which suited her best.

If we made it clear that we should fight to preserve the integrity of the Netherlands East Indies, Japan might very well decide against attack. The danger of having to take on both this country and the United States of America was a powerful deterrent. Russia also might be added to the number of Japan's enemies.[68]

Attlee spoke of the blow to prestige of permitting Japan to capture the East Indies. Alexander, the first lord of the Admiralty, reminded his colleagues that the Burma road had been closed because the struggle with Germany and Italy came first. Churchill dismissed the comparison: the Burma road crisis had not threatened the Singapore base. Pound staunchly repeated that the board of Admiralty had to consider if the recommendations of the chiefs of staff were consonant with the existing naval programmes.[69] Sinclair, the secretary of state for air, thought Japan would probably refrain from

arguments being voiced; the position was now more urgent and the arguments sharper.
[68] War cabinet conclusions, 29 July 1940, confidential annex, 214(40)7, Cab.65/14.
[69] Ibid.

aggression but held that it was important to decide that an attack on the Netherlands East Indies would be a *casus belli* and that the Dutch should, in this contingency, destroy their oilfields. Caldecote drew attention to the fears of Australia and New Zealand just as convoys were about to sail from Australia; he suggested that the views of the Dominions be sought. Churchill said the kernel of the question was whether Britain possessed the resources to prevent Japanese occupation of the East Indies, and thought the chiefs of staff should produce a paper explaining what action would be involved in opposing Japan. The cabinet agreed and the chiefs of staff were requested to submit a paper.[70] In addition, Halifax was asked to see the Netherlands minister and suggest that the United States should be approached to see what aid she could give.

The chiefs of staff reviewed the position in a paper dated 7 August and concluded there was very little that could be done to assist the East Indies:

So far as the Navy is concerned, it would be confined to the provision of facilities for their Navy at Singapore. On land we could not provide them with any assistance. Our air force in Malaya could afford some degree of protection against any Japanese approach by the route West of Borneo, which would free Dutch forces for action further East. In this connection it is possible that Australia might be willing to operate air forces from Dutch bases to defend key positions on the Eastern flank, but preliminary preparations will be necessary.[71]

If the United States intervened actively and warned Japan not to attack the East Indies, she could be dissuaded from taking action. If war nevertheless came, Britain could still contribute little in the defence sphere but could offer the United States the use of the Singapore base, which would in any event be essential for the American campaign.

The cabinet discussed the gloomy document on 8 August. Churchill felt that no decision could be taken on assistance to the East Indies; he proposed that the discussion be confined to deciding whether the paper should be sent to the Dominions.

[70] Ibid.
[71] 'Assistance to the Dutch in event of Japanese aggression in Netherlands East Indies', 7 Aug. 1940, W.P.(40)308, Cab.66/10; also in F3765/193/61, F.O.371/24708.

Caldecote was apprehensive of the repercussions in Australia and New Zealand. The prime minister breezily rejoined that the matter could be presented in such a way as to inspire confidence in the Dominions. This should be achieved by arguing that the primary aim was to defeat the Italians in the Mediterranean; it was hoped to avoid war with Japan but the contingency had to be recognized as a possibility. It was most unlikely that Japan would attack Australia and New Zealand; attacks on Hong Kong, Singapore, and the East Indies were, however, likely. If such attacks occurred, Britain would send one battle cruiser and one aircraft carrier to the Indian Ocean, based on Ceylon, to protect vital sea routes. If a full-scale invasion of Australia or New Zealand was threatened, the United States would, it was hoped, intervene to save matters. 'In the last resort, however, our course was clear. We could never stand by and see a British Dominion overwhelmed by a yellow race, and we should at once come to the assistance of that Dominion with all the forces we could make available. For that purpose we should be prepared, if necessary, to abandon our position in the Mediterranean and the Middle East.'[72] Caldecote thought such a declaration would prove an admirable answer to Dominion fears. Pound intervened to remind the cabinet of the consequences of leaving the Mediterranean. Gibraltar would presumably have to be given up and the direct trade route to the Cape could be endangered by Italian warships. Shipping would have to be routed further out to sea and additional ships provided in the Atlantic to defend the new routes. Caldecote and Halifax criticized the odd assumption by the chiefs of staff that it was quite possible that Japan and China would shortly come to terms; it was hard to tell the source of the observation and it did not correspond with the views of the Foreign Office. The cabinet deferred the strategic issue for later consideration, invited Caldecote to consult the Dominions, and requested the chiefs of staff to reconsider political aspects in conjunction with the Foreign Office.

The Dominions were duly consulted. Australia believed that war between the British Commonwealth and Japan would be virtually certain if Japan moved against the East Indies, but

[72] War cabinet conclusions, 8 Aug. 1940, confidential annex, 222(30)4, Cab.65/14.

agreed with the Admiralty that chronic defence weaknesses rendered it impossible for Britain to enter into a binding unilateral commitment to help the East Indies. South Africa gave no direct reply but Smuts regarded Japanese aggression as unlikely and advocated reliance on diplomacy involving cooperation with the United States. Canada sent no reply. With regard to opening staff conversations with the Dutch, only New Zealand supported the idea unequivocally. The joint planning staff reviewed matters once more in late September and concluded that while Britain could give no guarantee of support, it would be wise to begin secret defence talks with the Dutch, as urged by the service chiefs in the Far East.[73]

The Burma road crisis stimulated much thought and anxiety but few solutions. The war cabinet and chiefs of staff were agreed in identifying the severe weaknesses in the Far East and the importance of rectifying the worst omissions where possible. Churchill, however, was less alarmed since he thought it on balance improbable that Japan would move and was encouraged by a false conception of the strength of Singapore. He endeavoured to console the southern Dominions with promises of help, just as he had done in November 1939 and was to do again in December 1940, which would involve withdrawing from the Mediterranean — in all, consequences which he had not properly assessed. The controversy over aiding the East Indies marked the beginning of a tedious and repetitive argument which continued to the eve of Pearl Harbor.

Events in September and early October 1940 were dominated, as regards East Asia, by the interrelated crises connected with Japan's advance into Indo-China, her adherence to the tripartite pact, and the decision to reopen the Burma road at the expiration of the three-month agreement. In an interim assessment of the Burma road situation, Halifax informed his colleagues in the war cabinet that Japan was attempting to interpret the agreement as widely as possible, to such an extent that a Japanese official in Burma was trying to prevent the internal transport of goods banned from export

[73] 'The Far East: policy with regard to the Netherlands East Indies', report by the joint planning staff, 25 Sept. 1940, C.O.S.(40)772, J.P., Cab.80/19.

to China and was urging the suppression of manifestations of hostility to Japan from the Chinese community in Burma. British and American public opinion was firmly in favour of reopening the road. The decision would depend on the outcome of the 'Battle of Britain' and on progress in the Middle East. It was necessary to take preparatory measures to prepare Japan for reopening: this should be achieved by emphasizing the temporary character of the agreement and that its existence had been conditional on a serious attempt to resolve the Sino-Japanese war. Halifax pointed out that Japanese public opinion was not aware of the latter condition because it had been incorporated in a confidential memorandum signed just before the fall of the Yonai government. It was important that the reopening be accompanied by as little publicity as possible, and Chinese co-operation should be enlisted in this context. Roosevelt, Hull, and Welles had all expressed interest in the matter to Lothian; probably the Americans would do little while the presidential campaign was being waged but consultations should certainly take place. The Dominions supported reopening, if with apprehension in Australia's case.[74] The probability was, in early September, that the road would be reopened.

The subject was then overtaken by developments in Indo-China and the signing of the tripartite pact. The position of French Indo-China had been delicate from the start of the Sino-Japanese struggle, and the government in Paris and the local administration had shown growing alarm at the extent of Japanese expansion and the imminent threat to Indo-China. The collapse of France rendered the position much worse. Tentative plans for mutual Anglo-French support, resulting from the Singapore conference of June 1939, existed but became invalid in the changed circumstances of June-September 1940. The French community and forces were split between the supporters of Pétain, the supporters of de Gaulle, and those who supported neither side. The deciding factor with the majority was the desire to save the colony from outright annexation. Such an outcome would obviously be precipitated by a Gaullist triumph so that the local administration, which in the main supported Vichy, proceeded

---

[74] Memorandum by Halifax, 2 Sept. 1940, F4115/43/10, F.O.371/24669.

with pragmatism and caution. The governor-general at the time of the collapse, General Catroux, was fundamentally opposed to Vichy but disguised the fact while he devised a viable diplomatic policy to outmanoeuvre the Japanese. He was, however, soon replaced by Admiral Decoux, loyal to Vichy, mildly antagonistic to Britain, and prepared to fulfil the Vichy policy of making greater concessions to Japan. From Japan's viewpoint, infiltration of Indo-China was valuable as a means both of facilitating the war against China and of consolidating Japan's gains in preparation for the subsequent advances in south-east Asia. Sumner Welles told Lothian on 5 August that Japan was demanding bases in Tongking with right of passage for troops; Welles doubted if the United States could advance beyond a statement deploring changes in the far eastern *status quo*.[75] The Far Eastern department viewed the position with concern but also felt that Britain could not afford to intervene; Craigie was, however, instructed to see Matsuoka and convey the anxiety of the government.[76] Admiral Decoux followed the established diplomatic technique of delaying the talks for as long as he could. Japanese patience gave way at the beginning of September and an ultimatum was handed to the governor-general threatening a Japanese attack unless an agreement was swiftly concluded. The Foreign Office decided to consult Washington urgently to compare assessments on the contingency of a Japanese attack; Lothian was asked to inquire if an American squadron could visit Singapore.[77] It appeared that an agreement had been reached on 30 August between the Vichy ambassador in Tokyo and the Japanese government of which Decoux was at first ignorant. At least this was the allegation made by Matsuoka to Craigie on 16 September when the foreign minister refuted any intention of exerting pressure on Indo-China.

Lothian visited Hull on the same day and received a more forthright statement than usual when he inquired what support Britain could expect on reopening the road. Hull replied that it depended on the outcome of Britain's current

---

[75] Lothian to Foreign Office, 5 Aug. 1940, F3710/3429/61, F.O.371/24719.

[76] Foreign Office to Craigie, 9 Aug. 1940, ibid.

[77] Foreign Office to Lothian, 5 Sept. 1940, F4109/3429/61, F.O.371/24719. See also *I.M.T.F.E.*, Record, Exhibit 618-A, pp. 6844–6853, and Exhibit 620, pp. 6874–6894.

desperate fight for survival: if Britain could hold out until 1941, the United States could pursue a much firmer policy in the Pacific. He said that the administration was considering a 25 million dollar loan to China and was examining ways of strengthening the limited embargo on exports to Japan, including the possibility of discontinuing silk purchases. According to Lothian, Hull implied that the United States might be willing to go to war with Japan, although Hull appreciated this would not be to Britain's advantage as it would reduce supplies to Britain.[78] Hull expressed the fervent wish that the road be reopened. The secretary of state's trenchant remarks were encouraging and reflected the developing American suspicion of Japan, amidst the new evidence of expansion, and America's determination eventually to oppose this trend. On 23 September it was learned that Japanese forces had entered northern Indo-China to occupy the bases reluctantly ceded by Vichy. It was a profoundly significant development, not least for British defence policy which, until very recently, had not contemplated a threat to Malaya and Burma emerging from Japanese occupation of territories adjacent to British possessions. The French administration ostensibly remained in complete control but in practice a form of joint rule, characterized by incessant intrigue and rumour, had been inaugurated.

Almost simultaneously Japan signed the tripartite pact with Germany and Italy.[79] Hitler had been pressing for the agreement for some months and was unsuccessfully to urge Japan to attack Singapore in 1940-1. The Führer harboured no affection for the Japanese, who did not fit easily into his ideal racial world. The tenacity and power of Japan could not be ignored, however, particularly when their might could be turned against Britain and the United States. The concept of the tripartite pact was extremely attractive to most elements within the Japanese army and to the more belligerent nationalist circles. Matsuoka Yosuke, the eccentric and devious foreign minister, supported the pact with all of his not inconsiderable loquacity. Matsuoka is a puzzling figure to

---

[78] Lothian to Foreign Office, 16 Sept. 1940, F4290/193/61, F.O.371/24709.
[79] For the text of the pact and exchange of letters, see *D.G.F.P.* D, xi, 204-7.

assess.[80] He had been educated in the United States and was
generally regarded as one of the most promising younger diplomats in the 1920s and 1930s. He had worked for the South
Manchuria Railway Company during a break from his diplomatic career, and struck useful connections with nationalist
and military factions. Matsuoka represented Japan at the
debates in the League of Nations on the Lytton Report. He
became a popular hero in Japan by leading the walk-out of the
Japanese delegation in a final gesture of defiance at the
censure of the international community. He personified the
bizarre decade of the 1930s and first half of the 1940s, when
most Japanese opinion accepted and identified itself with
vociferous nationalism and moved sharply away from the
tenuous links with the 1920s. Matsuoka's foreign policy envisaged effective domination of East Asia and of the western
Pacific as quickly as possible and compelling the other powers,
by a combination of persuasion and coercion, to accept the
new order. Matsuoka believed the old order was dying
throughout the world—with the possible exception of the
American continent—and Japan's aim should be to help it on
its way with a well-aimed kick. He did not want to involve
Japan in war with the United States, however. Matsuoka
wished to gain his ends by diplomatic means. The tripartite
pact was a boastful and overt proclamation of confidence in
the new order; Japan hoped the pact would discourage the
United States from opposing her expansion by force and, less
importantly, from intervening directly in the European war.
The terms of the pact bound the partners to support each
other if attacked by a power not involved in the European conflict. Hitler hoped the pact would prevent the United States
from going too far in her aid to Britain, further, that is, than
she had already gone in the destroyers-bases deal with Britain
in September 1940. Hitler ardently longed for Britain and the
United States to become embroiled with Japan: in the end the
hope was realized, but much later than he had anticipated
and at a time when he himself was increasingly preoccupied

[80] See J. W. Morley (ed.), *Dilemmas of Growth in Prewar Japan*, especially the essay by
Hosoya Chihiro, pp. 81–105. For a reappraisal of Matsuoka see B. Teters, 'Matsuoka
Yosuke: The Diplomacy of Bluff and Gesture', in R. D. Burns and E. M. Bennett
(eds.), *Diplomats in Crisis: United States-Chinese-Japanese Relations, 1919–1941*
(Clio Press, Oxford, 1974), pp. 275–96.

with the vast conflict with Russia. Most opinion in Japan felt few qualms about the tripartite pact or about the certainty of ultimate German victory in Europe. There were, however, some who doubted whether Germany would win, the Japanese ambassador in London, Shigemitsu Mamoru, being one example. There were others, too, who feared the consequences of a German victory. If Hitler won in Europe, might not his attention turn to Asia with a demand for the return of Germany's former colonies? Scepticism was fed by recollections of Hitler's extreme racialism and unpredictability; in the latter context, the Nazi–Soviet pact was still a living and embarrassing memory. Prince Konoe Fumimaro, the prime minister, was one of the sceptics. An enthusiastic nationalist himself, Konoe's ardour had diminished somewhat from the heights of 1937–8, when he had been instrumental in transforming the early stages of the Sino-Japanese conflict into a major war. Konoe was uneasily aware of the danger of war with the United States, which he feared might be brought nearer by the tripartite pact. Although subtle and devious, Konoe was not a domineering man and certainly not inclined at this point to hold out against the army and his masterful foreign minister. Konoe assented to the pact. Ironically enough, he was to be joined by Matsuoka in December 1941 in lamenting the outbreak of the Pacific war; Matsuoka belatedly reached the conclusion that the tripartite pact had been a terrible blunder.

Sir Robert Craigie reported that there was much silent questioning of the pact behind the façade of popular enthusiasm. The pact was a logical consequence of the fall of France and of the more authoritarian atmosphere in Japan in recent months.[81] M. E. Dening philosophically remarked that it was a culmination to the trend of Japanese history since 1931. The Japanese were, he observed, great believers in symbolism and the pact connoted a new direction in foreign policy. A number of Japanese would deplore the pact but, since they were fatalists, they would accept it. The pact might be a stimulus to Japan to proceed to war at once; in Dening's opinion, the best course was to ignore the pact with disdain and not give the Japanese the impression that Britain was

---

[81] Craigie to Foreign Office, 28 Sept. 1940, F4469/626/23, F.O.371/24736.

afraid.[82] Sir Stafford Cripps, now ambassador in Moscow, thought the pact was intended to intimidate the Soviet Union. It was vital, he urged, that Great Britain and the United States should follow a vigorous policy in the Far East and that they should encourage Russia to join them.[83] Halifax entirely concurred and immediately told Cripps that co-operation with the Soviet Union would be most welcome, 'I should hope that it might not be impossible to get Molotov to realise that they backed the wrong horse from Russian point of view last year, and that next year is very likely to see the gravity of their miscalculation.'[84] This observation was prophetic enough. Halifax continued that a combination including Turkey and China would be highly desirable. The government had decided not to renew the agreement on the closure of the Burma road. Pursuance of a resolute anti-Japanese policy was conditional on the participation of the United States, and the subject was being pressed by Lord Lothian in Washington.

Lothian urged that the Burma road be reopened as a counter-blast to the tripartite pact and as a means of conveying Britain's determination to the American people. If Japan took drastic action against Britain, he thought the United States would be quickly drawn into the war. The Foreign Office was inclined to share Hull's view that it was preferable for the United States to keep out of war for the present and concentrate on assisting Britain economically. Lothian dissented, because participation in war was the only way to rally the American nation.[85] The same view was taken by the prime minister who, at the war cabinet on 2 October, 'questioned the statement that it was not in our interests that the United States should be involved in war in the Pacific.'[86] To Churchill, full American participation in the war was essential and he did not worry unduly over the circumstances in which the involvement occurred; in the Pacific he overestimated, as so many did in Britain, the ability of the United States to react quickly and effectively for war. The fact was that defence preparedness was proceeding slowly and the

---

[82] Minute by Dening, 30 Sept. 1940, ibid.
[83] Cripps to Foreign Office, 28 Sept. 1940, F4472/626/23, F.O.371/24736.
[84] Foreign Office to Cripps, 3 Oct. 1940, ibid.
[85] Lothian to Foreign Office, 2 Oct. 1940, F4533/626/3, F.O.371/24736.
[86] War cabinet conclusions, 2 Oct. 1940, 264(40)4, Cab.65/9.

American defence chiefs opposed an early clash with Japan unless absolutely unavoidable.

Meanwhile, in late September and early October, the chiefs of staff and the cabinet considered the reopening of the road but delayed an announcement until nearer the deadline of 18 October, when the agreement expired.[87] In cabinet on 3 October Halifax urged that the most satisfactory procedure would be to reopen the road as from 18 October. Churchill warmly supported Halifax:

THE PRIME MINISTER was clear that this was the right decision. He did not believe that the Japanese would declare war upon us as a result. We should be fully justified in taking the line that, whereas we had expected the Japanese during the interval afforded by the currency of the Burma road agreement to make a genuine effort to reach an all-round agreement, all they had done was to make the German-Italian-Japanese Pact. In these circumstances, we had no option but to carry out our duties as a neutral in the Sino-Japanese conflict.[88]

The war cabinet agreed: the road would be reopened on 18 October. Craigie called on Matsuoka to acquaint him of the decision on 8 October.[89] The foreign minister did not seem surprised and stressed the Japanese wish for peace with the whole of China; he promised to do what he could to discourage the agitation against Britain. Craigie reported that the Japanese press interpreted the decision as an American - inspired reprisal against the tripartite pact.[90] Chiang Kai-shek rejoiced at the news, and there was an exchange of telegrams between the generalissimo and Churchill praising each other and the huge struggle in which each country was involved.[91]

The crisis over the Burma road in the summer and autumn of 1940 therefore ended with the position markedly happier for Britain than had seemed possible in July. The original decision to comply with the demand was most likely unnecessary but it was still wise to have submitted and avoided the risk, when matters were so grave in Europe. The diplomacy of the surrender had been conducted with great skill by Craigie, and Japan compromised, too, in the form of

[87] Chiefs of staff committee, 27 Sept. 1940, 326(40)3, Cab.79/7.

[88] War cabinet conclusions, 3 Oct. 1940, 265(40)5, Cab.65/9.

[89] Craigie to Foreign Office, 8 Oct. 1940, F4596/43/10, F.O.371/24670.

[90] Craigie to Foreign Office, 9 Oct. 1940, F4623/23/10, F.O.371/24670.

[91] Halifax to Clark Kerr, 20 Oct. 1940, F4859/43/10, F.O.371/24671.

the confidential formula confirming closure for three months. A full assessment of the problems involved in securing a peace settlement had been made and the conclusions emerging from it were that it would be extremely difficult to reach a settlement, given the political and strategical realities. It was clearly more in Britain's interest that the Sino-Japanese war should continue than that it should end. The likelihood of war between Japan, Great Britain, and the United States loomed ever larger. The defence reappraisal of July 1940 revealed the sombre state of British defences. The Foreign Office urged, as before, that defences be improved, as did local defence personnel; the chiefs of staff vaguely sympathized but reluctantly agreed with Churchill that the Far East came last in the order of priorities. The attempt to square the circle by diplomacy would have to be continued.

VI

DEFENCE, AID FOR CHİNA, AND EXCHANGES WITH JAPAN

IN the period between October 1940 and June 1941 developments that were both encouraging and disturbing for Great Britain's war effort occurred. On the positive side was the fact that the 'Battle of Britain' had been won and the threat of German invasion had receded; it remained a contingency to be anticipated and guarded against but was less urgent than in the summer of 1940. Anglo-American relations continued to grow closer, a trend exemplified in the passage of the Lend-Lease bill (January-March 1941) and in the more active intervention of the American navy in the Atlantic. However, there was little immediate likelihood of full-scale American intervention in the war. Franklin D. Roosevelt's overwhelming victory in the presidential election (November 1940) was most reassuring for the British government and people since he was immensely experienced in government, an astute politician of the first order and the rallying symbol for Americans wishing to send more aid to Britain. Wendell Willkie was liked and respected in Britain but was comparatively unknown, and a Republican victory would have disrupted Anglo-American relations while the new administration acclimatized itseÏf. In Europe Mussolini launched his ill-considered attack on Greece (October 1940) and had to be rescued by Hitler; Britain became unwisely but perhaps inevitably involved. In north Africa the struggle between Italy and Great Britain swung decisively in favour of Britain (January-March 1941), but was soon to swing equally decisively in favour of Germany following Rommel's appearance on the scene. The defence of Egypt, the Suez Canal, and oil supplies in Iraq constituted a heavy and onerous commitment, which came second in the list of priorities after the defence of Britain itself and the battle of the Atlantic. In April 1941 Yugoslavia was subjugated, following the *coup* that removed Prince Paul. Relations between Germany and Russia slowly deteriorated: Hitler was determined to attack Russia soon in fulfilment of his racial ideals but the planning of the German general staff was perfunctory for such a huge enterprise.[1] In East Asia it was a phase of ominous quiescence punctuated by occasional rumours of a Japanese offensive in south-east Asia, rumours which were pronounced in February 1941 but lacked validity at this juncture. Matsuoka visited Europe in March-April 1941 and met Hitler for a rambling discussion. Matsuoka was delighted to meet the Führer but little that was concrete came of his visit to Berlin. He met Stalin in Moscow and quickly negotiated a non-aggression pact between Japan and the Soviet Union. Talks between the United States and Japan began in the spring of 1941 in a bid to find an acceptable solution to the growing differences between the two powers. The role of these talks and Britain's attitude towards them will be pursued in the next chapter. For the development of British policy, the principal aspects concern the various appreciations of defence problems, notably the staff talks held in Washington early in 1941; the reassessment of China's ability to maintain the resistance to Japan and the importance of fostering it; and the exchanges between Eden, Butler, and Shigemitsu in London and between Craigie and Matsuoka in Tokyo.

Developments in defence included consultations with the United States and reorganization of the structure of British defence in the Far East on a more efficient basis; a whole string of defence conferences met, involving primarily Britain, the southern Dominions, and the Netherlands, with the United States present as observers or participants. Singapore was the headquarters of the far eastern defence effort. Originally conceived as a great naval fortress, Singapore was less significant than Malaya itself; Singapore could not be held unless Malaya was defended successfully, as the chiefs of staff had recognized in the defence review in July 1940. The prime minister refused to accept this view, and minuted that it was

---

[1] For two convincing accounts of Russo-German relations at this time, see B. Leach, *German Strategy Against Russia, 1939–41* (Clarendon Press, Oxford, 1973), and J. Erickson, *The Road To Stalingrad* (Weidenfeld and Nicolson, London, 1975).

MAP II

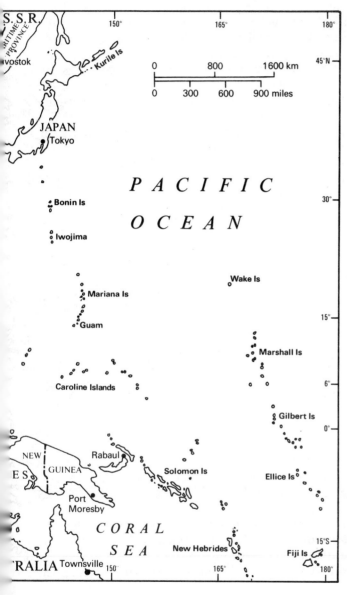

East Asia and the western Pacific

absurd to try to defend a country as large as Malaya.[2] Churchill did not believe valuable forces could or should be diverted to Malaya and he regarded the Japanese menace as remote. A fundamental division of opinion therefore existed between Churchill and the chiefs of staff, which was never properly settled. An appreciation by the commanders in the Far East was long overdue, and arrangements were made to convene a conference in October 1940. At first it was hoped the United States would participate. After the announcement of the tripartite pact at the end of September 1940, Cordell Hull advocated a firm approach to Japan and welcomed the prospect of staff talks with Britain. The chiefs of staff naturally enthused at the prospect, but the United States then declined to participate in the Singapore conference, instead supporting private talks between the respective defence staffs: political complications would render it impossible to take part and the presidential campaign was nearing its climax. Preparations for the Singapore conference were in any case proceeding. The conference was to be presided over by the C.-in-C., China station, Vice-Admiral Sir Geoffrey Layton, and he was to be assisted by the G.O.C. Malaya, General Sir Lionel Bond, and the A.O.C., Far East, Air Vice-Marshal J. T. Babington. Representatives from Australia, New Zealand, India, Burma, and Malaya would be present. The terms of reference were that the conference should provide a tactical appreciation of the situation in the event of war with Japan; that it should assess the defence requirements of India and Burma in the light of the Japanese threat via Thailand; that it should prepare points requiring discussion with the Netherlands East Indies if staff talks were authorized; and should perform a similar task for consideration jointly with the United States whenever full consultation took place on the Far East.[3]

The report of the conference accepted and followed the principles stated in the July 1940 report by the chiefs of staff, concentrating on emphasizing even more starkly the poverty of defences and the urgent importance of strengthening them.

---

[2] W. S. Churchill, *The Second World War*, ii (Cassell, London, 5th edition, 1955), 591-2, minute, 10 Sept. 1940, also cited in Cab.80/18.
[3] Report of the Singapore Defence Conference, 1940, Cab.80/24.

The enemy would most probably attack some or all of the following: Hong Kong, Malaya, British Borneo, Burma and the Netherlands East Indies or Timor. The seizure of islands in the Pacific and attacks on trade routes were certain. It was possible but unlikely that Australia and New Zealand would be assailed. The absence of adequate naval forces would dictate a defensive strategy. As regards priorities:

Our first and immediate consideration must be to ensure the security of Malaya against attack. The Tactical Appreciation shows that the army and air forces in Malaya (including reinforcements now being provided) are, both in numbers and in equipment, far below those required in view of the inadequacy of the naval forces available. *This deficiency must obviously be remedied immediately* and we recommend that the further cooperation of India, Australia and New Zealand be sought without delay.

What air forces are available we must use to prevent or at least to deter the Japanese from establishing naval and air bases within striking distance of our vital interests in Malaya, Burma, the Dutch East Indies, Australia, and New Zealand. By using advanced operational bases throughout the area, we should aim at being able to concentrate aircraft at any point from our collective air resources in the Far East, Australia and New Zealand . . .[4]

It was estimated that the minimum number of aircraft required in Burma and Malaya was 582, apart from air forces stationed in the Netherlands East Indies, Australia, and New Zealand. It was stressed that the number of aircraft in Australia was 'dangerously small' and the aircraft in New Zealand 'of obsolete type'. In sea communications the priority was to protect convoys across the Indian Ocean to the Middle East. Capital ships would be essential for escorting convoys and at least seven cruisers should be available in Australian waters. Considerable attention was paid to the threat of invasion of Burma, which could be accomplished by a combination of land and air attack from Thailand and Yunnan, in the event of Japanese advances into these areas. The immediate threat to Burma and eastern India was held to comprise an air attack on vital oil refineries and docks at Rangoon and possibly on vulnerable points in eastern India, including Digboi and Calcutta. In a detailed investigation of air defence the report envisaged that attacking Japanese air-craft would, as indicated by the chiefs of staff, be between 617 and 713 in number. Since it was unlikely that carrier-borne aircraft would operate against Burma, additional air forces, anti-aircraft defences, local naval defence, and artillery were recommended.

The chief deficiencies were:[5]

MILITARY

Units	Malaya	Burma
Infantry Battalions	12	7
Field or Mountain Regiment R.A.	6	1 field
		¼ mountain
Anti-Tank Batteries	8	1
Infantry Brigade Anti-Tank Companies	6	-
Field Companies, R.E.	3	3
Heavy A.A. Guns	120	24
Light A.A. Guns	98	68
Searchlights	138	
Light Tank Companies	3	1

AIRCRAFT

Present Strength	Recommended Strength	Deficiency in Modern Aircraft at 1 November 1940
Malaya and Burma 88 (48 modern)	582	534
Australia 82 (42 modern)	312	270
New Zealand 24 (obsolete)	60	60
New Guinea 4 (converted civil type)	8	8
Solomons-New Hebrides Fiji and Tonga 6 (converted civil type)	9	9
Indian Ocean 4 (obsolete)	87*	87

*Including two land-based squadrons in East Africa as striking force.

Approximately 346 aircraft were thought necessary in the Netherlands East Indies, of which only 159 were already stationed there, thus leaving a deficiency of 187 aircraft. As regards resources available for meeting deficiencies, the report suggested that India might provide four divisions to be ready at various stages during 1941 and that one strong brigade group and ancillary troops might be obtained from Australia by the end of December 1940, assuming agreement between the British and Australian governments. Limited supplies should be available from India and Australia. Detailed points

[5] Ibid.

for co-operation with the Dutch were listed, including mutual protection for shipping routes and planning of minefields. A longer section discussed aspects relevant to co-operation with the United States. One of the most important concerned the length of time that would elapse before the Americans could produce a battle fleet in the western Pacific equal or superior to the Japanese. The United States could contribute most significantly through assailing Japanese communications and any Japanese expeditions proceeding against the Netherlands East Indies, Malaya, or Hong Kong.

The report was examined by the joint planning staff in a commentary finally dated 1 January 1941.[6] In general terms the report was approved. It was agreed that an ultimate land strength of twenty-six battalions for Malaya and Borneo was reasonable and the emphasis given to Burma was acknowledged, since the chiefs of staff had not pursued the latter area in their assessment. The joint planning staff criticized the excessive pessimism of the report, however. 'We consider . . . that the views of the Commanders on the general defence situation are unduly pessimistic, and that they have in particular tended to over-estimate the minimum air forces necessary for reasonable security.'[7] The detailed recommendations were approved regarding the provision of extra aerodromes, the provision and preparation of a brigade group, and the availability of anti-aircraft guns. It was believed that the likelihood of a seaborne expedition against Burma from the west coast of Thailand had to be kept in mind. While fully conversant with the numerous weaknesses indicated, it was felt that Japanese prowess had been overestimated. In an appendix dealing with air forces, comparisons were drawn between difficulties experienced in the Middle East and the Far East, and an attempt was made to minimize the problems in the air:

Both the Defence Conference and the Commanders themselves appear to take far too pessimistic a view and to overestimate the Japanese. Thus, even in their final estimate, when they propose a first-line of 566 aircraft [actually raised to 582 at the conference] to

---

[6] 'Far East-Tactical Appreciation and Report of Singapore Defence Conference', report by joint planning staff, 1 Jan. 1941, Cab.79/8.
[7] Ibid.

meet the Japanese total of 600 to 700, some 300 of which are carrier-borne . . . they allege that they will still be 'heavily outnumbered' and may have to scale up their estimate of Japanese forces [*sic*] increase. This appears to be entirely divorced from reality. The Japanese have never fought against a first-class Power in the air and we have no reason to believe that their operations would be any more effective than those of the Italians.

In the very successful campaign in Egypt we started with 92 bombers and 44 fighters against an enemy total of 220 bombers and 240 fighters. Our success in countering the air attacks on Malta and on this country are even more significant. Moreover, as the Chiefs of Staff pointed out in the Far Eastern Appreciation, grave risks are involved in venturing a seaborne expedition within range of modern air forces, and it further appears to us entirely unnecessary to attempt to counter a spasmodic attack by carrier-borne aircraft at anything like terms of parity.

We agree that the final figure suggested in the Reports is probably a reasonable target to be aimed at establishing our position in the Far East and we feel that a first-line of 336 aircraft as proposed in the Far East Appreciation is one that should give us a reasonable degree of security. Any numerical weakness in our forces must be offset by endowing them with the maximum ability and power of concentration.[8]

The joint planning staff optimistically added that Dutch aid might be available. The shortage of fighters was considered 'perhaps our most serious weakness' and there was no prospect of an improvement within the near future.[9] It was important to allow maximum mobility in Malaya and a meticulous programme of aerodrome planning was needed.

The observations on the air situation have been cited at some length, since they illuminate clearly the grave underestimation of Japanese air power which was a consistent feature of defence thinking in London and the Far East. Erroneous comparisons were drawn between the Italians and the Japanese. It appears remarkable that no accurate information on Japan's air strength was obtained by intelligence operations. As the Malayan campaign was to demonstrate at the start of the Pacific war, Japan was supremely effective in the air. Presumably the prolongation of the Sino-Japanese war

---

[8] Ibid., appendix ii.
[9] Ibid.

encouraged fallacious comparisons and miscalculations.

One of the consequences of the worsening relations between Britain and Japan in 1940 had been the decision to reorganize the defence structure in Malaya with particular reference to the army and air force. With the navy so weak in far eastern waters, and little hope of improving it in the foreseeable future, attention was concentrated upon the other two services. A most unfortunate situation prevailed in Malaya in the defence establishment, where there were chronic disagreements affecting the civilian and service authorities and the military and air commanders. It resulted from the easygoing atmosphere of luxurious complacency that characterized the colonial administration and service establishment; it was the product of the unhurried and placid routine of life in Malaya, which seemed so remote from the ugly menace of Japanese aggression. Malaya was divided administratively into the Straits Settlements and then into the Federated and Unfederated Malay States, some of which enjoyed considerable independence. The governor of the Straits Settlements, Sir Shenton Thomas, was a worthy official but lacking in the drive and dynamism needed to galvanize Malaya in the new situation facing it in 1940–1; he was also away on leave in Britain for a lengthy period in 1940.[10] His defence secretary, C. A. Vlieland, was an able man but better at identifying problems than at solving them. The C.-in-C., Far East, Vice-Admiral Layton, had arrived only recently in succession to Sir Percy Noble and was initially not involved directly in the clash between General Bond and Air Vice-Marshal Babington.[11] The sharp differences between Bond and Babington were communicated to London in June 1940 by the colonial secretary in the Straits Settlements, S. W. Jones, who was in charge in the governor's absence. The argument between Bond and Babington was partly the result of personal acrimony; the major point at issue was whether aerodromes on the Malayan peninsula could be defended by the army or not. Babington held that Japanese forces must be

[10] For a concise discussion of the issues summarized here, see S. Woodburn Kirby, *Singapore: the Chain of Disaster* (Cassell, London, 1971), pp. 37–47, 71–7. See also I. Simson, *Singapore: Too Little and Too Late* (Leo Cooper, London, 1970) and Duff Cooper's final report on his mission to the Far East in 1941, 29 Oct. 1941, Cab.66/20.
[11] Babington later changed his name and became Air Marshal Sir J. T. Tremayne.

opposed in the air from aerodromes situated throughout the peninsula, for which purpose military co-operation was essential. Bond maintained that he did not possess enough troops to provide such co-operation, and accordingly opposed Babington. The chiefs of staff committee discussed the matter on 26 June 1940 and concluded that the controversy 'was due more to the lack of resources than to questions of principle'.[12] The chiefs of staff added that they were about to reassess far eastern strategy, and the local commanders must manage as best they could in the interim period. Babington was extremely critical of the failure in London to give proper recognition to the gravity of the situation. He also feared, in the summer of 1940, the appointment of a military dictator in Singapore; such an appointment might threaten his independence. In a private memorandum, dated 9 August 1940, Babington referred to the uneasiness over defence matters in Malaya as distinct from Singapore:

It is quite another matter as to whether, for instance, the obvious recent intensification of passive defence measures on Singapore Island is calculated to inspire confidence. No intelligent observer can fail to notice that after eleven months of war such measures are being suddenly applied and concentrated almost exclusively on the Island of Singapore. Corresponding measures or other similar preparations are conspicuous by their relative absence. It is only too easy to infer that ground defences are concentrated upon a Fortress basis. All the best European troops as well as the bulk of military equipment are concentrated on Singapore Island: they are nowhere in evidence on the Mainland.

It may well be, if there is uneasiness concerning military matters or military methods, that this situation accounts for some of it. The population on the Mainland may quite conceivably be wondering if they are to be left to their fate.[13]

Babington added, in the accompanying letter to Admiral Noble, that there was much dissatisfaction, 'and I think it is really quite clear that the sort of policy imposed upon us by the Home Government is not one which can possibly be clearly and publicly stated.'[14]

[12] Chiefs of staff committee, 26 June 1940, C.O.S.195(40)1, Cab.79/5.
[13] 'Notes on policy and public morale', 9 Aug. 1940, enclosed in Babington to Noble, 9 Aug. 1940, Air 23/1865.
[14] Ibid.

As a result of the greater likelihood of war and of the divisions of opinion in Malaya, it was decided in London that a commander-in-chief, Far East, should be appointed with supreme authority over the army and air force in Malaya; the navy would, however, continue under the direction of the C.-in-C., China. The man chosen to take up the appointment was Air Chief Marshal Sir Robert Brooke-Popham. After the disasters of the first phase of the Pacific war in December 1941, Brooke-Popham was unkindly described in the House of Lords as a 'nincompoop'.[15] This was unfair, and illustrated the popular desire to find a scapegoat at times of disastrous setback. Equally Brooke-Popham was no genius. As with many officers who subsequently entered the R.A.F., he had started his career in the army, having served in the Oxfordshire (later Oxfordshire and Buckinghamshire) Light Infantry from 1898 until 1912, when he joined the Royal Flying Corps as captain. After active service in the first world war, Brooke-Popham held a number of senior appointments in the R.A.F., including that of director of research at the Air Ministry (1919–21); commandant of the R.A.F. staff college (1921–6); A.O.C., Fighting Area Air Defence, Great Britain (1926–8); commandant, Imperial Defence College (1931–3); A.O.C., Defence, Great Britain (1933–5); and A.O.C. Middle East (1935–7). Brooke-Popham retired from the R.A.F. in 1937 and became governor of Kenya, a post which he occupied until his appointment as commander-in-chief, Far East in October 1940. Brooke-Popham seems to have been a typical higher service officer of his day — bluff, hale, and hearty with a certain shrewdness in weighing-up men and problems. He was rather too old and lacking in sufficient vigour for the demands of a difficult post in a taxing climate; he not infrequently fell asleep at meetings he was chairing.[16] While in Malaya he sent a number of private letters to the secretary of the chiefs of staff committee, General Sir Hastings Ismay, giving his opinion of developments. Ismay sent a smaller number of letters in return. The correspondence does not cast profound light and in general confirms the impressions derived from other sources. To capture the flavour of the correspondence and

---

[15] See *H. L. Deb*, 121, 381 for 8 Jan. 1942. The remark was made by Lord Addison.
[16] Kirby, p. 56.

to illustrate Brooke-Popham's views when he arrived in Singapore, it is worth noting the following extract from one of his early letters to Ismay:

To my mind the main thing that stands out about Singapore is the lack of touch and indeed the latent hostility between the Central Government, the Services and the Civilian Community.

With regard to the first and last there is here, and in many other colonies, a tradition of antagonism between officials and unofficials, an article of faith that each must mutually distrust the other.

The Heads of the Services get pretty wild at times with the Civil Government because of their procrastination, whilst the officers generally, who are paying a heavy Income Tax without complaint, feel that they have a grievance against the Civil Community who appear to be accumulating fortunes from War profits and scream out when any suggestion is made to impose an Income Tax on them.

The result of all this is that the three don't mix as they should and don't understand each other's point of view; I feel quite certain that the great majority of civilians and some of the Government officials don't grasp the realities of the situation and, possibly deliberately, close their eyes to the fact that, say, a naval defeat in the Mediterranean might bring bombs to Singapore in a few days. Just as an instance, I was arguing with a Resident over lack of Air Raid Precautions in his area and after a good deal of talk he finally brought up what was meant to be a conclusive argument and said, 'I am convinced that the possibilities of War with Japan are at least 500 to 1 against'.

I feel that until one can break down the walls dividing the different sections progress will be slow and difficult. But I also feel convinced of this, that once we can break the walls down, got [sic] the Government to take the leaders of the Civil Community into their confidence, and establish increased points of contact, that things will go well.

As you know there is a War Committee in Singapore which should be capable of doing very useful work. I put myself on it temporarily and attended the only meeting that there has been since I arrived. I was surprised to find that not only do they have no Agenda but that no Minutes are kept; individuals merely make notes on scraps of paper on any point in which they are particularly interested. On expressing my views on this, I found, to my surprise, a certain amount of opposition on the part of Government officials to keeping any record. I merely mention this to show the peculiar attitude of mind that exists . . .[17]

---

[17] Letter from Brooke-Popham to Ismay, 5 Dec. 1940, V/1/3, Brooke-Popham papers, Liddell Hart Centre for Military Archives, King's College, London.

Brooke-Popham therefore worked to secure a more cohesive and constructive atmosphere. He reached the conclusion that personalities were too abrasive for this to be achieved;[18] he forced the resignation of Vlieland in January 1941 and organized the replacement of Bond and Babington by General A. E. Percival and Air Vice-Marshal C. W. Pulford respectively.[19] Some improvement in mutual co-operation was secured as a result, but there was still excessive complacency and lethargy among civilians and military personnel, with consequences that were obvious enough when war began.

In November-December 1940 the chiefs of staff prepared the instructions for the British delegation which was about to visit Washington for wide-ranging, confidential discussions on world defence problems. The chiefs of staff expected disagreement on naval issues to be one of the key aspects of the coming exchanges. The British naval staff believed that it should be feasible for the allied forces to fight Germany, Italy, and Japan simultaneously, whereas the American staff held that if the European front came first, the United States could not with confidence expect to halt Japanese aggression in the south-west Pacific; another cause of dissension would arise from the American wish to use Hawaii as the principal base while the British preferred Singapore. The general instructions to the delegation emphasized that the discussions should be conducted 'in a spirit of complete frankness'.[20] The objective was to co-ordinate joint policy on the assumption of a war between Germany, Italy, and Japan on one side and the British Empire, her allies, and the United States on the other. Great Britain considered that the European theatre must have priority and that the defeat of Germany and Italy should be accomplished first. The security of the Far East, extended to embrace Australia and New Zealand, came next, with Singapore as the headquarters. Assistance given by the United States should not be at the expense of reducing British

[18] Letter from Brooke-Popham to Ismay, 6 Jan. 1941, V/1/4, Brooke-Popham papers.
[19] Brooke-Popham considered Vlieland to be intelligent but handicapped because he was distrusted.
[20] Chiefs of staff committee, 'British–United States Technical Conversations', note by the chiefs of staff submitting draft instructions for British delegation, 15 Dec. 1940, C.O.S.(40)1043, Cab.80/24.

armament orders. In the Far East powerful naval reinforcements were urgently required, as were fighter aircraft.[21] Churchill, who was most anxious that the delegation
should not pursue its case with undue zeal, added his personal
instructions:

It was most important that the attitude to be adopted by our
Delegation in the discussions on the naval strategy should be one of
deference to the views of the United States in all matters concerning
the Pacific theatre of war. It would be unwise to try and force our
views on naval strategy in that theatre upon the United States Naval
Authorities. Our Delegation should open the discussion by saying
that they recognised that the United States navy will be in charge of
the Pacific and that the American views on strategy in that theatre
must prevail. They would not be asking the Americans to come and
protect Singapore, Australia and India against the Japanese, but
would offer the use of Singapore to the Americans if they required
it.[22]

The British delegation proceeded to Washington in January
1941 and the talks were held over the ensuing two months.
The American military attaché in London, Brigadier-General
Raymond E. Lee, who was a fervent Anglophile, accompanied
the delegation on their outward journey, as did the American
naval attaché, Admiral Ghormley; Lee regarded the discussions as overdue and criticized the British in his journal for
not moving more quickly in beginning them.[23] The chiefs of
staff in London considered that the talks must be carefully
prepared in advance, however, and that it would be unwise to
advance prematurely. The most prominent members of the
British delegation were Rear-Admirals R. M. Bellairs and V.
H. Danckwerts, Air Vice-Marshal J. C. Slessor, and Major-
General E. L. Morris. The American chiefs of staff, General
George C. Marshall and Admiral Harold Stark, attended the
opening and closing sessions but otherwise left their subordinates to represent the United States; the most prominent
of the latter were Rear-Admiral R. K. Turner, Major-General

[21] Ibid., annex.
[22] Chiefs of staff committee, 'British–United States Technical Conversations', note by
the secretary, 19 Dec. 1940, C.O.S.(40)1052, Cab.80/24.
[23] J. Leutze (ed.), *The London Observer: the Journal of General Raymond E. Lee,
1940–1941* (Hutchinson, London, 1972), pp. 192–3.

S. D. Embick, and Brigadier-Generals S. Miles and L. T. Gerow.

At the first meeting, on 29 January 1941, Marshall and Stark formally welcomed the British and emphasized the importance of maintaining strict secrecy: leakage of information might jeopardize future co-operation and the passage of the Lend-Lease bill through Congress.[24] At the next meeting the American delegates stated that it was likely that the United States would become involved in war as a result of an act of policy by Japan, Germany, or Italy: it appeared that Japan was continuing to advance southwards, possibly avoiding attacks on American or Dutch territory.[25] On the British side it was made clear that British policy had stiffened and there would be no further concessions. A Japanese advance against the Netherlands East Indies would be most serious and, despite her own problems, Britain would have to assist the East Indies if attacked. The importance of Malaya was stressed, together with the need to keep the Japanese out of the Indian Ocean; the Americans expressed some scepticism on this supposed threat.

One of the primary aims of the British delegation was to convince the United States of the magnitude of the world struggle and that Britain's priorities were correct. To achieve this end, it was essential to appraise the relative significance of the Middle East and the Far East. A memorandum was produced giving the comparison. The repercussions of a withdrawal from the Middle East would be 'almost incalculable'.[26] The Middle East had to be held because Germany would otherwise be able to exploit Romanian and Russian oil supplies and might reach Iraqi supplies: a fleet had to be maintained in the eastern Mediterranean to implement the blockade and to encourage Turkey, which might be tempted to permit German penetration; the Italians had been defeated in Cyrenaica and British forces were rapidly closing in on Ethiopia. Retention of the Middle East was essential to the defeat of Germany. In comparison the Far East was valuable because of the implications for Australia and New Zealand

---

[24] British–United States staff conversations, B.U.S.(J)41, Cab.99/5.
[25] Ibid., 31 Jan. 1941.
[26] Ibid., 'Relative Importance of the Middle and Far East Theatres', 31 Jan. 1941, B.U.S.(J)(41)6.

and their present role in the war; Malaya was vital for strategic and economic reasons and its loss would connote 'the disintegration of the British Commonwealth and a crippling reduction in our war effort'.[27] The conclusion reached was that neither theatre could be abandoned but, in the long term, the Far East was more important than the Middle East. At the meeting on 3 February Rear-Admiral Turner stated that the United States would be willing to protect Anglo-American interests in the Pacific east of the 180th meridian, and in the south Pacific to support the Dominions as far west as 155 degrees east.[28] The functions of the American Pacific fleet would be to cut Japanese communications east of the 180th meridian and to assist associated forces holding the Malay barrier. The American Asiatic fleet would operate in defence of the Philippines and subsequently to resist the Japanese as far as possible. It was agreed that the Japanese should be kept north of the Malay barrier. Looking at the Far East in world perspective, Turner believed peace should be preserved with Japan if possible. The United States' line of communications to East Asia was itself hazardous and American policy would try to strengthen the British in the Atlantic and the Mediterranean so that Britain could then send additional forces to the area. There was no intention of strengthening the Asiatic fleet. Replying for the British delegation, Rear-Admiral Danckwerts explained the existing total commitments of the navy; it was imperative to avoid weakening the Mediterranean fleet. Britain desired the American Pacific fleet to play an active role against Japan so as to reassure the Dominions. Britain pressed for unity of command in the Pacific and Asiatic theatres, but this was opposed by the United States. At the request of the Americans, a paper was prepared summarizing the outcome of talks between the British and Dutch over the defence of Malaya and the East Indies. Consultations had not gone far for political reasons, but it had been agreed that the only significant co-operation could come through exchanges of air forces. If the Dutch were attacked, four squadrons could be dispatched from Malaya and in the reverse contingency three squadrons

---

[27] Ibid., 3 Feb. 1941.
[28] Ibid.

sent to Malaya.[29] Reconnaissance areas had been allocated. In an assessment of probable Japanese air strength by the British, it was stated that Japan was thought to possess a total air strength, as of 31 July 1940, of 2,419 aircraft.[30]

On 11 February the principal British appreciation of the situation in East Asia was produced. This was the fullest explanation of British thinking and was, in part, to be rejected by the United States. The first section of the memorandum outlined the strategic significance of the whole area and the second section examined in more detail the measures required to defend Singapore. Since the decision to terminate the Anglo-Japanese alliance, the development of a major fleet base at Singapore had been a fundamental constituent of British policy:

This has been based, not only upon purely strategic foundations, but on political, economic and sentimental considerations which, even if not literally vital on a strictly academic view, are of such fundamental importance to the British Commonwealth that they must always be taken into serious account. Just as the United States strategy has to take account of the political factor and the element of public opinion in relation to the integrity of their Western seaboard, so British strategy must always be influenced by similar factors in the Dominions of Australia and New Zealand, to whom we are bound, not only by the bond of kinship and a common citizenship, but by specific undertakings to defend them. But the retention of a Fleet base in the Far East means far more than that. We are a maritime Commonwealth, whose various Dominions and Colonies are held together by the communications and trade routes across the oceans of the world. Our population in the United Kingdom depend for their very existence upon imported food and upon the fruits of trade with the overseas Dominions and colonies, with India and with foreign countries, including the vast area of China. Finally, we are trustees for the security and prosperity of the sub-continent of India . . .[31]

British policy had until recently rested on being able to dispatch a fleet to Singapore as soon as war broke out but, in

[29] Ibid., 'Result of British staff conversations with the Dutch', 4 Feb. 1941, B.U.S.(J)(41)10.
[30] Ibid., 'British estimates of German, Italian and Japanese air strengths', 4 Feb. 1941, B.U.S.(J)(41)11.
[31] Ibid., 'The Far East. Appreciation by the United Kingdom Delegation', 11 Feb. 1941, B.U.S.(J)(41)13.

existing circumstances, this would be impossible. In reply to an American inquiry as to the consequences should the United States be unable to participate in the war, it was stated that British forces would hold out for as long as they could until a British fleet could be sent, even if this would mean surrendering the British position in the Mediterranean. American intervention would change the situation radically. It would remove the threat of invasion of the southern Dominions, and, even if Singapore fell, it was highly unlikely that the Japanese main fleet would be based there for operations further west. The fall of Singapore would involve the loss of the extremely valuable raw materials of Malaya and would correspondingly make Japan self-sufficient. The morale and prestige of the British Commonwealth would suffer an immense blow.

The second section of the memorandum contemplated the practical measures which could be taken to defend Singapore. It was foreseen that Japan might launch a land and air attack on Malaya from Indo-China and Thailand — this was considered an immediate menace in February 1941; it might be accompanied by an attack on the East Indies and the Philippines. It was correctly estimated that Japan had enough resources to handle three offensives simultaneously. In calculating the length of time the British forces could hold out, American intervention would be of first importance; in addition, there was no firm understanding between Britain and the Netherlands on mutual assistance. The commitment to the Atlantic and the Mediterranean would preclude any attempt to hold all possessions: it would be unrealistic, for example, to expect to retain Hong Kong, the Philippines or Borneo — 'the irreducible minimum that we must retain, as we see it, is our own capacity to hold Singapore as a card of re-entry for the main fleet into the Far East, and in order to do this we must be able to deny to the Japanese uninterrupted freedom of action to carry out sustained operations in the waters and from the territories surrounding Singapore'.[32] The most satisfactory solution would be to base a naval force, including capital ships, at Singapore; there would be numerous difficulties in this course, however. In the absence of capital

---

[32] Ibid.

ships, the minimum reinforcements to challenge Japanese sea communications in the south China Sea would comprise one carrier, a division of heavy cruisers, and appropriate auxiliary naval craft. Naval reinforcements of the Asiatic naval forces should not be at the expense of the Atlantic and Mediterranean, which would mean they would come from the American Pacific fleet. Hawaii and Singapore offered two first-class bases: if the Pacific and Asiatic fleets faced powerful opposition, it would be possible for them to fall back on these bases. In answer to the American suggestion that British forces might be sent to the Far East if American forces were sent to European waters, the sensible reply was made that such a development would be uneconomical owing to the wide redistribution inherent in it. The British memorandum concluded with the hope that the United States would accept the validity of the case that had been made out.

The American rejoinder was presented eight days later. The United States staff committee believed that if the United States became involved in war with Japan, it would at once also engage in war with Germany and Italy. Similarly if the United States first entered upon war with Germany and Italy, it would become involved against Japan, assuming that Japan was then at war with the British Commonwealth. If Japan occupied Indo-China and Thailand, however, it was unlikely that the United States would fight her. There was also considerable doubt that the United States would act if Japan moved against Malaya, Borneo, or the East Indies. Such doubt was indeed to persist until the eve of Pearl Harbor, when President Roosevelt at last promised American aid in these eventualities. The staff committee emphasized the limitations on freedom of action imposed by the political problems within the United States; it would be unwise for Great Britain to count upon American assistance.[33] There was no intention of sending a battle fleet superior to the Japanese fleet because it would be contrary to the responsibilities in and near the American continent; because far eastern bases could not satisfactorily accommodate such a fleet and the naval situation in the Atlantic required maximum strength to defeat Germany.

---

[33] Ibid., 'Statement by the United States staff committee. The United States Military Position in the Far East', 19 Feb. 1941, B.U.S.(J)(41)16.

Since neither Britain nor the United States could operate strong land and air forces in the theatre, it would be impossible to mount a counter-offensive against Japan. The aims of the two powers would necessarily be limited to a defence of the Malay barrier; a restricted offensive against the Japanese eastern naval flank; and an economic blockade of Japan together with Chinese offensives against Japanese garrisons. Japan's policy would most probably aim at defeating France, Great Britain, the Netherlands, the United States, and Russia, perhaps in that order. 'The possibility cannot be dismissed, however, that in case of necessity Japan may simultaneously attack the United Kingdom, the Netherlands, and the United States. But Japan unquestionably would prefer to avoid the difficulties of a war against all three powers at the same time.'[34] Japan would certainly attempt to capture the whole of Malaysia. The paper then investigated the controversial issue of Singapore and the importance of retaining it. The staff committee was less pessimistic than the British delegation about the consequences of its loss, while admitting they would still be considerable:

The general moral effect of the loss of Singapore and the Philippines would be severe. Singapore has been built up in public opinion as a symbol of the power of the British Empire. The eastern Dominions, the Netherlands East Indies and China look upon its security as the guarantee of their safety. Its value as a symbol has become so great that its capture by Japan would be a serious blow. But many severe blows have been taken by these various nations and other severe blows can be absorbed without leading to final disaster.

There is no question that the loss of Malaysia to Japan would be unfortunate from moral, economic, and strategic viewpoints. Nevertheless, the United States Staff Committee holds the view that this loss need not have a decisive effect upon the issue of the war.[35]

Strategy for the defence of the Malay barrier would include submarine, mine, and air operations, especially in the passes and shallow waters of the Philippines and the East Indies; cruiser offensives against minor forces supporting troop landings or escorting convoys; cruiser offensives south of the Malay barrier; land defence of Java and Malaya; and the des-

---

[34] Ibid.
[35] Ibid.

truction of oil wells, refineries, military stores, and foodstocks. The staff committee was opposed to the dispatch of appreciable reinforcements to East Asia. The battle in the Atlantic came first, and it would be foolish to divert resources to the Pacific. A clear distinction was drawn between the far eastern interests of the British and Dutch and those of the United States:

Territorial considerations should have a governing influence in the disposition of a nation's armed forces. In the Far East, British and Dutch territorial interests are paramount to those of the United States. The paramount territorial interests of the United States are in the Western Hemisphere. Consequently, the dispositions of the armed forces of the United Kingdom ought to provide for the defence of its interests in the Far East, and the dispositions of the United States ought to provide for the defence of its own interests in the Western Hemisphere, so that, if either associate is compelled to withdraw from the war, the deployment of the other remains fundamentally sound.[36]

The Washington talks improved mutual understanding and awareness of the peculiar problems of the two countries. Britain tended to exaggerate the ability of the United States, within the near future, to play a dominant role in blocking Japanese expansion. Rearmament was in its early stages and, more significant than the narrowly strategic aspects, was the political situation in the United States illustrated in the statements made by the staff committee.[37] Neither the American public nor the Roosevelt administration was prepared for involvement in war as yet. Isolationist sentiments were clamorous, and the United States could not be seen as advancing into war to protect the colonial possessions of other powers. The old anti-imperial legacy of the American people, bequeathed by the Founding Fathers, was still potent. While British and Dutch imperialism was certainly preferable to Japanese imperialism, it was nevertheless offensive. If the United States became involved in war, it must be because it was necessary in the defence of American interests. There could be no question of an American fleet basing itself on Singapore. Possibly the United States staff committee pushed

---

[36] Ibid.
[37] Ibid.

the argument that Singapore was not as vital as the British maintained for ulterior purposes, to avoid the contingency of having to use Singapore. They were right, if arguably for the wrong reasons, in holding that the British attached excessive importance to the retention of Singapore. The British were mildly obsessed with the notion of Singapore as the in-domitable fortress that governed everything. The Pacific war was to show that the Americans were correct in stating that grave setbacks could be surmounted. However, neither the British nor the Americans seemed fully to comprehend that it was Malaya rather than Singapore that was vital and for economic rather than strategic reasons. As regards East Asia and the Pacific, the achievements of the talks were limited.

Australia applied consistent pressure in 1940–1 to build up defences in the Pacific. The prime minister, Robert Menzies, was in a tenuous political situation, faced with dissension within his coalition government and vocal opposition from the Labour party. Despite repeated promises by Churchill to send large-scale reinforcements to the Far East in the event of an urgent crisis involving a direct threat to Australia, there were justified doubts in Australia as to how and when these would materialize. Menzies visited London in March-April 1941 to explore the problem further, and no doubt to convince his fellow-countrymen that he was doing all he could to advance the nation's cause. It was feared in London and Canberra, in February 1941, that Japan might go to war very soon. The Australian chiefs of staff reported that Japan possessed over-whelming superiority in each service and posed a grave threat to sea communications in the Indian Ocean, the south China Sea and the western Pacific bordering Australia and in the south-western Pacific. Since the Australian war effort was con-centrated in the area of the Tasman Sea, the transport of troops and supplies could be seriously reduced or halted by enemy action. Japan was unlikely to attack Australia or New Zealand, at least in the early stages of a war, but would probably attack Malaya or the East Indies instead. However, the Australian government would have to make arrangements for its own defence, in accordance with the conclusions of the 1940 Singapore conference that the minimum naval forces required in Australian and New Zealand waters could only be found by the return of all Australian and New Zealand naval forces currently serving overseas. The Australian chiefs of staff wished the subject to be studied at the forthcoming Singapore defence conference (in April 1941) and, if necessary, would want the forces released from their existing commitments. While in London, Menzies held detailed discussions with the prime minister, relevant ministers, and the chiefs of staff.[38]

Menzies emphasized the manifest dissatisfaction of his defence chiefs with the forces and equipment necessary for the effective defence of Malaya.[39] The British chiefs of staff produced a memorandum answering the various criticisms and questions raised by him. They stated that while it was not feasible to give definite dates for the arrival of arms and equipment, steady improvements were being made; apart from anti-aircraft and anti-tank guns, S.A.A. and artillery ammunition, the deficiencies in army equipment were not serious. In the air, a total of 336 aircraft remained the target but it was improbable that it could be attained by the end of 1941. In a bid to reduce Menzies's scepticism, the chiefs of staff explained that the existing air situation was not critical:

For the close defence of Malaya and Burma alone we have at present 118 aircraft, not including the two fighter squadrons (32 aircraft) now forming. The Netherlands East Indies now possess 162 aircraft (with reasonable reserves), of types at least equal in performance to those of the Japanese. Thus the Dutch and ourselves already possess for defence a total of 280 aircraft, and this figure does not include any of the 170 fighters which are now arriving in Malaya from the United States of America and takes no account of Dutch orders for 245 aircraft from the United States of America, deliveries of which were due to begin last month.

The majority of the 450 shore-based aircraft which the Japanese can marshal against us are of obsolete types, and, as we have said, we have no reason to believe that Japanese standards are even comparable with those of the Italians.[40]

[38] For a discussion of the background, see P. Hasluck, *The Government and the People*, pp. 264–332.

[39] 'Appreciation of the situation in the Far East by the Australian Chiefs of Staff', note by the secretary, 22 Feb. 1941, enclosing Fadden to Casey, 19 Feb. 1941, B.U.S.(41)17, Cab.99/5. This was one of the papers provided for the information of the British delegation at the Washington talks.

[40] Chiefs of staff committee, 'Visit of the Australian Prime Minister. Reply by Chiefs of Staff to memorandum by the Prime Minister of Australia', 11 Apr. 1941, Cab.80/27.

Menzies had inquired whether Hurricanes could be sent to the Far East, but the chiefs of staff ruled this out owing to the demands of the Middle East. In the naval sphere, the Australian prime minister pressed for the vague promises given in the past, such as Churchill's famous 'kith and kin' telegram of 23 December 1940, to be transformed into a specific plan of action, covering the withdrawal of Australian forces from the Middle East. The chiefs of staff reminded Menzies of the profound consequences of abandoning the Middle East:

The security of our position in the Middle East remains essential to our strategy for the defeat of Germany. Loss of that position would give our enemies such overriding advantages, strategic, economic and diplomatic, that the course of the war would be considerably prolonged.

Any withdrawal, however small, would involve the movement of forces by sea, and the necessity for retaining a strong fleet in the Mediterranean would be increased rather than lessened during the period of such withdrawal. Even if it were decided to abandon our Mediterranean interests, the fleet would have to remain until the end in order to cover the withdrawal of the armies.[41]

All that could be said with assurance was that a battle cruiser and carrier would be sent to the Indian Ocean at the outbreak of war with Japan. Whether a stronger force could be sent could only be determined according to circumstances at the time. A great deal depended on the attitude of the United States, which remained uncertain.[42] A more optimistic gloss was put on the situation to some extent, but the reality remained that unhappily little could be done while other theatres absorbed such a formidable proportion of the limited resources. The only solace was that an actual invasion of Australia was not likely and that the United States might intervene. This was cold comfort for Menzies in his political dilemma; the turmoil of Australian domestic politics continued, and uneasiness over the Japanese menace plus distrust of Menzies contributed to his resignation and replacement by Fadden.

Meanwhile Brooke-Popham presided over a series of con-

[41] Ibid.
[42] Ibid.

versations and conferences at Singapore between February and April 1941. These consultations involved the Dutch, Australians, and Americans and were intended to clarify what action should be taken by each country in the contingency of a Japanese attack. The first conference, held in February, was attended by delegates from the general headquarters at Singapore; from the China station; Malaya Command (army); R.A.F., Far East; Netherlands East Indies; and Australia, which also represented New Zealand. American observers were present. At the beginning of their report, the members of the conference emphasized the need for all governments to co-operate wholeheartedly in the event of any of the countries concerned being attacked. In an assessment of probable developments, it was thought that Japan would continue to expand gradually, initially into Indo-China and Thailand and then to attack Malaya. In contrast to the opinion of the British delegation at the Washington talks, Japan was considered to lack sufficient strength to implement simultaneous major attacks on Malaya and the East Indies. The position of the United States was regarded as the decisive element in determining Japan's policy:

The attitude of the U.S.A. is clearly a governing factor. If Japan is certain that the U.S.A. will intervene to support the N.E.I. or the British Empire, the chances of war breaking out are reduced to very small proportions. Unless Japan is certain that the U.S.A. will not intervene at all, at any stage, she will be compelled to retain considerable forces in Japan, and the major portion of her fleet to guard against the probability of subsequent intervention.[43]

The reaction of the United States was, however, a matter for conjecture. It would be necessary to meet the contingencies of Japan attacking Malaya or the East Indies. If Malaya were attacked, the Netherlands East Indies was willing to release air squadrons and submarines (three bomber squadrons, one fighter squadron, and six to eight submarines). Australia was willing to provide army units and an air striking force at Darwin to reinforce Ambon and Koepang. If the East Indies were the victim of aggression, it would be essential to hold the bases in North Borneo, North Celebes, and Ambon. Malaya

---

[43] 'Anglo-Dutch-Australian Conference', 27 Feb. 1941, C.O.S.(41)406, Cab.80/29.

would release four bomber squadrons to help the Dutch, and Australia would assist in the same way as she would if Malaya were attacked. The conference decided that the detailed administrative implementation of these plans should be pursued at once. The Japanese threat to sea communications between India, Malaya, the East Indies, and Australia should be resisted by attacking Japanese vessels and convoys through the outer line North Borneo–North Celebes–North-western New Guinea, supported by whatever forces could be based on the southern line Java–Timor–Darwin. Steps would have to be taken to prevent Japan from establishing a base in the New Guinea–New Hebrides–New Caledonia–Fiji area, because such a base would hinder the transport of American naval re-inforcements. It was thought possible but not likely that Japan might concentrate all her attention on attacking allied sea communications rather than attack Malaya or the East Indies. Sea communications would be defended by a combination of escort cover for troop convoys, air reconnaissance, and re-routing. Spheres of activity for the respective naval and air forces were approved.

Collective united action was of the utmost importance in combating Japan. The members of the conference expressed the hope that their governments would accept a full political commitment to assist each other; this was aimed at Churchill and the British chiefs of staff (especially the chief of the naval staff), who were continuing to procrastinate on a British promise of support to the East Indies. It was also hoped that this point would be taken by the American observers. The conference decided to recommend that military counter-action should be taken if Japan attacked any British, Dutch, Australian, New Zealand, or mandated territory; if Japanese forces advanced into any part of Thailand to the west of 100 degrees east or south of ten degrees north; if a considerable number of Japanese warships or merchant ships escorted by convoy warships was detected moving towards the Kra isthmus or the east coast of Malaya or had crossed the parallel of six degrees north between Malaya and the Philippines; if Japanese forces occupied Portuguese Timor, New Caledonia, or the Loyalty Islands; or if the Philippines were attacked. The conference made useful progress but underestimated the Japanese ability to launch a formidable, all-embracing offensive on the lines of the opening phase of the Pacific war. Full and effective co-ordination was handicapped, as before and subsequently, by the refusal of the United States to give a political commitment to defend British and Dutch possessions and, more surprisingly, by the British refusal to promise support to the East Indies.

The next conference met in April with delegates from the same countries but with the United States sending full delegates rather than observers. The conference was charged with constructing a plan of operations on the basis of the Washington talks, the particular points to be resolved concerning the functions and dispositions of forces in the entire area of the Indian Ocean, Pacific, Australian, and New Zealand waters before and after the arrival of the Far East fleet and also the detailed arrangements for co-operation, for example, in communications and exchange of liaison officers.[44] The assumption would be that the British Commonwealth, its allies, and the United States would be engaged in war with Germany, Italy, and Japan; no political commitment would be implied and decisions reached would have to be ratified by the respective governments. The report of the conference began by recalling that strategy against Japan would be defensive, relying on economic pressure, until Germany had been defeated; when the latter had been achieved, a comprehensive counter-offensive could be launched. The most important interests in the Far East lay in the maintenance of sea communications and the defence of Singapore. Luzon in the Philippines should be held if possible, owing to its favourable geographical position for employing submarines and air forces to attack Japanese expeditions against Malaya or the East Indies. Japan's policy was understood to connote the establishment of the new order throughout south-east Asia and the islands in the Far East area, in fulfilment of Japan's political and economic objectives. It was felt that if Japan realized that any act of aggression would be met by a united response by the powers, then such aggression might be pre-

---

[44] 'Report of the American–Dutch–British Conversations held at Singapore, April 1941', C.O.S.(41)387, Cab.80/28.

vented. Japan would still be involved heavily in China and would have to keep troops in Manchukuo and Mongolia despite the recently signed non-aggression pact between Japan and Russia. Japan might attack the Philippines, Hong Kong, the Netherlands East Indies, or, more remotely, Australia and New Zealand.[45] In the case of Malaya, there should be some warning of aggression unless an expedition were sent directly to the east coast; however, this development would entail greater control of communications than Japan presently enjoyed. Japan should be discouraged by the strengthening of Malayan defences in recent months:

It must be obvious to Japan that the forces available for the defence of Malaya have been greatly reinforced during the last six months, and an attack on them is becoming a much more formidable proposition than it was in October [1940] even taking into account only the British forces available on the spot . . .[46]

Apart from the other areas of probable Japanese aggression, attacks on sea communications would be a prominent part of Japanese action and could prove most dangerous. The conference believed it would be a considerable gamble for Japan to move into Malaya, the East Indies, or other areas further south before defeating the forces in the Philippines. It is a reasonable deduction that the conference again underestimated Japan's ability to wage a wide offensive. It was also reiterated that if Japan knew that she would encounter a united response from the powers, she would most likely not go to war:

The only situation which would be likely to appeal to her as offering outstanding chances would have to be concentrated in that theatre for a considerable time.[47]

However, it was imperative, to be prepared:

On the other hand, such is the national psychology of the Japanese that acts of hysteria which might lead to the plunging of Japan into war must be faced. It is for this reason in particular that it is necessary for combined plans to be made by the Associated Powers to meet

[45] Ibid.
[46] Ibid.
[47] Ibid.

threats to their interests which may occur at very short notice.[48]

Paragraph 26 of the report touched on delicate ground by outlining the different circumstances in which the powers should fight Japan; the circumstances were direct aggression against the possessions of any of the powers; a Japanese advance into Thailand to the west of 100 degrees east or to the south of ten degrees north; the advance of a large number of Japanese vessels or of merchant ships escorted by warships towards the Philippines, the Kra isthmus or the east coast of Malaya; occupation of Portuguese Timor, New Caledonia, or the Loyalty Islands. The United States subsequently objected firmly to this paragraph because it trespassed on political territory; the reaction to such developments would have to be decided by the highest authorities at the time. This was a natural response, but underlined the problem of properly co-ordinating strategy.

In contemplating the course of action open to the powers, the conference became unrealistic in thinking that operations could be launched against Japan herself: air bombardment of the Japanese islands should take place and, in conjunction with an economic blockade and naval pressure, should produce the defeat of Japan. It was recommended that the defences of Luzon should be strengthened; that financial aid and equipment be extended to the Chinese navy; that guerrilla activities should be stimulated in China; and, rather oddly, that subversive activities should be organized in Japan. Agreement was reached on the different areas for which the powers assumed responsibility. As decided at the Washington talks, the United States Pacific fleet at Hawaii would be used against the Japanese mandated islands and against Japanese sea communications in the Pacific; the C.-in-C. of the Pacific fleet would have to determine the assistance to be rendered to British forces south of the equator. The United States Asiatic fleet would at first be based on Manila; if Japanese movements became threatening, auxiliaries would be sent to Singapore. If the Manila base became untenable, forces would retire south to come under the command of the British C.-in-C., China. In sea links numerous routes would require protection,

[48] Ibid.

particularly to safeguard transport of troop reinforcements and supplies. When the British far eastern fleet arrived in the eastern theatre, the balance of naval power would move in favour of the allies and Japan would probably be in an inferior position. The British fleet would use Singapore as its base; if this was not possible — considered an unlikely contingency — the fleet would operate from bases in the Indian Ocean. The only land frontiers to be defended were those of Burma and Malaya; the northern border of Malaya was undeniably hard to defend. In other areas enemy forces could only advance by sea. Sea and air bases must be adequately guarded. Protected air bases would be set up on the line Burma–Malaya–Borneo–Philippines–New Guinea–Solomons–New Hebrides–Fiji–Tonga. This would be reinforced by a second line from Sumatra through the East Indies and the east coast of Australia to New Zealand. Spheres of air operations were approved. The conference urged that air strength should be built up as far as possible in order that operations could take place against Japan. Arrangements were made for the use of common ciphers and codes.

The second conference in April 1941 involved the British, Dutch, and Australians, with the Americans present as observers.[49] The conference adhered to the fundamental agreement reached at the previous Anglo-Dutch-Australian conference in February 1941, but reassessed certain issues. The terms of reference were to settle matters arising from the earlier conference and to prepare plans for the employment of British and Dutch forces. The plans would be subject to the British deciding on what constituted an act of war by Japan according to the circumstances. Although the United States was officially neutral, it was probable that the position of the United States would affect Japanese strategy. Japan would almost certainly aim to conquer Hong Kong; attack sea communications; attack Malaya, after consolidating her hold on Indo-China and Thailand; and attack Borneo, preparatory to moving against the East Indies. The most important interest was the retention of Singapore. 'A Japanese attack on the Netherlands East Indies, however, presents such a serious

---

[49] 'Report of the British–Dutch conversations held at Singapore, April 1941', C.O.S.(41)388, Cab.80/28.

threat to our position in the Far East and to the defence of our sea communications that, in as far as our forces permit, provision should be made for reinforcement of any threatened point in that area.' Hong Kong could not be expected to hold out for long and should be regarded as significant only in containing part of the Japanese forces. To ensure flexibility and swiftness of response in the naval sphere, it was recommended that the C. in C., China station should assume strategical direction of naval forces. Land forces should be utilized for the defence of naval and air bases; it was thought that land forces could not be used for offensive action. As regards air power, it was vital that air forces should concentrate quickly; to achieve this result, the British commander-in-chief, Far East, based at Singapore, should exercise such authority. The division of spheres of action for naval and air forces was agreed. In other respects the report covered the same ground as the American-Dutch-British conference with the same conclusions being reached.

Brooke-Popham was generally satisfied with the progress achieved at the conferences. After the conference in February 1941 he wrote to Ismay that it was imperative that the Dutch fight stubbornly in the event of war; he had visited Java and held private consultations with the Dutch commanders. He had also visited Australia but was not impressed with the calibre of Australian politicians; he liked John Curtin, the opposition leader, but considered Menzies more impressive. He wrote that the A.D.A. conference had been successful, although there had been some argument: the conclusions of the conference were, in his opinion, sound.[50] Brooke-Popham regretted that the Dominions and the United States had not been better represented at the two conferences in April. When he had visited Manila, he had invited General Grunert and Admiral Hart to attend but they had not done so:

Further, we were very anxious to bring home to the Americans the necessity for their Pacific Fleet taking a more active part in a Far East war than appears to be their intention at present, and it would have been much more useful to have done this through an Admiral than

[50] Letter from Brooke-Popham to Ismay, 28 Feb. 1941, V/1/7, Brooke-Popham papers.

through a Captain. I think they went away fully impressed with the importance of Singapore and the whole of the Far East.

The U.S.A. representatives seemed remarkably afraid of the Civil authorities in Washington and were very shy of expressing any opinions on any subject that touched on the political sphere . . .[51]

The United States chiefs of staff, whether or not they feared their political superiors, criticized the report of the A.D.B. conference. They had a number of objections. The report tried to lay down political commitments which the officers concerned were not competent to pursue; the strategic range of the report was too broad, for instance involving the East Indies station—the United States had not wished the conference to go beyond the A.B.C.-1 agreement; they could not see why it was necessary to appoint a C.-in-C. of the Eastern fleet to replace the C.-in-C., China, and the chief of naval operations was not willing to permit naval forces to be used outside the far eastern area as stipulated in A.B.C.-1 except under extraordinary circumstances; the report did not, in their view, give sufficient emphasis to retaining the line Malaya, Sumatra, Java and eastward and thus gave undue priority to defending the sea communications of the British Empire; the report was wrong to contemplate the employment of American naval and air forces for non-naval tasks; and the report did not provide a practical operating plan for naval forces. The American chiefs of staff were always hypersensitive of advancing too far in accepting commitments; their reaction was naturally governed by the instructions issued by President Roosevelt, and in this sense was wholly understandable, if unavoidably disappointing to the British chiefs of staff.[52] As always, political implications and the prior claims of other theatres of war handicapped progress in effectively producing a unified policy towards Japanese expansion.

In the diplomatic sphere the principal problems, now more closely linked than before, following the signature of the tripartite pact, revolved around aid to China and avoidance of

---

[51] Letter from Brooke-Popham to Ismay, 16 May 1941, V/1/12, Brooke-Popham papers.
[52] Chiefs of staff committee, 'U.S.A. Attitude to Report of Singapore Conference (A.D.B.). Report By Rear-Admiral Danckwerts', 5 July 1941, C.O.S.(41)414, Cab.80/29.

war with Japan. Conflict with Japan was obviously more probable than at any previous time, and it was, therefore, necessary to give urgent consideration to extending economic and perhaps military assistance to China. It was essential to keep China in the struggle as this tied down such vast numbers of Japanese troops. Chiang Kai-shek had long sounded periodical anguished warnings of China's inability to continue fighting without substantially improved aid. In the past the Foreign Office had regarded them sceptically; the reservations had been justified, for there was always deliberate exaggeration on Chiang's part. However, the duration of the war and the deteriorating economic situation in China, accentuated by the gravity of Britain's predicament, required a new approach. On 19 October Sir Archibald Clark Kerr reported on two lengthy talks with Chiang: the generalissimo called for generous treatment of China and her acceptance as an equal by Great Britain. He warned that co-operation could not succeed while China was regarded as 'semi-colonial'. 'China had now become a force to be reckoned with, not only in Far Eastern politics but in world politics also.'[53] Chiang said that China possessed a large and strong army, and equality with Britain should be recognized. In contrast, he added subsequently that China could not continue to drift in future and that she urgently needed support; if this did not materialize, she would have to extricate herself from her difficulties as best she could. Clark Kerr observed that Chiang desired an understanding and it was important that this be reached if Chinese resistance was to continue.[54] Sir John Brenan minuted that while there was much sympathy for China it was difficult to see what help could be given, since China's forces were weak (contrary to Chiang's bold words) and Britain herself could not provide large-scale assistance; there was, in addition, the difficulty of maintaining secrecy in discussions with Chiang. R. A. Butler concurred, but thought that reference should be made to the role of guerrilla warfare when a reply was sent to Chiang. B. E. F. Gage held that it was essential for the 400 million Chinese to march in step with Great Britain against

[53] Clark Kerr to Halifax, 19 Oct. 1940 (three telegrams), F4817/57/10, F.O. 371/24674.
[54] Clark Kerr to Halifax, with minutes, 19 Oct. 1940, F4826/57/10, F.O.371/24674.

Japanese aggression but the present time was awkward: forward action could not be taken until the American presidential election was over. Halifax replied to Clark Kerr on 28 October stressing that while Britain appreciated the value of the Chinese contribution, it was not easy to see what form of co-operation was feasible; however, the War Office was contemplating the dispatch of a military mission to Chungking.[55] Clark Kerr responded by urging that economic and military missions be sent and that Britain and the United States should join together, assuming Roosevelt's re-election, in supplying aircraft, artillery, ammunition, loans, and credits.[56] He did not believe that conclusion of an alliance with China would encourage a Japanese attack on British possessions, because Japan was basically frightened. Ashley Clarke minuted that the entire subject was being reviewed by the economic sub-committee of the Far Eastern committee. It might be possible for credits to be given to cover purchase of materials but it was doubtful whether the Treasury would assent to a loan; after consulting Sir Frederick Leith-Ross, he commented that credits of approximately £10 million were apparently feasible, of which £2 million could constitute a loan. It was not likely that an Anglo-American alliance could be secured, given Roosevelt's reluctance to enter into binding commitments.

Early in November Chiang Kai-shek applied further pressure, emphasizing to Clark Kerr that he must know by the end of the year where he stood with Britain; the morale of the people was suffering as a result of recent air raids and he expressed concern at the growing strength of the communists and the fact that Russia had stopped sending supplies to China while the Burma road was closed. Clarke minuted that the Far Eastern committee was still considering matters and that the priority lay in extending a loan for currency stabilization or export credits. Brenan philosophically noted that it was the third annual appeal from Chiang; it was true that the situation in China was worsening but a collapse was improbable. Chiang was soon encouraged by a telegram of support from Roosevelt, although the president stressed that the United States could

[55] Halifax to Clark Kerr, 28 Oct. 1940, ibid.
[56] Clark Kerr to Halifax, 31 Oct. 1940, F4971/57/10, F.O.371/24674.

not enter into alliances in peacetime. In mid-November the War Office decided to send a military mission to China. It was felt that the mission should be headed by Brigadier Dennys, currently in India, who would become the new military attaché in Chungking. Dennys would assess the state of the Chinese army and the scope for mutual assistance, but it would have to be made clear that no large-scale aid could be sent. The War Office deemed China's assistance against Japan as 'of immense value'.[57] The Foreign Office welcomed the proposal, holding that Dennys should be promoted to the rank of major-general since the rank of brigadier meant nothing outside Britain. An exchange of views took place with the United States later in November. Chiang had by then put forward proposals to Washington broadly similar to those suggested to London. The British view, as submitted to Washington on 21 November, was that a joint Anglo-American alliance with China would not be acceptable to the United States and an Anglo-Chinese alliance would lack sufficient strength and would greatly antagonize Japan.[58] Chiang naturally desired huge loans, but Britain could not contemplate them. Instead, the Treasury envisaged an agreement with China which would permit sterling held by Chinese residents to be made available for expenditure in the sterling area and Britain would make further advances to the stabilization fund. Britain's views were communicated to the Dominions. General Smuts warmly endorsed them. 'If the Chinese resistance to Japan were to collapse effects would almost immediately be felt by Britain and Dutch territories in the Far East. Chiang kai Shek [*sic*] has proved himself a great leader who has done wonders and may continue to do wonders if assured of British and American support.'[59]

At the end of November news of the treaty signed between Japan and the puppet Nanking government of Wang Ching-wei was received. Chiang told Clark Kerr that it would lead to a redoubling of efforts to resist Japan in free China; he was less

[57] Sinclair (War Office) to Sterndale Bennett, 16 Nov. 1940, F5179/57/10, F.O.371/24674.
[58] Minute by Clarke and telegram to N. Butler (Washington), 21 Nov. 1940, F5205/57/10, F.O.371/24674.
[59] High Commissioner, South Africa, to Dominions Office, 25 Nov. 1940, F5206/59/10, F.O.371/24674.

sanguine about reactions from Chinese occupied areas. Chiang added that he had heard from the American State Department that, while the United States could not ally herself with Britain and China, there was full approval for an Anglo-Chinese alliance; Chiang was disappointed at the American reply, since there seemed to be doubt as to whether the Americans would even offer a vague declaration of support.[60] Halifax decided against making a declaration of support. 'We are inclined to think that the announcement of further financial aid to China by both United States of America and ourselves will be sufficient notice of our joint determination to support China's fight for independence against Japanese aggression, and that any declaration would be unnecessarily provocative to the Japanese, unless of course the United States Government were willing to make a joint declaration.'[61] The Foreign Office was anxious to assist China within reason, but harboured no illusions as to Chinese military prowess. When the Foreign Office heard indirectly that ten divisions of Chinese troops were available for service outside China, perhaps in Burma, should Japan launch an offensive, Brenan mordantly remarked:

The suggestion that ten divisions of Chinese troops could be lent us for use in Burma is typical of the loose talk that we get from Chinese intellectuals. But since the idea might appeal to those who know nothing of China it may be as well to point out that we should be expected to equip these men from the feet up and pay all their expenses. Far from being trained troops in our sense of the phrase, they would probably be an unruly rabble of coolies with incompetent officers and of little fighting value. They might be useful as guerrillas in their own country but if transferred to a foreign land they are likely to be more of a menace than a help to our military defence.[62]

Gage dissented and believed that the troops could prove valuable. Sterndale Bennett tended to side with Brenan, but warned that Britain could not afford to alienate Chiang Kai-shek or to treat Japan openly as an enemy.[63]

[60] Clark Kerr to Halifax, 30 Nov. 1940, F5387/57/10, F.O.371/24674.
[61] Halifax to Craigie, 10 Dec. 1940, ibid.
[62] Minute by Brenan, 9 Dec. 1940, on letter from Professor E. W. Mead to Brenan, 3 Dec. 1940; Mead reported the views of Yui Ming, counsellor of the Chinese embassy and formerly a postgraduate student at Oxford, F5405/57/10, F.O.371/24674.
[63] Minutes by Gage and Sterndale Bennett, 10–12 Dec. 1940, ibid.

Britain and the United States therefore moved slowly towards giving more economic aid to China. The pace of Britain's progress was dictated by Roosevelt's unpredictable decision-making, as had so often been the case. Reports from China indicated that the economic situation within the Kuomintang-controlled areas was seriously deteriorating. The fundamental cause was the inflationary effect of the three-and-a-half-year-old war, exacerbated by the chronic inefficiency and corruption of the Kuomintang. Leith-Ross was opposed to an economic mission being sent to China unless there was some prospect of success.[64] Inflation was developing rapidly; the solution was either to reduce government expenditure, improvise a satisfactory means of raising additional revenue, or obtain extra real loans. Treasury authorities were agreed that nothing could be achieved while H. H. Kung remained at the Ministry of Finance. 'This is due not only to the corruption with which he is charged, but to the fact that he does not understand the fundamental difficulties and is always thwarting the effective execution of reform by his control of the machine. I feel that the situation is so dangerous that we must not reject any proposal which holds out any prospect of improving it.'[65] Leith-Ross believed that T. V. Soong would be the obvious replacement for Kung. No mission could, in his view, be sent until Roosevelt's emissary, Lauchlin Currie, had returned from China; Currie saw clearly enough how important it was to remove Kung, but his attempts to attain this objective were prevented by the redoubtable Madame Chiang Kai-shek. E. L. Hall-Patch of the British Treasury was in Shanghai and fully confirmed the depressing state of affairs in a private letter to S. D. Waley; the only comforting feature was the serene and indomitable faith of Chiang Kai-shek in the midst of the galloping inflation and corruption that were inexorably undermining his regime. On 10 December 1940 the sum of £5 million was granted to the China stabilization fund, together with additional export credits of £5 million.

[64] Letter from Leith-Ross to Sterndale Bennett, 22 Feb. 1941, F1227/1/10, F.O.371/27591.
[65] Letter from Hall-Patch to Waley, 7 Dec. 1940 (received 21 Mar. 1941), F2135/1/10, F.O.371/27591. For a statement of British aid to China in 1940–41 see Appendix D.

Brigadier Dennys was duly promoted to major-general and dispatched from India to China at the beginning of 1941. He was authorized to hold discussions with the Chinese government on a non-committal basis. Decisions would subsequently be taken in London on Britain's ability to render assistance in specified circumstances. Dennys held a series of meetings with Chiang Kai-shek and General Ho Yau-tzu between February and April 1941. The principal aspects pursued were the possible operation of a British air squadron in China, following the outbreak of war between Britain and Japan, and British co-operation with Chinese guerrillas. The Chinese were anxious for the R.A.F. to use Chinese facilities, and Dennys was enthusiastic at the proposal. It was optimistically envisaged that squadrons could proceed from Malaya as required; there would be some liaison with the American-led International Air Force but the R.A.F. squadrons would function independently. With regard to guerrillas, Chiang wished for British advisers, not commanders. There was, in addition, discussion of possible British co-operation in Yunnan on a covert basis before the outbreak of war; this was unsurprisingly rejected. The defence of the Burma road was also debated.[66] In a conversation with Chiang and Ho on 17 March, Dennys explained that the involvement of Britain in Europe and the Middle East would compel a defensive strategy in the Far East in the initial stages of war. Dennys emphasized the importance of holding Singapore and of China preventing Japan from withdrawing forces from China to permit strengthened offensives against south-east Asia:

Provided we can hold Singapore the ultimate defeat of Japan is certain, for Japan's already straitened economic situation is very susceptible to British and American pressure and would in time result in a serious shortage of essential materials for waging war. Obviously the harder we can make Japan fight on all fronts the quicker will that shortage begin to take effect.

On the other hand the loss of Singapore would leave British and Dutch possessions in the Far East open to Japanese attack and would have a most serious effect on China's war situation.

One of the dangers facing us is that the Japanese may be able to withdraw large numbers of troops from China as reinforcements for

[66] Reports by Dennys, F5281/26/10, F.O.371/27609.

their initial striking forces directed against Malaya, Borneo, N.E.I. etc.

Consequently the greatest contribution China could make to the common cause would be to contain the maximum Japanese effort in China by increased all round pressure on Japanese forces there.

China's difficulties in this respect, such as shortage of military equipment, is [*sic*] fully appreciated, but we feel that in her guerrilla forces she has an offensive weapon worthy of exploitation and one which, used with the greatest vigour, may produce situations favourable for offensive action by the main Chinese armies. The British desire to assist to the greatest possible extent and to make pre-war preliminary preparations to do so.[67]

Dennys stated that Britain would like six aerodromes made available for use against Japanese air forces in the Han-kow–Indo-China area and for use in the Hong Kong–Canton area. The British air forces would comprise bomber and fighter squadrons and would form a detachment from the forces employed in 'the main battle in the South Seas'. It was essential to improve the organization and air defence of the Burma road in order to facilitate transport. Britain would be unable to provide fighters to defend the road at the start of the war. Chiang Kai-shek reiterated the vital role that British air assistance could play in the defence of Yunnan; Japan must not be permitted to capture Kunming.

Dennys's military consultations were intended to bolster Chinese morale with the hope that Britain would be able to render some assistance in the later stages of a conflict. It was undeniably ironical for Dennys to refer to Britain requiring aerodromes in China when the commander-in-chief, Far East, had few aircraft for the essential purpose of defending Singapore. Chiang Kai-shek can have entertained no illusion about the direct help he would receive in the foreseeable future, but his position was so desperate that he had no option but to press his claims with mechanical repetition. It is, how-ever, unlikely that Chiang anticipated the swift collapse of British power that occurred in the first phase of the Pacific war. There was a greater awareness in London of the significance of China by the spring of 1941, as evidenced in the provision of more economic aid and the dispatch of the

---

[67] Record of tenth conversation, 17 Mar. 1941, ibid.

Dennys mission, but it was felt that the United States would have to play the principal part. In the United States there was deep sympathy for China and more willingness to give economic assistance, but it was limited by Roosevelt's determination not to advance too quickly in undertaking new commitments and by his more immediate concern over developments in Europe.

Relations between Britain and Japan in 1940–1 were governed by the apprehension arising from the Japanese advance into Indo-China and by Japan's closer relationship with Germany in the tripartite pact. As Craigie reported on 10 October, Japan's move south was aimed ultimately at Malaya but there was no likelihood of a sudden Japanese attack within the near future. Anglo-Japanese relations were rendered more volatile by the mercurial personality of Matsuoka Yosuke whose combination of loquacity, threatening language, intense nationalism, and bizarre pronouncements encouraged constant speculation as to Japan's future policy. Matsuoka's unpredictable qualities were illustrated by the fact that he condemned the arrest of various British nationals in Tokyo in July 1940; the arrests had included that of Melville Cox, Reuter's correspondent, who died in mysterious circumstances. Sir Robert Craigie reported that Matsuoka had deplored the arrests privately and publicly.[68] The answer here possibly lies in Matsuoka's concentration on developing relations with Germany at this point, and his irritation at events that distracted his attention from the task in hand.[69] The British Foreign Office not surprisingly disliked Matsuoka and sought to convey their grievances to Shigemitsu Mamoru, the Japanese ambassador in London. Shigemitsu believed firmly in the justice of Japan's mission in enhancing her place in the world but he wished to proceed with some care and tact; he was opposed to reckless, ill-prepared expansion which entailed grave risks for the future of the nation. Shigemitsu was favourably regarded by officials in London; he proved adept in his personal relationships with Churchill, Halifax, Eden,

[68] Craigie to Foreign Office, 10 Oct. 1940, F4661/193/63, F.O.371/24710; Craigie to Foreign Office, 11 Oct. 1940, F5294/653/23, F.O.371/24741.
[69] For a concise, lucid assessment of Matsuoka, see B. Teters, 'Matsuoka Yosuke: the Diplomacy of Bluff and Gesture', in R. D. Burns and E. M. Bennett (eds.), *Diplomats in Crisis: United States-Chinese-Japanese Relations, 1919–1941*, pp. 275–96.

and Butler.[70] Shigemitsu originally hoped that Matsuoka could handle foreign policy with the requisite blend of skill, subtlety, and opportunism. This was the general feeling about Matsuoka at the time he took office under Konoe in July 1940. Matsuoka after all came from an unusual background, which included living and studying for some years in the United States, service as a diplomat, being a Seiyukai party member of the Diet, and holding office in the South Manchuria Railway Company. Matsuoka was to disappoint and baffle his fellow countrymen as much as he alienated foreign leaders. A new study of Matsuoka is badly needed but, on the evidence at present available, it is reasonable to conclude that Matsuoka was ambitious, scheming, and erratic and became increasingly unbalanced in the later stages of his term of office at the *Gaimusho*. Shigemitsu frequently visited the Foreign Office and on 1 November he raised with R. A. Butler the topic of British policy in China, which he regarded as the key to improving Anglo-Japanese relations. Shigemitsu asked if Britain's purpose was to prolong the Sino-Japanese war so as to embarrass Japan or whether Britain desired a just settlement. While Britain paid lip-service to the latter objective, Shigemitsu was doubtful about the honesty of statements to this effect. Butler professed astonishment and alluded to British policy at the time the Burma road was closed. Britain had hoped Japan would take steps to secure a lasting peace, but nothing had been done. Shigemitsu inquired if Britain would leave negotiations to Japan and China, to which Butler replied that any settlement reached must be a fair one. Butler in turn asked the ambassador what was happening to Wang Ching-wei. 'Mr. Shigemitsu said that Mr. Wang Ching-wei was "getting along quietly". I said that we certainly did not appear to hear much of him.'[71] Shigemitsu thought Matsuoka's diplomacy to be shrewd and implied that the tri-partite pact could be interpreted as Japan wished. Sir Horace Seymour remarked of Shigemitsu's conduct, 'He is playing a difficult hand skilfully.'[72]

---

[70] For a useful discussion of Shigemitsu, see A. D. Coox, 'Shigemitsu Mamoru: the Diplomacy of Crisis', in Burns and Bennett (eds.), pp. 251-73.

[71] Minute by Butler, 1 Nov. 1940, F4992/23/23, F.O.371/24726.

[72] Minute by Seymour, 18 Nov. 1940, ibid.

Craigie had a lengthy interview with Matsuoka on 9 November which consisted in essence of a monologue by the foreign minister. Matsuoka spoke of a desire to improve relations with Britain, exemplified by his attempt at suppressing anti-British agitation. Japan's adhesion to the tripartite pact should not be regarded as connoting a more belligerent policy:

His compelling motive in concluding this pact had been his conviction that the United States entry into the war would inevitably involve other States including Japan. Thus in due course the war would quickly become worldwide and this in turn would mean Armageddon. Furthermore the entry of the United States into the war might be the signal for general use of those terrible engines of destruction, such as thermite, which belligerents had hitherto abstained from employing. The suggestion frequently made that he had been gambling on a British defeat was absolutely untrue: on the contrary he felt that Japan should play her part in preventing the general collapse of civilisation, even at the cost if necessary, of sacrificing certain Japanese interests. He had all his life been opposed to any policy of narrow Japanese Nationalism which took no account of general interest of humanity and this was as true of his and Prince Konoye's policy to-day as it has ever been. His earnest desire was that, when Great Britain felt her military position was of sufficient security to justify such a step, the principal Powers should meet round a table and thus rescue the world from descent into the abyss. He was sure that Germany was prepared to withdraw her troops from areas she had occupied.[73]

Craigie mentioned the difficulty of interrupting Matsuoka's flood of rhetoric but said he had told the foreign minister that Britain could only regard the tripartite pact as aimed at Great Britain. When Craigie referred to the need for mutual confidence, Matsuoka made a typically strange rejoinder:

On the question of 'confidence' the Minister for Foreign Affairs made the somewhat surprising admission that, having regard to the many broken assurances for which Japanese policy had been responsible since the Manchuria affair, he was not the least surprised that foreign Powers should no longer place the same reliance on Japan's word as they had done in the past (e.g. at the time of the Anglo-Japanese alliance). Some of his predecessors had given assurances which they had promptly been forced to disregard, and their right course should then have been to resign at once. He himself intended

[73] Craigie to Foreign Office, 9 Nov. 1940, F5063/23/23, F.O.371/24726.

to adopt an entirely different line. If he gave an assurance or a promise which was not honoured by other elements, he would at once resign. But he had no intention of offering assurances which he felt he could not keep, and it was from this point of view that he asked us to regard the expression of his fervent desire to avoid war with either Great Britain or United States. Nothing would provoke this except American entry into the European war or some serious provocation such as the visit of a powerful American squadron to Singapore.[74]

Matsuoka gave his word that the Japanese presence in Indo-China was solely designed to assist operations against China and was not intended as a prelude to a move south. Craigie objected to Matsuoka's observation about the provocative nature of an American visit to Singapore. Matsuoka closed the interview by requesting Craigie to regard certain of his remarks as confidential. When the Foreign Office received Craigie's account, Dening aptly commented:

Mr. Matsuoka, in addition to being very talkative and at times astonishingly frank, is also like many of his countrymen, a little mad . . .

Mr. Matsuoka has a habit of speaking earnestly and with conviction, and he has an attractive personality. Unfortunately his convictions vary, and he does not always remember what his last conviction was.

What Mr. Matsuoka was actually saying was, of course, what the Japanese so frequently say if a prospective victim shows signs of restiveness: 'Do please be patient while I cut your throat'.[75]

Seymour believed that Matsuoka's true objective was to dissuade Britain and the United States from deciding that American ships should visit Singapore.[76]

In a reply to Craigie, the Foreign Office maintained that while little could be hoped for from arguing with Matsuoka, it might be wise to make a statement for the record based on the contents of the telegram. The Foreign Office recalled the unhappy tone of Matsuoka's first interview with Craigie after taking over the *Gaimusho*: he had then implied that differences between Britain and Japan were unbridgeable. Subsequent developments had confirmed this interpretation,

---

[74] Ibid.
[75] Minute by Dening, 12 Nov. 1940, ibid.
[76] Minute by Seymour, 13 Nov. 1940, ibid.

notably the conclusion of the tripartite pact. The United
States had reacted with more vigour than had been expected
within Japan to the news of the pact, and Matsuoka had endeavoured to explain away foreign questionings. The Foreign
Office, therefore, held that the aims of Japan's policy
remained constant but that her strategy had been modified,
since Japan did not want war with the United States and Great
Britain as yet. Instead Japan would await developments in the
European struggle and choose her moment to act; if this
assessment of Japan's position was accurate, then it afforded
confirmation of the wisdom of the policy pursued by Britain
and the United States in recent weeks.

Meanwhile it would be unwise to assume that we have unlimited time
at our disposal to strengthen our position, or that it is unlikely to be
assailed. For the present Japanese Government have shown a certain
capacity for errors of judgement, while Germany on her part seems
to display considerable aptitude in persuading Japan to do things
which it is not in her real interests to do. As long as we remain largely
on the defensive in Europe, and until both we and the United States
can convince Japan that we have both the will and the power to resist her by force if need be, our position in the Far East and in the
Pacific is likely to remain insecure.[77]

Matsuoka's remarks about Singapore were manifestly meant to
discourage any American initiative; such a visit did not seem
probable given current American policy but the Japanese attitude should not be permitted to influence an eventual decision.

Anglo-Japanese relations slowly worsened. Captain Hiraide
of the Japanese navy stated at a public meeting in mid-
November that the period from February 1941 would be
critical in the Pacific region: Hiraide denied any aggressive
intent on Japan's part but said that Japan would act if the
United States took action affecting Japan or if the Americans
used Singapore as a base. In early December Matsuoka told
Craigie that Japan might shortly have to take action which
might strike Britain as incompatible with the obligations of a
neutral.[78] It was uncertain as to Matsuoka's meaning, but
Dening deduced that he was referring either to attempts to
avoid the British blockade or to more direct Japanese

[77] Foreign Office to Craigie, 20 Nov. 1940, ibid.
[78] Craigie to Foreign Office, 9 Dec. 1940, F5542/23/23, F.O.371/24726.

collaboration in German attacks on Britain's seaborne trade. 'We must, I am afraid, regard ourselves more and more as in a state of undeclared war with Japan, which may eventually culminate in total war . . . The general situation in the Far East is deteriorating, and the mere fact that minor pinpricks against us are rather fewer than they were, should be taken as a sinister rather than encouraging sign. For if the Japanese are out to do one a major injury, sentiment disposes them to avoid inflicting minor ones.'[79] Dening thought it important to strengthen British defences more speedily; Seymour gloomily added that it was improbable that defences could be significantly improved.[80] Britain would have to rely on the skill with which the Americans could handle matters.

British suspicion of the trend of Japanese policy came to a climax in February 1941, in blunt exchanges between London and Tokyo amidst rumours of an imminent Japanese attack. Fear of a Japanese attack arose in part from the steady deterioration in relations since the fall of the Yonai government and in part from faulty intelligence information reaching British authorities. In an interview with an Australian journalist on 17 January and in a speech in the Japanese diet in late January, Matsuoka inflamed the already delicate situation. At the press interview he speculated on the dangers of war in the Pacific. Japan would only fight after careful reflection on the issues. Japanese expansion would be inherently peaceful and economic in character, but Japan was determined to participate in opening the areas of the Netherlands East Indies, Thailand, Burma, and Indo-China. Craigie immediately protested at the reference to Burma, since it inferred a Japanese claim to a British territory; Matsuoka replied in vague terms but remarked that Japan did not enjoy equality of economic opportunity in Burma.[81] On 20 January Matsuoka made an extreme speech in the diet, described by Dening as 'without exception the most undiplomatic ever delivered by a Japanese Foreign Minister in the past 20

---

[79] Minute by Dening, 14 Dec. 1940, ibid.
[80] Minute by Seymour, 15 Dec. 1940, ibid.
[81] Craigie to Foreign Office, 20 Jan. (two telegrams), 21 and 23 Jan. 1941, F298/12/23, F.O.371/27883. In the controversial speech Matsuoka spoke vigorously on Japan's imperial mission and defended his country's policy in unnecessarily offensive language.

years'.[82] Shigemitsu called to see R. A. Butler on 31 January and assured him that the speech should be regarded as for domestic consumption; the ambassador promised to inform Butler if his personal assessment of Matsuoka's meaning proved to be erroneous.[83] Craigie consulted his embassy colleagues on the danger of war and sent a statement of their views to Brooke-Popham, the commander-in-chief, Far East, on 11 February. In their opinion it was certainly feasible for Japan to launch an offensive reasonably soon and this had to be expected; there was, however, a chance that if the United States took resolute action, war would not occur. The new foreign secretary, Anthony Eden, who had succeeded Lord Halifax in December, had never been well disposed to Japan and was now thoroughly exasperated. He considered Butler's interview with Shigemitsu to be unsatisfactory, and determined to see the ambassador personally to emphasize Britain's confidence in victory and warn Japan against drifting further into the German orbit. Cadogan warmly assented: Shigemitsu had been uttering 'the most blatant nonsense' and it was desirable that he should be gently rebuked. Eden saw Shigemitsu and spoke frankly and strongly to him.[84]

The defence situation was examined by the chiefs of staff at the beginning of February. In their view Japan was considering extreme action with the encouragement of Germany. The consequences would be grave for the whole British war effort; communications with Australia and New Zealand would be jeopardized, as would trade routes and links with the Middle East. If the threat to Singapore became grave enough, it might be necessary to retire temporarily from the Mediterranean in order to permit naval forces to go to the Far East. The chiefs of staff supported a joint Anglo-American warning to Japan in an effort to stave off war. Eden, in a minute for Churchill written on 8 February, regarded the warning as desirable but unattainable; he added that he had spoken to Roosevelt's special emissary, Harry Hopkins, at

---

[82] Minute by Dening, 25 Jan. 1941, F390/12/23, F.O.371/27879.

[83] Minute by Butler, 31 Jan. 1941, F529/12/23, F.O.371/27878.

[84] Minutes by Eden and Cadogan, 1-3 Feb. 1941, F648/17/23, F.O.371/27886. L. S. Amery wrote to Auchinleck that the Japanese meant 'mischief' and that a firm policy must be pursued, see letter from Amery to Auchinleck, 19 Feb. 1941, Jan.-June 1941, item 125, Auchinleck papers, John Rylands University Library of Manchester.

lunch and Hopkins thought it might be most advisable for Roosevelt to summon the Japanese ambassador and talk to him candidly.[85] In the light of the urgent situation Halifax, now ambassador to Washington, visited the president on 9 February. Roosevelt observed that he had been devoting much thought to the problem of Japan but his feeling was that American public opinion would not allow an American declaration of war if Japan attacked only British or Dutch possessions. Even if the United States became involved in war with Japan, it was doubtful if it could be other than a holding operation; it was vital to bear in mind the primacy of European supplies.[86] Apart from his customary practice of carefully gauging the state of domestic opinion, Roosevelt was conscious of the importance of not damaging the passage of the Lend-Lease bill through Congress and of heeding the views of his defence chiefs that the United States must not become involved in war with Japan at this juncture. On 10 February Halifax saw Cordell Hull and informed him that the position was more alarming than it had been a day or two before; it was imperative that the United States demonstrate its concern. Hull said it would be made abundantly clear to the Japanese that the United States was hostile to an attempt to dominate East Asia. He added, however, that caution was needed so as not to precipitate Japanese seizure of the Netherlands East Indies.[87] While the position of the United States was not without some encouragement, determined action was not likely.

Churchill decided to send a personal appeal to Roosevelt. He dispatched one of his personal messages to Roosevelt on 15 February. Japanese intentions were by no means clear but an attack on British possessions was definitely possible. The prime minister did not consider an offensive directed at Singapore to be likely at first; it was more probable that Japan would act against the East Indies and proceed against Singapore afterwards. Churchill was most worried at the potential activities of Japanese raiders on trade routes in the Pacific and Indian Oceans. The effect would be most serious in the economic and

---

[85] Minute by Eden, 8 Feb. 1941, with *aide-mémoire* from chiefs of staff, F677/17/23, F.O.371/27886.
[86] Washington to Foreign Office, 9 Feb. 1941, F7957/17/23, F.O.371/27886.
[87] Washington to Foreign Office, 11 Feb. 1941, F741/17/23, F.O.371/27886.

military spheres. If Japan threatened an invasion of Australia or New Zealand, the British fleet would have to be withdrawn from the Mediterranean and sent to the Far East. Churchill ended with an appeal for support:

Some believe that Japan in her present mood would not hesitate to court or attempt to wage war both against Great Britain and the United States. Personally I think the odds are definitely against that, but no one can tell. Everything that you can do to inspire the Japanese with the fear of a double war may avert danger. If however they come in against us and we are alone, the grave character of the consequences cannot easily be overstated.[88]

Craigie visited Matsuoka on 15 February and found the foreign minister in a rather less bellicose frame of mind. Matsuoka admitted that Japanese forces in Indo-China were being strengthened. With regard to his earlier suggestion of Japanese mediation in the European war, he denied that Japan would require a *quid pro quo* for any role she might play. He agreed that there were currents of opinion urging a different policy but such attitudes were contrary to the wishes of Konoe and himself:

He wished me to believe . . . that both the Prime Minister and he were irrevocably opposed to schemes of adventure or aggression and if necessary they would go to the Emperor to secure support for their policy. Should such a step prove insufficient they would resign. The leadership which he and the Prime Minister desired was, as he had frequently stated, a spiritual leadership and, if Japan could make herself worthy of it, he would wish this kind of leadership to prevail not only in East Asia but throughout the world.

I pointed out, that, however high might be His Excellency's morals, they did not appear to be understood by the majority of people in Japan who seemed bent on achieving more materialistic ambitions. His Excellency admitted the truth of this assertion — in fact, he said jokingly that he was sometimes doubtful whether anyone in Japan understood his policies except the Prime Minister.[89]

Towards the close of the interview, Matsuoka agreed with Craigie that it was important to prevent rival action by both sides which might terminate in a collision. Dening minuted

---

[88] Former Naval Person to Roosevelt, 15 Feb. 1941, F1068/17/23, F.O.371/27887.
[89] Craigie to Foreign Office, 15 Feb. 1941, F1009/12/23, F.O.371/27878.

that Matsuoka was a liar and it was regrettable that Craigie, on this occasion, seemed to place some credence in the foreign minister's assurances. Cadogan, who usually took a more favourable view of Craigie, concurred.[90]

Eden was away from the Foreign Office in mid-February and Churchill took over. Shigemitsu visited Butler on 17 February and handed him a memorandum from Matsuoka, in the course of which the foreign minister defended Japanese policy against accusations of being too bellicose and instead attempted to lay the responsibility of the crisis on the shoulders of Britain and the United States in his inimitable way. Matsuoka professed surprise at the concern over Japanese policy and alluded darkly to misleading information emanating from the British embassy in Tokyo. He stated that he had explained to Craigie and to the public at large that the purpose of the tripartite pact was peaceful. Warlike preparations by the British and Americans were regarded with much concern in Japan to such an extent that some Japanese believed counter-measures to deal with 'the worst eventuality' should be taken. In the latter part of his memorandum, Matsuoka emphasized his sincere devotion to peace and his wish to help in terminating the European conflict:

Having had the privilege of forming personal acquaintanceship at Geneva with His Britannic Majesty's Principal Secretary for Foreign Affairs and, prompted by the belief that an exchange of frank views in a general way at this juncture will be of some service in enabling the two peoples to see eye to eye, the Minister for Foreign Affairs wishes to take the liberty of making further observations. The uppermost thought in his mind has always been the world peace. He sincerely hopes that, on the one hand, the China affair will be brought to an end as soon as possible, and, on the other, the European war will see an early termination. It is his earnest and constant prayer that the Powers may gather again to discuss at a round table their differences and disputes and deliberate on the great question of organising an enduring peace upon a just and equitable world order. In this connexion he desires to assure his eminent colleague that, far from aspiring to control the destinies of, and to dominate other peoples, it is Japan's established policy to inaugurate an era of peace and plenty and of mutual helpfulness of Greater East Asia by promoting the spirit of concord and conciliation. As

[90] Minutes, 19–21 Feb. 1941, ibid.

repeatedly affirmed, Japan's motto is 'no conquest, no oppression, no exploitation'. He therefore strongly deprecates those biased reports designed to calumniate Japan . . .

Lastly, the Minister for Foreign Affairs would like to make it clear that Japan, deeply concerned as she is with an early restoration of peace, is fully prepared to act as a mediator or to take whatever action calculated to recover normal conditions, not only in Greater East Asia but anywhere the world over. The Minister for Foreign Affairs trusts that His Britannic Majesty's Principal Secretary for Foreign Affairs will not hesitate to share the conviction that upon the shoulders of the leading powers rests the great and grave responsibility of restoring peace and saving modern civilisation from impending collapse . . .[91]

Churchill was not one to resist a splendid opportunity to reply in typically Churchillian terms. Indeed the curious personality of Matsuoka seems to have fascinated Churchill, for he developed an enthusiasm for communicating with him and for endeavouring to outwit him in paper exchanges. The prime minister saw Shigemitsu, talked with him, and handed him a memorandum for transmission to Matsuoka. In conversation with Shigemitsu, Churchill dwelt, as was his custom, on the long history of amicable relations between Britain and Japan. Japan could not, he said, expect Britain to condone her conduct in China but stressed that an impartial attitude of neutrality had been followed by Britain since 1937. Churchill pursued the points outlined in the *aide-mémoire* handed to Shigemitsu. The ambassador replied that he understood Britain's views well enough and Japan intended no attack on Britain or the United States. 'The only complaint which Japan had, he said, was our attitude to China, which was encouraging China and adding to her difficulties. It might be they had made mistakes in entering into China, but even we made mistakes sometimes, and it was our attitude of partisanship for the Chinese which had led to some estrangement between Britain and Japan.'[92] Churchill described Britain's

---

[91] Churchill to Craigie, 20 Feb. 1941, enclosing note by Butler and memorandum from Matsuoka, F1069/17/23, F.O.371/27887. The worsening of relations with Japan helped to concentrate Auchinleck's mind on the weak defences of India. He commented on the air threat to eastern India — '. . . we have left ourselves very naked indeed as regards aircraft — dangerously so in fact', letter from Auchinleck to Dill, 20 Feb. 1941, Jan.-June 1941, item 126, Auchinleck papers.
[92] Churchill to Craigie, 24 Feb. 1941, F1239/17/23, F.O.371/27887.

military measures as wholly defensive. When Shigemitsu protested at the current British press campaign against Japan, Churchill denied any responsibility but held that it had clarified the situation 'because instead of the grave dangers of war becoming apparent only to the small military circles who largely control the Japanese Government, the whole Japanese nation knew what was going on and of the dangers lying ahead, and I had confidence that the Japanese did not wish to embark upon such a tremendous struggle as would be inevitable if they went to war with the British and Americans.'[93] At the close of the interview, Churchill reiterated that the tripartite pact had been a major blunder for Japan. He described the meeting to Craigie as having been most cordial, adding 'we have no doubt where he [Shigemitsu] stands in these matters'.[94]

In his memorandum Churchill began by noting Matsuoka's promises about the peaceful aims of Japanese policy. He denied any warlike intentions on the part of Britain or the United States. He went on to expound Britain's objectives in the European war: Britain had been compelled to go to war and it had naturally taken some time to organize British defences. The United States was aiding Britain because Britain was pledged to defeat 'the system of lawlessness and violence abroad and cold, cruel tyranny at home which constitutes the German Nazi regime'. Britain had no ulterior aims and did not wish to conquer or annex territory; she was solely concerned with eliminating nazism and restoring true peace to the world. Churchill skilfully repudiated Matsuoka's offer of mediation:

Mr. Matsuoka, with the loftiest motives, has hinted at his readiness to act as the mediator between the belligerents. The Prime Minister is sure that, in the light of what he has said and upon further reflection, Mr. Matsuoka will understand that in a cause of this kind, not in any way concerned with territory, trade or material gains, but affecting the whole future of humanity, there can be no question of compromise or parley . . .[95]

Thus the danger of war breaking out in February 1941

[93] Ibid.
[94] Ibid.
[95] Ibid.

receded amidst the verbiage of diplomatic exchanges. Matsuoka was extremely well disposed to Germany, and viewed the course of world progress as resting with Japan and Germany in the era of the respective 'new orders' in East Asia and Europe. He did not desire war with the United States, and the tripartite pact was designed to prevent it. He regarded Britain with contempt, but felt war could not be waged against her for fear of involving the United States. Matsuoka did not appreciate that relations between Germany and Russia were deteriorating and that Hitler had decided to attack Russia within the near future. Matsuoka's purpose in visiting Europe was to strengthen ties with Germany and thereby to improve his chances of succeeding Konoe as prime minister. He also wished to reach an agreement with Stalin if possible. The Foreign Office in London deliberated whether to invite Matsuoka to visit London. It was doubtful whether much would be achieved thereby, apart from impressing the erratic Matsuoka with the indomitable spirit and zeal of the British people. It was decided to sound out American opinion.[96] Sumner Welles told Halifax that it was not desirable that Matsuoka should visit London but if he expressed the wish to come, it should be arranged.[97] Matsuoka did not ask to visit London and confined his tour to Moscow, Berlin, and Rome. Craigie, whose patience with Matsuoka appeared at an end, suggested that it would be an excellent idea to arrange a bombing raid over Berlin during Matsuoka's stay, so as to demonstrate British air power. Craigie remarked, 'In his conversations with me he has always tended to take my statements in regard to the growing power of the R.A.F. with a grain of salt and I consider that the effects of heavy raid would be very salutary.'[98] Cavendish-Bentinck, who represented the Foreign Office on the joint intelligence sub-committee to the chiefs of staff, commented that a light raid would be futile. 'If this operation is done at all, it should be done properly and a heavy attack should be made on Berlin, with the district in which it is expected that Mr. Matsuoka will be staying in the target area. A land mine on his hotel would be most

[96] Foreign Office to Halifax, 27 Mar. 1941, F1980/17/23, F.O.371/27889.
[97] Washington to Foreign Office, 2 Apr. 1941, F2536/17/23, F.O.371/27889.
[98] Craigie to Foreign Office, 18 Mar. 1941, F2073/137/23, F.O.371/27926.

gratifying.'[99] Sterndale Bennett expressed the qualification 'that our objective is to impress rather than to extinguish Mr. Matsuoka.'[100] Cadogan stated that the proposal had been raised in cabinet 'and met with general approval'.[101] It was not, however, subsequently implemented, perhaps wisely.

Churchill had reached the decision to address a list of questions to Matsuoka, with the aim of compelling him to reflect more carefully on the perils of closer identification with Germany. The prime minister was filled with enthusiasm at the thought of a further duel with Matsuoka but the Foreign Office showed less zeal. Churchill wanted the message given to Matsuoka by Sir Stafford Cripps, the ambassador in Moscow. Dening minuted respectfully that the impact would be lost through transmission in Moscow and that it would be preferable to send it to Konoe.[102] R. A. Butler dissented, adding significantly that Churchill was very proud of his questions.[103] It would have been better for the message to have gone to Konoe, in fact, especially as moves were being fostered by Konoe to open full-scale talks with the United States in a bid to resolve their differences. Matsuoka was far too committed to his Germanophile policies to contemplate alternatives. Matsuoka replied to Churchill in late April in verbose and woolly terms, again proclaiming Japan's dedication to peace, opposition to exploitation, oppression, and suffering and fealty to the great racial design of Hakko-ichiu, the Japanese conception of universal peace. In presenting Matsuoka's response to Eden, Shigemitsu stated that there was no need for Anglo-Japanese conflict and that the problem hinged on Britain's inability properly to comprehend Japan's policy in China.[104] He also criticized economic restrictions on trade with Japan; such restrictions were applied and regulated under the authority of the Far Eastern committee chaired by R. A. Butler. Eden responded that Japan's treatment of China was wrong. The discussion ended on a friendlier note, with Shigemitsu indicating his genuine respect for Great Britain

[99] Minute by Cavendish-Bentinck, 19 Mar. 1941, ibid.
[100] Minute by Sterndale Bennett, 20 Mar. 1941, ibid.
[101] Minute by Cadogan, 20 Mar. 1941, ibid.
[102] Minute by Dening, 1 Apr. 1941, F2554/17/23, F.O.371/27889.
[103] Minute by Butler, 1 Apr. 1941, ibid.
[104] Eden to Craigie, 25 Apr. 1941, F3424/17/23, F.O.371/27891.

and his admiration for the heroism of the British people.

Matsuoka returned from Europe flushed with the triumph of his meetings with Hitler and Stalin. The most tangible symbol of his mission was the signature of the non-aggression pact with the Soviet Union. Matsuoka brushed aside hints from Ribbentrop of worsening relations with Russia; he was determined to secure a personal victory and this was the most obvious sign of it. Hitler continued to urge a Japanese attack on Singapore, as he had done for six months. Matsuoka was becoming more dictatorial and seemed to regard himself as complementary to the European totalitarian leaders. British and American leaders were not alone in their dislike of Matsuoka; the feeling was shared by the foreign minister's colleagues, who believed that his extreme admiration for Germany was going to culminate in a clash with the United States unless he was restrained. They were not yet prepared to dispense with his services, but the time was approaching.

For Great Britain the significance of the period from October 1940 to June 1941 lay in the closeness with the United States revealed most clearly in the passage of the Lend-Lease bill in March 1941. Senator Burton K. Wheeler (Democrat, Montana), one of the leading opponents of the bill and of Roosevelt's foreign policy, alleged during the debate in Congress that Britain was intriguing to involve the United States in the European war via the Far East.[105] Roosevelt was edging his country nearer to Britain, but the movement was gradual. In East Asia Britain could not rely on American assistance if Japan attacked British and Dutch possessions; British policy was bound to rest on a combination of as much verbal firmness as her exposed position allowed and of limited strengthening of defences. The Foreign Office believed that urgent steps were required to improve defences in the Far East; it was in this context that Sterndale Bennett described British policy as 'fumbling'.[106] The defence chiefs were pre-occupied with wars nearer home and constantly reiterated, as did their American counterparts, that war with Japan should be avoided. The crucial aspect was that Churchill, although

---

[105] Letter from N. Butler to Sterndale Bennett, 26 Feb. 1941, F2099/86/23, F.O.371/27908.
[106] Minute by Sterndale Bennett, 3 Feb. 1941, F540/9/61, F.O.371/27760.

periodically worried about the Far East, did not regard war with Japan as likely and opposed any radical reinforcement of defences in the area. As was to become even clearer in the final phase of the Pacific crisis, Britain would not pursue a policy of appeasement towards Japan and depended on the United States to handle the climax of the confrontation with Japan—and whatever the Americans eventually decided would have to be accepted.

VII

THE APPROACH OF WAR

IN the final phase of the Pacific crisis, culminating in the outbreak of war in December 1941, the latent confrontation between the United States and Japan at last became overt. Great Britain had shouldered the burden with increasing difficulty but in the six months before Pearl Harbor Britain moved to the side of the stage, as the vital decisions were taken in Washington and Tokyo. This is not to maintain that the situation was clear-cut: it was in fact opaque. British and American leaders remained preoccupied with events in Europe and the Middle East; a limited amount of time and thought was devoted to the Far East. Winston Churchill placed reliance on the growing involvement of the United States throughout the world, and regarded a Japanese attack as improbable. Churchill did vacillate and there were moments when he contemplated the Japanese threat more soberly, but fundamentally he believed that even if Japan were foolish enough to launch an offensive, she could be held. Anthony Eden's attitude was similar. The defence chiefs were primarily concerned with avoiding any additional commitments, which could only be met at the expense of other theatres. The Foreign Office wanted defences in and adjacent to Malaya strengthened, and shared the widespread underestimation of Japan. In the United States President Roosevelt largely delegated the task of handling the protracted talks with Japan to his secretary of state, Cordell Hull. Hull was slow, ponderous, and fiercely attached to his cherished principles: he did not want war but was adamant that it should not be avoided at the cost of sacrificing the moral stand which the United States was taking in the world. Roosevelt intervened decisively only in the last days of peace in the Pacific, when it was obvious from information derived from the intercepted 'Magic' code that war was imminent. It was in this closing period that Roosevelt gave the elusive promise of concrete support so long sought by Churchill. The assurance of support for Britain and the Netherlands in the event of a Japanese attack on their possessions came late in the day; only on the eve of Pearl Harbor was the apprehension that had haunted British policy-makers of having to fight Japan without American participation laid to rest. The period from June to December 1941 exhibits a variety of moods and attitudes: confusion, uncertainty, periodic hopes that an agreement with Japan might yet be reached, and ultimate resignation to whatever fate had in store. Such were the feelings common in London, Washington, Tokyo, and Singapore.

The catalyst was the American decision in July 1941 to impose rigorous, full-scale economic sanctions against Japan, a decision swiftly followed by the British and Dutch. In London it had long been felt that the United States should demonstrate unmistakably to Japan that deeds would eventually follow the torrent of words. However, when the United States announced the application of sanctions, there were fears that it was an over-reaction. Roosevelt's decision to enforce the freezing measures was precipitated by the Japanese advance into southern Indo-China in July 1941; the Japanese advance was significant, for it would manifestly facilitate offensives against Malaya, the Netherlands East Indies, and the Philippines. Japanese leaders approved the move south in a series of liaison conferences of top leaders held in late June and ratified at an imperial conference presided over by the emperor on 2 July. The situation had been complicated by the German attack on Russia, which had begun on 22 June. The attack had come as a surprise in Tokyo, and prompted reassessment of Japan's prospects in the world context. Hitler wanted Japan to join Germany in overthrowing Stalin and eliminating the bolshevik menace. However, he had previously urged Japan to attack Singapore and, furthermore, had not consulted Japan with the frankness to be expected under the tripartite pact. While the advance of the German forces into Russian territory did not arouse the profound emotions of August 1939, when the Nazi–Soviet pact had been announced, it did resemble it in the lack of prior consultation. The majority of Japanese leaders accordingly regarded Hitler with some reservations, rightly suspecting that his sole interest in

Japan lay in the extent to which Japan could aid his designs at a particular time. Matsuoka Yosuke, the garrulous foreign minister, favoured a Japanese advance into Siberia. He was entirely willing to shed his recent ardent protestations of friendship with Russia, exemplified in his meeting with Stalin in April and signature of the non-aggression pact with the Soviet Union. Matsuoka wished to avoid war with the United States, and had seen the tripartite pact as a diplomatic weapon to deter American intervention. At a liaison conference on 30 June, Matsuoka observed: 'I have never made a mistake in predicting what would happen in the next few years. I predict that if we get involved in the South it will become a serious matter. Can the Army Chief of Staff guarantee that it won't? Furthermore, if we occupy southern Indo-China it will become difficult to secure oil, rubber, tin, rice etc. Great men will change their minds. Previously I advocated going south, but now I favour the North.'[1] Muto, the chief of the bureau of military affairs, and Nagano, the chief of the naval staff, pointed out that the road south would bring valuable raw materials, notably rubber and tin, and that the navy had based its recent actions on the assumption of expansion south — it would be difficult to reverse this policy now. Sugiyama, the army chief of staff, tried to reassure Prince Higashikuni and Prince Asaka, who voiced doubts about proceeding south. 'There are several possible timetables and methods for moving south; but for the purpose of survival and self-defence, we are thinking of going as far as the Netherlands East Indies. Territory is not our objective. We are going forward in such a way that the worst possible eventuality — i.e. Britain, the United States and the Soviet Union attacking us simultaneously — will not happen. However, we cannot stop if we are confronted by Britain and the United States alone.'[2]

The imperial conference met on 2 July and formally endorsed the southern strategy:

Our Empire is determined to follow a policy that will result in the establishment of the Greater East Asia Co-Prosperity Sphere and will thereby contribute to world peace, no matter what changes may occur in the world situation.

---

[1] Ike, p. 72, 36th liaison conference, 30 June 1941.
[2] Ike, p. 74.

Our Empire will continue its efforts to effect a settlement of the China Incident . . .

In order to guarantee the security and preservation of the nation, our Empire will continue all necessary diplomatic negotiations with reference to the southern regions, and will also take such other measures as may be necessary.

In order to achieve the above objectives, preparations for war with Great Britain and the United States will be made. First of all . . . various measures relating to French Indochina and Thailand will be taken, with the purpose of strengthening our advance into the southern regions. In carrying out the plans outlined above our Empire will not be deterred by the possibility of being involved in a war with Great Britain and the United States . . .

In accordance with established policy, we will strive to the utmost, by diplomatic and other means, to prevent the entry of the United States into the European war. But if the United States should enter the war, our Empire will act in accordance with the Tripartite Pact. However, we will decide independently as to the time and method of resorting to force . . .[3]

In the discussion at the conference, Hara, the president of the privy council, had doubts about advancing into Indo-China. He stated: 'What I want made clear is whether the United States would go to war if Japan took action against Indochina.'[4] Matsuoka replied, 'I cannot exclude the possibility.'[5] Sugiyama commented firmly: 'Our occupation of Indochina will certainly provoke Great Britain and the United States. After our successful mediation of the dispute in Indochina earlier this year, our influence has become quite strong there and in Thailand. At present, however, the intrigues of Great Britain and the United States in Thailand and Indochina have increased steadily, and we cannot tell what will happen in the future. At this juncture, Japan must resolutely carry out the policy she now has in mind: this policy is absolutely necessary in order to stamp out the intrigues of Great Britain and the United States.'[6] Sugiyama added that great care would be exercised so as to minimize the dangers of conflict with other powers, but his determination to fulfil expansion south was

---

[3] Ike, pp. 78-9, imperial conference, 2 July 1941.
[4] Ike, p. 88, ibid.
[5] Ibid.
[6] Ibid.

undoubted. Japan wanted to avoid war in the Pacific if possible and for this reason the diplomatic exchanges in Washington would be continued: the primary purpose of Japanese policy was to advance the new order in East Asia and the Pacific and to secure an adequate place in the sun and, whatever happened, there would be no retreat from this policy. A treaty between Japan and the Vichy regime was signed on 21 July, permitting the Japanese forces to proceed with the occupation of Indo-China.

For some time the Roosevelt administration had reflected on the response to be made to a new Japanese aggressive initiative. Economic measures were the most obvious and drastic method of retaliation. The Achilles heel of the Japanese economy was reliance on crucial imports of raw materials, above all oil. Discreet economic pressure had been employed against Japan by Britain and the United States since the summer of 1940; in London this had been co-ordinated for the British Commonwealth by the Far Eastern committee, chaired by R. A. Butler.[7] The committee reviewed economic relations with Japan and determined what measures could be taken to slow down or prevent exports of commodities to Japan; there were divisions of opinion in Washington as to the wisdom of enforcing extreme sanctions but it was decided to press ahead.[8] The British government certainly supported some retaliation against Japan but the war cabinet did not contemplate full-scale economic measures beforehand. On 7 July the cabinet considered a memorandum from Eden containing proposals on the strategic, political, and economic courses of action that could be taken if Japan moved into southern Indo-China.[9] Eden advocated consultations with the Dominions and with Sir Robert Craigie in Tokyo as to the desirability of denouncing the Anglo-Japanese commercial treaty of 1911, so as to allow the government to act more swiftly in the event of Japan occupying the whole of Indo-China. The war cabinet authorized the preparation of measures but emphasized that caution was required. 'In dis-

---

[7] For the records of this committee, see Cab.96/1-4,7-8. See also Appendix C.
[8] J. M. Blum (ed.), *From the Morgenthau Diaries: Years of Urgency 1938-1941* (Houghton Mifflin, Boston, 1965), p. 377.
[9] War cabinet conclusions, 7 July 1941, 66(41)4, Cab.65/19.

cussion it was agreed that the general situation did not justify us in taking strong deterrent measures to prevent further Japanese encroachments. Our policy must therefore be, for the present to take appropriate counter-action after each encroachment, calculated to play on Japanese reluctance to come into the war against an unbeaten and still formidable country.'[10] After the Japanese advance had taken place, Eden informed his colleagues that the United States intended to freeze Japanese assets in the United States, to render all imports from Japan subject to licence, and to limit petroleum exports. It would require a few days for the measures to be formulated, and Eden proposed delaying announcements on British action until the situation had been clarified. He would then proclaim denunciation of the Anglo-Japanese commercial treaty of 1911 and freezing of Japanese assets. The war cabinet approved Eden's policy. The demands of over-all war policy necessitated full British co-operation in whatever decisions were taken in Washington, regardless of whether or not such measures were the most fitting in the circumstances.

There was much confusion concerning the action being taken by the American administration. It took a surprising time to clarify the ambiguities: this was due to a not untypical failure on Roosevelt's part to instruct his subordinates as to the precise nature of the measures and to put an end to bureaucratic wrangling. On 31 July Eden told his colleagues in cabinet that 'although at the outset, the United States had taken a firm line in freezing Japanese assets, there were now indications that while bringing to an end special trade and war supplies, they might intend to allow normal trade with Japan to continue. The Foreign Secretary thought it was both dangerous and unwise to follow a bold decision by feeble and ineffective action. We, at any rate, should enforce the freezing order strictly and only grant licences in the exceptional cases where it was in the interests of our war effort to do so.'[11] The

---

[10] War cabinet conclusions, 24 July 1941, 73(41)4, Cab.65/19.
[11] War cabinet conclusions, 31 July 1941, 76(41)4, Cab. 65/19. See also W. N. Medlicott, *The Economic Blockade*, ii, 106-20, and H. Feis, *The Road to Pearl Harbor*, p. 229. It has been argued that Roosevelt did not originally intend to implement a full embargo of Japan but that the bureaucracy made up his mind for him, see I. H. Anderson, Jnr., 'The 1941 *De Facto* Embargo on Oil to Japan: A Bureaucratic Reflex', *P.H.R.* xliv, No. 2 (May 1975), 201-31.

cabinet authorized Eden to intimate British views to Washington. It was, however, essential to proceed warily and give no scope for the vociferous isolationist lobby in the United States to accuse Roosevelt of being manipulated by the machiavellian British. Lord Halifax reported on 25 July remarks made by Senator Walter George of Georgia, chairman of the Senate Foreign Relations Committee, to the effect that while Britain would probably be consulted on economic co-operation, American policy would be devised for the best interests of the United States. Halifax urged that it was politically expedient to continue to depict the policies of the two countries as being 'parallel' rather than 'joint':

While we should avoid on the one hand, giving the impression that the United States Government have taken the lead as a result of pressure from His Majesty's Government and on the other hand, that His Majesty's Government are not likely to back the United States up, we should I think take the line that it is only natural that the two Governments should have reacted in very similar fashion to the Japanese move in view of the fact that the interests of both are equally affected by Japanese action.[12]

Sir Frederick Leith-Ross wrote from the Ministry of Economic Warfare to Sterndale Bennett on 31 July that in his opinion a complete embargo on trade with Japan would not be feasible. The repercussions on Japan would be so grave as to compel Japan to go to war. Leith-Ross pointed out that British defence spokesmen were constantly reiterating that Britain was not prepared for war: 'If we are ready for war with Japan, well and good; but the Service representatives at the Far Eastern Committee have frequently stressed that we are by no means ready. Even today they emphasized that we must do everything to avoid a Japanese advance into Thailand, which we are in no position to stop.'[13] Leith-Ross suggested a more gradual approach to the enforcement of the freezing order. In the Foreign Office L. H. Foulds observed that the problems in deciding policy resulted from the uncertain position of the United States; B. E. F. Gage expressed it more succinctly when

---

[12] Washington to Foreign Office, 23 July 1941, F6743/1299/23, F.O.371/27972.
[13] Letter from Leith-Ross to Sterndale Bennett, 31 July 1941 (received 1 Aug. 1941), F7153/299/23, F.O.371/27973. See also minutes by Leith-Ross and Dalton, 31 July–1 Aug. 1941, F.O.837/534.

he wrote that Britain simply had to follow the American lead.[14]

During August the departments of the British government principally involved, the Foreign Office, the Treasury, and the Ministry of Economic Warfare, proceeded to draw up and apply the British economic measures. In a telegram sent to Washington on 7 September, the Ministry of Economic Warfare provided details of the freezing action implemented throughout British possessions.[15] Magnesium was the only indispensable import from Japan at present; no new licences were being granted in the United Kingdom. All exports from Britain, India, Burma, and the colonies had been subjected to export licence. Inquiries were made in Washington in an attempt to resolve the continuing uncertainties over the full extent of the American actions. Halifax reported shortly afterwards that Cordell Hull had given explicit orders, within the previous two days, that there must be absolutely no weakening on the economic front against Japan; however, Hull did not want to offer public definition of the comprehensiveness of the measures, since he preferred to keep the Japanese guessing.[16] Hull desired maximum British and Dutch co-operation. Ashley Clarke pointed out that the chief difficulties were being encountered with India and Burma: the economies of both were to some extent dependent on trade with Japan and the problems would have to be surmounted.[17] Eden minuted: 'We must act as drastically as U.S.A. This should be impressed on Govt. of India.'[18] The Netherlands government in exile felt that closer co-ordination in economic action was needed and deprecated the uncertainties in Washington. The foreign minister, Van Kleffens, visited Eden on 17 September. 'M. Van Kleffens complained a good deal about the difficulty of obtaining from the United States any clear indication of their policy towards trade with Japan. This attitude was proving very embarrassing to the Netherlands Government in respect of the Netherlands East Indies. American officials in

[14] Minutes by Foulds and Gage, 1 and 2 Aug. 1941, ibid.
[15] Ministry of Economic Warfare to Washington, 7 Sept. 1941, F9238/1299/23, F.O.371/27980.
[16] Washington to Foreign Office, 14 Sept. 1941, F9322/1299/23, F.O.371/27980.
[17] Minute by Clarke, 16 Sept. 1941, ibid.
[18] Minute by Eden, 19 Sept. 1941, ibid.

Washington were apt to be both secretive and pontifical. They would say nothing in their offices about their policy, and even in private houses it was only about the time of the third cocktail that they ever became really communicative.'[19] Eden replied that 'it was quite true that the United States Government had not given us much time or opportunity to co-ordinate their policy with ours, but in fact they had virtually stopped all their trade with Japan, and this was the most important factor in the situation.'[20] Dean Acheson, who was occupied in enforcing the sanctions policy in Washington, recognized the need to produce a more coherent strategy and signed a memorandum on 22 September to this effect, requesting Roosevelt and Hull to give firmer directives.[21]

By October 1941 the extent and character of the sanctions were clear enough. While Roosevelt was willing to reopen talks with Japan, there would be no retreat from the policy of inexorably tightening the economic screw on Japan. Japan was faced with various alternatives. She could accept the slow strangulation of her economy and the consumption of her valuable oil reserves; she could advance to war in a desperate bid to rescue herself before it was too late; or she could modify her policies substantially and retreat from the new order. The mood of the United States had changed; Roosevelt and Hull were moving away from appeasement and were determined to show that aggression would not be passively tolerated. In Britain the forthright American policy was naturally applauded and followed, but it was felt that Roosevelt had perhaps given insufficient thought to the danger of Japan going to war eventually. Japan would have to modify her policies or accept the challenge.

Winston Churchill welcomed the more positive American response, but did not consider it to be enough in itself. He wished to secure a promise of help from the United States should Japan invade British and Dutch possessions, and had decided to travel across the Atlantic to meet Roosevelt at Placentia Bay, Newfoundland, for a frank exchange on war issues, with the Pacific crisis prominently to the fore in his

[19] Eden to Bland, 17 Sept. 1941, F9501/1299/23, F.O.371/27981.
[20] Ibid.
[21] *F.R.U.S. 1941*, iv, 881–4, memorandum by Acheson, 22 Sept. 1941.

mind. Eden prepared a minute to assist Churchill in his cogitations:

Our main purpose in the Far East is to keep Japan out of the war. The best way to ensure this is by means of a warning from the United States, the Dutch and ourselves of the consequences of further acts of aggression by Japan. This warning will probably be most effective if delivered privately but this is a matter which can be discussed. The United States have always been reluctant to take joint action. The warning would be as effective if the representations were parallel instead of joint. The most probable next victim is Thailand whose Government has already appealed to us to know what help we could give. We cannot reply until we know the attitude of the United States.

The Dominions, especially Australia, are concerned by the fact that though we have acted with the United States in freezing Japanese assets, the United States has not given us any assurances of help should any part of the Empire or the Dutch in consequence become embroiled with Japan.

The difficulty of the President's position is that he can give no undertaking to come to the help of any foreign power without the authority of Congress. At the same time, it is most desirable to secure some assurances in the interests of ourselves and the Dominions. It would satisfy us if the President could go so far as to tell you that in the event of ourselves or the Dutch becoming involved in hostilities with Japan while we were pursuing a policy parallel to that of the United States he would then be prepared to ask Congress to authorise him to take measures to give us all possible help.[22]

Churchill duly crossed the Atlantic on the ill-fated *Prince of Wales*. His discussions with Roosevelt were cordial and mutually beneficial; the British defence chiefs appreciated for the first time how rudimentary was the state of rearmament in the United States and that the Americans could not meet the demands of the British and Russians. Churchill strongly urged the president to give a blunt and unequivocal warning to Japan on his return to Washington that any additional act of aggression on Japan's part would be met with force. Roosevelt agreed but was persuaded soon afterwards by Cordell Hull to

[22] Minute by Eden, 2 Aug. 1941, F7072/1299/23, F.O.371/27973. For a general survey of the meeting, see T. A. Wilson, *The First Summit: Roosevelt and Churchill at Placentia Bay* (MacDonald, London, 1970). See also D. Dilks (ed.), *The Diaries of Sir Alexander Cadogan, 1938-1945*, pp. 397-402.

modify it, since the secretary of state feared that it might
seriously exacerbate relations with Japan if issued as originally
conceived.[23] Churchill was understandably disappointed but
accepted the outcome with good grace, consoling himself with
a radio broadcast on 23 August in which he referred, with
splendid Churchillian rhetoric, to the fact that:

For five long years the Japanese military factions, seeking to emulate
the style of Hitler and Mussolini, taking all their posturing as if it
were a new European revelation, have been invading and harrying
the 500,000,000 inhabitants of China. Japanese armies have been
wandering about that vast land in futile excursions, carrying with
them carnage, ruin and corruption and calling it 'the Chinese incident'. Now, they stretch a grasping hand into the southern seas of
China. They snatch Indochina from the wretched Vichy French.
They menace by their movements Siam, menace Singapore, the
British link with Australasia, and menace the Philippine Islands,
under the protection of the United States.

It is certain that this has got to stop. Every effort will be made to
secure a peaceful settlement. The United States are laboring with in-
finite patience to arrive at a fair and amicable settlement which will
give Japan the utmost reassurance for her legitimate interests. We
earnestly hope these negotiations will succeed but this I must say:
that if these hopes should fail we shall, of course, range ourselves un-
hesitatingly at the side of the United States.[24]

Churchill failed to realize that the Japanese paid more heed to
deeds than words and that strengthening Britain's chronically
weak air position was the best method of convincing the
Japanese of British determination. Churchill's unrealistic
appraisal of Japan was sagaciously questioned by General
Smuts in a telegram sent to London on 29 August. Smuts
thought that a more cautious approach might be advisable:

Question arises whether, if war with Japan does come, we shall not
have to bear brunt of it at a time when we may be most heavily
committed in both Europe and Africa.
   What really is position of United States of America? How far is she

---

[23] See C. Hull, *The Memoirs of Cordell Hull*, ii, 1017-18. For the text of the warning
as given to Japan, see *F.R.U.S. Japan 1931-1941* ii, 556-7. Ismay considered the
meeting between Churchill and Roosevelt to have been valuable but confessed to being
'a little disappointed' at the tangible results, see letter from Ismay to Auchinleck, 28
Aug. 1941, July-Aug. 1941, item 308, Auchinleck papers.

[24] *F.R.U.S. 1941* iv, 394, Hull to Grew, 25 Aug. 1941. See also entry for 26 Aug.
1941, Dalton diary, xxv, London School of Economics.

in fact prepared for war and in particular for first class war in South Pacific? In spite of much propaganda about American production and preparedness we have little definite information to go on and provocative ultimatum to Japan may have to be made good by us while United States of America takes further months of preparation and organisation for war. Even now American declaration to Japan is tempered with further discussions and negotiations and question arises whether we should not hold our hand until finality in these exchanges has been reached.

Is it not possible to leave matter for present where American declaration has placed it and avoid language which may touch face of Japan and provoke conflict for which America is perhaps not yet ready?[25]

In Japan the prime minister, Prince Konoe Fumimaro, decided in August to make a personal attempt to obtain an agreement with the United States by meeting President Roosevelt. Konoe had moved away from his previous extreme nationalism as the perils of Japan's predicament influenced him more forcefully. He had removed the obdurate Matsuoka from the *Gaimusho* in July: Matsuoka was not only an obstacle to an American–Japanese *rapprochement*, a fact not disguised by Cordell Hull in his talks with the Japanese ambassador, but had become a thorn in the side of his colleagues, too. The cabinet resigned and reconstituted itself without Matsuoka, who was replaced by Admiral Toyoda. Konoe pinned his hopes on being able to persuade Roosevelt to make major concessions on China and upon his own ability to impose Japan's concessions on the recalcitrant armed forces through the intervention of the emperor. Roosevelt was initially attracted by the suggestion of a meeting with the Japanese prime minister. He always liked personal meetings and oral discussion of problems. Hull was not enthusiastic, however, for he was conversant, through his lengthy exchanges with Admiral Nomura, with the deep divisions between the two countries and with the problems of surmounting them. Hull feared that Roosevelt might accept Konoe's invitation without careful prior contemplation; he, therefore, emphasized to the president that it was essential to secure some agreement before embarking on a personal meeting. Roosevelt reconsidered his

---

[25] Union of South Africa to Dominions Office, 29 Aug. 1941, communicated to Foreign Office, 30 Aug. 1941, F8621/86/23, F.O.371/27910.

position and accepted Hull's advice. The meeting did not take place, owing to the impossibility of making adequate progress beforehand. While Konoe's proposal had a superficial plausibility, Hull's reservations were justified. The two powers were so far apart that it is most unlikely that a Roosevelt–Konoe conference could have produced a viable settlement.[26]

Japanese leaders continued to hope that relations with the United States might improve but simultaneously pressed forward with their approval of policies leading to war. This dual attitude was well illustrated in the deliberations of the liaison conference on 3 September, which approved the document entitled 'The Essentials for Carrying Out the Empire's Policies'.[27] The document combined a decision to continue the discussions with the United States with a provisional decision that if the Washington negotiations did not succeed by the last ten days of October, Japan would go to war. The curious feature about this lengthy meeting and its outcome is that Konoe and Toyoda both supported the resort to war, although they were working strenuously to avoid it. The most convincing explanation is that Konoe was gambling on the meeting with Roosevelt taking place and saving the situation for him. An imperial conference was held on 6 September to endorse the decisions reached on 3 September. Before it met, the emperor saw first Konoe and then Sugiyama and Nagano, in separate interviews to express his doubts about the trend of events. Hirohito stressed that diplomacy must come before war. Sugiyama, in particular, was embarrassed at the emperor's words, but it was recognized and accepted that diplomacy must take priority. At the imperial conference Konoe stated the dilemma in which Japan found herself:

As you all know, the international situation in which we are involved has become increasingly strained; and, in particular the United

---

[26] For a discussion of these issues, see R. J. C. Butow, 'Backdoor Diplomacy in the Pacific: the proposal for a Konoye-Roosevelt meeting, 1941', *J.A.H.* lix (1972), 48–72. For the setting of the suggested meeting in the broader context of the Washington talks, see Professor Butow's admirable account of the bizarre origins and course of the discussions in R. J. C. Butow, *The John Doe Associates: Backdoor Diplomacy for Peace, 1941* (Stanford University Press, Stanford, 1974).

[27] Ike, pp. 129–33, 50th liaison conference, 3 Sept. 1941.

States, Great Britain and the Netherlands have come to oppose our Empire with all available means. There has also emerged the prospect that the United States and the Soviet Union will form a united front against Japan as the war between Germany and the Soviet Union becomes prolonged.

If we allow this situation to continue, it is inevitable that our Empire will gradually lose the ability to maintain its national power, and that our national power will lag behind that of the United States, Great Britain, and others. Under these circumstances our Empire must, of course, quickly prepare to meet any situation that may occur, and at the same time it must try to prevent the disaster of war by resorting to all possible diplomatic measures. If the diplomatic measures should fail to bring about favourable results within a certain period, I believe we cannot help but take the ultimate step in order to defend ourselves.[28]

Admiral Nagano referred to Japan's dwindling resources, particularly oil, and to the effort being made by the British, Americans, and Dutch to strengthen their defences:

By the latter half of next year America's military preparedness will have made great progress, and it will be difficult to cope with her. Therefore, it must be said that it would be very dangerous for our Empire to remain idle and let the days go by.

Accordingly, if our minimum demands . . . cannot be attained through diplomacy, and ultimately we cannot avoid war, we must first make all preparations, take advantage of our opportunities, undertake aggressive military operations with determination and a dauntless attitude, and find a way out of our difficulties.[29]

Sugiyama expressed the same sentiments. The outbreak of the Pacific war, while still not certain, was becoming increasingly likely.

Meanwhile in Britain the debate over the state of defences in the Far East persisted in desultory fashion. Weaknesses in the air were the most disturbing aspect. There was much ignorance over the skill and might of the Japanese in the air. The numerical inferiority of the British was manifest and grave, but the air chiefs consoled themselves with the belief that the types of aircraft possessed by the British, obsolete though some were, were yet almost certainly superior to the

---

[28] Ike, p. 138, imperial conference, 6 Sept. 1941.
[29] Ike, p. 139.

Japanese. The confidence was sadly misplaced. A booklet produced by Air H.Q. (India) and issued by the general staff in India in December 1941 stated that accurate information on Japanese air power was hard to obtain. 'Never yet having been faced with any opposition it is impossible to offer any valuable assessment of the operational efficiency of the Japanese Air Force. All that can be said is that the Navy Air Service, shore-based, is the most efficient of the three services.'[30] The secretary of state for air, Sir Archibald Sinclair, and the minister of aircraft production, Lord Beaverbrook, agreed on few issues and their relationship was frequently tempestuous: however, they were in accord in holding, in the spring of 1941, that the dispatch of planes to distant regions must be restricted.[31] The commander-in-chief, Far East, Sir Robert Brooke-Popham, pressed for reinforcements. He ruefully reflected on the scene in a letter to Ismay:

My principal worry at present is the repeated postponement of our Glen Martin bombers and our Beauforts. Wasn't it the elder Moltke who said that the art of war consists in the practical adaptation of the means at hand to the attainment of the object in view. And I wish I could see more clearly how to adapt Vildebeests to attain the object of sinking Japanese troopships if they're escorted by cruisers and covered by fighters off carriers bearing in mind that we've got to keep squadrons going for six months, so we can ill afford heavy casualties.[32]

No significant addition was made to air strength; the Far East remained bottom in the list of priorities.

Australia became more vocal in expressing dissatisfaction with the British attitude to the Pacific area. There was nothing new in this response, for Robert Menzies had conveyed the unhappiness of his government on numerous occasions. The bitter state of Australian domestic politics had caused the downfall of Menzies; he was succeeded transiently by Arthur Fadden and then by a Labour administration

[30] 'Japanese Service Aircraft', produced by Air H.Q. (India), Dec. 1941, Air.23/5076.
[31] Letter from Sinclair to Beaverbrook, 16 Mar. 1941 and letters from Beaverbrook to Sinclair, 16 Mar. and 11 Apr. 1941, Sinclair papers, Air 19/510. For the differences between Sinclair and Beaverbrook, see A. J. P. Taylor, *Beaverbrook* (Hamish Hamilton, London, 1972), pp. 416, 419-21, 433-4.
[32] Letter from Brooke-Popham to Ismay, 3 July 1941, V/1/14, Brooke-Popham papers.

headed by John Curtin. Curtin was more nationalistic and critical of British policy; Anglo-Australian relations became more acrimonious. The Fadden government had already dispatched the veteran politician, Sir Earle Page, to London to argue Australia's case. Page attended a number of meetings of the British war cabinet and did his best to urge the claims of the Far East; on 5 November he stated that urgent measures were required to strengthen Singapore by December or early January at the latest.[33] Page was especially alarmed by the state of air defence. Churchill commented that it had not been possible to increase air strength owing to the demands of the Russian and Middle Eastern theatres and home needs.[34] Sinclair said that matters were not as bad as depicted by Page. He made the curious statement that there were about 250 aircraft at Singapore serviceable either immediately or within fourteen days; the number of aircraft in Malaya at this time was 141.[35] In the naval sphere, Churchill drew attention to the detachment of the *Prince of Wales* from Home Fleet; the *Prince of Wales* was to proceed to Singapore as the basis of the newly projected battle squadron. On 12 November Page returned to the charge with a long statement on the need to build up resources in the Far East speedily; he advocated a guarantee of support to the Netherlands East Indies and support for Russia if Japan should attack her.[36] Page thought that a combination of military and political pressures would force Britain into war with Japan. He felt that Britain was leaving too much of the political leadership in the Pacific to the Americans. The chiefs of staff commented on Page's remarks. The first sea lord indicated that naval talks with the United States would take place in December and these would be followed by joint conversations with the Americans and Dutch. The chief of the air staff held that a force of 200 aircraft should be adequate as a defensive force — a most

[33] War cabinet conclusions, confidential annex, 5 Nov. 1941, 109(41)2, Cab.65/24. For a discussion of the Australian dimension, see P. Wright, 'Great Britain, Australia and the Pacific Crisis, 1939–41', unpublished M.A. thesis, Manchester University (1974).

[34] War cabinet conclusions, confidential annex, 5 Nov. 1941, 109(41)2, Cab.65/24.

[35] Ibid.

[36] War cabinet conclusions, confidential annex, 12 Nov. 1941, 112(41)1, Cab.65/24. For further discussion of naval aspects, see P. Haggie, 'The Royal Navy and the Far Eastern Problem, 1931–1941', pp. 430–8.

optimistic and misleading statement — and referred to the absence of 'extreme danger' in the Far East.[37] The chief of the imperial general staff stated that the garrison at Singapore was over 63,000; there were shortages in field and anti-tank guns. Churchill repeated his familiar promise that if Australia were threatened with invasion, Britain would act promptly. He added, however, that it would be a major strategical error to send forces to the Far East at this moment since they might remain inactive for a year. The Middle East was the vital theatre in comparison with the claims of East Asia. Churchill did not believe Japan could invade Australia but if Japan made such an attempt, the Middle East would have to be sacrificed — 'Such a decision, however, was not to be taken lightly.'[38] Page professed contentment with these assurances. Little was done or, in the few remaining days of peace, could be done in practical terms to improve British defences. The dispatch of the *Prince of Wales* and *Repulse*, on Churchill's initiative, was the only tangible sign of British concern, and their arrival was soon to be cast into a tragically lurid light in the opening hours of the Pacific war.

Sir Earle Page had alluded to the importance of establishing a close working relationship with the Netherlands East Indies.[39] He had touched upon a sensitive and strange aspect of British policy, in which Great Britain behaved towards the Netherlands government in exile in a manner remarkably similar to that of the United States towards Britain herself. This masked a serious division of opinion between the Foreign Office on the one side and the prime minister and defence chiefs on the other side. The argument centred on the desirability or feasibility of giving an undertaking of full support to the East Indies if attacked by Japan. The Foreign Office consistently contended that since Britain enjoyed close relations with the Netherlands and since the defence of the East Indies was vital to Malaya and other British possessions, a guarantee of support should be extended. The chiefs of staff, in contrast, stubbornly maintained that Britain was in no position to accept new commitments whatever the political

---

[37] War cabinet conclusions, confidential annex, 12 Nov. 1941, 112(41)1, Cab. 65/24.
[38] Ibid.
[39] Ibid.

justification for doing so; the chief of the naval staff, -Admiral Sir Dudley Pound, was the most obdurate and was fully supported by Churchill. The Netherlands government in exile wanted an unequivocal statement of British support, which accorded with the emphasis attached to this subject at the Singapore defence conferences in February and April 1941. Anthony Eden repeatedly pressed for a guarantee to be extended, to no avail. On 21 July he told the war cabinet:

that the idea had been dropped of making a public declaration that we should go to the help of the Dutch East Indies if they were attacked by Japan. All that was now proposed was that we should tell the Dutch privately that we would do so, and would inform the United States of what we had done . . .

On the merits of the case, he could not see that if Japan attacked the Dutch East Indies, we should not go to their aid. He found difficulty in postponing a decision on this matter further, as the Dutch were pressing us to ratify the conversations. The Governments of Australia and New Zealand were in agreement with the course proposed . . .[40]

Churchill trenchantly dissented:

As for a Japanese attack on Singapore, he did not believe anything of the sort was contemplated. It might well be that, even if Japan encroached on the Dutch East Indies, the right policy would be that we should not make an immediate declaration of war on Japan. Once war had been declared, Japanese cruisers would attack our sea communications, and none of our shipping would be safe unless heavily protected by convoys. At the present moment we were not in a position to send an adequate fleet to the Far East.[41]

Churchill's attitude was governed by the fundamental belief that the United States must take the lead in the Pacific and that the Admiralty were correct in resisting the pressure from the Foreign Office to act contrary to this policy. It was recognized that this would create growing difficulties in relations with the Netherlands East Indies. It was agreed, as a compromise, that Eden could state that the British government considered that it had, in effect, assumed responsibility for defending the East Indies but that the form that this co-operation would take could not be defined. Not surprisingly

[40] War Cabinet conclusions, confidential annex, 21 July 1941, 72(41)10, Cab.65/23.
[41] Ibid.

the Netherlands government was unenthusiastic, and urged that a clear agreement should be reached. The Foreign Office was exasperated at the interminable nature of the embarrassing issue. Ashley Clarke minuted in ironic vein:

The salient points to bear in mind are (1) that we shall have to defend the Dutch East Indies anyway and (2) that the United States can give us no prior guarantee of support although the probability of such support amounts almost to a certainty. We therefore lose nothing by having an unambiguous agreement with the Dutch and we gain nothing by making further appeals to the United States. The reluctance which is felt by the Chiefs of Staff to make a frank agreement with the Dutch seems to me like saying that when an invasion comes we will defend Hampshire and of course Devonshire, but we are short of anti-tank guns and will therefore not commit ourselves to defend Dorsetshire unless we get some backing from the President of the United States.[42]

Eden concurred but pointed out that Churchill's opposition was the problem. 'It is not only or even mainly the Chiefs of Staff (C.I.G.S. happens to agree with us) but Admiralty and above all P.M. who take this view . . .'[43] The position remained unchanged until the eve of war, when Britain at last received the promise of American support. A wholly clear and unambiguous undertaking of military support was only extended to the Netherlands government on 5 December. The issue of the Netherlands guarantee exemplifies the inflexibility of Churchill and the Admiralty. The failure to respond more encouragingly to the Dutch imposed a strain upon relations and hindered co-ordination of defence. There was little point in the refusal to give the guarantee sooner for, as the permanent under-secretary at the Foreign Office, Sir Alexander Cadogan, had observed in May 1941, the cynical answer to saying that little help could be given was that there was therefore nothing to be lost by promising it.[44]

The principal development in the evolution of the Pacific crisis in 1941 was the protracted diplomatic exchanges in Washington between the United States and Japan. The talks originated in the well-intentioned but misleading activities of

[42] Minute by Clarke, 7 Nov. 1941, F11734/4366/61, F.O.371/27847.
[43] Minute by Eden, 9 Nov. 1941, ibid.
[44] Minute by Cadogan, 6 May 1941, F4128/54/61, F.O.371/27777.

two American Roman Catholic missionaries, Bishop James
Walsh and Father James Drought. The two priests, perturbed
at the sharp deterioration in American-Japanese relations in
1940, had determined to try to arrest and, indeed, reverse this
decline. Although their intervention was a joint one, it is clear
from research that the key role was played by Drought, who
was dominated by an intense sense of personal mission and by
a misguided faith in his own talents for reconciling the
irreconcilable.[45] Thanks to their highly placed contacts in
Tokyo and Washington, the activities of Drought and Walsh
met with initial success. The contacts extended via inter-
mediaries to the Japanese prime minister and the American
president. The efforts of Drought and Walsh led the American
and Japanese governments each to believe that the other was
far more willing to contemplate concessions in the cause of
reaching a settlement than was in fact the case. The
Drought-Walsh mission assisted in the opening of the
Washington talks, but the subsequent revelations of the extreme differences between the United States and Japan created
an atmosphere of disillusionment and resentment that contributed to the final crisis. Cordell Hull was not sanguine
about the prospects of success but was prepared to conduct the
discussions in the hope that something might be achieved and
in the knowledge that, even if the talks ultimately failed,
valuable time would have been gained for improving defences
in the Pacific and for aiding Great Britain in other spheres.
Time was all-important to both sides. The indefinite prolongation of the discussions would cause no problems for the
United States but Japan could not tolerate such a development. Britain was not consulted adequately by the United
States in the course of the Washington conversations. The exchanges began in earnest in April 1941, but it was only in the
final month before Pearl Harbor that Hull expanded to Lord
Halifax on the nature of his discussions with Admiral Nomura
Kichisaburo. Hull's attitude was that he was conducting exploratory conversations to ascertain if sufficient common
ground existed to justify formal negotiations. While Japan
initially accepted this definition, the length of the talks and

[45] The most thorough, cogent, and entertaining account of the activities of Drought
and Walsh is to be found in R. J. C. Butow, *The John Doe Associates*.

the urgency of the position transformed matters so that Japan maintained that formal negotiations were actually in progress. In conformity with his understanding of the talks, Hull intended to consult other interested powers, meaning Britain, the Netherlands, and China, when formal negotiations began.

In one sense Hull's determination to conduct the talks personally, without proper discussion with Britain, fulfilled Churchill's oft-reiterated view that the United States should bear the brunt of the Pacific crisis. It was gratifying that this was now happening. However, it was extremely desirable that Britain should be acquainted with the state of play so that she could pursue the most appropriate policy in her own dealings with Japan. The Foreign Office officials voiced dissatisfaction at their relative ignorance; they were not alone, for the American ambassador, Joseph C. Grew, was not consulted by his own government either and was not in touch with the thinking of the State Department.[46] In May the Foreign Office decided that Halifax should see Hull and warn him that Matsuoka might be seeking to drive a wedge between London and Washington and that this should be kept in mind. Halifax saw Sumner Welles, the assistant secretary of state, on 24 May and gave him an *aide-mémoire*. Welles stated that particular care was being exercised but it would be better for the ambassador to see Hull to pursue it further. Hull sent for Halifax on the morning of 25 May and an unpleasant interview occurred, as a result of which the Foreign Office concluded that it was best to refrain from pressing Hull in future. Halifax reported:

Mr. Hull sent for me this morning and I found him in a state of pained and reproachful indignation. He very much resented what he evidently felt to be the implicit criticism in your telegram . . . on which my aide memoire was based, vis-à-vis his good faith with us or his sagacity in dealing with the Japanese. He had been careful to explain to me that conversations with Nomura were quite informal, and that he did not rest any exaggerated hopes on them, and against this background, to receive what he termed a lecture from His Majesty's Government was something that he found it very difficult to accept. I have never seen him so disturbed.

He then proceeded to say that they had very good information to

[46] For a concise account of Grew's mission, see E. M. Bennett, 'Joseph C. Grew: the Diplomacy of Pacification' in R. D. Burns and E. M. Bennett (eds.), *Diplomats in Crisis: United States-Chinese-Japanese Relations, 1919-1941*, pp. 65-89.

show that Matsuoka was fighting a pretty lone hand for his full Axis policy in Japan, and that Hitler was, in his phraseology, beating him black and blue. In the present situation in the Atlantic and Mediterranean, he could not understand why, unless we permit doubts either as to the intelligence or bona fides of the United States Government in this matter, we should be disturbed at the very cautious steps he had been taking to try out the situation with the object at least of postponing any Japanese action to add to our embarrassments.[47]

Halifax was upset at Hull's blunt words and told him that he had misunderstood the position. Halifax had informed Eden that the United States was involved simply in informal exchanges with Japan, and Halifax stated that Eden had merely wanted to transmit information in Britain's possession to Washington:

As to the aide-memoire which I had given to him, based on your telegram, I had only done this to save him trouble, and if, as he had suggested, it was a distasteful surprise to have my communication on record, in such form, I would immediately remove it from his table in my box. To this he said I could do what I liked about that, and I accordingly took it away.[48]

Halifax continued that Hull was not mollified and proceeded to refer to the hoary legend of Sir John Simon's alleged rebuff to Henry L. Stimson in 1932 during the Manchurian crisis, which was always cited whenever Americans were in bad humour with Britain. Halifax concluded in chastened mood, 'I think perhaps that I made a mistake not being sufficiently alive to the sensitiveness of the State Department on this particular matter, having regard to past history, and if I had been, it would have been wiser not to give him anything on paper.'[49] He urged that a conciliatory message be sent to him for transmission to the State Department; he ended his telegram by hinting that Stanley Hornbeck might have been responsible for Hull's verbal onslaught.

The Foreign Office was alarmed at the news. Ashley Clarke regretted that the ambassador had not been instructed to approach the topic with more care. The British view was that

[47] Washington to Foreign Office, 25 May 1941, F4430/86/23, F.O.371/27908.
[48] Ibid.
[49] Ibid.

it was preferable for the United States not to reach any agreement with Japan while Matsuoka remained at the *Gaimusho*; instead the egregious foreign minister should be allowed to discredit himself. Clarke added, 'However all that may be, it is obviously deplorable that we should have any disagreement with the Americans over our Far Eastern policy: the Japanese initiative was in fact designed to produce such a result and it must not be allowed to succeed.'[50] R. A. Butler was critical of Halifax, who should have 'jumped' on Hull's allusion to the Stimson–Simon controversy.[51] The ambassador's advice that a message in suitably contrite terms should be addressed to Hull was acted upon:

I am deeply distressed to learn of Mr. Hull's reception of what was intended in no sense as a formal communication, still less as a lecture. You may assure him at once that I had no thought whatever of questioning either the good faith of the United States Government or the good sense with which we here know that they will handle the Japanese. In your reports moreover you have made it clear that Mr. Hull's exchanges with the Japanese Ambassador were of a most informal nature and that he himself placed no high hopes on their outcome.

Our reason for asking you to speak to the United States Government was that we had received certain information which indicated that, contrary to what had apparently been the case at the outset, the Japanese approach was now being sponsored by Mr. Matsuoka himself in pursuit of his own ends. We thought it our duty to pass on this important information . . . in case they had not received it, together with the conclusions which we drew therefrom. We also had in mind that last year we had ourselves, through Lord Lothian, put forward the question of a general Far Eastern settlement and we were anxious that the United States Government should be informed of the view we took of this problem in the light of developments which have occurred since then . . .

Please communicate the above immediately to Mr. Hull. You should add that I know he will understand our natural anxiety in regard to happenings in the Far East and our desire to keep in the closest touch with him regarding all developments in that area.[52]

Halifax saw Hull again on 27 May and found the secretary of

---

[50] Minute by Clarke, 26 May 1941, ibid.
[51] Minute by Butler, 29 May 1941, ibid.
[52] Foreign Office to Washington, 26 May 1941, ibid.

state in a more amenable frame of mind. Hull accepted the apology and told Halifax there were three basic points upon which he was insisting in his discussions with Nomura — a satisfactory settlement of the war in China, an assurance that Japan would follow peaceful policies in future, and an assurance that Japan would not attack the United States if she became involved in war with Germany. Hull said the chances of the talks achieving success were about one in ten. He observed that the problem in transferring the American fleet from the Pacific to the Atlantic was the psychological consequence for China if Japan were given a free hand in the Pacific.[53]

Thereafter, Hull persevered with the conversations and conveyed little information to Britain. Debate continued in the Foreign Office minutes on the wisdom of the Americans and of the probable outcome. L. H. Foulds commented on 14 June, 'The State Department's question as to the likelihood of an understanding being accepted by extreme circles in Japan may be hypothetical but one has the uncomfortable feeling that they are playing with fire in continuing these discussions with the Japanese Ambassador.'[54] Ashley Clarke agreed: 'Yes. These talks are a menace. But we have entered our caveat and got our heads bitten off for so doing.'[55] The head of the Far Eastern department, J. C. Sterndale Bennett, wrote: 'I think we should ask Lord Halifax to make an inquiry as to the present position if he has a suitable opportunity. Diffidence in dealing with the U.S. Govt. is understandable but the matter is one of considerable importance and we are I think entitled to expect more information and greater frankness than we have hitherto been shown.'[56] Halifax was instructed to pursue the subject unless information was forthcoming soon. Halifax spoke to Summer Welles, but obtained only scant information.[57] Suspicions festered in the Foreign Office. Foulds minuted: 'The State Dept's lack of frankness persists: can it be that Mr. Hull is hoping to achieve some coup of historic importance, such as detaching Japan from the Axis,

[53] Washington to Foreign Office, 27 May 1941, F4570/86/23, F.O.371/27909.
[54] Minute by Foulds, 14 June 1941, F5174/86/23, F.O.371/27909.
[55] Minute by Clarke, 16 June 1941, ibid.
[56] Minute by Sterndale Bennett, 18 June 1941, ibid.
[57] Washington to Foreign Office, 26 June 1941, F5655/86/23, F.O.371/27909.

and in such a way that he will be able to claim all the credit?'[58] Clarke found it 'decidedly puzzling' and perhaps 'ominous'.[59] The talks between Hull and Nomura meandered on in repetitive fashion but achieved nothing concrete. Hull adhered rigidly to his 'four principles' — the territorial integrity and sovereignty of all nations, non-intervention in the internal affairs of other countries, economic equality, and non-disturbance of the *status quo* in the Pacific, unless modified peacefully. The Japanese contemplated minor concessions, but these could not satisfy the United States. The insuperable difficulties concerned Japan's 'holy war' in China and Japanese membership of the tripartite pact; China, however, was the most fundamental issue.[60]

On 8 September Hull spoke to Halifax and remarked that the talks were not progressing satisfactorily. He believed that Prince Konoe possibly desired a settlement but the four principles would have to be accepted before real progress could be made. Hull assumed Britain would welcome a settlement if it could be secured on acceptable terms. He recognized the importance of gaining more time. 'He went on to say, however, that his conversations had not approached the point where they would justify consultation with His Majesty's Government and by a friendly reference . . . hinted that you need not be anxious.'[61] It was felt in the Far Eastern department that Britain must take what comfort she could from Hull's comments; Japan might be playing for time, too, and could be hoping for the collapse of Russia in the face of the German invasion. Foulds noted that Hull now gave the talks one chance in twenty-five or fifty of succeeding, which led on to the question of what would happen if the talks failed. The subject should be discussed with the United States. The same thought struck the British embassy in Washington: a telegram was sent to London on 14 September stating that Hull could be drawn on to dangerous ground through being persuaded to concur in a vague solution that would bring solace to Japan; it

---

[58] Minute by Foulds, 29 June 1941, ibid.

[59] Minute by Clarke, 2 July 1941, ibid.

[60] The course of the talks has been covered fully elsewhere; see in particular, Feis, pp. 171–270, R. Wohlstetter, *Pearl Harbor: Warning and Decision* (Stanford University Press, Stanford, 1962), and Butow, *The John Doe Associates*.

[61] Washington to Foreign Office, 9 Sept. 1941, F9173/86/23, F.O.371/27910.

was also pointed out that uneasiness was being caused in China by the talks, which was regrettable. The embassy suggested that an approach be made to John G. Winant, the American ambassador in London.[62] Ashley Clarke minuted that it was inevitable that Britain and China harboured doubts, since the talks were obviously going badly and the Americans gave such inadequate information. Clarke thought it possible that the chances of American-Japanese agreement were brighter than appeared likely in Washington.[63] Sterndale Bennett held there was more cause for confidence in the United States than formerly but 'it is impossible not to have serious misgivings about the whole business'.[64] Britain could contribute little in economic terms to a general settlement in East Asia and there was a danger that Britain could be asked at short notice to pay a price that was beyond her power. Sterndale Bennett quoted a sentence from a private letter he had received from M. E. Dening, who was currently attached to the Washington embassy; 'My feeling is that there is quite a dangerous tendency in the highest quarters to toy with the idea that something may come of the talks with Japan and that this tendency is violently opposed (though how successfully I do not know) by reasonable people below.'[65] It was considered somewhat awkward to approach Winant, and preferable to leave the position as it was. Halifax had arrived in London for consultations and Eden decided to see Halifax before taking any action. Care was patently necessary in contacting Hull.

Sir Robert Craigie had, earlier in 1941, adhered firmly to the opinion that no concessions should be made to Japan and that a tough policy was the most sagacious in the circumstances. Craigie had adopted this view largely because of his disapproval of Matsuoka. In September 1941 he changed his mind: Matsuoka had gone and Craigie was convinced, as was his colleague Grew, that Konoe was making a sincere effort to reach a settlement. Craigie reported that 'a very considerable — though not yet a radical change — has occurred in the political situation here, and there exists a more real

[62] Washington to Foreign Office, 14 Sept. 1941, F9321/86/23, F.O.371/27910.
[63] Minute by Clarke, 17 Sept. 1941, ibid.
[64] Minute by Sterndale Bennett, 18 Sept. 1941, ibid.
[65] Ibid.

prospect . . . of setting in action a steady swing away from the Axis and towards more moderate policies.'[66] He castigated the American preoccupation with tying down the Japanese to a detailed settlement. 'If persisted in, it bids fair to wreck the best chance of bringing about a just settlement of Far Eastern issues which has occurred since my arrival in Japan.'[67] Craigie recognized there were risks in concluding an agreement, 'But risks must be faced either way, and my United States collea- gue and I are firmly of the opinion that on balance this is a chance which it would be the hight [*sic*] of folly to let slip.'[68] Sterndale Bennett described Craigie's telegram as 'highly con- troversial'.[69] He enclosed a commentary by P. D. Butler, who was about to go to Singapore as diplomatic liaison officer. Butler thought that Craigie's suggestions would connote a reversal of policy, to the encouraging of 'liberal' elements in Japan;[70] he considered it unlikely that there could be so signi- ficant a switch in policy as to involve a retreat from the belli- cose policies followed by Japan in recent years. It was under- standable that Japanese leaders were alarmed, for economic sanctions were biting:

Nevertheless the inherent Japanese conviction that cooperation means 'You give and I take' remains unshaken. The negotiations are at present entirely in American hands. If the views of Mr. Grew are as represented by Sir Robert Craigie, he will no doubt represent them to the State Department from whom the initiative should come. Any initiative on our part would be dangerous, since it would lay us open to a recrudescence in the United States of the criticisms of our Far Eastern policy which have been so damaging to us ever since the Stimson proposals of 1932, and have only recently been partially allayed.[71]

Sterndale Bennett was similarly critical of Craigie's recom- mendations and advocated the continuance of the resolute policy towards Japan.[72] Sir Alexander Cadogan observed:

We must let the Americans try out their talks. Pres. Roosevelt and

---

[66] Tokyo to Foreign Office, 30 Sept. 1941, F10117/12/23, F.O.371/27883.
[67] Ibid.
[68] Ibid.
[69] Minute by Sterndale Bennett, 1 Oct. 1941, ibid.
[70] Note by Butler, enclosed in minute by Sterndale Bennett, ibid.
[71] Ibid.
[72] Minute by Sterndale Bennett, ibid.

Mr. Welles, at the Atlantic meeting, never pleaded that they would do more than 'gain time'. And, unless America goes back on all she has said, they won't. America does sometimes, suddenly, go back on all her principles. But we must hope that in this case she will not. It may be something to 'gain time'. What we do gain, beyond that, is that America is engaging herself in a discussion of the Pacific situation. I have no great hopes of it, but I subscribe to all that Mr. P. D. Butler has written. America is drawing up a claim to the table and is taking up a hand of cards. We must lend Japan no 'chips'.[73]

Eden assented, 'I agree with these minutes which clearly and, I am convinced, accurately assess the situation.'[74] Craigie's telegram exemplified the growing divergence between the British and American ambassadors in Tokyo, on the one side, and their home governments on the other side. Craigie and Grew believed that the prospects for an acceptable, as distinct from an ideal, agreement existed and that the opportunity should not be missed. British policy was dependent on the United States in any event, and there was broad agreement that the existing policy should be pursued.

On 4 October Cordell Hull saw Halifax, who described his policy as follows:

He said what United States Government had been concerned to do was to try and gain time. He did not conceive that he had been as yet engaged upon negotiations, but rather upon exploratory talks to see whether later negotiations would or would not be profitable. Should this situation develop, he had made it plain to Japanese that Chinese, Dutch and ourselves would have to be brought in.

In exploratory conversations he had consistently taken the line that Japanese policy was a wrong road, and that while United States would do their best to assist Japan in economic field if the Japanese policy got back on the right road, the United States had nothing to offer unless and until essential principles were recognised and put into force. By this he meant, and had made plain to the Japanese, that they should withdraw their troops from China, give up their expansionist policy to the south, recognise the open door in China, and, in short, accept everything for which American policy had stood in China.

Although he had not told the Japanese so and would deny it if any public suggestion to this effect were made at this stage, his own mind was in favour of distinguishing between the assertion of the above

[73] Minute by Cadogan, 2 Oct. 1941, ibid.
[74] Minute by Eden, 3 Oct. 1941, ibid.

principles in regard to China and position existing in Manchukuo, which traced from earlier date. The implication was that if by any chance United States could get settlement on the lines they deemed acceptable for China they would not quarrel about Manchukuo.[75]

Hull, therefore, revealed that he was willing to some extent to modify the pronounced moral disapproval of Manchukuo, which had been a prominent feature of American policy since promulgated by Stimson in 1932. Hull stated at the close of the interview that it was hard to assess how Japanese policy would develop but it would be affected appreciably by the fighting in Russia and the Middle East.[76] Hull's remarks on Manchukuo surprised the Foreign Office, but it was decided not to comment. Eden wrote, 'We must let the Americans play the hand, and I would not give them advice about Manchukuo.'[77]

In mid-October, a watershed was reached in Japan with the resignation of Konoe's government and the emergence as prime minister of the outgoing war minister, General Tojo Hideki. Joseph C. Grew did not regard the advent of Tojo as ominous, since he was an active general, renowned as a disciplinarian, and he should prove capable of controlling the army.[78] However, Tojo was a hardliner where war was concerned, and alarm was warranted. In London it was feared that Japan might attack Russia, following the grave reverses inflicted by the German forces and the retreat of the government from Moscow. A telegram was sent to Washington stressing the dangers and emphasizing that Russia must be supported if Japan attacked her.[79] Hull was not as worried as the British Foreign Office, and pondered how the elusive moderates in Tokyo could be encouraged; he considered the wisdom of a limited barter exchange offering American cotton against Japanese silk. Halifax told Hull that Eden would regard the preservation of a united front as extremely important.[80] The reactions in London were critical. Churchill sent one of his magisterial minutes to Eden: *'Foreign*

[75] Washington to Foreign Office, 4 Oct. 1941, F10329/86/23, F.O.371/27910.
[76] Ibid.
[77] Minute by Eden, 8 Oct. 1941, ibid.
[78] *F.R.U.S. 1941*, iv, 541-3, and J. C. Grew, *Ten Years in Japan*, pp. 256-61.
[79] Foreign Office to Washington, 18 Oct. 1941, F10885/86/23, F.O.371/27910.
[80] Washington to Foreign Office, 18 Oct. 1941, F10969/86/23, F.O.371/27911.

Secretary. This is the thin end of the appeasement wedge.'[81] The composition of the Tojo government was less extreme than originally expected, and consequently less alarming; however, appeasement should not be adopted. A period of watchful vigilance was indicated. 'Pending this our own inclination is to believe that there is greater hope of inducing a reasonable frame of mind in the Japanese by keeping up the pressure rather than in relaxing it even in so small a measure.'[82] Halifax visited the State Department on 22 October to discuss the contingency of a Japanese attack on Russia. Hull was vague in his response, but said that in his opinion little could be achieved beyond improving allied defences in the Philippines. Hull did not consider a sudden Japanese move to be likely; if action against Japan had to be taken at a later date, he thought that a naval blockade offered possibilities.[83]

Craigie had a series of meetings with Japanese officials in late October and early November. On 22 October he warned of a possible Japanese advance south, remarking perceptively that the Japanese had a genius for secrecy and for making surprise moves.[84] Craigie stated that Britain must be ready for action, especially from the beginning of 1942. He felt that the Foreign Office sometimes underestimated the tenacity and desperation of Japan; Japan was powerful enough to move against Russia, south-east Asia, and the Pacific simultaneously. Soon afterwards Craigie had a frank exchange with the new foreign minister, Togo. Togo put forward the standard explanation for the presence of Japanese troops in Indo-China and south-east Asia, as necessary to the security of Japan and as protection of her economic interests.[85] Craigie refuted the arguments, and observed that Japanese troops were not far from British territories. Britain could only regard the Japanese consolidation in Indo-China as a threat to her position. He stressed that there was no wish in Britain for conflict with Japan. There were limits, however, to what Britain

---

[81] Minute by Churchill, 19 Oct. 1941, ibid.
[82] Foreign Office to Washington, 21 Oct. 1941, ibid.
[83] Washington to Foreign Office, 22 Oct. 1941, F11204/86/23, F.O.371/27911.
[84] Tokyo to Foreign Office, 22 Oct. 1941, F11231/12/23, F.O.371/27884.
[85] Tokyo to Foreign Office, 29 Oct. 1941, F11593/12/23, F.O.371/27884.

would tolerate. At their next meeting Togo stated that Britain should participate in the Washington talks with the United States.[86] He referred to the importance of the time factor: 'He had the strong impression that the United States Government, for reasons best known to themselves, were deliberately dragging out the negotiations, in which case, of course, it would be impossible for the Japanese Government to continue.'[87] Craigie naturally denied that the United States was acting in this manner, reminding Togo that the task of securing a lasting settlement in the Far East was indeed an ambitious one. A week later Craigie informed the Foreign Office that a Japanese contact had warned him of the growth of extremist opinion; this opinion pointed to the Anglo-American policy of economic strangulation, which it was impossible for Japan to accept any longer.[88] The contact thought Britain and the United States should play for time and avoid a showdown but, at the same time, they could display some sympathy for Japan's problems. Ashley Clarke was unimpressed, minuting that the latter exhortation was the old familiar Japanese refrain.[89] On 6 November Craigie sent his considered views on the greater likelihood of a Japanese offensive:

Of all the causes which might project Japan into a world war at the present juncture e.g. article 3 of Tripartite pact, designs on maritime provinces, ambitions in Thailand . . . and effects of foreign economic restrictions, I regard the latter as most likely the determining factor. Assuming this to be correct, I arrive, by the following process of elimination, at the conclusion that the occupation of parts of the Netherlands East Indies is likely to be the primary objective: Indo-China being already under Japanese control and Thailand being already in process of furnishing bulk of her resources to Japan, the convenient resources close at hand are thus in Burma, Malaya and the Netherlands East Indies: Burma being inaccessible as a first step and Malaya a hard nut to crack, we are left with the Netherlands East Indies as the most likely object of attack. And in Netherlands East Indies the most likely objective would seem to be Borneo. This theory is supported by our belief that Japan's greatest need is oil and that she would be able to put forward the specious plea that it was our own restrictive measures which would have rendered the use

[86] Tokyo to Foreign Office, 30 Oct. 1941, F11651/12/23, F.O.371/27884.
[87] Ibid.
[88] Tokyo to Foreign Office, 5 Nov. 1941, F11874/12/32, F.O.371/27884.
[89] Minute by Clarke, 14 Nov. 1941, ibid.

of force inevitable. Such an expedition could be prepared in complete secrecy in the Japanese mandated islands, and the idea would doubtless be to face both the United States and ourselves with a fait accompli . . . of seizure of oil wells in the belief that neither Power would, in fact, carry the matter to the point of war.[90]

Craigie added that strong precautionary measures would be taken by Japan to contain the British forces in Malaya as soon as it appeared probable that Britain would intervene. He believed that Japan would be prepared, if necessary, to accept involvement in a world war. He concluded by referring to the underestimation of the United States in Japan:

One of the tragedies of the situation is that most Japanese, including many in high places, appear to under-estimate America's naval and air strength and endurance of Japan. The belief I have frequently expressed in the past year that Japan would avoid war with America at almost any cost, no longer holds good to-day.[91]

The Foreign Office, the chiefs of staff, and the war cabinet were most concerned, in early November, at the rumour of a Japanese offensive in Yunnan, aimed at undermining Chiang Kai-shek. T. E. Bromley of the Far Eastern department considered an offensive in Yunnan to be probable, with seizure of Borneo next on the list followed by the threat to Thailand.[92] L. H. Foulds believed the Foreign Office would agree with Craigie that the economic measures being applied against Japan were likely to precipitate conflict. 'It would certainly be unwise to underestimate the possibility that she may decide to strike directly towards this goal: since the initiative for making war lies with Japan she can choose both the time and the direction of her initial blow and we have to be ready for whatever she decided to do.'[93] Foulds agreed with Bromley that the first move would be against Yunnan, but this could be combined with a seaborne campaign to take Borneo.

In Japan preparations for war proceeded, but it was decided to make a final diplomatic attempt to reach agreement with the United States. Like Hull, General Tojo gave varying estimates as to the chances of avoiding war, in his more

[90] Tokyo to Foreign Office, 6 Nov. 1941, F11947/12/23, F.O.371/27884.
[91] Ibid.
[92] Minute by Bromley, 8 Nov. 1941, ibid.
[93] Minute by Foulds, 9 Nov. 1941, ibid.

optimistic moments putting the odds at fifty-fifty and on other occasions as three chances out of ten. An imperial conference met on 5 November to approve decisions taken at preceding liaison conferences. In the fundamental policy document before the conference it was stated:

I. Our Empire, in order to resolve the present critical situation, assure itself preservation and self-defence, and establish a New Order in Greater East Asia, decides on this occasion to go to war against the United States and Great Britain and takes the following measures:
1. The time for resorting to force is set at the beginning of December and the Army and Navy will complete preparations for operations.
2. Negotiations with the United States will be carried out in accordance with the attached document.
3. Co-operation with Germany and Italy will be strengthened.
4. Close military relations with Thailand will be established just prior to the use of force.
II. If negotiations with the United States are successful by midnight of December 1, the use of force will be suspended.[94]

The attached document comprised alternative proposals, A and B, intended as a basis for settlement. Japan was prepared to offer some concessions in connection with Indo-China and the tripartite pact, but the termination of 'the China incident' was axiomatic and Japan must have a free hand for this purpose.[95] In opening the meeting, Tojo stated that eight liaison conferences had been held to consider policy.[96] 'As a result of this, we have come to the conclusion that we must now decide to go to war, set the time for military action at the beginning of December, concentrate all of our efforts on completing preparations for war, and at the same time try to break the impasse by means of diplomacy.'[97] Togo, the foreign minister, made a lengthy statement reviewing Japan's experiences since the start of the Undeclared War in 1937. During this period the British and American governments had consistently worked to thwart Japanese ambitions and bolster the regime of Chiang Kai-shek. Initially Britain was most obstructive, having more interests in East Asia than any other

[94] For the text see Ike, pp. 209-11.
[95] Ike, p. 211.
[96] Ike, p. 214.
[97] Ike, p. 214. See also *I.M.T.F.E.*, Record, Exhibits 1202A, 1203, 1204, pp. 10482-10504.

power, but in the last twelve months the United States had assumed the leading role in opposing Japan's justified policies. The situation was becoming more serious daily and the foreign minister emphasized that the time element meant that negotiations with the United States could not continue for much longer. He described the prospects for a settlement as 'dim'. After prolonged discussion, including a number of questions asked by the president of the privy council, Hara, the document was approved.

As part of the final diplomatic effort, Japan dispatched a career diplomat, Kurusu, to assist the ambassador in Washington, Admiral Nomura. For some time there had been doubts in Tokyo as to Nomura's competence, doubts which were correct in that Nomura did not always report swiftly or accurately. This was not because of any peculiar deviousness on Nomura's part but rather because of his very sincerity. Nomura was a naval man by background, and came from that faction in the navy which had always favoured amicable relations with the United States and Britain. Nomura had accepted the appointment to the Washington embassy because of his deep desire to prevent war. He had become involved in the complications unleashed by the Drought-Walsh mission, and was reluctant to think that his mission would end in failure. He was not a trained diplomat and erred in a number of respects; however, his sincerity was patent and was recognized by Cordell Hull. In the second half of November Japan proposed a *modus vivendi* and the United States contemplated a counter-offer, which was not subsequently transmitted to Japan. Japan envisaged withdrawing troops from southern Indo-China in exchange for the suspension of the freezing measures. This was not acceptable as presented, but Cordell Hull approached Great Britain, the Netherlands, and China about the possibility of proposing a *modus vivendi* for three months incorporating the withdrawal of Japanese troops from southern Indo-China in return for the modification of the freezing measures.[98] Britain at first cautiously welcomed the news of the Kurusu mission. Ashley Clarke commented that 'if the Kurusu suggestion (of possible withdrawal from Indo-China) is genuine there seems to be

[98] See *F.R.U.S. Japan 1931–1941*, ii, 755–6 and *F.R.U.S. 1941*, iv, 661–4.

some ground for a (very cautious) response on the part of the
Americans.'[99] Sterndale Bennett responded similarly: 'We
cannot of course rule out the possibility that a piecemeal
settlement may merely give the Japanese a breathing space.
But to get them really moving in reverse would be a great gain
for us.'[100] However, when more information reached London
the Foreign Office concluded that neither Kurusu's proposal
nor Hull's possible alternative was satisfactory: vague formulas
were dangerous because they would provide loopholes for the
Japanese to exploit. The freezing regulations should only be
lifted if Japan was willing to make significant concessions.
Britain was worried about Chiang Kai-shek's ability to with-
stand setbacks, for Chiang had been loudly complaining that
the needs of China were being overlooked, and the information reaching London on the situation in China was
not encouraging. China was hardly waging an effective
struggle against Japan, but it was undeniable that large numbers of Japanese troops were tied down in retaining possession
of approximately 40 per cent of China and these forces might
otherwise be released for operations in south-east Asia. This
consideration was never far from the minds of the chiefs of
staff.[101] A certain amount of guilt could be discerned in
British reactions, since moral support for China had not been
followed by any significant material assistance. Churchill felt
that the Americans might be losing sight of the importance of
continued Chinese resistance. In a minute to Eden on 23
November he showed less enthusiasm than before for an unyielding approach to Japan, since Britain had enough war to
contend with already, but upon receiving Chiang's appeal,
Churchill dispatched a personal message to President Roosevelt expressing sympathy for Chiang and alluding to the 'thin
diet' upon which the generalissimo was subsisting.[102] Chiang
himself vociferously protested to his American friends, and
addressed appeals for support to members of the cabinet in

[99] Minute by Clarke, 19 Nov. 1941, on Washington to Foreign Office, 18 Nov. 1941,
F19475/86/23, F.O.371/27912.
[100] Minute by Sterndale Bennett, 20 Nov. 1941, ibid.
[101] See 'The Burma Road, report by chiefs of staff committee', 20 Aug. 1941,
C.O.S.(41)81, Cab.80/29.
[102] Churchill, iii, 529.

Washington.[103] Henry L. Stimson was deeply disturbed to receive Chiang's message and firmly opposed the *modus vivendi*. Hull was thoroughly exasperated at the turn of events. He had conducted the interminable exchanges with Nomura for months with little having been achieved other than gaining time; he had not been in good health for much of the time. It was clear from the intercepted 'Magic' code[104] that war was looming. Hull washed his hands of the position, in effect, and dropped any idea of sending the *modus vivendi*. Instead he put forward a long statement of American principles, requiring a complete reversal of Japanese policy.[105] In Japan the tough American response was regarded as an ultimatum. Hull's feelings were not dissimilar: the statement was the definitive record of American principles, and the diplomatic efforts of the United States were virtually at an end. Halifax saw the secretary of state on 29 November and informed London:

I saw the Secretary of State this morning. He said that the situation had not changed, but he thought it was pretty well inevitable that Japanese would take some early action under what he felt certain must now be the increased pressure of the military extremists. He had been impressing on the United States Service Departments that they should prepare themselves for all eventualities. He did not expect that the Japanese would make any reply to the communication the President had given Chargé d'Affaires, and saw no hope of reviving modus vivendi plan.

In a post-mortem of what had passed he spoke with considerable bitterness of the part played by T. V. Soong, both in unbalanced advice given to Chiang Kai-shek and also for breach of confidence with the press.

This had had the immediate effect of swinging Stimson, who had been forward in pressing to gain time, on to the other tack of supporting the Chinese view. He did not reproach His Majesty's Government, but said that they too had been unduly impressed by what he continued to feel unreasoned and unreasonable attitude of Chiang Kai-shek reached on partial information and picture supplied by T. V. Soong. Except as regards T. V. Soong, the Sec-

[103] *F.R.U.S. 1941*, iv, 661-5.
[104] The Magic code was the Japanese code which had been brilliantly unravelled by the Americans. For a discussion of the cracking of the code and an explanation of why the information obtained was not put to better use, see R. Wohlstetter, *Pearl Harbor: Warning and Decision* (Stanford, Calif., 1962).
[105] *F.R.U.S. Japan 1931-1941*, ii, 768-70.

retary of State spoke more in sorrow than in anger.

The plain answer to all this of course is that the Secretary of State had not brought us into consultation at an early enough stage, and I told him that I thought many of these difficulties had arisen because of the extreme rapidity with which things had moved after he had pointed out a stage when he thought he could bring us in.[106]

Halifax told Hull that Britain would have been willing to accept an interim agreement and had simply voiced certain considerations that should be borne in mind. Hull agreed, but made it clear that he regretted Churchill's message to Roosevelt. With regard to China, Hull stated what was true and had been the case since the beginning of the Sino-Japanese conflict, 'He said Chiang Kai-shek obviously had always wanted to get us embroiled with Japan and that he looked like being successful.'[107] The lack of close Anglo-American consultation on the Pacific was admirably illustrated when Halifax observed to Hull that he would like to see the lengthy document given to Japan. Hull assented but rummaged through the pile of papers on his desk without being able to find it, and remarked that it was 'couched in purely general terms and reiterated general principles'.[108] Halifax assured Eden that he would endeavour to locate a copy. Halifax seized the opportunity to emphasize the need for close co-operation in defence:

In regard to what he had said about the importance of the Services preparing themselves for eventualities, I told him that while it was no doubt quite possible for our staffs to get together in regard to hypothetical developments, it would be necessary, before any general action would be taken, for our two Governments to be absolutely together on policy, and I again asked him what would be the United States attitude in the event of a Japanese attack on Thailand . . . To this, however, he would make no direct reply, saying in effect that as Stimson had played a considerable part in busting his diplomatic effort, the situation was no longer one for diplomatic treatment.[109]

Halifax suggested that Eden should send him definite proposals to put before the United States, indicating what action Britain was considering and addressing relevant questions to the Americans.

[106] Washington to Foreign Office, 29 Nov. 1941, F12992/86/23, F.O.371/27913.
[107] Ibid.
[108] Ibid.
[109] Ibid.

Upon receiving Halifax's telegram, Ashley Clarke commented that Hull seemed to resent representations by Britain and China 'which had saved him from making a Munich Settlement with Japan'.[110] Clarke pondered the problem of determining British policy when it was not known what precisely Hull had said to the Japanese in his latest statement. 'Now that Mr. Hull has taken the course of putting a proposal on the widest basis before the Japanese we must be ready to back him. For this purpose it would be very advantageous if Mr. Hull would give us a sight of the proposals which he has made to the Japanese. Indeed we are greatly handicapped by not knowing what this proposal was and Lord Halifax would surely be justified in pressing for a copy . . .'[111] It was urgently necessary to discuss matters frankly with the United States, and Churchill had already, before Clarke's minute was written, sent a personal message to Roosevelt suggesting a joint Anglo-American warning to Japan. To judge from the prime minister's remarks in cabinet, he was not optimistic on the answer.[112] Halifax believed that the United States would almost certainly support a British move into the Kra isthmus to forestall Japanese operations against Malaya. This was the aspect that had vexed the chiefs of staff and the commander-in-chief, Far East, for some months; the political complication was that the government of Thailand could not be relied on to accept the British advance into Thai territory. The British minister in Bangkok, Sir Josiah Crosby, did not want any action taken that might affect the internal balance of power in Thailand and push the Thais into the arms of the Japanese. In fact, it could be forecast that Thailand would support Japan if the crunch came, since Japan was the power in the ascendant.

At this point, from the end of November onwards, matters began to develop rapidly. Roosevelt at last intervened decisively. He knew that the crisis was coming to a head, as was obvious from the intercepted 'Magic' code. The president handled the position skilfully but in typical, almost relaxed,

---

[110] Minute by Clarke, 1 Dec. 1941, ibid. See also entries for 26 and 28 Nov. 1941, Dalton diary, xxv, London School of Economics.

[111] Ibid.

[112] War cabinet conclusions, confidential annex, 1 Dec. 1941, 122(41)3, Cab.65/24.

manner. Halifax described his meeting with Roosevelt and
Harry Hopkins on 1 December:

The President sent for me at lunch time and I had an hour and a half
with him, Hopkins also present.

His information was that the Japanese Government was a good
deal disturbed by his return to Washington. He told me that in the
interview with the Secretary of State Japanese had returned to the
subject of interim arrangement, presumably on their own responsibility and Secretary of State had replied to the effect that
interim arrangement was not possible on a unilateral basis, which
was the basis on which the Japanese were proceeding, in as much as
they were continuing to move troops all the time.[113]

Roosevelt then discussed Japanese reinforcements of Indo-
China at great length, and said he had been considering
making a 'concerted parallel statement' with Britain. He felt it
would be wiser to address a question to the Japanese over the
troop movements in Indo-China:

We discussed what would be the next step, since the Japanese reply
would certainly be either mendacious or evasive, seeing that there
could be no possible legitimate reason for such reinforcement of
Japanese strength in Indo-China.

Hopkins emphasised the danger of impression being created that
the Japanese acted while we only sent notes and talked.

President agreed and said that it was of great importance that His
Majesty's Government and the United States Government should be
clear in their minds as to what they would do in the various hypothetical situations that were likely to arise . . .

He wished me accordingly to ask you what His Majesty's Government would do in the event of

(a) Japanese reply being unsatisfactory, reinforcements not yet
having reached Indo-China; and

(b) reply being unsatisfactory, reinforcements having in the
meantime reached Indo-China; and

(c) Japanese attack on Thailand (Siam) other than attack on Kra
Isthmus, attack covering, in his mind, such Japanese pressure on
Thailand as to force concessions to the Japanese dangerously det-
rimental to the general position.[114]

Halifax then came to Roosevelt's promise of support, given in

[113] Washington to Foreign Office, 30 Nov. 1941, F13001/86/23, F.O.371/27913.
[114] Ibid.

characteristically casual manner, 'At one point he threw in an aside that in the case of any direct attack on ourselves or the Dutch, we should obviously all be together, but he wished to clear up the matters that were less plain.'[115] In the event of a Japanese attack on British possessions, 'we could certainly count on their support, though it might take a short time, he spoke of a few days, to get things into political shape here.'[116] Roosevelt mentioned that he was thinking of sending a message directly to the Japanese emperor in the hope that this would avert confrontation, but he had not yet decided to do so. According to Halifax, Hopkins had been very helpful in the meeting.

It was a most encouraging development. A rapid reply was sent to the president's queries.[117] The first two questions seemed inseparable for practical purposes, as information available confirmed that reinforcements were still arriving. What was necessary was to decide on a response should the Japanese reply to Roosevelt's inquiry be unsatisfactory. Britain believed that simultaneous American, Dutch, and British warnings to Japan would be the most effective method.[118] If the warnings were disregarded, Britain would prepare to activate the operation to take the Kra isthmus. While Roosevelt's third hypothetical question did not involve a direct threat to Singapore, it would be advisable to take the Kra isthmus. Roosevelt's promise of support was warmly welcomed.[119] Britain was reflecting on the feasibility of reaching agreement with Thailand under which Britain would advance into the Kra isthmus by invitation, but Britain was unable to offer a guarantee of the integrity of Thailand. It was pointed out that the Thai prime minister had stated emphatically that the only way to save Thailand was through an Anglo-American public warning to Japan.[120] Halifax spoke to Roosevelt and Welles on the evening of 4 December. Roosevelt agreed that the first two hypothetical questions were in-

---

[115] Ibid.
[116] Ibid.
[117] Foreign Office to Washington, 3 Dec. 1941, ibid. See also minute by Churchill, 2 Dec. 1941, ibid.
[118] Ibid.
[119] Foreign Office to Washington, 5 Dec. 1941, F13219/86/23, F.O.371/27914.
[120] Foreign Office to Washington, 5 Dec. 1941, ibid.

distinguishable; he asked whether the suggested warning to Japan over Indo-China should refer to an actual act of aggression or preparation for aggression. Halifax said he believed Eden meant the former; the ambassador thought Roosevelt favoured a warning when Japan embarked on a forward move. The president confirmed that his earlier promise of support connoted military support, although the form would have to be decided by the defence chiefs. Roosevelt indicated that he would support the implementation of the Kra isthmus operation, 'and I have no doubt in this case you can count on armed support of the United States.'[121] Roosevelt stated that information in the possession of the Americans suggested that Japan might attack the Netherlands East Indies, particularly an island north of Sumatra. He then stressed his concern with the impact of decisions taken on American public opinion. 'He made comment on this that any action of the kind would prove easy of presentation to United States public opinion on the ground of threat to the Phillipines [*sic*] by encirclement.'[122] Roosevelt concluded by recommending that Britain should consider intimating to Thailand that she did not intend to invade but that, if the Japanese invaded, Britain would follow suit in self-defence. In addition, Britain might contemplate issuing a public statement to the effect that Britain did not intend to attack Thailand and was solely concerned with preserving her sovereignty and independence.

Roosevelt's assurances met with 'very deep appreciation' in London. Halifax was told to notify the president that a warning would apply to a Japanese attack on Thailand, Malaya, or the Netherlands East Indies and to an attack on the Burma road from Indo-China. As regards Thailand:

Our proposed action . . . must of necessity be of a forestalling nature. Consequently we cannot technically give Thais . . . a guarantee of non-aggression. But we do wish to encourage them to resist Japanese encroachment, and we should like therefore to assure them that in the event of attack by Japan we will both help them to the best of our ability.[123]

---

[121] Washington to Foreign Office, 4 Dec. 1941, ibid.
[122] Ibid.
[123] Foreign Office to Washington, 5 Dec. 1941, ibid.

It was decided to extend the guarantee of support to the Netherlands East Indies, and the United States was informed. Halifax met Roosevelt for a further long discussion. Roosevelt explained that he did not wish to include an attack on the Burma road in the proposed warning:

On the question of warning . . .he was very doubtful about the wisdom of including attack on Burma Road. Apart from the fact that the Chinese war stood on a different footing to some new aggression, his recollection was that in the summer of 1940, the Japanese had blocked Indo-China route to China at Hanoi where the United States had had supplies for China which had consequently been obstructed, without he thought, any serious protest in the United States. This precedent made it difficult for him to take stiffer . . . line now over an attack on the Burma Road. Moreover, if hostilities came, he will have to make his case . . . which he feels he can well do on the other cases you mention, but not (repeat not) on the Burma Road issue. He hopes, therefore, that you may not think it necessary to include this in the warning.

Subject to above and to paragraph 5 below, he agrees to warning covering any attack by Japan on Thailand (Siam), Malaya or Netherlands East Indies. He thinks that if the warning is given by the United States, ourselves and the Dutch, we should act independently all within 24 hours using different language to mean the same thing . . . He would prefer the United States to get in first. On account of political considerations here, it was important that their action should be based on independent necessities of United States defence and not appear to follow on ourselves. He assumed that you would be concerting with the Dutch.

Paragraph 5. He said, however, that he had received indirect communication from Kurusu that matters were not yet hopeless and that direct appeal to the Emperor might produce result. Kurusu had also said that if the President would make move it might still not be impossible to secure a truce and even settlement between Japan and China.[124]

Roosevelt said Kurusu had described the possible form of an agreement including a truce, withdrawal of the bulk of Japanese forces from Indo-China and north China on a basis to be determined. Roosevelt thought the Japanese would require economic relief. The president was not impressed with the chances of success, 'but was naturally reluctant to miss any

[124] Washington to Foreign Office, 5 Dec. 1941, F13280/86/23, F.O.371/27914.

chance and thought communication with Emperor would
strengthen his general case if things went wrong'.[125] Halifax
spoke of the importance of avoiding delay in communicating
with the emperor and Roosevelt agreed that it should serve as
a definite warning. The ambassador also referred to the need
to handle the Chinese diplomatically so as to avert a repetition
of the recent altercation with Chiang Kai-shek. Roosevelt
stated that he would soon decide whether or not to contact
Hirohito; if he did so, he hoped that the three-power warning
could be deferred until he had received the reply. Where
Thailand was concerned, he thought it best to tell the Thais
that if their sovereignty was temporarily destroyed by Japan,
Britain would work with the allies to restore it.

Churchill personally approved the reply, which expressed
great relief at Roosevelt's views and support for the procedure
proposed.[126] Late on 5 December Welles telephoned the
British embassy in Washington to say that the president had
changed his mind and wished to suspend an approach to
Thailand for the moment.[127] Halifax attempted to contact
Roosevelt but urged that Britain should press ahead, for the
American attitude was clear enough. Roosevelt sent his
personal message to Emperor Hirohito, but it came too late to
influence events and was held up in Tokyo so that the emperor
did not receive it.[128] In the final days of peace in the Pacific,
Britain had succeeded in obtaining what she had so long
desired—an unambiguous promise of American support if
Japan attacked. As Roosevelt revealed in his discussions, he
was preoccupied with presenting Japanese aggression in the
way that would have the greatest influence on American
public opinion. In the circumstances that accompanied Pearl
Harbor, Roosevelt's objective was attained to his complete
satisfaction.

In Japan, liaison and imperial conferences met in November and continued the deliberations pointing inexorably to war. The naval task force responsible for carrying
out the attack on Pearl Harbor set sail on 26 November from
the Kurile islands on its lonely journey into the central Pacific.

[125] Ibid.
[126] Foreign Office to Washington, 6 Dec. 1941, ibid.
[127] Washington to Foreign Office, 5 Dec. 1941, F13282/86/23, F.O.371/27914.
[128] For the text of the appeal, see *F.R.U.S. 1931-1941*, ii, 784-6.

An imperial conference gathered on 1 December to ratify the final decisions. The prime minister, General Tojo, opened it by summarizing the attempts made in recent weeks to obtain a diplomatic solution. The United States had, however, refused to compromise and had remained adamant; the American attitude had been an insult to the dignity of the empire and threatened its existence. The United States, Britain, the Netherlands, and China had intensified economic and military pressure against Japan:

Under the circumstances, our Empire has no alternative but to begin war against the United States, Great Britain and the Netherlands in order to resolve the present crisis and assure survival.

We have been engaged in the China Incident for more than four years and now we are going to get involved in a great war. We are indeed dismayed that we have caused His Majesty to worry.

But, on further reflection, I am thoroughly convinced that our military power today is far stronger than it was before the China Incident; that the morale of the officers and men of the Army and Navy is high; that unity in domestic politics is greater; that there is willingness on the part of individuals to make sacrifices for the nation as a whole; and that as a result, we can anticipate that we will overcome the crisis that confronts the nation.[129]

Togo and Nagano confirmed Tojo's assessment. It was unanimously agreed that there was no alternative to war. There were no doubt private reservations as to what the future held in store for Japan, but the public spirit of unity was maintained. Tojo closed the meeting by expressing the determination of the nation and its profound sense of responsibility to the emperor:

We are fully prepared for a long war. We would also like to do everything we can in the future to bring the war to an early conclusion. We also intend, in the event of a long war, to do our utmost to keep the people tranquil, and particularly to maintain the social order, prevent social disorganisation, and block foreign conspiracies.

We have now completed our questions and remarks. I judge that there are no objections to the proposal before us.

I would now like to make one final comment. At the moment our Empire stands at the threshold of glory or oblivion. We tremble with fear in the presence of His Majesty. We subjects are keenly aware of

---

[129] Ike, pp. 263–4.

the great responsibility we must assume from this point on. Once His Majesty reaches a decision to commence hostilities, we will all strive to repay our obligations to him, bring the Government and the military even closer together, resolve that the nation united will go on to victory, make an all-out effort to achieve our war aims and set His Majesty's mind at ease.[130]

All had been settled. The outbreak of the Pacific war could not be averted: Japan was about to strike at the United States, Great Britain, and the Netherlands. Britain, despite her vast territorial and economic interests in East Asia and the Pacific, was not of outstanding significance in the climax of the events culminating in war. The United States and Japan were the principal determining powers and both, for their own reasons, had decided that there would be no retreat. Britain naturally fell in with the United States but there was no doubt that the United States had taken over the role of decisive leadership in the Pacific in confronting Japan in 1941.

[130] Ibid.

CONCLUSION

PEARL Harbor and the events immediately ensuing settled a number of problems at the expense of creating others of a formidable nature. Great Britain, the United States, and the Netherlands East Indies were allied against the advance of the Japanese empire, but the comforting knowledge of common resistance to the enemy was vitiated by the absence of plans for immediate co-ordination of defences and by the paucity of strength. The euphoria induced by the Japanese attack on the United States (and Hitler's maladroit declaration of war on the United States) gave way to a sober realization of the truly world dimensions of the war now being waged. The first phase of the Pacific war, from December 1941 to the battles of the Coral Sea and Midway (May-June 1942), constituted a picture of unrelieved gloom for the allies, with Japan constantly possessing the initiative and seizing her opportunity with brilliant enterprise. A bitter and humiliating price was paid for the superficial dismissal of the Japanese menace in the years before the war. The full extent was not appreciated until February-March 1942, with the surrender of Malaya, the Netherlands East Indies, and the Philippines.

Immediately after Pearl Harbor the British ambassador in Washington could still discern some sense of distance and wariness in American attitudes. Lord Halifax wrote that as soon as he had heard of Japan's attack, he was conscious of Churchill's earlier ringing declaration that Britain would be at war 'within the hour'. In addition:

. . . there was the consideration that it was essential to avoid anything which might suggest that Great Britain was pushing the United States into war with Japan. Accordingly while keeping in close touch with the State Department in order to discover whether the United States Government intended to issue any formal statement declaring that a state of war with Japan was in existence, I thought it better to refrain from asking to see any member of the Administration or from making any public statement, although I was frequently asked to do the latter by representatives of the press and the broadcasting companies.[1]

[1] Halifax to Eden, 10 Dec. 1941 (received 1 Jan. 1942), F3/3/23, F.O.371/31807.

In a telegram to Churchill sent on 9 December, Halifax commented that while Roosevelt was certainly enthusiastic at the prospect of a further meeting with Churchill within the near future, he sensed that there was a slight feeling that the prime minister's arrival in Washington might be 'too strong medicine' for public opinion as yet. 'I seem to be conscious of a still lingering distinction in some quarters of the public mind between war with Japan and war with Germany, but this obviously won't last long.'[2] Whatever doubts may have existed, Churchill made up his mind that he must visit Roosevelt and exchange views with him; there were too many issues requiring discussion to delay a meeting. Churchill therefore proceeded to Washington, accompanied by the chiefs of staff. The meeting was successful in terms of the consolidation of friendship between Churchill and Roosevelt and the frank discussion of outstanding difficulties.[3] Churchill adhered to his long-held view that the Pacific was primarily an American responsibility, while the Atlantic and European theatre should be directed from London. He expressed reservations about the American zeal for a vast area of command against the Japanese but, despite his doubts, agreed to the creation of the A.B.D.A. (American-British-Dutch-Australian) command with a British general, Wavell, as supreme commander. The unfortunate Wavell added another daunting challenge to the list with which he successively grappled, from the Middle East campaigns to the diplomacy of the closing stages of British rule in India. The A.B.D.A. command stretched from Burma to northern Australia and was an impossible commitment for any one to handle. It was improvisation of a ludicrous nature in the face of a crumbling defence. However, Churchill's visit triumphantly succeeded in stimulating confidence in Washington. According to Halifax:

You have the principal share in the recovery of American morale that these last two or three weeks have seen. Perhaps one had to be here to have the wide sense of unsureness and loss of confidence immediately after December 7th. It is all very different now and the

[2] Halifax to Churchill, 9 Dec. 1941, Prem.4/27/9.
[3] For details of the defence deliberations at the Washington talks, see ' "Arcadia". Record of Proceedings, Washington War Conference, December 1941-January 1942', Cab.99/17.

immense usefulness of your personal contacts with F.D.R. will remain and grow, as the field of joint action widens.[4]

The campaign in Malaya started badly and grew progressively worse. The calibre of command in the army was poor, with a notable absence of the decisiveness and inspiration so essential to leadership. The commander-in-chief, Air Chief Marshal Sir Robert Brooke-Popham, had been about to leave Singapore and hand over his command to General Sir Henry Pownall when the attack on Malaya occurred. Brooke-Popham then had to continue until Pownall arrived on 23 December. The army commander, General A. E. Percival, was not suited to the tasks that confronted him and did not inspire. The unsatisfactory relationship between Percival and his fellow commanders is illustrated by the controversy over the decision of the Australian, Gordon Bennett, to leave Singapore before the surrender became effective without obtaining Percival's authorization.[5] The army in Malaya comprised British, Australian, and Indian troops, including some raw men—in all, difficult to weld into a cohesive fighting machine. Air strength was totally inadequate: only 141 aircraft at the beginning of the campaign. The result was that airfields on the Malayan peninsula could not be defended properly and Japan possessed air superiority from the start. This did not excuse the hasty evacuation of airfields and frequent failure to render them unusable by the enemy. Brooke-Popham was so unhappy with the morale and efficiency of the R.A.F. that he prepared a statement to be issued to all units, reminding personnel of service traditions.[6] The navy was not seriously involved after the abrupt and

---

[4] Halifax to Churchill, 11 Jan. 1942, Prem.4/27/9.

[5] See notes by General A. E. Percival, C.B., D.S.O., O.B.E., M.C., on 'Certain Senior Commanders and other matters', no date, box 5, item 42, Percival papers, Imperial War Museum, London.

Gordon Bennett's action in escaping from Singapore was regarded critically by General Sturdee, the chief of the Australian general staff, and his colleagues. Bennett encountered more sympathy from the prime minister, John Curtin. Mr. Justice Ligertwood conducted an investigation in 1945 and concluded that Bennett was not justified in leaving his command but added that there were extenuating circumstances. See L. Wigmore, *The Japanese Thrust* (Australian War Memorial, Canberra, 1957), pp. 384-5, 650-2.

[6] Confidential memorandum, Dec. 1941, marked '2 copies given personally to AOC for issue to all units', V/5/50, Brooke-Popham papers.

devastating sinking of the *Prince of Wales* and *Repulse* on 10 December. Churchill had insisted that the two ships be sent to East Asia with the aim of impressing Japan. It had been intended originally to send the aircraft carrier *Indomitable* to afford air cover, but she had run aground in the West Indies. The Admiralty had not wished to send the ships because of their vulnerability. Admiral Sir Dudley Pound gave way to Churchill's pressure with the tragic consequences feared by the Admiralty. Japan controlled the sea, and faced a diminishing and ineffectual challenge in the air from the obsolescent British machines. General Yamashita Tomoyuki skilfully directed the land offensive with the steady advance down the Malayan peninsula towards the island of Singapore. To the British civilians—and indeed to most servicemen—the unbelievable had happened. The calm of a placid existence had been rudely and irrevocably shattered. The prewar defects of unsatisfactory co-ordination between military and civilian authorities, rudimentary arrangements for defensive action, and grave underestimation of the Japanese reaped the appropriate reward. The Malayan campaign became a rout, ending in the surrender of Singapore after a brief siege on 15 February 1942: more than 100,000 men surrendered to the Japanese army of 30,000. Ironically, the Japanese had almost run out of ammunition and the final stage of their campaign was based on bluff. The speed and flexibility of the attacking force led General Percival to believe that he was actually outnumbered instead of facing a numerically inferior foe. General Pownall was at once struck by the dismal atmosphere upon his arrival.[7] Nearly two months later he sadly reflected:

I fear that we were frankly out-generalled, outwitted and outfought. It is a great disaster for the British arms, one of the worst in history, and a great blow to the honour and prestige of the Army. From the beginning to the end of this campaign we have been outmatched by better soldiers. A very painful admission, but it is an inescapable fact.[8]

Shortly afterwards he added:

[7] B. Bond (ed.), *Chief of Staff: the Diaries of Lieutenant-General Sir Henry Pownall*, ii, 67, entry for 24 Dec. 1941.
[8] Ibid. 85, entry for 13 Feb. 1942.

There's no doubt that we've underestimated the Jap. He is far more efficient, a far better fighter than we ever thought. We thought (I among them) that when they got up against something other than the Chinese they would begin to quail. Therein we underestimated the Chinese too. But suppose we'd made a better shot and had got the Jap at his true worth, would it have made any difference? I very much doubt it. Our policy was to avoid a war with Japan as long as we could (or to make America cause it, if it was to happen) and we gambled on that policy succeeding (or if it didn't succeed on America bearing the brunt). With all our other commitments I don't believe that, however highly we had rated the Japs as fighters, we would have been caused thereby to improve the condition of our Services in the Far East. We just hoped it wouldn't happen. And it did . . .[9]

Pownall's observations were accurate enough. The swiftness of the Japanese victory was a fitting commentary on the bankruptcy of the 'Singapore strategy' as it had developed from the abrogation of the Anglo-Japanese alliance to 1941.

Japanese victory in Malaya was followed by victories soon afterwards in the East Indies and the Philippines and by advances to the border of India and to New Guinea. The A.B.D.A. command predictably failed, and was replaced by the dual American counter-offensives headed by General MacArthur and Admiral Nimitz and by the British counter-attack from Burma. Chiang Kai-shek was generalissimo of the remaining and least important theatre. The Pacific war lasted a little over three and a half years and was extremely brutal. By August 1945 the Japanese empire, which had grown with such spectacular speed in recent years, lay in ruins. The importance of the intervening period is difficult to exaggerate for its repercussions on the western colonial territories. Japan had long conceived of herself as having a mission to lead East Asia and to free native peoples from occidental hegemony. The colonial empires proved to be even more vulnerable than Japanese leaders had expected. Native populations in the captured territories greeted the Japanese with a mixture of respect and indifference. Japanese propaganda stressed that the Japanese army came as liberators and that conditions in the former colonial territories would improve dramatically.

[9] Ibid. 92, entry for 25 Feb. 1942. For further reflections by Pownall on the defeat, see pp. 96–100.

The harsh reality was different. It quickly became clear that the interest of Japanese soldiers was confined to the role peoples could play in assisting the Japanese empire: one kind of imperialism had been exchanged for another and it did not necessarily become more bearable because the oppressor had a yellow skin. It might have been thought that this lesson would have been learned from Japanese policy in China from 1937 onwards, but this was not the case. China was remote to the nationalist leaders of south-east Asia and they were pre-occupied with their own problems. Japan set up a Greater East Asia Ministry, to the chagrin of the *Gaimusho*, and General Tojo presided over a conference of nationalist leaders convened in Tokyo in 1943. Japan's policy lacked coherence beyond the simple objective of decisively discrediting the former colonial administration.[10] The combination of the rapid disintegration of the colonial governments in the face of Japan's onslaught and the callous and humiliating treatment meted out to white prisoners by their captors ensured that Japan succeeded in this aim.

Japan gave little genuine freedom to the lands she conquered, but she had encouraged and given credence to nationalist movements. Thus Japan's defeat permitted vicarious satisfaction at the repudiation of the former colonial masters. In Indo-China, and the East Indies, the French and Dutch respectively failed in their attempts to restore some semblance of their old positions. In India the presence of the Japanese army on the eastern frontier accelerated the trend to independence. In Burma Britain transiently reappeared until Burma opted out of the British Commonwealth in 1948. Only in Malaya was there less desire for autonomy, and Malaya constituted the one example of a guerrilla movement being defeated; immediately afterwards Britain gave independence to Malaya in 1957.[11] The Philippines became independent in 1946 in fulfilment of American policy before 1941. The Pacific war therefore contributed most significantly to the

---

[10] On Japanese policy towards nationalist movements, see F. C. Jones, *Japan's New Order in East Asia, 1937-1945* (Oxford Universty Press, London, 1954), chs. 11 and 12, and J. C. Lebra, *Japan's Greater East Asia Co-Prosperity Sphere in World War II: Selected Readings and Documents* (Oxford University Press, Kuala Lumpur, 1975).

[11] On the counter-insurgency campaign in Malaya, see A. Short, *The Communist Insurrection in Malaya, 1948-60* (Frederick Muller, London, 1975).

changing map of East Asia. The delayed fall of the anti-communist regimes in south Vietnam, Cambodia, and Laos in the spring of 1975 and the withdrawal of the United States from intervention in these areas was in part the last vestige of the historical process unleashed by the Pacific war: ironically the principal victor of the war suffered some of the ultimate consequences.

In China Chiang Kai-shek aimed to do the minimum necessary to fight the Japanese and to husband his resources for the developing confrontation with the communists under Mao Tse-tung. The communists employed guerrilla warfare ably against the Japanese, but were fundamentally more concerned in the struggle with the Kuomintang. Japan's holy war in China was supposed to be designed to save China from the horrors of communism but instead helped to ensure that China became communist within four years of the end of the Pacific war. While the reasons for the collapse of the Kuomintang remain a source of controversy and, in certain respects, of obscurity, there is no doubt that the Sino-Japanese war aided the communists by driving the Kuomintang from the coastal provinces into the more reactionary interior and by stimulating the raging inflation that sapped the vitality of Chiang's regime.

For Great Britain the Pacific war hastened the pace of change, as all wars do. Britain's traditional interests in China, diminishing before 1941, declined rapidly during the war and after it. The Japanese took over the treaty ports and extinguished extraterritoriality: the formal end of extraterritoriality was approved by Churchill, Roosevelt, and Chiang Kai-shek in 1943. Britain's standing with Chiang had suffered serious blows as a result of the crises over Tientsin and the Burma road in 1939 and 1940. It was manifest that the British star was falling, and Chiang looked instead to the United States for succour and encouragement. The United States took the lead in handling relations with Chungking from Pearl Harbor onwards: it proved an exasperating and unrewarding task. Roosevelt was correct in realizing that China was assuming more importance in the world and that she could not be treated in the manner to which westerners had become accustomed in former years. He was, however, wrong in believing that Chiang Kai-shek and the Chungking government would direct the regeneration of China. Churchill's basic contempt for Chiang was justified up to a point, but Churchill erred in dismissing China altogether. After 1945 British capitalists returned briefly to Shanghai, but the communist victory in 1949 finally terminated the remnants of imperialism (except in Hong Kong and Macao where it was convenient for the communists to allow the British and Portuguese to remain). Britain remained important in south-east Asia for two decades after the Japanese surrender, but this was due to co-operation with other countries against the menace of communism as an external and internal threat. The exigencies of Britain's own increasing economic and social difficulties, together with the realization that the governments of the area must solve the problems confronting them largely by their own efforts, caused the progressive with-drawal of British forces so that, by 1975, Britain's military presence had almost disappeared. Such developments would no doubt have occurred at some time, in any case, but the Pacific war produced a swifter pattern of change.

This study has examined Great Britain's involvement in the origins of the Pacific war. The origins stretch back a long way, certainly into the nineteenth century, but in the present work the emphasis has been placed on the crucial years of climax from the minor incident at the Lukouchiao bridge in July 1937 to the Japanese offensives beginning on 7 December 1941. Was Britain responsible to some extent for the outbreak of war? Could the war have been avoided? Most major participants in wars bear some share of responsibility for the eventual dis-aster. Insufficient understanding of Japan was shown by the British government and British society in the 1930s. The forces impelling Japan forward, the underlying tenacity, self-confidence, and willingness to endure profound hardship, were not properly recognized except by a few astute observers such as Sir George Sansom. Most British policy-makers believed that Japan lacked the ability to wage large-scale war for a prolonged period and that the Japanese economy could not stand the strains imposed. It was, therefore, maintained that Japan could not afford to become involved in conflict with the United States and Great Britain. Japan could not, however, retreat from the policy of expansion upon which she had embarked: to do so would be a betrayal of values and a humiliating reversal at the dictation of foreign powers. The most serious error made in Britain — and in the United States — was the comfortable belief that, if war came to the Pacific, Japan could be contained without undue difficulty. It would be most unfortunate to become embroiled in an additional conflict when the wars in the Atlantic, the Middle East, and Russia absorbed such vast resources but, if the worst occurred, it was unlikely that Japan would break through decisively. Such illusions contributed to the margins of error allowed for in the decisions taken not to make significant concessions to Japan in 1941. It is true that the decisions were effectively taken by Roosevelt, Hull, and their subordinates in Washington but Churchill was always vehemently opposed to concessions and had conveyed this view unmistakably to the Americans; the Foreign Office on the whole followed this line, if less stridently, and the chiefs of staff (although opposed to an additional war) felt that Japan could be held. A more accurate and realistic assessment of Japan's capacity to inflict damage would perhaps have led to greater caution in 1941 and to a more careful judgement of the likely repercussions of such actions as the freezing measures in July 1941.

Britain did not pursue a policy of appeasement to Japan because she did not believe that Japanese expansion beyond Manchuria was reasonable or that Japan would be satisfied by any concessions made. There are three examples of individual acts of appeasement made under pressure: the customs agreement of May 1938, the Craigie–Arita formula over Tientsin in July 1939, and the temporary closure of the Burma road in July 1940. In addition, British policy-makers always had to consider the response of the United States to British decisions. As the threat of war with Japan loomed larger, so it was generally recognized that the United States would occupy the chief role in facing Japan and that Britain must try to avoid taking action that would antagonize Washington. Was Britain right not to attempt a general policy of appeasing Japan? Japan would not have been satisfied with less than effective western acquiescence in Japanese domination of China. One of the leading elements in the developing Japanese resentment of Britain from 1937 onwards was the belief that Britain was encouraging Chiang Kai-shek and thus thwarting Japan's aims. Subsequently the United States adopted a similar approach. Japan was convinced of the need to sustain her divine mission in China and was determined not to retreat. Britain and the United States were just as determined not to make appreciable concessions in China, because of the moral implications for allied policy of submitting to a power identified with the European Axis. Moral factors entered more prominently into American policy and were axiomatic to Roosevelt's strategy of selling his policy of supporting the allies to the American electorate. The British were conscious of the revulsion in public opinion against blatant acts of appeasement, after Munich, but were influenced more by the belief that appeasement would not achieve its objectives and that much of the Japanese army was preoccupied in China. Appeasement would have postponed a showdown with Japan but it was most unlikely that it would have avoided war in the Pacific. Japanese society was geared to expansion and it would not stop or compromise significantly. The only way in which conflict could have been avoided was by British and American withdrawal from East Asia and the western Pacific. Such a withdrawal would have been easier for the United States than Britain, for American territorial interests were confined to the Philippines and the American economic stake in China was not large. For Britain, on the other hand, it would have connoted surrender of the portions of the British empire lying east of India, would have encouraged the collapse of British authority in the Indian sub-continent, and have had disastrous consequences on relations with Australia and New Zealand. Furthermore it would have included the liquidation of investments in China. Looked at from the vantage point of the 1970s, it might be argued that such a policy would have been sensible. The United States has learned painful lessons from overextending herself in East Asia and is intervening in the area less than at any time since 1941; the British empire has vanished into history and Britain sees her future as part of the European Community. Was it all worthwhile? Would Japanese hegemony perhaps have been preferable? These questions are unhistorical and in essence irrelevant. Politicians and diplomats have to resolve the problems of today and let tomorrow take care of itself. The world was in turmoil in 1941, experiencing conflicts of unprecedented scale and savagery. Errors of a grave character were unquestionably committed by British and American leaders in their far eastern policies before Pearl Harbor. However, Britain and the United States were not primarily responsible for the outbreak of the Pacific war. The application of the freezing measures in July 1941 definitely affected the timing of the commencement of the struggle with Japan, but this simply quickened the pace of development. Japanese leaders were prepared to risk the destruction of their country, if necessary, rather than give way. The European war, with the ascendancy of Hitler and the German attack on Russia, again affected the timing and brought the war nearer. The origins of the Pacific war are firmly to be located in East Asia and the Pacific; the war was quite distinct from that in Europe, although the two obviously merged to form a world struggle. The responsibility for beginning the Pacific war was chiefly that of Japan; British and American responsibility was unwittingly to ensure that the war started on 7 December 1941 rather than at some date in 1942.

APPENDIX A
BRITISH DIPLOMATS AND MEMBERS OF THE FOREIGN OFFICE

BENNETT, John Cecil Sterndale, b. 1895. Entered Foreign Office, 1920 and served at Stockholm, Santiago, Peking (1927–30); first secretary, 1930; served at Cairo, 1937–40; transferred to Foreign Office, May 1940; acting counsellor, Sept. 1940; head of Far Eastern department, 1940–2 and 1944–6; served at Ankara, 1942–4; minister at Sofia, 1947–9; deputy commissioner-general at Singapore, 1950; head of British Middle East office, 1953; retired 1956; died 1969.

BRENAN, Sir John Fitzgerald, b. 1893. Student interpreter, Siam, 1903; transferred to China, 1905; served Tientsin; Foochow, Nanking, Shanghai; employed in Far Eastern department of Foreign Office, 1923–4; consul-general at Canton, 1929; transferred to Shanghai, 1930; employed in Far Eastern department of Foreign Office from Nov. 1937; acting counsellor, Nov. 1938; retired 1943; died 1953.

CADOGAN, Sir Alexander George Montagu, b. 1884. Entered Foreign Office, 1908, and served at Constantinople, Vienna; minister and then ambassador to China, 1933–6; deputy under-secretary of state, 1936–8; permanent under-secretary, Jan. 1938–46; representative to United Nations, 1946–50; retired 1950; died 1968.

CLARK KERR, Sir Archibald John, b. 1882, Entered Foreign Office, 1905 and served at Berlin, Buenos Aires, Washington, Rome, Teheran, Tangier, Cairo; counsellor, 1925, minister to Guatemala, 1925; consul-general for Guatemala, Honduras, Nicaragua, and Salvador, 1925; transferred to Santiago, 1928; served at Stockholm, 1931–5; ambassador to Iraq, 1935–8 and ambassador to China, Feb. 1938–Feb. 1942; ambassador to Moscow, 1942–6, and Washington, 1946–8; created Baron Inverchapel, 1946; retired 1948; died 1951.

CLARKE, Henry Ashley, b. 1903. Entered Foreign Office, 1925 and served at Budapest, Warsaw, Constantinople, Tokyo; first secretary at Tokyo, 1936–8; transferred to Foreign Office, Sept. 1938; acting counsellor, 1942, and counsellor, 1944; served at Lisbon and Paris; assistant under-secretary of state (administration), 1949, and deputy under-secretary of state (administration), 1950; ambassador at Rome, 1953–62; retired 1962.

CLIVE, Sir Robert Henry, b. 1877. Entered Foreign Office, 1902; served at Rome, Tokyo, Cairo, Berne, Stockholm, Peking, Munich,

Tangier, Teheran; minister at Teheran, 1926–31, to Holy See, 1933; ambassador to Japan, May 1934–July 1937; ambassador to Belgium, Aug. 1937–Dec. 1939; retired 1939; died 1948.

CRAIGIE, Sir Robert Leslie, b. 1883. Entered Foreign Office, 1907 and served at Berne, Sofia, Washington; counsellor, 1928; assistant under-secretary of state, 1935; ambassador to Japan, Aug. 1937–Dec. 1941; retired 1944; died 1959.

CROSBY, Sir Josiah, b. 1880. Student interpreter, Siam, 1904; served at Bangkok, Chiengmai, Saigon, Batavia; minister to Panama, 1931; minister to Thailand, May 1934–Dec. 1941; retired 1943; died 1958.

CRIPPS, Sir Richard Stafford, b. 1889. Labour M.P. for East Bristol, 1931–51, ambassador at Moscow, June 1940–Jan. 1942; Lord Privy Seal and Leader of the House of Commons, Jan.–Nov. 1942; Minister of Aircraft Production, 1942–5; President of Board of Trade, 1945–7; Minister of Economic Affairs, 1947; Chancellor of Exchequer, 1947–50; died 1952.

DENING, Maberly Esler, b. 1897. Student interpreter, Japan, 1920, and served at Seoul, Manila, Dairen, Osaka, Kobe; acting consul-general, Harbin, 1936–7; promoted as consul in Foreign Office, Nov. 1938; given rank of first secretary while at Washington, 24 July–15 Nov. 1941; promoted consul-general, 1943, and political adviser to Supreme Allied Commander, S.E. Asian Command; assistant under-secretary of state, 1946; ambassador to Japan, 1952–7, retired 1957; died 1977.

DODDS, James Leishman, b. 1891. Entered Foreign Office, 1919, and served at Tokyo, Madrid, Stockholm, The Hague, Berne; acting counsellor at Tokyo, Mar. 1936; counsellor at Tokyo, Mar. 1938; Minister to Peru, 1940–4, and to Cuba, 1944–9; ambassador to Peru, 1949–51; retired 1951; died 1972.

GAGE, Berkeley Everard Foley, b. 1904. Entered Foreign Office, 1928; served at Rome, 1928; second secretary, 1933; transferred to China, Sept. 1941; served in Foreign Office, The Hague, Chicago; ambassador to Thailand, 1954–8, and to Peru, 1958–63; retired 1963.

HOWE, Robert George, b. 1893. Entered Foreign Office, 1919, and served at Copenhagen, Belgrade, Rio de Janeiro, Bucharest, Peking; acting counsellor at Peking, 1936–8; counsellor of embassy, 1936; transferred to Foreign Office, Mar. 1938, and head of Far Eastern department, 1938–40; minister to Ethiopia, 1942–5; seconded to Sudan government, 1947, and governor-general of Sudan, 1947–55; retired 1955; died 1975.

LINDSAY, Sir Ronald Charles, b. 1877. Entered Foreign Office, 1898 and served at St. Petersburg, Teheran, Washington, Paris, The Hague; first secretary at Washington, 1919, and Paris, 1920; assistant under-secretary of state, 1921; ambassador to Turkey, 1925–6, and to Germany, 1926–8; permanent under-secretary, 1928–30; ambassador to United States, 1930–9; retired 1939; died 1945.

LOTHIAN, Philip Kerr, Marquess of, b. 1882. Liberal politician; ambassador to United States, Aug. 1939–Dec. 1940; died in office.

MOUNSEY, Sir George Augustus, b. 1879. Entered Foreign Office, 1902; served at The Hague, Berlin, Constantinople, Rome; first secretary, 1915; counsellor, 1924; assistant under-secretary of state, 1929; seconded to Ministry of Economic Warfare, 1939; retired June 1940, died 1966.

ORDE, Charles William, b. 1884. Entered Foreign Office, 1909, and served in Foreign Office until 1938; counsellor, 1929; head of Far Eastern department, 1930–Mar. 1938; minister at Riga, Tallinn, and Kovno, 1938–40; ambassador at Santiago, 1940–6; retired March 1946.

PRATT, Sir John Thomas, b. 1876. Student interpreter, China, 1898; served at Wuchow, Tientsin, Shanghai, Tsinan; consul-general, Tsinan, 1919; in charge of consulate at Nanking, 1922–4; acting consul-general, Shanghai, 1924–5; employed in Foreign Office from Oct. 1925; acting counsellor, Apr. 1925; retired Apr. 1938; died 1970.

RONALD, Nigel Bruce, b. 1894. Entered Foreign Office, 1920, and served at Berne, Oslo; transferred to Foreign Office, 1936; first secretary, 1930; acting counsellor, Nov. 1939, and counsellor, Nov. 1941; ambassador at Lisbon, 1947–55; retired 1955; died 1973.

SANSOM, Sir George Bailey, b. 1883. Student interpreter, Japan, 1903; served at Yokohama, Chemulpo, Hakodate, acting Japanese counsellor, Jan.–Nov. 1920; commercial secretary, Sept. 1923; commercial secretary (grade I) with local rank of commercial counsellor, Jan. 1930; adviser to Indian government in Indo-Japanese negotiations, Sept.–Nov. 1933; retired Sept. 1940; employed on special service at Singapore and Java, 1941–2; adviser to ambassador at Washington, Sept. 1942; distinguished historian and authority on Japanese culture; died 1965.

SEYMOUR, Sir Horace James, b. 1885. Entered Foreign Office, 1908 and served at Washington, The Hague, Rome; counsellor 1929; minister at Teheran, 1936–9; assistant under-secretary of state, Jan. 1940; ambassador to China, Feb. 1942–Jan. 1947; retired 1947.

VANSITTART, Robert Vansittart, Lord, b. 1881. Entered Foreign Office, 1902, and served at Paris, Teheran, Cairo, Stockholm, Paris Peace Conference Delegation; counsellor, 1920; assistant under-secretary, 1928; permanent under-secretary, 1930–Dec. 1937; chief diplomatic adviser, Jan. 1938–June 1941; raised to peerage, July 1941; died 1957.

APPENDIX B
JAPANESE PRIME MINISTERS AND FOREIGN MINISTERS

Prime Minister
Konoe Fumimaro
(4 June 1937–4 Jan. 1939)
Hiranuma Kiichiro
(5 Jan. 1939–28 Aug. 1939)
Abe Nobuyuki
(30 Aug. 1939–14 Jan. 1940)
Yonai Mitsumasa
(16 Jan. 1940–16 July 1940)
Konoe Fumimaro
(28 July 1940–16 Oct. 1941)
Tojo Hideki
(18 Oct. 1941–18 July 1944)

Foreign Minister
Hirota Koki
(4 June 1936–26 May 1938)
Ugaki Kazushige
(26 May 1938–30 Sept. 1938)
Arita Hachiro
(29 Oct. 1938–28 Aug. 1939)
Nomura Kichisaburo
(25 Sept. 1939–14 Jan. 1940)
Arita Hachiro
(16 Jan. 1940–16 July 1940)
Matsuoka Yosuke
(22 July 1940–16 July 1941)
Toyoda Teijiro
(18 July 1941–16 Oct. 1941)
Togo Shigenori
(18 Oct. 1941–Sept. 1942)

APPENDIX C
THE FAR EASTERN COMMITTEE

The Far Eastern Committee was set up in October 1940 'to keep under review our policy in the Far East, with particular regard to co-operation with the Dominions and other interested governments.'[1] The committee was chaired by the parliamentary under-secretary for foreign affairs, who was R. A. Butler in the formative stage of the committee's work (October 1940–August 1941); Butler was succeeded by Richard Law. The committee comprised representatives from each government department concerned with East Asia; issues of common interest were discussed with the aim of securing better understanding of the different perspectives. The committee was concerned essentially with co-ordination. The principal pre-occupation of the committee lay in relations with Japan involving the economic sphere—'to concert measures of precaution or pressure against Japan; to facilitate resistance to her and to diminish her war potential, while bearing in mind the great importance of avoiding action likely to provoke Japan into aggression against our own possessions in the Far East or the Netherlands East Indies.'[2] The committee proceeded to increase restrictions on trade with Japan with the aim of preventing Japan from assisting Britain's enemies and from building up stocks. Machinery was erected throughout the Commonwealth in the form of licensing control with the intention of limiting exports to Japan to normal figures in respect of all goods which were regarded as German, Italian or Japanese deficiencies, as for example with tin and rubber from Malaya, except where stricter embargoes were already being applied, as with jute from India and nickel from Canada. British policy diverged from that of the United States, which had imposed complete embargoes on a few special commodities, for example molybdenum, aluminium and scrap iron. A full comprehensive range of restrictions was developed and applied in the period down to the American decision to enforce full-scale economic sanctions in July 1941. The restrictions were intended to conserve for Britain raw materials essential to the war effort; to prevent materials reaching Britain's enemies and to prevent Japan from accumulating stocks and thus facilitating a Japanese campaign

---

[1] 'Report of the Far Eastern Committee', 17 Dec. 1940, enclosed in memorandum by Halifax, 18 Dec. 1941, W.P.(40) 484, Cab.66/14.
[2] Ibid.

against British, American and Dutch possessions. In a report to the war cabinet it was stated:

That our restrictions should produce some reactions in Japan is inevitable. In so far as such reactions indicate a realisation on the part of the Japanese of the disadvantages of their allying themselves with the Axis, they are not necessarily undesirable; indeed, it is our hope that we may bring home to an increasing number of Japanese the solid advantages to be gained by renewing Japan's former relations with us and renouncing her connexion with the Axis. Meanwhile constant care and vigilance is being exercised by the Far Eastern Committee, in the prosecution of their policy, not to push restriction to the point of provoking Japan to war either by reducing too drastically and suddenly her supplies, *e.g.*, of oil, considered vital by the Japanese Government or by striking too brusquely at Japanese enterprises within British territory. It must be realised, however, that if and when Japan judges—for whatever reasons—that the moment has come to strike at Malaya and the Netherlands East Indies she will in all probability seize on our restrictions as a justification of her action.[3]

The economic restrictions were enforced by the Treasury and the Ministry of Economic Warfare, under the overall supervision of the Far Eastern Committee. In a memorandum prepared by the Ministry of Economic Warfare, it was stated that the United States had subjected the majority of significant commodities to export licence; the American practice was more drastic than the British in certain respects with the qualification that some important commodities, such as cotton and mineral oils, were not subject to restriction at all. The Americans had extended their licensing system to goods transshipped in the United States, which seriously affected Japanese imports from Latin America. In addition, this had been extended to include the Philippines. In the British Commonwealth restrictions had gradually been tightened. Some commodities were embargoes entirely on supply lines, for example, nickel and ferro-alloys. Other embargoes, such as scrap iron, had been imposed to conform with American policy. Elsewhere restrictions had been increased for solely economic warfare reasons. No further licences were to be issued for rubber and tin from Malaya in 1941 in the light of the excessive quantities which Japan had obtained from other sources. An embargo had been placed on exports of copra from most parts of the Commonwealth because of Japan's abnormal imports, especially from the Philippines and of the evidence that copra and other fats had been sent to Germany. Additional restrictions had recently been put on other exports to Japan, for example pig iron, lead and zinc, and possible restrictions on manganese, jute and other commodities were under con-

[3] 'The Nature and Extent of our Economic Restrictions Against Japan', memorandum by Eden, 7 July 1941, W.P.(41)155 and F.E.(41)136, Cab.66/17.

sideration. India and the colonies had co-operated fully but the Dominions, and notably Canada, had shown more independence. Care was being taken not to impose such restrictions as to provoke Japan to war:

Thus, with the exception of copra and an embargo placed by the Canadian Government on wheat, little has been done to interfere with Japan's food supplies. For example, Burmese rice is open to her to buy at will. Japanese reactions to date may be summed up as follows: the Canadian embargo on wheat was followed by a veiled threat to withdraw the Japanese Diplomatic Mission in Canada. The embargo on copra led to urgent appeals and protests in Tokyo, Canberra and London. An embargo imposed in Hong Kong on exports of scrap iron, wolfram and gall nuts caused a similar outburst, and the Japanese intimated that Hong Kong should be regarded as having some special relationship in economic matters with the Japanese Empire. This suggestion was finally rejected.[4]

The mounting Japanese protests, together with the menacing Japanese attitude to the East Indies, pointed to the efficacy of British policy. 'While it would be foolish to claim that they are as yet seriously weakened, it would be equally foolish to deny that they are becoming increasingly alarmed.'[5]

The Far Eastern Committee improved understanding and co-operation between government departments but individual departments continued to be responsible for the implementation of policy.

[4] 'Economic Restrictions against Japan', memorandum by Dalton, (minister of Economic Warfare), enclosed in memorandum by Eden, 7 July 1941, ibid.
[5] Ibid.

APPENDIX D

AID TO CHINA, 1940-41

British assistance to China in 1940-41 was limited in scope but did increase gradually. It was governed by the prior claims of the European and Middle Eastern theatres, in which Britain was so heavily engaged, and by the view that Britain wished to sustain the Chinese war effort without provoking Japan to attack British possessions. British aid may be concisely summarized as follows:

(a) An advance of £5 million to the China Stabilization Fund, made on 10 December 1940, and additional export credits of £5 million, for use within the sterling area, additional to the sum of nearly £3 million granted on 18 August 1939.

(b) The transfer of the Chinese government's Loiwang aircraft factory to Bangalore in India, the assembly of Chinese military aircraft in Burma and the export of aircraft from Burma and India provided that they were not in a condition to engage in combat en route. The war cabinet decided on 17 July 1941 that fully armed aircraft could fly from Burma to China.

(c) Facilities were made available in Burma for the assembly of aircraft and transport of supplies for the International Air Force, under the command of the American Claire Chennault, and the war cabinet authorized full operational training of pilots for this force in Burma.

(d) Britain made available for the International Air Force 100 Tomahawks and 144 Vultees out of the allocation made to Britain in the United States.

(e) After lengthy consideration, it was agreed to provide funds for the construction in Burma of the Burma-Yunnan railway. This had been under discussion for a prolonged period; the Foreign Office had supported the project since 1938 but the Burma Office and the government of Burma were not enthusiastic because the railway was unlikely to prove commercially viable and Burma had a continuing quarrel over the frontier with China. However, these reservations were swept aside in the interests of bolstering Chinese morale and keeping large numbers of Japanese troops tied down in China.

(f) Road communications in Burma were improved in 1941 and new road projects planned so as to facilitate more rapid communication with China. The quantity of goods passing over the Burma road rose from 5,220 tons in October 1940 to 9,100 tons in January 1941, to 14,000 tons in May 1941 and to 18,544 tons in September 1941. Delays in transporting goods from Lashio to Kunming resulted from the incompetence of the Chinese traffic controllers and was not the responsibility of the authorities in Burma. This was clearly established in an investigation conducted by an American, Arnstein, in the summer of 1941.

(g) General Dennys was sent to Chungking as military attaché and empowered to pursue talks with Chiang Kai-shek to achieve a better understanding of mutual defence problems. In addition, a military mission was formed in Burma so as to move into China on the outbreak of war with Japan and engage in guerrilla warfare.

(h) A Chinese freight air service from Kunming to Lashio was authorized but the Chinese government subsequently decided not to proceed with it. A number of proposals for improving air communications between China and India/Burma were under consideration.

(i) A party of Chinese staff officers had been allowed to visit Burma and Malaya.

(j) Sir Otto Niemeyer of the Bank of England had been sent to China to report on financial and economic aspects of China's position.

(k) Six junior Chinese naval officers had been accepted for service with British ships on the East Indies station.

(l) Naval guns from H.M.S. *Falcon*, laid up at Chungking, had been given to the Chinese for anti-aircraft defence of the Burma road.

(m) A grant of £50,000 was under consideration, in September 1941, to help in treating wounded Chinese soldiers.

(n) At the request of the Chinese government, a freezing order was imposed on all Chinese balances as from 29 July 1941, so as to enforce economic pressure on Japan.[1]

Chiang Kai-shek pressed stridently for increased aid in monetary and material terms in the last few months of 1941. He stepped up his earlier warnings of the looming threat to China's continued participation in the war against Japan and referred explicitly to the dangers of a vigorous Japanese offensive in Yunnan to cut the Burma road. Sir Otto Niemeyer regarded the situation in China with gloom, for the combination of prevailing corruption and accelerating inflation was insidiously undermining China's war effort. Sir John Brenan accurately minuted on a report from Niemeyer: 'Sir O. Niemeyer does not think that the Chinese are in danger of entire collapse, at least for some time to come. I think we must expect, how-

---

[1] This is largely based on a memorandum by A. L. Scott, 3 Sept. 1941, F8674/145/10, F.O.371/27642; some information is also derived from military attaché, Chungking, to War Office, 8 Nov. 1941, communicated by War Office to Foreign Office, 12 Nov. 1941, F12115/196/10, F.O.371/27658.

ever, that they will tend more and more to sit back and leave Japan to the United States and ourselves . . .'[2]

---

[2] Minute by Brenan, 8 Dec. 1941, on Chungking to Foreign Office, 4 Dec. 1941, F13300/1/10, F.O.371/27604.

BIBLIOGRAPHY

The bibliography is divided according to the nature of sources used; critical comment is attached where necessary.

A. OFFICIAL PAPERS
I. Public Record Office, London.

(a) *Foreign Office Records*

The principal Foreign Office source comprises political correspondence for the years 1937–41. Each volume begins with the index number F.O.371/.

1937   F.O.371/20944–21027 (China)
        F.O.371/21028–21044 (Japan)
1938   F.O.371/22037–22164 (China)
        F.O.371/22165–22176 (General)
        F.O.371/22177–22193 (Japan)
1939   F.O.371/23395–23537 (China)
        F.O.371/23538–23553 (General)
        F.O.371/23554–23575 (Japan)
        F.O.371/23586–23598 (Thailand)
1940   F.O.371/24646–24704 (China)
        F.O.371/24705–24722 (General)
        F.O.371/24723–24743 (Japan)
        F.O.371/24750–24757 (Thailand)
1941   F.O.371/27590–27757 (China)
        F.O.371/27758–27876 (General)
        F.O.371/27877–28063 (Japan)
        F.O.371/28108–28165 (Thailand)
        F.O.371/26143–26287 (United States)
1942   F.O.371/31616–31725 (China)
        F.O.371/31726–31806 (General)
        F.O.371/31807–31847 (Japan)

The Foreign Office files constitute a most important source with a vast amount of information on the formulation of British policy, including correspondence with embassies, other government departments, and internal minutes and memoranda. The major source is the political correspondence in F.O.371/ but a selection of important documents is to be found in the printed volumes of Confidential Print.

F.O. Confidential Print, Far Eastern Affairs, 1937–41 F.O.436/1–11. (The volumes from 1942 onwards are closed for fifty years.)

(b)   *Cabinet Office Records*
These include conclusions of cabinet discussions and accompanying memoranda; the papers of the Committee of Imperial Defence; the records of the chiefs of staff committee; and papers emanating from other cabinet committees. A large and important collection.
(i) Cabinet conclusions and memoranda. A valuable source at times of particular crisis.

Cab.23/73-101   for conclusions, 1937-9.
Cab.24/233-288   for memoranda, 1937-9.
Cab.65/1-25   for war cabinet conclusions, 1939-42.
Cab.66/1-20   for war cabinet memoranda, 1939-42.

(ii) Committee of Imperial Defence. A useful source down to the outbreak of war.
Cab.2/6-9   for minutes of discussions
Cab.3/6-9 and Cab.4/26-30 for memoranda.
(iii) Chiefs of Staff Committee. Important for revealing the full dilemmas of defence.

Cab.53/8-11   for minutes, 1937-9.
Cab.53/32-54   for memoranda, 1937-9.
Cab.79/1-18   for conclusions, 1939-42.
Cab.80/1-34   for memoranda, 1939-42.

(iv) Reports of further committees concerned with defence problems.
Cab.16/181-183A and B for Defence Plans (Policy) 209.
(v) Miscellaneous files relating to defence.
Cab.21/702-708, 893, 999, 1007-1014, 1024-1029, 1369, 1414-1420.
(vi) War Cabinet Defence Committee (Operations)
Cab.69/1-4, 8.
(vii) Far Eastern Committee. Valuable for pursuing the implementation of increasing economic measures against Japan in 1940-1.
Cab.96/1-4, 7-8.
(viii) Visit of Australian Prime Minister, 1941.
Cab.99/4.
(ix) British-United States Staff Conversations in Washington, January-March 1941.
Very significant for revealing Anglo-American strategic ideas.
Cab.99/5.
(x) Anglo-Dutch-American Technical Conversations, 1940-1.
Cab.99/8.
(xi) 'Arcadia', Visit of Churchill and Chiefs of Staff to Washington, December 1941.
Cab.99/17-18.
(xii) 'Riviera' talks, August 1941, between British and American

defence chiefs during Churchill's visit to Placentia Bay, New-foundland.

Cab.99/18.

(xiii) British Joint Staff Mission: Washington Office Files.

Cab.122/1, 4, 5-9, 25-26, 30-31, 43, 52, 60, 72-73, 86, 95-97, 120, 148, 161-64, 185-87.

(c) *Prime Minister's Office*

A source of intermittent value. Many papers may be located in the original Foreign Office or Cabinet Office files and some are trivial. However, there are some important minutes and a small number of papers not encountered elsewhere.

Prem.1/277-78, 305, 309-10, 314-16, 345-48, 366-67.

Prem.3/90/1; 3/142/6; 3/252/1-6A; 3/462-63; 3/467-69; 3/474/1; 3/476/10; 3/485/1-5; 3/486/1-2; 3/488/1-2; 3/489/1-5.

Prem.4/20/1; 4/25/2-3; 4/28/9; 4/50/4A; 4/50/7A; 4/50/5; 4/71/1; 4/43A/11-13; 4/50/4A; 4/71/2; 4/83/1A-2; 4/84/1-2A; 4/84/3-4.

Indexes Prem.4/102/135.

(d) *Treasury*

The office papers of Leith-Ross are valuable for financial aspects: T.188/187-90, 205, 208, 234-37, 248, 249 and 284.

T160/Box 764/File 14435; T160/Box 782/File 3420/05; T160/Box 850/File 14375/1-2; T160/Box 1033/File 15194/026/1-3; T160/Box 1036/File 15255/05/03/1-2; T160/Box 1094/File 16244/1-5; T160/Box 1098/File 16829/1-2.

The T160 series includes some files of interest but much of the material is available in the Foreign Office files.

(e) *Ministry of Economic Warfare*

F.O. 837/530-539 and 995-6.

These files include numerous papers dealing with economic pressure against Japan in 1940-1. The papers are detailed; some are to be found, in addition, in the Foreign Office files and in the Cab.96/ category. The files were being recatalogued and it was not possible to use them fully in this study. The files were used to some extent by W. N. Medlicott in *The Economic Blockade* (see list of secondary sources).

(f) *Admiralty*

A source of some value but less easy to consult owing to the chaotic order of files. The following were significant: Adm.1/9822; Adm.116/3922; 2953-55; 4087; 4302; 4348; 4393; 4396; 4657; 4806; Adm.199/1149, 1156, 1228, 1928-34.

(g) *War Office*

Little of significance but the following files were consulted: W.O.32/3644, 4183, 4186, 4187-89.

(h)   *Air Ministry*
Some files are illuminating, notably those concerning the correspondence between the A.O.C., Far East, Babington, and the Air Ministry. Some of the correspondence of Sir Archibald Sinclair, Secretary of State for Air, is of interest, too.
Air 2/2130, 2225, 2616, 3558, 4128, 5249, 7174–77.
Air 23/1863–69, 4643, 4661–62, 5076, 5422.
Sinclair papers, Air 19/185, 227, 242, 246, 274–75, 287–88, 302, 449, 453–54, 461, 500, 502, 510.
(i)   *Colonial Office*
The files for the Straits Settlements in 1941 were consulted but there was little of interest.
C.O.273/666–71.
II.   *India Office Library, London*
The papers of the viceroy, Lord Linlithgow, are of some interest (for details, see below under private papers).

B.   PRIVATE PAPERS
AUCHINLECK. The John Rylands University Library of Manchester.
Little of direct relevance but useful for illuminating strategic issues.
BROOKE-POPHAM. The Liddell Hart Centre for Military Archives, King's College, London (by permission of the Trustees).
Includes a number of letters of interest exchanged with Ismay.
CADOGAN. F.O.800/293–94, Public Record Office, London.
Little of interest.
NEVILLE CHAMBERLAIN. Birmingham University Library.
Contains a considerable number of papers, the most interesting being letters to his sisters. In the main, the papers confirm rather than modify the impression of Chamberlain's attitude to far eastern issues derived from the official archives. This source became available to researchers at too late a stage for me to be able to use it fully.
CHATFIELD. National Maritime Museum, Greenwich.
A useful source, demonstrating the range of defence problems with particular reference to the navy.
CRANBORNE. F.O.800/296, Public Record Office, London.
Little of interest.
DALTON. London School of Economics.
Dalton's voluminous diary contains the occasional comment of interest but he was not apparently interested particularly in relations with Japan.
GODFREY. Churchill College, Cambridge.
Includes Admiral Godfrey's unpublished autobiography with some interesting observations.

HALIFAX. F.O.800/309–327, Public Record Office, London.
Most of the correspondence deals with European issues, but there are some items of value.
HANKEY. Cab.63/series, Public Record Office.
Hankey's 'magnum opus' files including some relevant papers.
INVERCHAPEL (CLARK KERR). F.O.800/298–99. Public Record Office, London.
Contains some useful material.
ISMAY. The Liddell Hart Centre for Military Archives, King's College, London (by permission of the Trustees).
Little of interest.
KNATCHBULL-HUGESSEN. F.O.800/297, Public Record Office, London.
Little of importance.
LINLITHGOW. India Office Library, London, MSS. Eur.
Includes some material of interest relating to defence and policy towards Japan in 1940–1. The letters exchanged between the viceroy and the secretary of state for India are significant.
LLOYD GEORGE. Formerly Beaverbrook Library, London, but now at House of Lords Library.
Contains a few letters from the Chinese ambassador but otherwise little of use.
MAZE. School of Oriental and African Studies, London University.
Interesting in showing the workings of the Maritime Customs Service but not of great use for broader aspects.
PERCIVAL. Imperial War Museum, London.
Includes some material of interest on defence problems in Malaya but the bulk of the collection comprises papers dating from after 1945 concerning the surrender of Singapore in 1942 and the planning of the official history of *The War Against Japan*.
TEMPLEWOOD (HOARE). University Library, Cambridge.
Little of value.
VANSITTART. Churchill College, Cambridge.
Nothing of interest.

C.   NEWSPAPERS AND CONTEMPORARY JOURNALS
The Times
Manchester Guardian
The Economist
The Round Table

D.   PRINTED SOURCES
Documents on British Foreign Policy, 1919–1939 (H.M.S.O.,

London) selected volumes from second and third series, edited by E. L. Woodward, D. Dakin, J. P. T. Bury, and W. N. Medlicott.
Documents on German Foreign Policy 1918-1945 (H.M.S.O., London), selected volumes from series D.
Foreign Relations of the United States (Government Printing Office, Washington) volumes dealing with the Far East from 1931 to 1941.
Parliamentary Debates, Commons and Lords, 1937-42 (5th series).
International Military Tribunal for the Far East (Tokyo, 1946-48).
Imperial War Museum, London, and St. Antony's College, Oxford.

ADAMS, F. C., 'The Road to Pearl Harbor: A Re-examination of American Far Eastern Policy, July 1937-December 1938', *J.A.H.* (1971), 73-92.

ALLEN, L., *The End of the War in Asia* (Hart-Davis, MacGibbon, London, 1976).

ANDERSON, I. H., Jr., *The Standard-Vacuum Oil Company and United States East Asian Policy* (Princeton University Press, London, 1975).
'The 1941 *De Facto* Embargo on Oil to Japan, A Bureaucratic Reflex', *P.H.R.* xliv (1975), 201-31.

AVON, Earl of, *The Eden Memoirs: Facing the Dictators* (Cassell, London, 1962) and *The Reckoning* (Cassell, London, 1965).

BERGAMINI, D., *Japan's Imperial Conspiracy* (Heinemann, London, 1971).

BLUM, J. M., *From the Morgenthau Diaries: Years of Crisis, 1928-38* (Houghton Mifflin, Boston, 1959) and *Years of Urgency, 1938-41* (Houghton Mifflin, Boston, 1965).

BOND, B. (ed.), *Chief of Staff: the Diaries of Lieutenant-General Sir Henry Pownall, 1933-1944*, 2 vols. (Leo Cooper, London, 1972, 1974).

BOORMAN, H. L., 'Wang Ching-wei: China's Romantic Radical', *Political Science Quarterly*, lxxix (1964), 504-25.

BORG, D. M., *The United States and the Far Eastern Crisis of 1933-1938* (Harvard University Press, Cambridge, Mass., 1964).
'Notes on Roosevelt's Quarantine Speech', *Political Science Quarterly*, lxxii (1957), 405-33.
and OKAMOTO, S. (eds.), *Pearl Harbor as History: American-Japanese Relations 1931-1941* (Columbia University Press, New York, 1973).

BOYLE, J. H., *China and Japan at War 1937-1945: The Politics of Collaboration* (Stanford University Press, Stanford, 1972).

BUHITE, R. D., *Nelson T. Johnson and American Policy Toward China 1925-1941* (Michigan State University Press, East Lansing, 1968).

BUNKER, G. E., *The Peace Conspiracy: Wang Ching-wei and the China War, 1937–1941* (Harvard University Press, Cambridge, Mass., 1972).

BURNS, J. M., *Roosevelt: the Lion and the Fox* (Secker and Warburg, London, 1956), and *Roosevelt: the Soldier of Freedom 1940–1945* (Weidenfeld and Nicolson, London, 1971).

BURNS, R. D. and BENNETT, E. M. (eds.), *Diplomats in Crisis: United States-Chinese-Japanese Relations, 1919–1941* (European Bibliographical Centre—Clio Press, Oxford, 1974).

BUTLER, J. R. M., *Grand Strategy*, vol. ii (H.M.S.O., London, 1957).

　　Lord Lothian, 1882–1940 (Macmillan, London, 1960).

BUTLER, Lord, *The Art of the Possible* (Hamish Hamilton, London, 1971).

BUTOW, R. J. C., *Tojo and the Coming of the War* (Princeton University Press, Princeton, 1961).

　　The John Doe Associates: Backdoor Diplomacy for Peace, 1941 (Stanford University Press, Stanford, 1974).

　　'Backdoor Diplomacy in the Pacific: the Proposal for a Konoye-Roosevelt Meeting, 1941', *J.A.H.* lix (1972), 48–72.

CHURCHILL, W. S., *The Second World War*, vols. i–iii (Cassell, London, 5th edition, 1955).

CLIFFORD, N. R., *Retreat from China* (Longmans, London, 1967).

　　'Britain, America and the Far East, 1937–1940', *J.B.S.* iii (1963), 137–54.

　　'Sir Frederick Maze and the Chinese Maritime Customs, 1937–1941', *J.M.H.* xxxvii (1965), 18–34.

COLVIN, I., *The Chamberlain Cabinet* (Gollancz, London, 1971).

COOPER, A. D., *Old Men Forget* (Hart-Davis, London, 1953).

COSGRAVE, P., *Churchill at War: Alone, 1939–40* (Collins, London, 1974).

COWLING, M., *The Impact of Hitler* (Cambridge University Press, Cambridge, 1975).

CRAIG, G. A. and GILBERT, F., *The Diplomats: 1919–1939*, vol. ii (Princeton University Press, Princeton, 1953).

CRAIGIE, R. L., *Behind the Japanese Mask* (Hutchinson, London, 1946).

CROWLEY, J. B., *Japan's Quest for Autonomy: National Security and Foreign Policy, 1930–1938* (Princeton University Press, Princeton, 1966).

　　'Japanese Army Factionalism in the 1930s', *J.A.S.* xxi (1962), 309–26.

　　'A Reconsideration of the Marco Polo Bridge Incident', *J.A.S.* xxii (1963), 277–92.

DAVIES, E., 'Britain and the Far East, 1922-1931: A Study in Foreign and Defence Policy', unpublished University of Birmingham Ph.D. thesis (1973).

DILKS, D. (ed.), *The Diaries of Sir Alexander Cadogan, 1938-1945* (Cassell, London, 1971).

'Allied Leadership in the Second World War: Churchill', *Survey* 1/2 (94/95), Winter-Spring 1975.

DIRKSEN, H., *Moscow, Tokyo, London* (Hutchinson, London, 1951).

DRUMMOND, I. M., *British Economic Policy and the Empire, 1919-1939* (Allen and Unwin, London, 1972).

Imperial Economic Policy, 1917-1939: Studies in Expansion and Protection (Allen and Unwin, London, 1974).

EASTMAN, L. E., *The Abortive Revolution: China under Nationalist Rule, 1927-1937* (Harvard University Press, Cambridge, Mass., 1974).

ENDICOTT, S. L., *Diplomacy and Enterprise: British China Policy 1933-37* (Manchester University Press, Manchester, 1975).

ERICKSON, J., *The Road to Stalingrad* (Weidenfeld and Nicolson, London, 1975).

FALK, S. L., *Seventy Days to Singapore* (Robert Hale, London, 1975).

FEILING, K., *The Life of Neville Chamberlain* (Macmillan, London, 1946).

FEIS, H., *The Road to Pearl Harbor* (Princeton University Press, Princeton, 1950).

FRIEDLANDER, S., *Prelude to Downfall: Hitler and the United States, 1939-1941* (Chatto and Windus, London, 1967).

FRIEDMAN, I. S., *British Relations with China, 1931-1939* (Institute of Pacific Relations, New York, 1940).

GIBBS, N. H., *History of the Second World War: Grand Strategy*, vol. i (H.M.S.O., London, 1976).

GILL, C. H., *Royal Australian Navy 1939-1942* (Australian War Memorial, Canberra, 1957).

GILLISON, D., *Royal Australian Air Force, 1939-1942* (Australian War Memorial, Canberra, 1962).

GLENDEVON, Baron, *The Viceroy at Bay: Lord Linlithgow in India, 1936-1943* (Collins, London, 1971).

GORE-BOOTH, P., *With Great Truth and Respect* (Constable, London, 1974).

GREW, J. C., *Ten Years in Japan* (Simon and Schuster, New York, 1944) and *Turbulent Era: a Diplomatic Record of Forty Years 1904-1945*, 2 vols. (Houghton Mifflin, Boston, 1952).

GWYER, J. M. A. and BUTLER, J. R. M., *Grand Strategy*, vol. iii (H.M.S.O., London, 1964).

HACHEY, T. E., *Confidential Dispatches: Analyses of America by the British Ambassador, 1939-1945* (New University Press, Evanston, Ill., 1974).

HAGGIE, P., 'The Royal Navy and the Far Eastern Problem, 1931-1941', unpublished University of Manchester Ph.D. thesis (1974).

HAIGHT, J. McV., Jr., 'Franklin D. Roosevelt and a Naval Quarantine of Japan', *P.H.R.* xl (1971), 203-26.

HAMILL, I., 'The Strategic Illusion: the Singapore Strategy and the Defence of Australia and New Zealand, 1919-1942', unpublished University of Leeds Ph.D. thesis (1975).

HARVEY, J. (ed.), *The Diplomatic Diaries of Oliver Harvey, 1937-1940* (Collins, London, 1970), 203-26.

HASLUCK, P., *The Government and the People* (Australian War Memorial, Canberra, 1952).

HAVENS, T. R. H., *Farm and Nation in Modern Japan: Agrarian Nationalism, 1870-1940* (Princeton University Press, Princeton, 1974).

HERZOG, J. H., *Closing the Open Door: American-Japanese Diplomatic Negotiations, 1936-1941* (Naval Institute Press, Annapolis, Maryland, 1973).

HOOKER, N. H. (ed.), *The Moffat Papers: Selections from the Diplomatic Journals of Jay Pierrepont Moffat* (Harvard University Press, Cambridge, Mass., 1956).

HULL, C., *The Memoirs of Cordell Hull*, 2 vols. (Macmillan, New York, 1948).

IKE, N. (ed.), *Japan's Decision for War: Records of the 1941 Policy Conferences* (Stanford University Press, Stanford, 1967).

IKLE, F. W., *German-Japanese Relations 1936-1940* (Bookman Associates, New York, 1956).

ISMAY, Lord, *The Memoirs of General the Lord Ismay* (Heinemann, London, 1960).

ISSRAELJAN, V. and KUTAKOV, L., *Diplomacy of Aggression: Berlin, Rome, Tokyo Axis, Its Rise and Fall* (Progress Publishers, Moscow, 1970).

JANSEN, M. B., *The Japanese and Sun Yat-sen* (Harvard University Press, Cambridge, Mass., 1954).

JONES, F. C., *Japan's New Order in East Asia: Its Rise and Fall, 1937-45* (Oxford University Press, London, 1954).

Shanghai and Tientsin, with Special Reference to Foreign Interests (Oxford University Press, London, 1940).

KANE, H., 'Sir Miles Lampson at the Peking Legation, 1926-1933', unpublished University of London Ph.D. thesis (1975).

KENNEDY, M. D., *The Estrangement of Great Britain and Japan,*

1917-1935 (Manchester University Press, Manchester, 1969).

KIRBY, S. W., *The War Against Japan*, 5 vols. (H.M.S.O., London, 1957-69).

Singapore: the Chain of Disaster (Cassell, London, 1971).

KNATCHBULL-HUGESSEN, H., *Diplomat in Peace and War* (John Murray, London, 1949).

LANGER, W. L. and GLEASON, S. E., *The Challenge to Isolation, 1937-1940* and *The Undeclared War 1940-41* (Oxford University Press, London, 1952, 1953).

LARY, D., *Region and Nation: the Kwangsi Clique in Chinese Politics 1925-1937* (Cambridge University Press, Cambridge, 1974).

LEACH, B. A., *German Strategy Against Russia, 1939-1941* (Clarendon Press, Oxford, 1973).

LEBRA, J. C. (ed.), *Japan's Greater East Asia Co-Prosperity Sphere in World War II: Selected Readings and Documents* (Oxford University Press, Kuala Lumpur, 1975).

LEE, B. A., *Britain and the Sino-Japanese War, 1937-39* (Stanford University Press and Oxford University Press, London, 1973).

LEITH-ROSS, F. W., *Money Talks: Fifty Years of International Finance* (Hutchinson, London, 1968).

LEUTZE, J. (ed.), *The London Observer: the Journal of General Raymond E. Lee, 1940-1941* (Hutchinson, London, 1972).

LOEWENHEIM, F. L., LANGLEY, H. D. and JONAS, M. (eds.), *Roosevelt and Churchill: Their Secret Wartime Correspondence* (Barrie and Jenkins, London, 1975).

LONG, G., *The Six Years War: a Concise History of Australia in the 1939-1945 War* (Australian War Memorial, Canberra, 1973).

LOUIS, W. R., *British Strategy in the Far East, 1919-1939* (Clarendon Press, Oxford, 1971).

LOWE, P., *Great Britain and Japan, 1911-15: a study of British Far Eastern Policy* (Macmillan, London, 1969).

(ed.), *Proceedings of the British Association for Japanese Studies* Part 1 (1976), *History and International Relations* (Centre for Japanese Studies, Sheffield University, 1976).

'Great Britain and the Outbreak of War with Japan, 1941', in M. R. D. Foot (ed.), *War and Society: Essays in Honour and Memory of J. R. Western, 1928-1971* (Paul Elek, London, 1973).

'Great Britain and the Coming of the Pacific War, 1939-1941', *Transactions of the Royal Historical Society*, new series, vol. xxiv (1974), 43-62.

LU, D. J., *From the Marco Polo Bridge to Pearl Harbor: Japan's Entry into World War II* (Public Affairs Press, Washington, D.C., 1961).

MCALEAVY, H., *The Modern History of China* (Weidenfeld and Nicolson, London, 1967).

MARDER, A. J., 'Winston is Back: Churchill at the Admiralty, 1939–1940', *E.H.R.*, Supplement 5 (1972).

MEDLICOTT, W. N., *The Economic Blockade*, 2 vols. (H.M.S.O., London, 1952, 1959).

MORISON, S. E., *History of United States Naval Operations in World War II*, vol. iii: *The Rising Sun in the Pacific 1931–April 1942* (Little, Brown and Company, Boston, 1948).

MORLEY, J. W. (ed.), *Dilemmas of Growth in Prewar Japan* (Princeton University Press, Princeton, 1971).

Japan's Foreign Policy, 1868–1941: a Research Guide (Columbia University Press, New York, 1974).

NAYLOR, J. F., *Labour's International Policy* (Weidenfeld and Nicolson, London, 1969).

NICOLSON, N. (ed.), *Harold Nicolson: Diaries and Letters, 1930–1939* and *1939–1945*, 2 vols. (Collins, London, 1966, 1967).

NISH, I. H., *Alliance in Decline* (Athlone Press, London, 1972).

Japanese Foreign Policy 1869–1942 (Routledge and Kegan Paul, London, 1977).

PARKINSON, R., *Blood, Toil, Tears, and Sweat: The War History from Dunkirk to Alamein Based on the War Cabinet Papers of 1940 to 1942* (Hart-Davis, MacGibbon, London, 1973).

PELZ, S. E., *Race to Pearl Harbor: the Failure of the Second London Naval Conference and the Onset of World War II* (Harvard University Press, Cambridge, Mass., 1974).

PIGGOTT, F. S. G., *Broken Thread* (Gale and Polden, Aldershot, 1950).

POGUE, F. C., *George C. Marshall*, vol. ii, *Ordeal and Hope, 1939–1942* (The Viking Press, New York, 1966).

PRATT, J. T., *War and Politics in China* (Cape, London, 1943).

PRATT, L. R., *East of Malta, West of Suez: Britain's Mediterranean Crisis, 1937-39* (Cambridge University Press, Cambridge, 1975).

'The Anglo-American Naval Conversations on the Far East of January 1938', *I.A.* (1971), 745–63.

PRESSEISEN, E. L., *Germany and Japan: a Study in Totalitarian Diplomacy, 1933–1941* (Martinus Nijhoff, The Hague, 1958).

ROBERTSON, E. M. (ed.), *The Origins of the Second World War* (Macmillan, London, 1971).

ROSKILL, S. W., *Hankey: Man of Secrets*, vols. ii–iii (Collins, London, 1972, 1974).

Naval Policy Between the Wars, ii: *The Period of Reluctant Rearmament, 1930–1939* (Collins, London, 1976).

SANSOM, K., *Sir George Sansom: a Memoir* (Diplomatic Press,

Tallahassee, Fla., 1972).

SCHROEDER, P. W., *The Axis Alliance and Japanese-American Relations, 1941* (Cornell University Press, Ithaca, 1958).

SHAI, A., *Origins of the War in the East* (Croom Helm, London, 1976).

SHERWOOD, R. E., *Roosevelt and Hopkins* (Harper and Brothers, New York, 1948).

SHIGEMITSU MAMORU, *Japan and her Destiny* (Hutchinson, London, 1958).

SHORT, A., *The Communist Insurrection in Malaya, 1948-60* (Frederick Muller, London, 1975).

SILBERMAN, B. S. and HAROOTUNIAN, H. D. (eds.), *Japan in Crisis: Essays on Taisho Democracy* (Princeton University Press, Princeton, 1974).

SIMSON, I., *Singapore: Too Little and Too Late* (Leo Cooper, London, 1971).

SKED, A., and COOK, C. (eds.), *Crisis and Controversy: Essays in Honour of A. J. P. Taylor* (Macmillan, London, 1976).

SMETHURST, R. J., *A Social Basis for Prewar Japanese Militarism: the Army and the Rural Community* (University of California Press, London, 1974).

STORRY, G. R., 'Konoye Fumimaro: the Last of the Fujiwara', in G. F. Hudson (ed.), *St. Antony's Papers*, No. 7: *Far Eastern Affairs*, No. 2 (Oxford University Press, London, 1960).

TAYLOR, A. J. P., *The Origins of the Second World War* (Hamish Hamilton, London, 1961).

Beaverbrook (Hamish Hamilton, London, 1972).

(ed.), *W. P. Crozier: Off the Record, Political Interviews, 1933-1945* (Hutchinson, London, 1973).

TEMPLEWOOD, Viscount, *Nine Troubled Years* (Collins, London, 1954).

THORNE, C., *The Limits of Foreign Policy* (Hamish Hamilton, London, 1972).

TIEN, H-M, *Government and Politics in Kuomintang China, 1927-1937* (Stanford University Press, Stanford, Calif., 1972).

TOLAND, J., *The Rising Sun* (Cassell, London, 1971).

TROTTER, A., *Britain and East Asia, 1933-1937* (Cambridge University Press, Cambridge, 1975).

'Tentative Steps for an Anglo-Japanese Rapprochement in 1934', *M.A.S.* viii (1974), 59-83.

'The Dominions and Imperial Defence: Hankey's Tour in 1934', *J.I.C.H.* ii (1973-4), 318-32.

WATT, D. C., *Personalities and Policies: Studies in the Formulation of British Policy in the Twentieth Century* (Longmans, Green,

London, 1965).

Too Serious a Business: European Armed Forces and the Approach of the Second World War (Temple Smith, London, 1975).

WIGMORE, L., *The Japanese Thrust* (Australian War Memorial, Canberra, 1957).

WILSON, T. A., *The First Summit: Roosevelt and Churchill at Placentia Bay* (MacDonald, London, 1970).

WOHLSTETTER, R., *Pearl Harbor: Warning and Decision* (Stanford University Press, Stanford, 1962).

WOODWARD, E. L., *British Foreign Policy in the Second World War*, vols. i–ii (H.M.S.O., London, 1970, 1971).

WRIGHT, M. C. (ed.), *China in Revolution: the First Phase, 1900–1913* (Yale University Press, London, 1968).

WRIGHT, P., 'Great Britain, Australia and the Pacific Crisis, 1939–1941', unpublished University of Manchester M.A. thesis (1974).

YOUNG, A. M., *China and the Helping Hand, 1937–1945* (Harvard University Press, Cambridge, Mass., 1963).

INDEX

Abe Noboyuki, General, 100, 103, 113
Abyssinian crisis (1935–6), 9, 27, 80
Alexander, A.V. (1st Earl Alexander of Hillsborough), 164
Amau doctrine, 12
Ambon, 201
Amery, Leopold S., 142, 148n, 222n
Anderson, Sir John, 67
Anglo-Japanese alliance, 3–5, 106, 155
Anti-Comintern pact, 52, 99
Arita Hachiro, 50–1, 83, 88–9, 114, 120, 138, 150
Asaka Yasuhiko, Prince, 234
Attlee, Clement R. A., (1st Earl Attlee), 142, 164
Australia, concern over Pacific, 10; discussions on naval question (March–July, 1939), 67–9; Tientsin crisis (1939) and, 93–5; attitude to withdrawal of troops, 106; Burma road crisis and, 138–9, 142, 144, 146, 148, 153, 163; Churchill regards attack on as unlikely, 166; attitude to Netherlands East Indies, (1940), 164–7; defence conferences (1940–41) and 180–3, 189–92, 200–4; crisis of Feb. 1941 and, 198, 221, 222; visit of Menzies to London (1941), 198–200; fall of Menzies, 200, 246; visit of Page to London, 246–8; attitude to Netherlands East Indies (1941), 248

Beaverbrook, 1st Baron (Max Aitken), 246
Babington, Air Vice-Marshal J. T. (Sir J. T. Tremayne), 96, 180, 185–6, 189
Baldwin, Stanley (1st Earl Baldwin of Bewdley), 8
Belgium, 29
Bellairs, Rear-Admiral R.M., 190
Bennett, General Gordon, 279
Bennett, John C. Sterndale, 154, 156–9, 212, 255, 258–9, 288
Bingham, Robert, 17–18, 22
Bond, General Sir Lionel, 180, 185–6, 189
Borneo, 181, 201, 206, 263
Bradford chamber of commerce, 54

Brenan, Sir John, 38, 42, 47–8, 52, 53, 54–5, 72–3, 86, 105, 108, 118, 123, 124, 126, 128, 130, 132–3, 153–4, 209, 212, 288
Bromley, T. E., 263
Brooke-Popham, Air Chief Marshal Sir Robert, 187–9, 200–1, 207–8, 222, 246, 279
Bruce, Stanley, 43, 68–9, 93–5, 106, 146
Brussels conference (1937), 29–31
Butler, Paul D., 258–9
Butler, R. A. (Baron Butler of Saffron Walden), v, 100, 105–7, 109, 112, 114, 119, 126–7, 132, 151, 154–6, 209, 217, 222, 225, 229, 292
Burma, 139–40, 212, 221, 263, 278, 281, 294, 295
Burma road, 70, ch. v *passim* 214, 272–3, 295–6

Cadogan, Sir Alexander, 17, 23, 31, 34, 39, 40, 83, 88n, 105, 107, 119, 156, 225, 288
Caldecote, 1st Viscount (Sir Thomas Inskip), 68, 93–5, 144, 165, 166
Canada, 10, 146, 167, 292, 294
Catroux, General Georges, 169
Cavendish-Bentinck, V. F. W., 228–9
Celebes, 201, 202
Chamberlain, Neville, chancellor of the exchequer and views on East Asia, 7, 8; attitude to defence as chancellor, 9; on wounding of Knatchbull-Hugessen, 21; on Roosevelt's 'quarantine' speech, 26–8; on war in China, 28; on possible loan to China (1938), 43, 60–1; on European appreciation (1939) and East Asia, 68–9; on naval aspects and Dominions, 69; on worsening of Tientsin crisis, 78–80, 84–5; opposes economic sanctions, 79–80, 84–5; support for diplomatic solution to Tientsin, 85; criticizes Foreign Office, 85; praises Craigie, 88–9; on American denunciation of trade treaty, 91n; exchanges with Australia (1939), 93–5; resigns as prime minister, 136, 151n; supports compromise